D0207523

GENERATING CREATIVITY AND INNOVATION IN LARGE BUREAUCRACIES

GENERATING CREATIVITY AND INNOVATION IN LARGE BUREAUCRACIES

EDITED BY
ROBERT LAWRENCE KUHN

The IC² Management and Management
Science Series, Number 4
W. Cooper and George Kozmetsky, Series Editors

QUORUM BOOKS
Westport, Connecticut • London

Library of Congress Cataloging-in-Publication Data

Generating creativity and innovation in large bureaucracies / edited
by Robert Lawrence Kuhn.
   p.   cm.—(The IC² management and management science series,
ISSN 1058-5036 ; no. 4)
   Includes bibliographical references and index.
   ISBN 0-89930-774-4 (alk. paper)
   1. Creative ability in business. 2. Bureaucracy.
3. Organizational change—Management. 4. Technological innovations—
Management. I. Kuhn, Robert Lawrence. II. Series.
HD53.G46   1993
658.4'063—dc20   92-15684

British Library Cataloguing in Publication Data is available.

Library of Congress Catalog Card Number: 92-15684
ISBN: 0-89930-774-4
ISSN: 1058-5036

First published in 1993

Quorum Books, 88 Post Road West, Westport, CT 06881
An imprint of Greenwood Publishing Group, Inc.

Printed in the United States of America

The paper used in this book complies with the
Permanent Paper Standard issued by the National
Information Standards Organization (Z39.48-1984).

10 9 8 7 6 5 4 3 2 1

Contents

vi   Contents

Tables and Figures

TABLES

FIGURES

Orientation
and Overview
Robert Lawrence Kuhn

When, in 1982, we began this series of conferences on creative and innovative management, there was a sense of excitement as a new field of academic endeavor was formed. At the fourth conference in 1990, there was palpable realization of the critical relevance of creative and innovative management on a global scale: Creative and innovative management now affects the engines of world economics and the course of major nations.

Discontinuity, step-function breaks, sea changes, tidal shifts, Big Bang—these are the descriptors of creative and innovative management, and these are the descriptors of today's turbulent world. There has been more change in the past several years than in the previous forty. And while political liberation and battle have grabbed the headlines, the more fundamental discontinuities, step-function breaks, sea changes, tidal shifts, and Big Bangs are occurring in the economic arena, where personal freedom and individual initiative are amplifying each other to attain critical mass.

The plain truth is that no country can progress in the postindustrial era as a totalitarian state, and no company can prosper as a rigid organization. The nature of economic strength has changed dramatically and changed forever. Knowledge-based resources—those nurtured in the minds of the people, not nestled in the ground of the countries—have become the true wealth of nations. The quality of personal computer software, much more than the quantity of hot rolling steel, will define the leading economies of tomorrow's world.

CNN News and the fax machine have done more to conquer the world than all the tens of thousands of tanks churned out by the world's military-industrial complexes. New alliances of all kinds are being forged. Technologies are being researched in one country, developed in a second, commercialized in a third, produced in a fourth, financed in a fifth, and marketed in a sixth. In such a kinetic and interconnected environment, creative and innovative management has grown from being interesting and intriguing to being central and vital.

The First Conference on Creative and Innovative Management, held at the IC[2] Institute of the University of Texas at Austin in 1982, defined terms, set an agenda, and offered some specific applications. Papers were published in *Creative and Innovative Management,* edited by A. Charnes and W. W. Cooper (1984).

The Second Conference on Creative and Innovative Management, held at the Graduate School of Business of the University of Miami in 1984, focused on the management of knowledge-based institutions—universities, research institutes, and think tanks. Papers were published in *Frontiers in Creative and Innovative Management,* edited by Robert Lawrence Kuhn (1986).

The Third Conference on Creative and Innovative Management, held at the Graduate School of Industrial Administration of Carnegie Mellon University in 1987, stressed research methodologies and techniques for the new field interacting with actual organizational issues and cases. Papers were published in *New Directions in Creative and Innovative Management,* edited by Yuji Ijiri and Robert Lawrence Kuhn (1986).

The Fourth Conference on Creative and Innovative Management, held at the Anderson Graduate School of Management at the University of California at Los Angeles in 1990 in cooperation with the Graduate School of Business Administration of the University of Southern California,[1] looked at creative and innovative management in large-scale bureaucracies—national governments, public agencies, industrial corporations, and educational institutions.[2]

In 1988, the *Handbook for Creative and Innovative Managers,* edited by Robert Lawrence Kuhn, was published. Combining theoretical articles derived from these conferences with practical examples of creativity and innovation in action, brought new ways of thinking and doing to the attention of the general business community.

The chapters in *Generating Creativity and Innovation in Large Bureaucracies* are based on presentations made at the Fourth Conference on Creative and Innovative Management held at UCLA in cooperation with

USC. The conference was sponsored by the RGK Foundation whose president, Ronya Kozmetsky, played a critical role in organization and logistics. And, once again, it is entirely fitting that the agenda-setting paper was presented by George Kozmetsky, my mentor and friend, whose vision and persistence have transformed creative and innovative management from image into theory and from theory into practice.

Finally, I wish to thank two colleagues and close friends at the Anderson Graduate School of Management, University of California at Los Angeles, for their invaluable assistance in making the conference a success: Alfred E. Osborne, Jr., director of the Entrepreneurial Studies Center, and George T. Geis, professor of management science information systems and accounting. I would also like to express my appreciation to Jack Borsting, dean of the School of Business, University of Southern California, for his guidance and support.

NOTES

1. The cooperation between UCLA and USC, cross-town rivals in everything from football to business schools, was by itself a nice piece of creative and innovative management.

2. We credit Professor W. W. Cooper of the IC^2 Institute of the University of Texas at Austin for the prescient recommendation of the large-scale bureaucracy focus of the fourth conference. For a summary of some primary themes of the Conference, see "A Personal Summary" by Robert Lawrence Kuhn.

Part I

Creative and Innovative Management: Background and Setting

1

The Growth and Internationalization of Creative and Innovative Management

George Kozmetsky

The Fourth Conference on Creative and Innovative Management, the conference on which this volume is based, explored generating creativity and innovation in large bureaucracies. The conference provided a unique opportunity to explore the forces and factors that enhance or inhibit creative and innovative activities in large organizations in both the private and public sectors. During the conference, participants had the opportunity to examine these forces and factors in the context of a number of different nations, cultures, and institutions. They listened to and engaged in meaningful dialogue with speakers from China, Germany, Hungary, Japan, and the Soviet Union. They were joined by U.S. executives and administrators from large federal agencies and corporations, experts from consulting firms, and academic administrators and researchers.

The scope of the conference topic is in many respects intriguing, exciting, and awesome. The participants ranged from those actively involved in reforms in the communist world to those associated with the one hundred largest international corporations. Other participants managed large-scale international institutions, cooperative efforts, major research universities, and medium and small-size firms.

The word "bureaucrat" conjures up in the general public mind slow-moving, unresponsive, stick-to-the-letter-of-regulations-and-procedures employees in large-scale government agencies and departments, large corporations, and academic and educational institutions. Others may think of another type of bureaucrat—one who is aggressively successful in cutting costs and otherwise being efficient while simultaneously building an unnecessarily large, self-serving empire.

Bureaucracies are more than numbers of people or efficient administration. They are systems of values with goals and rewards. Bureaucracies have lifecycles and a propensity to stifle creativity and innovation, particularly as they grow over time or face an uncertain future. Bureaucracies are often thought to hold back progress, largely because of their rigid hierarchical formations, red tape, and paper-shuffling management. Bureaucracies are associated with the decay of civil infrastructures, lack of adequate quality education for tomorrow's technologically driven society, failure of individual commitment to sociopolitical values, loss of the ability to make high-quality products, acquisitions and mergers, loss of a nation's ability to be competitive or to be responsive to trade wars, and loss of scientific and technological dominance.

Many bureaucracies are perceived as entrenched resistance to change. To change them thereby raises many questions. Can the U.S. Congress reform its own budgeting process? Can large U.S. corporations and their domestic manufacturing divisions make their processes more efficient and flexible than those of their foreign competitors? Can those responsible for rearing and educating our children prepare them for the leadership and commitment required twenty years from now?

The underlying theme of this volume is the answer that these challenges require: the creative and innovative management of bureaucracies. Such management recognizes the need for new responses and new solutions that revitalize bureaucracies even if they must generate their own crises while they change their organization for the better.

Creative and innovative acts consist of two basic elements. The first element is new ways—new in that they are different from the established ways of doing things. Second, they must produce better results. Being both different and better is essential to generating creativity and innovation. Therefore, creative and innovative activities challenge established ways by being new and different and produce better results when they are evaluated in terms of established values.

Creative and innovative management involves three different constructs: creative management, innovative management, and creative and innovative management.

Creative management is much the same as the first element of a creative and innovative act—new ways. Creative management consists of new ideas, new directions, new methods, and new modes of operation.

Innovative management is much the same as the second element of creative and innovative activities—better results. Innovative management is involved with those innovation processes that implement creative ideas and move successfully in new directions. The operative words are "to implement" and "to move successfully."

A recent report issued by the U.S. Department of Commerce illustrates the need for innovative management:

> For most of the period following World War II, the U. S. was dominant internationally and nearly self-sufficient in science and technology. Our universities, industry, and government laboratories were the sources of the ideas for new products and processes which were produced by American factories using American workers and equipment and financed by American investors. . . .

> The dominance has eroded in recent years and U. S. supremacy has been challenged. . . .

> To remain competitive in this rapidly evolving international economic community, U.S. industry must match these developments by increasing emphasis on research and development of new products and emerging technologies and then on product commercialization and market share.[1]

Industrial management has the responsibility of commercializing innovations. The creative role of the government and university in conjunction with industry for global competitiveness is not explored in the report.

Creative and innovative management focuses on coupling; that is, linking the creative management and innovative management constructs. The operative words are "act of management." Acts of management involve linking strategy, organization, motivation and incentives, culture and environment, and institutional alliances. The means of measuring and evaluating these linkages in terms of their being better is on the cutting edge of creative and innovative management.

Identification of creative and innovative management performance is a major research need. In concept, this means that successful creative and innovative management must be superior to the accepted norm of management. As Yuji Ijiri noted, "there must be an established way of doing things and established values by which to evaluate creative and innovative activities."[2] The established ways and values permit benchmarking for assessing creativity and innovation. By the same token, activities can be creative and innovative when they are so new that there are no ways of benchmarking them.

The generation of creative and innovative activities can be directed to all levels of the means/ends hierarchy. These activities can also be directed to improve the established values. According to Ijiri:

> They may . . . be directed toward finding a path that will worsen several intermediate values but will improve at a higher level in the hierarchy. The latter, a roundabout method, is more difficult than the direct method because deliberate worsening of intermediate values require courage, persuasion, and understanding. Yet, if successful, it is the roundabout method that often leads to a significant improvement in the organization's value at the higher level by letting the organization move out of a local optimum.[3]

There are many ways to approach the subject of the growth and internationalization of creative and innovative management. Growth is development to maturity, not an increase in size. Internationalization is the globalization of the marketplace and a changing geopolitical environment.

Global markets and geopolitics are rapidly changing. They are outpacing established management thinking and traditional politics. Murray Weidenbaum referred to this phenomenon as both systems—geopolitics and geoeconomics—being out of synchronization.[4]

Many distinguished analysts have commented on the changing global marketplace as imports and exports are transacted between domestic companies and foreign subsidiaries or foreign parent companies. Any creative and innovative activity in such bureaucracies, when evaluated by established values, raises a dichotomy. Generating new ways of doing global business is better when it is evaluated based on a company's established values (higher profits). On the other hand, if the new ways of doing global business are evaluated in the traditional terms of international transactions (increased trade deficit), they could be worse. These dichotomies and others yet to be explored as well as defined issues present opportunities for the growth of the discipline of creative and innovative management.

The growth and internationalization of creative and innovative management shift the focus from rapid changes due to technology and ideology drivers per se to new ways of thinking creatively and innovatively—spontaneous and cultivated. Peter Drucker has captured the essence of why management needs to think differently:

> Rarely in human history has any institution emerged as quickly as management or had as great an impact so fast. In less than one hundred fifty years, management has transformed the social and economic fabric of the world's developed countries. It has created a global economy and set new rules for countries that would participate in that economy as equals. And it has itself been transformed. Few executives are aware of the tremendous impact management has had. . . . As a result, they are ill-prepared for the tremendous challenges that now confront them. The truly important problems managers face do not come from technology or politics; they do not

originate outside of management and enterprise. They are problems caused by the very success of management itself.[5]

If bureaucracies are to be more creative and innovative, they need to extend and transform themselves and their organizations to meet changing global needs.

BACKGROUND

Since 1982, the IC^2 Institute of the University of Texas at Austin has co-sponsored along with the Graduate School of Business at UT-Austin, the RGK Foundation, the School of Business at the University of Miami, the Graduate School of Industrial Administration at Carnegie Mellon University, the John E. Anderson Graduate School of Management at the University of California-Los Angeles, and the Graduate School of Business Administration at the University of Southern California, four international conferences on creative and innovative management. This series of conferences is unique in that it serves as the means for structuring a newer academic discipline for teaching and research: creative and innovative management. It also provides new managerial ways of achieving comparative advantages in a dynamic, global, hypercomplex, and ultracompetitive environment. The resultant conference proceedings have focused specifically on creative and innovative management as a means of changing the science, practice, and institutionalization of management.

The first conference—"Creative and Innovative Management"—made early contributions to identifying the foundations for continued system improvements in creative and innovative managerial practices. Three classes of preconditions were identified: the need to (1) drop a number of older distinctions among entrepreneur, manager, and administrator; (2) develop new approaches (e.g., flexibility and adaptability rather than only efficiency and effectiveness); and (3) redesign and design new institutions (e.g., ones that could deal with global problems of competition and cooperation as well as collaborations among business, government, and academia).[6]

The second conference—"Frontiers in Creative and Innovative Management"—was an exploratory effort to identify problems and opportunities for creative and innovative management in private enterprise, government, not-for-profit institutions, universities, and other societal activities. This conference established that it was possible for management to think spontaneously and to cultivate by focusing on two things: (1) successfully solving problems associated with society's crises, needs, and demands; and (2) dealing with challenges found in the public and nonprofit sectors.[7]

The third conference—"New Directions in Creative and Innovative Management"—emphasized the need for the takeoff of research methodology in creative and innovative management. This conference resulted in five themes: (1) differences among creativity and innovation and productivity must be identified (e.g., breakthrough and incremental advances); (2) traditional methods of management performance are inadequate (e.g., financial results, productivity, market standing, quality, innovation, accountability, R&D investments); (3) nonprofit institutions need better measures that are specific to their missions; (4) performance has to be built into any institution's strategy, organization, culture, and motivation in such a way that it can be continually measured for improvement; and (5) it is necessary to determine the optimal relationship between theory and practice in creative and innovative management.[8]

The fourth conference—"Generating Creativity and Innovation in Large Bureaucracies"—was IC²'s next step in linking the research and practice of creative and innovative management to large-scale bureaucracies in government, business, and academia in terms of the longer competitive status of economic and political systems. A series of unstructured problems engendered the selection of the issues that large bureaucracies face.

The IC² Institute has held over fifteen conferences on important elements of creative and innovative management, particularly relating to internationalization and global markets. These conferences were held in the United States, China, Western Samoa, England, Australia, and the Soviet Union. Important research by the IC² fellows that pertained to creative and innovative activities especially in technology transfer were conducted in the United States, Hungary, Japan, Australia, Germany, and Sweden. Five graduate seminars that bear on creative and innovative management have been taught by IC² Fellows who are faculty members of the Graduate School of Business at the University of Texas at Austin. Extensive knowledge-bases have been developed on "Technology Alliances for Competitiveness."

As a whole, it is clear that in a rapidly changing, competitive world, large-scale bureaucracies are more critical than ever. Small entrepreneurial businesses have been and still are important in the United States for maintaining economic growth and employment. However, their limited technical, human, and financial resources restrict their participation in the challenges that various international opportunities offer. It is clear that larger organizations need to take the leadership in developing opportunities in markets such as China, the former Soviet Union, Eastern Europe, and India. Large bureaucracies' resources and leadership are required to effectively compete within and with the emerging European Common Market and the Pacific Basin and North American markets.

The problems and issues that the IC[2] fellows encountered from their own research and gathered from other studies on U.S. competitiveness made it abundantly clear that large-sized bureaucracies in industry, government, and academia needed to generate creative and innovative responses if the United States was to be among the leadership nations in the 1990s and beyond. Small and growth firms will not be able to take the required leadership in sufficient time.

In the summer of 1986, Hans Mark of the University of Texas began to raise some interesting and provocative questions on technological risk assessments that are under the management of large-scale bureaucracies. In the original manuscript for a lecture that he presented at the University of Texas at Dallas's Andrew R. Cecil Lectures on Moral Values in a Free Society, Mark wrote:

> It may be too early to draw really definitive conclusions about the two accidents, but I do believe that it is worth starting the process at this time. The initiation of such an evaluation is the purpose of this paper. . . . There are longer term questions related to the accidents that have more general applications. What have we learned about the problem of risk assessment from these accidents? More important, what is the change, if any, in how the public perceives the risks involved in the operation of spacecraft and nuclear reactors? Finally, and this is perhaps the most fascinating question of all the ones that have been raised, how did the two vastly different political systems react? The fact that one accident occurred in the United States and the other one in Russia gives us a unique opportunity to make such a comparison.[9]

The *New Perspectives Quarterly* for winter 1988–89 confirmed that the communist world command and control management of bureaucracies was in the process of change. Evaluating these changes, subjecting them to scrutiny, and assessing them against other nations' economic systems became an imperative for IC[2] research. This landmark issue of *New Perspectives Quarterly* examines perestroika and communist reforms. Subsequent internal and external reports and studies recorded the need for reform because of the economic failure under communism in Eastern Europe, the Soviet Union, and China. The early reform trends for the countries under communism seemed to be a move from command and control planning to experimenting with a market economy. A few examples from China, the Soviet Union, and Hungary will illustrate why the direction of these trends caught the attention of the IC[2] Institute.

The China example is based on an interview with Hu Qili, a member of the Standing Committee of the Politburo of China's Communist party. His responsibilities include ideology, the press, and propaganda. He is quoted as follows:

> For a period of time, we thought highly centralized planning was the sole economic form of socialist system. We thought the market economy and commodity exchange were equivalent to capitalism....
>
> Now, it seems that the market is not a feature unique to capitalism. Capitalism doesn't have the patent right over the market economy....
>
> What we are trying to establish is a modality where the state regulates the market and the market guides the enterprises. Our planning must respect the "law of value," of supply and demand. We want to integrate the advantages of the planning and market economy. This is what we mean when we say socialism with Chinese characteristics.[10]

The Hungarian example is based on an interview with Janos Berecz, who was then a member of the Politiburo in charge of ideology.

> Our [Communist party] policies were both practically and theoretically hasty. Our central planning policies established monopolies instead of the competition that would have helped develop the economy. As a result, the people themselves started to lose interest in production. We reached a stage where we could not progress, and so we became underdeveloped.
>
> The system of political institutions built up during the "dictatorship of the proletariat" also contributed to stagnation. During that time, the Hungarian Socialist Workers party (HSWP) monopolized all activities in the political sphere and we are suffering the consequences: political and economic crisis, as well as the social explosion of 1956.
>
> Similar situations prevailed in 1968 in Czechoslovakia and in Poland in 1981 when Solidarity emerged and martial law was instituted. These explosions forced the respective parties to recognize that the contradiction between the relations of production and the development of the economy had to be resolved.
>
> Today, we see that a reform movement has developed across the socialist world. Our reforms, the Chinese reforms and Gorbachev's *perestroika* will result in unleashing productive forces and will prove more conducive to human creativity.
>
> We are all aiming to create conditions in which people don't just work, but also think and put those thoughts into practice. And, if the people put their ideas into practice, they should reap the benefits from their efforts. Such conditions are necessary in the age of scientific-technological revolution.[11]

The Soviet example is taken from an interview with academician Abel Aganbergyan, head of the Economics Department of the Soviet Academy of Sciences:

> Perestroika is a strategy for the qualitative transformation of all aspects of life in the USSR. In economics, it has three aims: the transition from bureaucratic order to performance-based management; a rapid economic transition to the scientific-technological revolution; and the creation of a consumer society. . . .

> In order to accomplish these objectives, we must end the autarkic [*sic*] tendencies in our economy and make foreign economic relations a priority. The administrative command economy must be replaced by a market economy with highly developed financial and credit mechanisms. Material encouragement and the economic self-reliance of enterprises must replace "wage-leveling" and neglected material incentives.

> Finally, we must move toward plural forms of property ownership, thereby disbanding the central economic system and replacing it with competitive economic units.[12]

From a creative and management perspective, these excerpts tend to focus on the failures of bureaucracies. They also raise the issue of how the failure of bureaucracies holds back social progress, and how one changes a bureaucracy when moving toward new directions and new value systems.

The problems of changing large bureaucracies underlie much of the LBO, merger, and acquisition controversy in the United States. Michael C. Jensen has suggested a creative and innovative way of transforming public companies into private, institutionally owned companies:

> New organizations are emerging in its [public corporation's] place— organizations that are corporate in form but have no public shareholders and are not listed or traded on organized exchanges. These organizations use public and private debt, rather than public equity, as their major source of capital. Their primary owners are not households but large institutions and entrepreneurs that designate agents to manage and monitor on their behalf and bind those agents with large equity interests and contracts governing the use and distribution of cash.

> Takeovers, corporate breakups, divisional spin-offs, leveraged buyouts, and going-private transactions are the most visible manifestations of a massive organizational change in the economy. These transactions have inspired criticism, even outrage, among many business leaders and government officials, who have called for regulatory and legislative restrictions. The backlash is understandable.

Change is threatening; in this case, the threat is aimed at the senior executives of many of our largest companies.[13]

For a number of years, the IC^2 Institute of the University of Texas at Austin has been involved in research in the area of large-scale programs. A large-scale program typically involves technological innovations and implementations that are costly and complex, involve some centralized planning, are politically and publicly sensitive, and are limited and managed by a complex of public and private sector bureaucracies. In general, they involve billions of dollars and require ten years or more for successful completion. Such programs are initiated when they meet the following criteria:

- *Need*—Is there motivation in terms of pride, security, and profit?
- *Vision*—Are there adequate mentors and facilitators to foster creative collaborative projects?
- *Timing*—Is there a real current market need?
- *Technical Feasibility*—Does the technology exist? Is the required research underway?
- *Skilled Personnel*—Is there sufficient quality and quantity?
- *Champion*—Is leadership available and in place?
- *Adequate Financial Resources*—Has the necessary capital been committed?
- *Public and Political Support*—Is there a consensus on key public policy issues? How will it be sustained?
- *Public/Private Sector Cooperation*—Are the institutional alliances viable and effective?
- *Intellectual Community Support*—Is the theoretical basis being developed in harmony with the new reality?

Successful large-scale projects usually take longer and cost more than anticipated, and setbacks will surely occur along the way. Consequently, there must be contingency planning to incorporate the following needs:

- Continuity of public and private support
- Capital infusion
- Parallel developments to alternative approaches and supporting technology
- More skilled personnel than originally planned.[14]

From a creative and management perspective, NASA is an example that conforms to the criteria for initiating large-scale programs. Lessons learned from the successful Apollo program have not been good enough to solve the problems in space station programs or to assure U.S. leadership in orbital space manufacturing. On the other hand, there are successful lessons to be learned from NASA's aeronautic research. The U.S. aerospace industry is still the world leader in terms of commercialization. Large-scale program management, which in effect is essentially a one-shot effort, is not enough in today's changing, internationally competitive global economy. The strategic risks involved are complex. When the United States was a creditor nation, its risk-taking capabilities were significantly different than today, when it is the world's leading debtor.

The culture of an agency's bureaucracy as well as the industrial complex bureaucracy under conditions of a creditor/debtor environment need to be carefully examined. Strategic risk becomes more crucial and demands a changed bureaucratic approach under constraints of economic conditions.

What all nations and leaders of bureaucracies are facing is a more perplexing problem than being efficient. How do they get a mature bureaucracy to change and to do what it ought to do in a better way? The changes are being forced by constraints of time, limited resources, and hypercompetition among nations, institutions, and industries.

THE SETTING

The decade of the 1990s will be a period of dramatic changes, upheavals, and events that pose unforeseen and unexpected challenges and opportunities for large-scale bureaucracies. Getting around to these opportunities involves understanding global trends. Global trends are driving forces that alter the shape and direction of a bureaucracy as well as a nation. The early identification and understanding of these trends are crucial to the development and growth of creative and innovative management as a discipline, enhancement of a nation's competitiveness, and generation of creativity and innovation in large-scale bureaucracies.

There are at least five major longer-term global trends that will affect large-scale bureaucracies in the future. These are:

1. Expansion of market-driven economies
2. Movement toward democracy and individual freedom
3. Emergence of revolutionary technologies
4. Creation of new infrastructures
5. Concern for accountable development

Any management that does not anticipate and respond to these global trends may not compete successfully in tomorrow's hypercompetitive global market.

Expansion of Market-Driven Economies. Planned economies do not work in an internationally competitive environment. Walt Rostow expects to see more and more of what he calls "regional federalism"—an economic global grouping of nations rather than the older but more popular One World of Wendell Wilke. Regional federalism primarily involves highly developed nations such as the Western European nations, the United States and Canada, and Japan. They are developing and strengthening the European Market, the North American Market, and the Pacific Basin Market. Some think that these regional economic federations are at best involved in a bashing economic war while others see it as a post-cold war bonus that will provide newer spheres of economic power that will both cooperate and compete among themselves.

Movement Toward Democracy and Individual Freedom. The dissolution of Stalin's Eastern European empire and the Soviet Union has posed many questions about the fragmentation and unity of different races, colors, cultures, religions, tribes, nationhoods, economic interests, or, simply, size. The problems of fragmentation and unity in the former USSR are also true in other nations: Canada, Belgium, Northern Ireland, most Eastern European nations, and a number of African states. Certain aspects of the fragmentation and unity problems are also to be found in the United States.

The Eastern Europe Revolution of 1989 has posed for the European Communities its greatest and most challenging task: to create a United Europe that provides economic prosperity and stability in a competitive and cooperative world.

From a business perspective, the movement toward democracy and freedom connotes that there is a rising trend toward innovation. Individuals need to be encouraged and supported in initiating and developing their own ventures. It is an entrepreneurial movement. It is a movement that encompasses all nations aspiring to market-driven economies.

Creation of New Infrastructures. There is an increasing trend to create new infrastructures that are characterized by smart cities and fast systems. A cadre of facilitators conversant in innovation, manufacturing, and servicing is essential for the smart city of the twenty-first century to compete in a hypercompetitive global environment. A recent study by David Aschauer has demonstrated that there is a linkage between the lack of public infrastructures and the slowdown in the private sector's productivity in the United States.

Fast infrastructure systems depend on easy and rapid access to areas and instantaneous communication. Consequently, the infrastructure must provide the latest appropriate transportation available and the most advanced telecommunications capabilities. Transportation and telecommunications must be interfaced with smart facilities, value-added networks, and modern building codes.

Tomorrow's smart infrastructures will require communities to rethink, reshape, and restructure their current infrastructure for a global context. Managers of private firms will need to participate in infrastructure improvements. The smart infrastructure will have to evolve over time. The global smart infrastructure is a set of interrelated human, technological, institutional, financial, and social links that accelerate access to information and resources.

Emergence of Revolutionary Technologies. A series of revolutionary technologies is creating the emerging industries of the 1990s and beyond. Developments in superconductivity, new materials, computers, communications, robotics, space utilization, and the medical field are occurring with increasing speed.

These technologies are revolutionary for several reasons. First, they reflect fundamental advances in the basic sciences. Our understanding of how the world works has been permanently changed through advances in the basic sciences, which in turn have resulted in a new wave of technologies.

Second, these technologies are widely diffused. Because they are so diverse, because they have so many applications, and because they have an impact on so many markets, no one region or country can dominate them completely. Consequently, many regions and countries will have increasing opportunities to develop and utilize these technologies for their own purposes.

These technologies spur new industries and regenerate traditional industries. Consequently, they are changing the nature of the workplace, making old abilities and skills obsolete, and requiring new capabilities in those affected by them.

These technologies are creating new types of institutional alliances among academia, business, and government. Given the requirements for research on these technologies and new types of demands for their transfer and commercialization, innovative organizational structures are being developed.

Ownership issues are becoming more important. These revolutionary technologies are requiring greater intellectual property protection. Indeed, the whole area of intellectual assets is becoming an emerging area of study and practice. For example, many of these revolutionary technologies are redefining the concept of what is man-made. Algorithms are now receiving patent protection, where only a few years ago they were considered unpatentable.

The development of these technologies is accelerated by the information age. Advances in transportation and communication now make technological changes known almost instantaneously anywhere in the world.

Finally, these technologies are revolutionary because they generate more creative or discontinuous innovations faster than ever before. Continuous innovations or traditional ways of innovating are modifications of, or variations to existing products, or they are new brands in an existing category. Discontinuous innovations, however, result in new products that significantly alter or create new consumption/behavior patterns. They create new approaches that make existing skills and competencies obsolete.

Accountable Development. There is a shift from laissez-faire development to accountable development. New constraints on the environment, health, and energy are forcing a new sensitivity to and respect for environmental impacts of economic development initiatives. Any major developmental project must, therefore, demonstrate not only that it will not threaten the environment but that it will positively contribute to enhancing the quality of life. Accountable development, therefore, must be incorporated into major economic development efforts from the very start of the process.

CONCLUSIONS

Global trends establish challenges for generating creativity and innovation for large bureaucracies. They also provide research challenges from a creative and innovative management perspective. Research challenges fall into two major classes of opportunities: one deals with methodologies and the other deals with issues to rethink, realign and restructure large-scale bureaucracies.

Newer methodologies are required to investigate empirically if the creative and innovative activities have provided better than average performances. Measuring a large-scale program's productivity and meeting its objectives with a constant level of real-dollar budgets is a continuing bureaucratic challenge. Measuring the risk of plans that coordinate and conform all activities to accomplish a bureaucratic strategy or mission is another opportunity. Methods are needed to measure the efficiency of large-scale bureaucracies as well as to compare them with other competing nations' bureaucracies.

A recent alternative to monolithic bureaucratization is to utilize free competitive market mechanisms. These mechanisms are utilized by capitalistic, socialistic large-scale bureaucracies. Such creative and innovative activities employ deregulation, privatization, and decentralization. Research opportunities abound in formulating an answer to the question of whether free competition markets are the only alternatives. China's Hu Qili believes they are developing an alternative when they integrate the advantages of central planning and a market economy.

Another alternative is to utilize information technology and automation for productivity, competitive advantage, and fast responsiveness. There are yet other alternatives to be discovered and utilized.

The second class of major research challenges includes rethinking, realigning, and restructuring large-scale bureaucracies.

1. Rethinking or changing bureaucracies from one set of established ways and values to another that creates and innovates. Think of this issue as "Gorbachev's problem." Changing large bureaucracies from a command and control system to a more market performance-based system requires more than perestroika or glasnost. They are necessary but not sufficient.

2. Realignment of policies and strategies to new realities that dominate worldwide activities and trends. Realignment will involve international cooperation, domestic regional economic development, promotion of risk-taking developments by the private sector, growth of global industrial standardization, and cooperative diffusion of science and technology.

3. Restructuring of private large bureaucracies without "big shocks." These issues involve transforming large bureaucracies without liquidation through operation, bankruptcy, or a takeover or by trade protection without an appropriate time frame to maintain their globally competitive edge.

Clearly, more needs to be done to research in creative and innovative management that can be extended to large-scale bureaucracies. Too often in the past bureaucracies took off on their own; they became preoccupied with regulations and procedures that facilitated the success of their own operations. There is a need to generate other alternatives to large-scale bureaucracies. Developing global infrastructures, exploiting new technologies for the benefit of all people, and providing more space and a better quality of life on a crowded planet place ever-increasing demands on creative and innovative ways to manage bureaucracies. New methods of accountability will be needed to ensure that creative and innovative activities are truly better than traditional ways.

NOTES

1. Technology Administration, U.S. Department of Commerce, *Emerging Technologies: A Survey of Technical and Economic Opportunities,* Spring 1990, p. 3.

2. Yuji Ijiri, "Creativity and Accountability in Management," in *New Directions in Creative and Innovative Management: Bridging Theory and Practice,* ed Yuji Ijiri and Robert Lawrence Kuhn (Cambridge, Mass.: Ballinger, 1989), p. 67.

3. Ibid.

4. Murray Weidenbaum, "Geopolitics and Geoeconomics: Systems Out of Sync," *Directors and Boards* 14 (4) (Summer 1990): 7.

5. Peter Drucker, *The New Realities: In Government and Politics/In Economics and Business/In Society and World View* (New York: Harper and Row, 1989), p. 221.

6. A. Charnes and W. W. Cooper, eds., *Creative and Innovative Management* (Cambridge, Mass.: Ballinger, 1984), pp. xvi–xvii.

7. Robert Lawrence Kuhn, ed., *Frontiers in Creative and Innovative Management* (Cambridge, Mass.: Ballinger, 1985), pp. xv–xviii.

8. Yuji Ijiri and Robert Lawrence Kuhn, eds., *New Directions in Creative and Innovative Management: Bridging Theory and Practice* (Cambridge, Mass.: Ballinger, 1988), pp. 1–2.

9. Hans Mark, "The Challenger and Chernobyl: Lessons and Reflections," in *Traditional Moral Values in the Age of Technology,* ed. W. Lawson Taitte (University of Texas at Dallas, 1987).

10. "Capitalism Has No Patent on the Market," *New Perspectives Quarterly* (Winter 1988–89): 7.

11. "From Big Brother to Big Mac," *New Perspectives Quarterly* (Winter 1988-89): 12–13.

12. "The Dictatorship of the Consumer," *New Perspectives Quarterly* (Winter 1988-89): 26.

13. Michael C. Jensen, "Eclipse of the Public Corporation," *Harvard Business Review* (September/October 1989): 61.

14. Michael Yarymovych unpublished lectures at the Large Scale Programs Institute, Austin, Tex.

Part II

Dynamic Change in Diverse Political and Economic Environments

2

The American Administrative Style: A Costly Inheritance

Walt W. Rostow

Several distinguished analysts have commented on the present unsatisfactory competitive status of the American economy against the long sweep of American history.[1] This chapter does not clash head-on with the analysis and conclusions of these analysts. The present argument, however, is somewhat more sharply focused on the relation of U.S. competitiveness to the four technological revolutions that have shaped the world economy over the past two centuries.

In the 1780s, the first revolution revolved around Watt's improved steam engine, power-driven textile machinery, and Cort's method for fabricating good iron from coke rather than charcoal. Then, starting in the 1830s, came the railroad-steel complex, which dominated the next half-century or so. Straddling the turn of the century, electricity, the internal combustion engine, and a new batch of sophisticated chemicals moved on stage. In its various elaborations this third cluster did not decelerate until the mid-1960s; although continuity was broken by the Great Depression and, to a degree, accelerated by the Second World War. The fourth technological revolution moved from invention to innovation in, roughly, the mid-1970s, and involved microelectronics, genetic engineering, the ubiquitous laser, and a range of new industrial materials. One of its results has been a remarkable transformation of communications.

The thesis of this chapter is simple: The United States was granted by geography, natural resources, and demography, two initial assets—a rapidly expanding market that quickly achieved great scale; and a higher average level of real per capita income than its major rivals. These assets carried the United States to global economic primacy by the end of the nineteenth century (by the close of the second technological revolution). In the third revolution a few industrial sectors—notably, electronics, chemicals, and aeronautics—learned to link R&D intimately to production; but most sectors did not. Nevertheless, the United States, aided by European vicissitudes, was able to achieve and maintain global economic primacy from 1900 until the late 1950s. From that time the twin relative advantages the United States had historically enjoyed progressively diminished. It was left to contest for status in a global arena governed primarily by the capacity for rapid, steady innovation where the American heritage from the past was distinctly mixed.

In that setting the initial American response to the coming of the fourth technological revolution was constrained in critical sectors by habits of mind and administration, built up over the previous two lucky centuries. This combination of altered external circumstances and a less than optimum response to new challenges and opportunities reduced the economic stature of the United States on the world scene. The constraints in responding to the fourth technological revolution were particularly severe in certain important sectors that had played an important role in the third technological revolution; but these weaknesses suffused public attitudes and policy on a wider basis as well, as an important part of the nation's economic leadership thrashed about searching for quick, easy profits with no clear consensus in either the economic or political communities on what had happened and what was to be done about it.

Prospects on the world scene make it most unlikely that any single country will again achieve the kind of economic primacy that Britain enjoyed from the 1780s to the 1880s and that the United States enjoyed in the subsequent eight decades. But the United States does have the potential to remain one of the major economic and technological powers of the twenty-first century. This will require, however, that American society discard some misleading residues from the past and gear its public as well as private policies and institutions to the task of absorbing promptly and efficiently, in all relevant sectors, the flow of potentially profitable innovations generated by R&D in the United States and abroad.

THE UNITED STATES IN THE FIRST
TECHNOLOGICAL REVOLUTION

An American style in manufactures had defined itself since Thomas Jefferson backed Eli Whitney's rifles with interchangeable parts in 1801 and Francis Cabot Lowell set up his first large-scale cotton textile plant in 1813. As in agriculture, the high cost of labor led Lowell to introduce capital-intensive methods from the beginning; and, with a bit of help from a tariff-minded Congress, relatively high-income farmers and workers provided a profitable mass market for his sturdy middle-grade textiles.

The United States was, of course, overwhelmingly an agricultural country in the first half of the nineteenth century; but, led by extraordinarily rapid expansion in cotton textiles, New England as a region exhibited all the major characteristics of takeoff, including backward linkages to machinery manufacture and lateral linkages reflected in rapid urbanization. Moreover, despite the predominance of rural life, Americans shared, even in the eighteenth century, European excitement over the scientific revolution and generated a Philosophical Society in Philadelphia, an answering Academy in Boston, and a tradition of inventive ingenuity associated, among others, with the names of Franklin, Jefferson, Whitney, and Fulton.

In 1851, at the time of the Crystal Palace Exposition in London, the United States was almost certainly outranked in industrial production by France and Germany as well as by economically hegemonic Britain. Nevertheless, the United States was the surprise of the show—like a precocious junior tennis player who unexpectedly does well in a major tournament. It not only produced a winning schooner in a prestigious race with the British, but also two products of its atypical population-resource balance and its relatively high real wage rates: McCormick's reaper hardly known in Europe, and a number of mass-produced products with interchangeable parts, including Colt's revolver.

In this first phase of modern industrialization the standard American business firm was a one-man or one-family affair, with an unambiguous boss who could oversee its affairs, expanding by the plow-back of profits; although Astor's elaborate fur empire, Biddle's Second Bank of the United States, and, as we shall see, the U.S. Army in peacetime foreshadowed a later administrative style.

THE RAILROAD AND THE MAKING OF INDUSTRIAL AMERICA: THE SECOND TECHNOLOGICAL REVOLUTION

Strictly speaking, the second technological revolution, centered on the railroad, began slowly in the United States (and Western Europe) in the 1830s. In the 1840s Britain laid out the main lines of its rail net with almost six thousand miles of track, while the United States slightly exceeded that total in providing the Northeast with a new transport system which, in turn, came to underpin a modern coal-iron-engineering base in Pennsylvania.

In the 1850s more than twenty thousand miles of track were laid in the United States, vaulting the Appalachians and uniting the Middle West and the Northeast. The expansion of the American railroad net to the Mississippi in the 1850s and its extension to the Pacific in the quarter-century after the Civil War created a massive continental market. Buttressed by a sustained if cyclical surge in immigration, this market provided the base for a large-scale diversified industry.

This process, in motion for a half-century, came to a climax in the 1880s when a working continental market was actually created. It was then that the bone structure of transcontinental railroads was filled in with feeder lines and double tracking. In that decade Gustavus Swift built the modern meat-packing industry; John D. Rockefeller created the Standard Oil Trust commanding the strategic oil-refining bottleneck; the St. Louis brewers moved out from their regional market to the national scene; James Duke, with a cigarette-making machine in hand, built national and international markets for his product. The familiar list can, of course, be extended. But it was due to this remarkable transformation in production, marketing, and the administration of large-scale units that the United States edged beyond Britain in its proportion of global industrial production (29 to 27 percent in 1881–85) moving on to 36 percent by 1913, as Britain fell to 14 percent.

Technical developments played a part in this process. Electricity and refrigeration as well as James Bonsack's machine that produced 125,000 cigarettes a day, leased by Duke, are examples. But Alfred Chandler has correctly emphasized that, in this stage of modern American industry, the exploitation of scale was primarily a matter of investment in production, marketing, and management—plus the legal (or occasionally illegal) exploitation of the advantages of "first-mover" pioneering in an inherently oligopolistic market.

The long-distance railroad building, which began its four-decade run in the 1850s, not only laid the basis for a continental industrial market, but also posed a new challenge to administration; and this fact was almost immediately perceived by thoughtful observers. Daniel C. McCallum in 1855, noted that

A Superintendent of a road fifty miles in length can give its business his personal attention and may be constantly on the line engaged in the direction of its details; each person is personally known to him, and all questions in relation to its business are at once presented and acted upon; and any system however imperfect may under such circumstances prove comparatively successful.

In the government of a road five hundred miles in length a very different state exists. . . . I am fully convinced that in the want of a system perfect in its details, properly adapted and vigilantly enforced, lies the true secret of their [large roads'] failure.[2]

On this perception a group of imaginative railroad engineers designed and installed the organizational structure of the first large-scale American industrial enterprise, based on the centralized management of specific functions, broken down by departments, its unity maintained by the prompt and uniform reporting and standardized operating instructions permitted by the telegraph.

Essentially, this was the administrative model, only gradually perfected, which was applied to the great continental business units made possible by the long-distance railroads. Indeed, the railroads were often an explicit model, and administrators moved over from them to industry. The central problem in industry was, once again, to combine the imperatives of unified management with the advantages of continental scale—notably in respect to the cost of raw materials; efficiency of plant operations; mobilization of labor supply; marketing; and working capital. Central operational units related to each function were created, with general managers for each department. Coordination and broad policy-making decisions governing finance, mergers, and efforts to extend markets fell to a small group of commanding figures supported by small staffs.

This administrative style had precedents before 1850 and applications beyond. The army in peacetime was, perhaps, the most significant example of a fairly large organization set up to do repetitive tasks efficiently with, if necessary, run-of-the-mill personnel. Although it did not heighten his qualifications as a field commander in a time of war, General George McClellan, a talented organizer and trainer of military units, was, for a time, chief engineer on the Illinois Central Railroad and briefly president of the Ohio and Mississippi Railroad. But the maximization of efficiency on repetitive tasks is, perhaps, best symbolized by the concept of scientific management as evolved by Frederick W. Taylor. He focused on efficiency in the small, not the large, on how, by specialization of function in a machine shop or other narrow operation, maximum efficiency could be achieved in routine, regularly repeated operations. Taylor's classic work is focused on shop management. His image of innovation was the small, incremental improvement, arising from imaginative men working in or directing the shop. His symbol was not the laboratory but the stop-watch.

Similar notions came to suffuse the organization of the public sector. In cumulative response to corrupt administration, Congress finally passed the Civil Service Act of 1883. The act defined functional tasks with precision and subjected applicants to examinations in these narrowly defined fields on the basis of which appointments were made.[3]

Thus, the classic American style of administration became in this period the large hierarchical organization, structured according to function and geared to the performance of repetitive tasks with maximum efficiency. Formally, there was no place for innovation except marginal improvements in an essentially static structure.

There was, of course, a good deal of technological change in this half-century, which included the massive and diversified exploitation, from the 1870s on, of the breakthrough in the making of cheap, high-quality steel. And, as noted earlier, the miracle of electricity began to spawn its many progeny, including the electric light bulb and refrigeration, in the last quarter of the nineteenth century. Edison's fecund laboratory, the creation of an extraordinarily gifted inventor, did not use science in, say, the later systematic style of the Bell laboratories; but it was, nevertheless, an anticipatory symbol of the third and fourth technological revolutions, not the second. Most innovations were modest if sometimes important refinements of familiar technologies. In a useful phrase, William Lazonick calls these "adaptive" as opposed to "formative" innovations.[4] The grand enterprise of the era was the exploitation on a continental scale of a market characterized by a still rapidly expanding population and a relatively high average level of real income.

THE ROAD DIVIDES, BUT LUCK CARRIES THE UNITED STATES FORWARD: THE THIRD TECHNOLOGICAL REVOLUTION

The technological revolution that took shape at the beginning of the twentieth century centered on the elaboration of a new sequence in chemicals (including petroleum refining), electricity, and the internal combustion engine. Defined broadly, these dynamic sectors required and attracted over a long period of time a high proportion of research and development resources (on the order of 80 percent in the United States and elsewhere). These sectors proved capable of more than incremental or "adaptive" technological refinement. After all, such refinement had also proved possible in the nineteenth century with respect to Watt's steam engine, cotton textile machinery, iron and steel manufacture with coke as fuel, and the railroad. The great new innovational sectors of the third technological revolution yielded, in addition, a succession of major new products. Thus, Chandler summarizes the century of dynamic industrial capitalism after 1870 as *Scale and Scope*. "Scope" refers to the switch of industry from single products (e.g., meat, cigarettes, etc.) or single services (e.g., rail transport) to a widening array of products generated progressively by the application of science and human ingenuity. Scope is mainly (not wholly) the story of the twentieth century. If one is prepared to include under chemistry post-1945 pharmaceuticals, synthetic fibers, plastics, and other petrochemicals; under the internal combustion engine, the sequence from the Model-T to jet aircraft and rockets; under electricity, radio, television, and the premicroelectronic computer, the third technological revolution did not sharply decelerate in the advanced industrial countries until the second half of the 1960s.[5]

The flow of diversified products yielded by the third technological revolution led some American industrial leaders to move to a new organizational structure. The pattern was set when three cousins of Eugene du Pont bought out and reorganized the family's century old explosives firm in 1903 after his death. Within the production department their reorganization set up separate relatively decentralized units for high explosives, black powder, and smokeless powder. Special development laboratories were created. By 1921 the technologically vital and inherently diversified nature of the chemical business had yielded departments for manufacturing cellulose, dyestuffs, and paints, as well as explosives. Decentralization by product, rather than merely by function, plus the acceptance of research and development as part of the firm, required greatly strengthened executive management at the top, supplied by an enlarged executive committee and staffs to mobilize essential data.

Of all the organizational creations in this period perhaps the most remarkable was the transformation of the laboratories of the Bell System into an instrument for a succession of major innovations. The transformation to a new organizational pattern occurred in 1907–19 under the leadership of Theodore Vail.[6]

The interest of du Pont in the automobile industry, via the investment of a substantial volume of its profits in General Motors in the period 1910–20, set the stage for the application of these principles, for a time at least, to the most important industry of the next stage of American development.

The mass production, sale, and use of the automobile was clearly the most powerful innovation of the first half of the twentieth century. Like the railroad a century earlier, the stature of the automobile in economic history flows from its multiple effects. It became a significant, if not dominating, market for steel and engineering products, rubber, glass, oil, and light electronics; it restructured American life along suburban lines; it linked rural to urban markets in new, more flexible ways; it created a requirement for large-scale sales and servicing industries; it set up extensive requirements for roads and parking facilities; it touched patterns of American life from courting habits to the get-away methods of bank robbers. It was accompanied by—and, in various indirect ways, related to—a surge in the production of various durable consumer goods and processed foods that came to fill American homes, as rising incomes and suburban life made personal service expensive and inaccessible: washers and dryers; vacuum cleaners; the electric ice box; the oil furnace and then air conditioning; canned and then frozen foods. It was the family car that inspired the supermarket and the shopping mall.

This wide-ranging transformation came logically first to the United States because of the persistence of higher per capita income. But it was triggered, against this background, by one of the great insights in the history of American enterprise—an insight into the potential income elasticity of demand. Henry Ford defined in 1908 (and announced in 1909) his immediate mission as the production and sale of a cheap, reliable, single model "for the great multitude" so that every man "making a good salary" could "enjoy with his family the blessing of hours of pleasure in God's great open spaces." Then, in 1913, the moving assembly line for the Model T was set in motion. Ford's strategic concept of 1908 was now matched by a working process derived not from a complex R&D process but an analogy with the moving belt in a slaughter house.

Ford's success—and the parallel success of others—posed major questions of industrial organization, as the number of private automobiles in use grew from 306,000 in 1909 to 8 million in 1920; 23 million in 1929; 26 million in 1945; 54 million in 1955; 78 million in 1966. The critical transition in scale was that which occurred in the decade before 1920, when a twenty-five-fold increase in private automobile ownership and something like a tenfold increase in annual sales occurred.

The motor car, which had begun as the plaything of the elite, became the liberator (and enslaver) of the common man.

But Ford's administrative style, remarkable as it was, essentially belonged to an earlier era: concentration on a single product, the rigorous exploitation of economies of scale, and vertical integration. He was not successful as an adaptive innovator. Ford expanded by enlarging his Model T factories, creating a vertical input production structure, and proliferating his sales operations, under essentially one-man control.[7] The other major innovator in the industry, William C. Durant, pulled together a holding company for making and selling automobiles, parts, and accessories. Ford's was an engineer's solution to the challenge and opportunity, Durant's that of an organizer of finance and people in a rapidly diversifying market.

Built into the General Motors structure under Durant was a considerable degree of autonomy for the various manufacturing units. A brief recession in 1910 suggested the financial vulnerability of this sprawling, loosely managed empire; and it was caught hard, in the midst of ambitious postwar expansion plans, by the sharp recession of 1920–21.

Durant withdrew and the du Ponts moved in to make sense of the operation, later putting up, with others, the funds necessary to avoid catastrophe. Chandler describes as follows the historic reorganization designed by Alfred P. Sloan, Jr., and put into effect by Pierre du Pont:

> The new organization was one which Sloan had already suggested to Durant.
>
> Under Durant each operation had been left completely to its own. . . . To bring some sort of order and unity into the corporation, Sloan had proposed the creation of a central office to coordinate, appraise, and plan policy for the different units and the corporation as a whole. The operating divisions were to remain responsible for market and financial performance. . . . Sloan recommended separating the divisions into four groups— motor car, parts, accessories, and miscellaneous. This structure, which was changed only in detail after its adoption in January 1921, became a model for structural changes at International Harvester, General Electric, and elsewhere in later years.[8]

The relative decline of Ford's sales from 40 to 50 percent of the market in 1920–25 to 20 to 30 percent in the 1930s and the rise in this period of General Motors' from 10 to 20 percent to 40 percent or better clinched the point. According to *Fortune* (May 1947) after the Second World War Henry Ford's grandson "clapped the G.M. organization garment onto the Ford manufacturing frame."

Thus, American enterprise found its way to a new pattern that went beyond the centralized management of functional divisions. The new structure balanced the financial and other advantages of centralization with quasi-autonomous product divisions. It provided the advantages of both manageable scale and clear accountability. The pattern was not universally accepted; and, where it was accepted, it was modified to fit the special requirements of particular markets and firms. But it commended itself in general, to an industrial complex that was moving to diversified lines of capital and consumer goods operating abroad as well as in the uniquely large American market.

These are the large but flexible structures, commanding vast resources of working capital, managerial skill in depth, a sense of competitiveness among their various divisions as well as in relation to other firms, which constituted *Le Défi Americain* that Europe and the world had to face after the Second

World War. But these firms, superficially rather uniform in style and ripe for textbook treatment in American business schools, were by no means uniform in their capacity to conduct "adaptive" let alone "formative" innovation.

The early evolution of automobile technology was a phenomenon shared in the Atlantic community; and the United States was not even primus inter pares. The organization of the European chemical and electricity-related industries matched their American counterparts. What the United States had was one old asset—relatively high average per capita income—plus Europe's bad luck, often self-generated. The level of American wages made it natural for the United States to be the first country to produce a car for a worker "making a good salary." Meanwhile Europe was greatly set back by the First World War and the sluggish interwar years, and then setback again by the Second World War. The United States only shared the setback of the Great Depression of the 1930s. The post-1948 boom in Europe—and, after 1955, in Japan—brought the rest of the advanced industrial world to levels of real per capita income and market scale in the same range as those of the United States.

Thus, as the great quarter-century boom of 1948–73 proceeded in a global environment of relatively liberal trade, the two classic pillars of American industry progressively weakened and disappeared: the relatively higher average level of American income and the unique scale of the American market.

The first signs that American primacy was waning came in the late 1950s when, in President Eisenhower's phrase, the United States experienced a "sputtering economy," balance of payments pressure, and, under the Bretton Woods arrangement, some gold loss. The outflow of gold was one of the two major problems President Eisenhower laid reluctantly on President-elect Kennedy on January 19, 1961. (The other was the situation in Laos, where Eisenhower urged, Kennedy would probably have to send U.S. forces "if possible with others, if necessary alone.") Kennedy, it so happened, was already well informed about the balance of payments problem, which pleased Eisenhower. To the surprise of some of his economic advisers, Kennedy took his responsibility for the balance of payments as second only to his responsibility to protect U.S. national interests without the use of nuclear weapons; and he understood, better than some of his advisers, that the balance of payments problem had arisen from the higher rate of productivity increase in Europe and Japan than in the post-1945 United States—a trend with profound long-run implications screened out by the reigning short-run framework of Keynesian macroeconomics. Kennedy took a number of steps designed to increase U.S. productivity; to gear wages to productivity increases; and to share military and foreign aid burdens more equitably in the Atlantic Alliance.[9]

Since then, pressures on the U.S. trade balance have been chronic, although it was not until 1982 that the over all balance on current account moved systematically into deficit.

From the present perspective, however, the central fact about American industry in the third technological revolution is that it evolved in two quite distinct patterns. Some sectors wove research and development departments intimately into their day-to-day operations and executive planning, including agriculture and food processing, electricity and electronics, and most branches of the ramified chemical industry. After its reorganization, General Motors, under Pierre du Pont and Alfred Sloan, developed a research department headed by Charles Kettering, inventor of the self-starter. Research was well linked to the executive and operating divisions and did useful work related to automobile manufacture and use. In the 1930s research was diversified, yielding a diesel-powered railroad locomotive as well as advances in the aircraft industry. But an effective research and development tradition did not persist at General Motors into the post-1945 generation, perhaps because of complacency among the oligopolistic Big Three about virtually unchallenged control over the bulk of a domestic market where gasoline was cheap, distances long, and cars big. In any case the American automotive industry was ill-prepared for the later challenges from Europe and Japan.

The aircraft industry, stimulated by the First World War, nurtured after 1917 by a strand of continued governmental interest through the National Advisory Committee for Aeronautics, and lifted to great heights in the Second World War, was sustained strongly in the cold war by ties to large-scale research and development as well as to a rapidly expanding commercial market.

In steel, machine tools, and, indeed, in most other sectors, steady and effective links between research and development and those conducting American industrial strategy were never built. There seemed to be a clash between the imperatives of innovation and the nation's reigning administrative style in industry.[10] In short, American industry taken as a whole—with a history of peculiarly easy triumphs and a heavy, rather static bureaucratic administrative style—was not well prepared for the rigors of the fourth technological revolution. Some sectors were to perform as poorly as General McClellan when he switched from the more or less predictable order of the Central Illinois Railroad to the shocks, surprises, and innovational requirements of the battlefield.

THE UNITED STATES IN THE FOURTH
TECHNOLOGICAL REVOLUTION

The relative performance of the major sectors in the fourth technological revolution was affected by its special characteristics:

- It is closely linked to areas of basic science that are themselves in a state of fast-moving revolution. The scientific revolutions underpinning the new technologies generate an accelerated pace of innovation. They also have the effect of requiring the scientist to join the team of inventor, entrepreneur, and worker. How closely the scientist, engineer, businessperson, and worker operate in partnership will determine the pace of technological change in each society.

- This revolution seems fated to transform virtually every sector in the economy: the older basic industries (e.g., textiles, steel, motor vehicles); agriculture, forestry, and animal husbandry; and all the services from education to military hardware, from medicine to banking.

- The new technologies are immediately relevant to developing countries, depending on their stage of growth and technological absorptive capacity.

- Each branch of the fourth technological revolution is so diversified that it is most unlikely that any one nation will establish unambiguous leadership as Britain did in the cotton textile revolution, or the United States did in the early days of the automobile. International competition there is and surely will be; but the diversity of each of the new technological fields means that different countries will develop a comparative advantage in one or another aspect of high-tech.

How, then, have the major sectors of the American economy fared in the first phase of the fourth technological revolution, with their classic advantages lost and the playing field leveled down to a race in innovation, including commercialization?[11] The relative sectoral performance is suggested in Figure 2.1, indicating major export surpluses and import deficits for 1988.[12]

Those sectors with a significant historical linkage to R&D, agriculture, aircraft production, and various branches of the chemical industry fared best; the performance of electronics was mixed; the motor vehicle industry was a disaster. Sectors without a strong institutionalized connection with R&D on the whole fared poorly.[13]

Figure 2.1. Top Ten Product Surpluses and Deficits, 1988

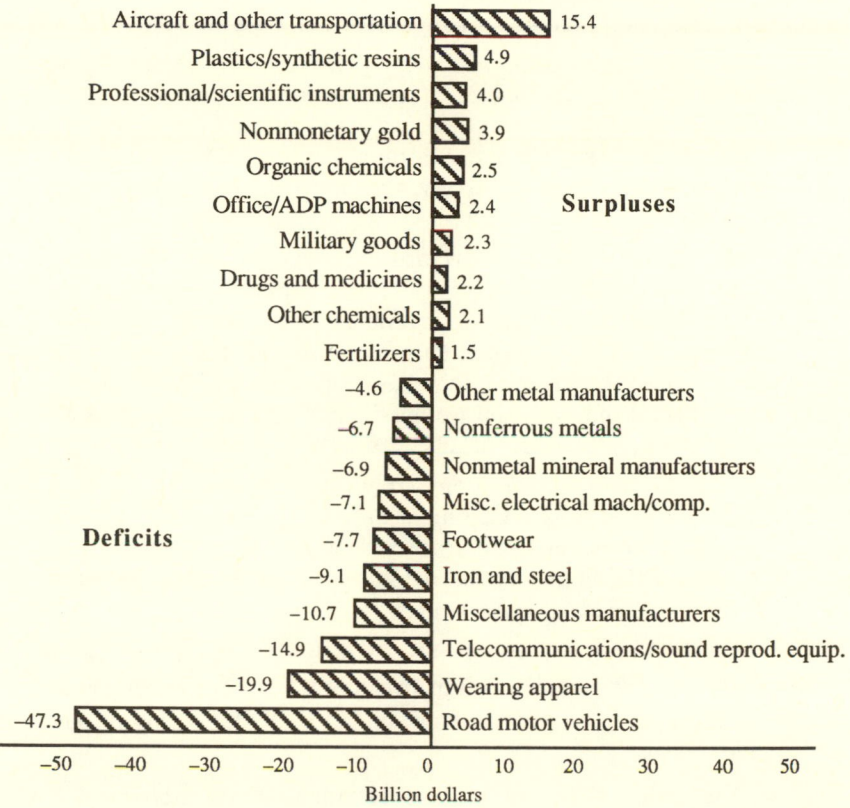

Aircraft and other transportation		15.4
Plastics/synthetic resins		4.9
Professional/scientific instruments		4.0
Nonmonetary gold		3.9
Organic chemicals		2.5
Office/ADP machines		2.4
Military goods		2.3
Drugs and medicines		2.2
Other chemicals		2.1
Fertilizers		1.5

Surpluses

Deficits

−4.6		Other metal manufacturers
−6.7		Nonferrous metals
−6.9		Nonmetal mineral manufacturers
−7.1		Misc. electrical mach/comp.
−7.7		Footwear
−9.1		Iron and steel
−10.7		Miscellaneous manufacturers
−14.9		Telecommunications/sound reprod. equip.
−19.9		Wearing apparel
−47.3		Road motor vehicles

−50 −40 −30 −20 −10 0 10 20 30 40 50

Billion dollars

The American aircraft industry, for example, has thus far sustained its primacy in world markets in a remarkable way. In part, of course, this was a result of the outcome of the Second World War, which left Germany and Japan inhibited with respect to military aircraft, and the national industries of France and Britain in a poor initial position to challenge American primacy. But there was another factor that carries a lesson for the future. Aircraft manufacturers of both military and civil aircraft know that they are caught up in an apparently endless competitive test that requires that each successive model represent an authentic improvement on its predecessor or meet a new requirement in the private or public market. Two things follow: Research and development are intimately linked; and, despite inevitable problems and the infinitely resourceful operation of Murphy and his Law, the bugs must be overcome and the development process yield a viable product.

Hans Mark has recently summed up the reasons for the continued competitiveness of the aircraft industry in terms that illuminate some of the principles he believes should govern an American industrial policy:

1. *The federal government has made a consistent investment in the development of aeronautical technology for more than 70 years.* . . . At the present time, we are investing between NASA and the military about $2 billion per year in aeronautical research. This is a small investment when you consider the return.

2. *There is no adversarial relationship between the government and the aeronautical industry.* This is extremely important. In other industries the federal government has attempted to break up the most successful corporations and has sometimes succeeded. Fortunately, this has not been tried yet in the aeronautical industry, and we must guard against attempts to do so.

3. *There is good technology transfer from research and development to manufacturing in the aeronautical industry.* This is also a consequence of the close relationship between the aeronautical contractors and the customer community, be it the federal government or the airlines.[14]

The quite different story of the VCR underlines once again the importance of development as well as invention. The American electronics industry failed to see its pioneering work on the VCR stubbornly through the development process:

> In the case of the VCR. . . Japanese firms achieved outstanding success in a global marketplace for products founded on basic technologies originated in the U.S. or Europe. But the Japanese leaders in VCR production did more than simply copy Western technology. . . . They pushed a difficult technology far beyond the limits thought practical by most U.S. and some Japanese competitors. . . .
>
> [T]he story of pioneering in VCRs is not an exceptional case. Strategic experimentation and disciplined learning at critical, early stages in the evolution of particular technologies, combined with stable teams of managers and engineers, has no doubt affected, if not determined, the current performance of a large number of firms in Japan.[15]

Unlike the U. S. electronic firms and the VCR, the chemical industry has put on a model performance in the fourth technological revolution. As Figure 2.1 shows, more than $13 billion in trade surplus was generated by various branches of the chemical industry in 1988. In characterizing American industry when it began to face increased foreign competition in the 1960s and thereafter, Chandler observes:

> An initial response to intensified competition . . . was the decision of top managers to have their industrial enterprises grow by acquiring companies in markets that were only distantly related or even unrelated to the core facilities and skills of their enterprise. . . . Not all managers responded in this way. Those in many of the large industrial enterprises reacted to the new competition, as they had done earlier to less intensive competition, by making state-of-the-art investments in production, distribution, and R&D, and by adjusting the roles and responsibilities of their management teams . . . to exploit fully their organizational capabilities.[16]

The chemical industry represents Chandler's second category. By and large it never lost its capacity to weave R&D and operations together dynamically. Since the du Pont reorganization of 1903, it has managed to hold a strong position in highly competitive world markets and seems likely to continue to do so as genetic engineering gathers momentum with wide-ranging applications.

Major events in history usually occur when independent forces converge to push things in the same direction.[17] The following forces or circumstances may have contributed to the sharp relative decline of the U.S. automobile industry and the scandalous balance of payments deficit of almost $50 billion in the motor vehicle sector.

- The post-1945 decline in the quality of R&D in the automobile industry
- Laxity in quality control perhaps stemming from both management and labor complacency about continued Big Three domination of a domestic market addicted to cheap gasoline and large cars
- The rise in the real price of gasoline in the oil crises of 1973–75 and 1979–81, increasing the American public's demand for smaller cars
- The takeover of management by experts in finance rather than production or R&D, encouraged by their business school training to focus on maximizing the bottom line in the short run, reproducing a century later the kind of management-operations fault-line Henry Varnum Poor identified in the early long-distance railroads

The critical missing element in the sectors that have contributed to the U.S. trade deficit is a lack of technological dynamism either because significant R&D has not been generated in that sector or its results have not been applied (as in the case of A. D. Little's clientele of the late 1950s).

The markedly uneven and, on average, mediocre performance of the United States in the first phase of the fourth technological revolution was affected negatively by six factors beyond the special character of the sectors themselves and inappropriate inherited styles of administration.

First, the tax cuts of 1981–82 and subsequent large federal deficits and the monetary policy then pursued raised real interest rates in the United States, attracted large flows of short-term capital from abroad, bid up the dollar, and radically diminished the competitive position of American exports while cheapening and stimulating imports. The overvalued dollar could not have come at a worse time. The Japanese, understanding the opportunity offered by this self-inflicted wound, drove to the wall the automobile, machine tool, and sections of the electronics industry, already rendered vulnerable by American technological sluggishness. A variety of factors have reduced the efficacy of the post-1985 devaluation of the dollar, including the ruthless drive of the Japanese to hold on to—if not to expand—market share in the United States, via differential low pricing of exports and other mercantilist devices.

Second, since President Kennedy's limited pioneering efforts, there has been no coherent American industrial policy; and in the 1980s, when the American competitive position became palpably precarious, with profound foreign policy as well as domestic consequences, the Reagan and Bush administrations (supported by a good many Democratic politicians and experts) mainly contented themselves with the rationale that "None of us is smart enough to pick winners," although this is precisely what we have had to do in military production for a half-century in order to survive. There is, however, much more to an industrial policy than picking winners—greater investment in education and in greatly neglected physical infrastructure as well as a reduction in the federal deficit, which would bring about a decline in real interest rates.

Third, the lack of political leadership has been compounded by business school teaching that almost totally lost touch with manufacturing and focused on the maximization of profits in the short run in a world that assumed fixed production functions or, at best, "adaptive" innovation. And these attitudes reflected the predominant views in the business and financial communities.

Fourth, starting in the 1960s, as European and Japanese competition mounted, the expansionary impulses from the third technological revolution waned, and before the fourth had declared itself, frustrated American business leaders converted their cash flow into diversified acquisitions. When these proved unmanageable, mergers and acquisitions gave way in the 1970s and 1980s to a wave of divestitures. Chandler describes this extraordinary phase in measured language:

> Such unprecedented diversification . . . often led to a separation, that is, a breakdown of communications, between top management at the corporate office . . . and the middle managers who were responsible for maintaining the competitive capabilities of the operating divisions in the battle for market share and profits. . . .
>
> The managerial weaknesses resulting from the separation of top from operating executives quickly led to still another new phenomenon— the selling off of divisions and other operating units in unprecedented numbers. The costs of unbridled diversification were soon learned.[18]

When historians take stock of this phase—from which Germany and Japan were largely spared—they may conclude that large parts of the American business and financial community ingested locoweed and went mad—a phase Galambos and Pratt characterize as "vulture capitalism."[19] Charles Kindleberger captures the strain of irrationality that clearly was part of this process:

> I have [an] interest in the theory we all bought about the internalization of external economies. . . . The multinational corporation on this showing was a bundle of synergy, one hand washing the other, coordinate planning that improved on atomistic competitive markets. . . . But the wave of takeovers leading to the selling off of various constituent parts of multinational corporations poses a question as to how wide and deep this motive for foreign direct investment has been. Many companies seem to be worth more dead than alive, butchered rather than in live weight. . . . The scrappy data I collected . . . showed company after company taking over others, both in hostile and friendly fashion, and then selling off bits and pieces—shoulders, hams, sides, steaks, whatever. These companies proved to be decomposable matrices rather than tightly woven integers. . . . Takeovers and selling bits and pieces seem to me to cast doubt on the generality of the internalization theory. . . .
>
> The initial direct investment may have been a mistake of the follow-the-leader mania, bubble, or overtrading variety; the company may be in trouble and forced to amputate to save the rest; inflation may have raised the value of bits, especially those with real estate; there may be a cyclical aspect to investment and disinvestment in the vertical chain . . . and there is a real possibility that some of the original acquisitions and subsequent reshuffling have been more concerned with simple-minded market share than with synergy.[20]

The Savings and Loan tragedy was, evidently, an element in this extraordinary American performance in which parts of the business and financial communities, unable or unwilling to face the discipline, long-term commitment, and sustained creativity required to cope with tough foreign competition, looked about in desperation for some other way to make easy profits. This included an extravagant building boom worthy of the seventeenth-century Dutch Tulip Mania.

Fifth, a narrower example of the disorientation of American economic thought and policy in the 1980s was the handling of Latin American debt. Clearly there was no rational basis either for the granting or acceptance of the loans—a piece of collective pathology that lies outside the scope of this chapter. As the consequence of these loans became clear after 1981, including economic stagnation or worse in Latin America, the United States had three interests in a resolution of the debt problem: the continued viability of the U.S. and international banking structure; the revival of U.S. exports to Latin America at a time of acute balance of payments pressure; and the encouragement of a remarkable resurgent movement toward democratic politics in Latin America.

The U.S. government for a time gave overriding priority to the maintenance of the fiction that the loans would be fully repaid, encouraging public and private banks to lend enough additional money to permit interest on the loans to be transferred. This cosmetic procedure permitted the banks to carry the loans on their books at 100 percent. In 1989–90, at long last, policy moved toward a limited writeoff of principal as well as a substantial writedown of the loans on the books of private American banks. All this proceeded at the cost of 20 to 40 percent of the American trade deficit while endangering the democratic process in critically important parts of Latin America. Overall American merchandise exports rose in current dollars about 30 percent between 1981 and 1988: exports to Latin America rose less than 5 percent. The proportion of manufactured exports to Latin America fell from 20 to 14 percent.

Finally, most fundamentally, the American political process at the highest national level failed to identify the critical nature of the transition through which the nation was passing and to focus the great energies of the continent on a satisfactory passage to a new phase in American and global history. The two major political parties continued a battle almost a century old: Should the marginal dollar go to the public or to the private sector? Should we seek lower taxes or greater equity in American society? In fact, the central issue of American society—now and in the foreseeable future—is whether it can rally in partnership to assure that the nation can pay its way in the world and continue to expand the common pie on which the standard of living, the quality of social services, and national security uniquely depend. In the 1980s, the foundations of American affluence eroded in physical and human infrastructure as well as in the balance of payments; social inequity increased; and the nation's capacity to influence its global environment diminished.

On balance, historians will probably regard the overall performance of American society in the 1980s as quite as bizarre. The story recalls the *bon mot* of the historian Lewis Namier, who wrote, "A neurotic, according to Freud, is a man dominated by unconscious memories, fixated on the past, and incapable of overcoming it: the regular condition of human communities."[21] And this is not surprising. Between the 1930s and the 1980s the United States had worked its way out of the Great Depression; emerged strong and honorably from the Second World War; used a real—if inherently transient—interval of global economic hegemony with some wisdom; accepted the costly and sometimes tormenting burden of leadership in the test of will and systems we call the cold war. It is understandable that the leaders of such a society, having transited successfully an extraordinary half-century, would tend to feel that their inherited ways of thinking and doing things had been vindicated and that little change—perhaps a bit of adaptive change—was all that was required. But history is not notably tolerant of nostalgia. It is more inclined to ask the famous question of Alben Barkley's constituent: "What have you done for me lately?"

In fact, this continental society has proved more complex than Namier's generalized human community, a bit more capable of reacting to reality with resilience rather than merely nostalgia. While the politicians of both parties fenced irrelevantly and indecisively in Washington over the federal budget, and the financial community played its pathological and often illegal games, serious business proceeded across the country in three major respects.

First, after a costly delay, a substantial array of business firms and sectors have taken on the fourth industrial revolution and the intensely competitive world the United States confronts and will confront as far ahead as anyone can foresee. The relative competitive performance of American firms has not only been sustained under heavy pressure in the aircraft, chemical, and electronics industries; but, to some degree, the automobile, steel, machine tool, and other industries that exhibited vulnerability to technological competition have exhibited considerable recuperative powers. This is peculiarly important because the fourth technological revolution has proved relevant, in different degrees, to virtually every manufacturing, agricultural, raw material, and service sector. Put another way, the perceptions of Theodore Vail, Alfred Sloan, and Edwin Land (Polaroid) will have to suffuse the outlook of virtually every American entrepreneur (and business school graduate) before we can be confident of the long-run viability of the American economy and the society it sustains.[22]

Second, the progressively acute competitive crisis of the last generation, climaxed by the debacle of the 1980s, has brought to the fore and strengthened the greatest relative asset American society possesses: the Morrill Act tradition.

When the transcontinental railroads were subsidized in 1862 by land grants, alternative squares of land were allocated to colleges in support of agriculture, mining, and industry. A cultural tradition was thus established in the United States linking in an easy, unembarrassed way the intellectual life of universities with the day-to-day tasks of men and women who were earning their living. In Europe, Japan, and elsewhere the fourth technological revolution has moved societies in this direction because the role of basic science in this revolution is uniquely direct. But it is the Morrill Act tradition that has not only sustained a high productivity agriculture, but has also facilitated the emergence of more than fifty high-tech centers in the United States, bringing into partnership scientists, engineers, entrepreneurs, and, where successful, the working force as well. These partnerships, sustained steadily for the long pull, will prove to be fundamental to U.S. competitiveness.

Third were the rather gallant politics of American states and cities in the 1980s. The federal government reduced in real terms both its own welfare payments and nonmilitary physical infrastructure investment, while reducing at the same time grants to state and local governments for both purposes. In the course of the decade, however, the local demand for social services and for infrastructure maintenance and expansion increased under pressure from expanded population, increased use of drugs, the diffusion of AIDS, increased crime, and growing concern for the level and quality of education at the primary and secondary levels. The almost universal requirement that state and local governments balance their budgets left little scope for state and local politicians to congratulate themselves on the state of the nation and play games with Gramm–Rudman.

Although performances varied by and large governors and mayors of both parties attempted to deal with their problems even at the cost of advocating higher taxes; and, overall, under existing bookkeeping procedures, they generated a budget surplus on the order of $50 billion per annum.

They also confronted the realities of the balance of payments deficit and the imperatives of the fourth technological revolution in a more direct and vigorous way than the federal government. The attenuation of manufactured exports in the older industries and the continued dynamism of certain high-tech sectors led to active local measures to stimulate exports and to attract high-tech firms. The latter, in turn, brought state and local governments into an organizing role in bringing universities, private sector firms, and financial institutions together to create the high-tech concentrations referred to above. The critical importance of the quality of education was dramatized vividly to politicians in the course of these efforts. The federal government may not have had an industrial policy in the 1980s; but many states and cities did and still do.[23]

All their enterprises did not succeed, but the competition among American cities and states in jobs, high-tech firms, the quality of research universities, and education in general may turn out to have been a fundamental dynamic force, partially insulating the society as a whole in the 1980s and beyond from the corrosive goings on in national politics and in important parts of the business and financial communities. If the United States succeeds, as it must, in once again paying its way in the world and holding its own in the gut-wrenching competitive world that lies ahead, a transfer of attitudes and policies from state capitols and city halls to Washington will be an essential part of that recovery of viability.

As of August 1990 there was solid evidence that the United States was bottoming out of the slide of the 1980s, including the narrowing of the rate of increase in manufacturing productivity in the course of the 1980s between the United States and its major competitors. But, evidently, we still have a long way to go.[24] (See Table 2.1.)

Table 2.1. Manufacturing Productivity in the United States and Its Major Competitors
(average annual percentage change)

	United States	Japan	Canada	France	Germany	United Kingdom
1981	2.2	3.7	4.8	3.1	2.2	5.1
1982	2.2	6.1	−4.5	7.0	1.4	6.1
1983	5.8	5.4	7.2	2.6	5.9	8.5
1984	5.4	7.2	10.8	3.0	3.8	5.5
1986	3.7	1.7	−0.3	2.4	1.7	2.8
1987	2.8	4.1	1.8	3.7	1.3	6.9
Average, 1961–70	3.0	17.9	4.9	9.1	7.7	4.4
Average, 1971–75	3.0	7.1	3.4	5.4	5.3	3.6
Average, 1976–80	1.8	7.1	2.2	4.6	3.9	1.4
Average, 1981–87	3.9	4.8	3.2	3.6	2.9	5.5

Source: Bureau of Labor Statistics, "Current Labor Statistics," *Monthly Labor Review* (August 1988).

As the process proceeds it is bringing about a piecemeal, uneven, but quite detectable change in labor relations parallel to that occurring in politics beyond the Beltway. As already noted, the governors and mayors are being forced by circumstances to take steps that are based less on class interests and somewhat more on authentic communal interest; and to make their appeal in terms of the need for communal partnership rather than a winning combination of special interests. Somewhat similarly, the traditional American labor-management confrontation over the division of a firm's income between an increment in distributed profits versus an increment in wages is being diluted by a common labor-management interest in higher productivity and preservation of competitiveness. This transition is, of course, not occurring because of a joint access of civic virtue. The loss of jobs to foreign competitors has both weakened the bargaining leverage of labor (and union membership) in many sectors; while the swift and efficient changes in technology required for international viability have helped persuade management that profits—indeed, staying in business—require a personnel policy that yields an intelligent, self-respecting workforce authentically committed to the common cause of survival.

In short, the fourth technological revolution is beginning to drive home, in the manufacturing sector at least, the lesson that American private affluence and public services are not guaranteed by history and some special dispensation of Higher Authority, but will have to be earned day-by-day by sustained cooperation among diverse groups in American society in a raw international struggle for productivity, in which the pace of innovation will be the determining variable.

CONCLUSIONS

The United States is more rather than less likely to assume and sustain a position of dignity and strength in the world economy. Posing the right question has always been 90 percent of good science and good policy making. Robert Kuhn has edited a handbook of over 650 pages on the subject with almost seventy ardent authors who obviously know at least a part of the answer.[25]

The fate of American society, stripped of its two grand initial advantages, depends and will continue to depend on the extent to which we can reconcile over a much wider front than in the past a high sustained rate of innovation with the order and continuity our inevitably bureaucratic civilization demands.

While the criteria for success and excellence differ as among profit-making, public policy, and academic bureaucracies, certain broad rules hold.

First, *the most important subject in which to train a young person with potentially executive capacities is history.* Lest this be thought special pleading by a historian, it is a matter of record that this was the overwhelming advice of a group of major CEOs interviewed by an MIT faculty committee when the Sloan School of Industrial Management was set up in the early 1950s. The outsiders were asked: "What would you teach young men who might be your successors?" They observed that a business leader must accept as normal an environment of endless change, never in equilibrium, demanding purposeful innovation and a long perspective for survival. History is the only way to teach such a perspective, because it requires the serious student to separate what is unique in historical circumstances from what carries abiding lessons, what is transient from a trend that may foreshadow the future.

Second, *the capacity of a business firm or other institution to reconcile innovation with the efficient management of routine functions depends overwhelmingly on its manager.* When President Kennedy called up an official four levels down from the cabinet secretary to let him know of his personal interest in an innovative project; or when President Johnson called the policy planner at the State Department on Wednesday asking for two new policy initiatives by Friday; or when Winston Churchill required every British wartime bureaucracy to examine and evaluate in writing every outside suggestion—even a proposal to use big butterfly nets hung on jet fighter planes to trap flying bombs and haul them out to sea—word got around. One of the mysterious qualities of a bureaucracy—even one as heavy and sluggish as the federal government in Washington—is its sensitivity to the style and values of the current chief executive.

Third, *innovative units, at every stage in the R&D spectrum, should be kept as small as possible.* Innovation is a job for first-rate people; and there are not many first-rate people. Moreover, innovative creativity is fostered by intense, mutually confident collegial exchanges. Such exchanges are difficult if not impossible in big units. Finally, every administrator should remember that each person hired will demand a significant chunk of time and attention from a superior. When hiring, the administrator should be confident that benefits outweigh costs, including the cost in administrator time.

Fourth, *inventors, at the initiating stage of the R&D spectrum, should be governed by two rules: (1) They must be willing to share the difficulties of development, helping translate an idea into a viable operation; and (2) they should be prepared to let the operator get the bulk of the credit.* Innovation is a painful, disruptive, and disturbing business to operators. They must feel they have a stake in an innovation's success and rewards will flow from that success. The point here is peculiarly important for the United States. At this stage in our history, we remain a highly creative society. Our weaknesses lie in moving rapidly from invention, through the stages of development, to successful innovation in the market. Ironically, for a nation caricatured around the world as obsessed with business, we are rather poor at commercialization in the global market.

Fifth, *managers should maintain close, regular relations with the leader of the R&D team, sharing their own dreams for the future, sharing the R&D team's intervals of frustration inevitable in a sustained creative process; but that tie should not be dramatized.* Every move or idea generated in the R&D process concerns an operator's business. Operators should not be made unnecessarily uneasy with the image of the executive and the R&D team getting excessively into operator affairs.

Sixth, *a great deal of extremely important innovation will be incremental, or "adaptive."* This means that all departments, not just R&D, should be geared to innovational possibilities and rewarded when they are demonstrated to be viable. This requires in turn an administrative style and method aimed to place individuals in settings in which they can and will perform at the full stretch of their creative capacities.

These simple rules are obvious enough; but they are not the rules by which the army in peacetime or long-distance railways or Taylor's machine shop were governed; nor the standard rules for either a functional or divisional table of organization; nor the rules to be found in a conventional administrative text in a business school; nor yet, at least, in a great many American bureaucratic institutions.

These rules are all heightened in importance by special characteristics of the fourth technological revolution—notably, the seamless web required to bind the whole spectrum from scientist through the R&D process to the market; the extraordinary pace of the revolution; and its ubiquity. As Mark and Levine note, these characteristics place a premium on lateral as opposed to the vertical communications spawned by the second technological revolution.[26]

This chapter encompasses, then, the story of four adjustments to four technological revolutions, one still incomplete. The first revolution required building an industrial base in competition with ample cheap land and an expensive urban workforce; the second required mastering, by specialization of function, efficient administration of large-scale operations, yielding a single product or service, in order to exploit a rapidly expanding continental market made possible by the long-distance railroad; the third required the reconciliation of R&D with the inherited style of bureaucratic order plus a shift over a wider front to organization by production division rather than by function; the fourth came at a time when the United States no longer enjoyed unique status because of market scale and high average affluence and required the extension across the board of attitudes and methods that balanced the creative requirements of R&D with the canons of reasonable bureaucratic order—a reconciliation hitherto confined to only a few sectors.

There is a deep reason for confidence in the long-run viability of this continental society—deeper, even, than the widespread concern with the pace of innovation and the setting down of rules, whether 101 or six, for creative and innovative management. The reason is that, confronted with a problem, Americans still argue, experiment, chew away at it until an approximation of an answer is found. We remain both proud and critical of our performance as a people. From earliest days foreign observers of the United States have noted that Americans were haunted by a "magnificent image" of the nation's ideals and its adventure;[27] although a long line of invaluable commentators— Mark Twain, Mr. Dooley, Will Rogers, and Harpo Marx among others— assured that their countrymen were also reminded that they were no better than they should be.

Both strands in our character remain alive and well.

A people driven by a restless pragmatic energy, haunted in its round of life by old ideals that it can neither abandon nor fully attain, maintaining a sense of proportion by self-depreciating humor, is likely to adjust constructively to new realities rather than go down in the style to which it has become accustomed.

NOTES

1. In particular, Louis Galambos and Joseph Pratt, *The Rise of the Corporate Commonwealth* (New York: Basic Books, 1988), esp. pp. 201–66; and Alfred D. Chandler, Jr., *Scale and Scope, The Dynamics of Industrial Capitalism* (Cambridge: Belknap Press of Harvard University Press, 1990), esp. pp. 593–628.

2. From *Reports of the President and the Superintendent of the New York and Erie Railroad to the Stockholders for the Year Ending September 30, 1855* (New York), p. 34, quoted in Thomas K. McGraw, ed., *The Essential Alfred Chandler* (Boston: Harvard Business School Press, 1985), p. 184. As McCallum's reference to the initial failure of the large railways lines suggests, the administrative revolution required was not quickly brought to pass. In the first of the short list of American classics in the field of administration, Henry Varnum Poor captured the problems posed by administration of large-scale business units, notably the problem of linking effectively financially oriented management, ignorant of railway operations, and the engineers of the line. See, notably, Alfred Chandler, "Henry Varnum Poor: Business Analyst," in *Essential Alfred Chandler*, pp. 23–45. The key

problem isolated by Poor characterized a good many of the overblown conglomerates of the 1960s and 1970s.

3. Read in the context of this paper Woodrow Wilson's famous essay, "A Study of Administration," with its explicit admiration of the Prussian and Napoleonic administrative styles, is typical of this period. It was first published in the *Political Science Quarterly* in June 1887, and reprinted in that journal in December 1941. Hans Mark and Arnold Levine thus characterize the kind of "mechanistic" organization Wilson (and Max Weber) had in mind. See *The Management of Research Institutions* (Washington, D.C.: NASA, 1984), p. 177: "The mechanistic organization is the classic hierarchical, bureaucratic system described by Max Weber nearly eighty years ago. A mechanistic system can be easily identified by the specialized differentiation of functional tasks, the precise definition of each person's rights and obligations, the elaborate code governing superior-subordinate relations, the greater importance attached to local rather than to general knowledge, and the concentration of information at the top of the hierarchy. Mechanistic organizations are appropriate to stable conditions."

4. Louis Galambos applies Lazonick's concept to the story of the Bell system in "Theodore N. Vail and the Role of Innovation in the Modern Bell System," citing Lazonick's manuscript "Theory, History, and the Capitalist Enterprise" (November 1987), esp. pp. 24–35. The contrast between "adaptive" and "formative" strategies obviously bears a family relation to Schumpeter's distinction between incremental changes and adaptation to external events permitted in his circular flow system and the dynamics of his great, irreversible innovational revolutions. For discussion, see my *Theories of Economic Growth from David Hume to the Present* (New York: Oxford University Press, 1990), esp. pp. 234–35. Galambos (p. 8) characterizes the "adaptive" phase of innovation in the Bell system in terms similar to Mark and Levine's "mechanistic organization" (above, p. 8, n. 1) as follows:

> As a mode of innovation it lacked the dynamic element that would come to characterize the Bell System in subsequent years. Instead of the development of new technologies, it envisioned the perfection through standardization of the existing array of equipment and lines in the various local exchanges. The same approach was applied to routine aspects of operations. This style of standardization would reduce risk, improve efficiency, and increase the System's income. But it was essentially an "adaptive" strategy of eliminating uncertainty in the process of producing equipment and providing services.

5. See, for example, W. W. Rostow, *Why the Poor Get Richer and the Rich Slow Down* (Austin: University of Texas Press, 1980), esp. pp. 284–88. Also see *The World Economy, History and Prospect* (Austin: University of Texas Press, 1978), esp. pp. 267–73.

6. Galambos, "Theodore N. Vail."

7. For a favorable evaluation of Ford's early administrative operation—different in emphasis, but not inconsistent with that presented here—see William Abernathy, Kim B. Clark, and Alan M. Kantrow, *Industrial Renaissance* (New York: Basic Books, 1983), pp. 69–71.

8. McCraw, *Essential Alfred Chandler,* pp. 92–93.

9. See, for example, W. W. Rostow, *The Diffusion of Power* (New York: Macmillan, 1972), esp. pp. 136–48, 234–37.

10. See, in particular, my *United States in the World Arena* (New York: Harper, 1960), esp. pp. 485–515.

11. The trade and payments playing field was by no means level in the anarchic post-Brettons Wood world of the 1970s and 1980s. That world permitted intolerable chronic surpluses for Japan, Germany, and Taiwan, and an intolerable chronic deficit for the United States. A system without a corrective mechanism is neomercantilist and not a system at all. But that fact should not be permitted to obscure the American failure in competitiveness.

12. James K. Galbraith documents the structural characteristic of the U.S. trade balance, in much greater detail in the excellent first chapter ("Capital Goods") of his *Balancing Acts* (New York: Basic Books, 1989), pp. 9–26.

13. For temperate, somewhat understated, but useful analyses of two gross failures, see David G. Tarr, "Steel: International Position and Mobilization Capabilities" and William J. Corcoran, "The Machine Tool Industry under Fire," Chapters 8 and 9 in Donald L. Losman and Shu-Jan Liang, *The Promise of American Industry* (New York: Quorum Books, 1990). This volume analyzes the present state and prospects of American industry in disaggregated, structural terms—a procedure mainstream economics has rarely followed.

14. Hans Mark, "The End of the Cold War and Its Consequences," Occasional Publication of the National Institute for Staff and Organizational Development (NISOD) (Austin: University of Texas, 1990), p. 3.

15. Richard S. Rosenbloom and Michael A. Cusumano, "Technological Pioneering and Competitive Advantage: The Birth of the VCR Industry," *California Management Review* 29(4) (Summer 1987): 171. See also Margaret B. W. Graham, *The Business of Research: RCA and the VideoDisc* (Cambridge: Cambridge University Press, 1986).

16. *Scale and Scope,* p. 622.

17. For two excellent studies of the discomfiture of the American automobile industry and its succession of responses, see Abernathy, Clark, and Kantrow, *Industrial Renaissance,* pp. 43–94; Marvin B. Lieberman, Lawrence J. Lau, and Mark D. Williams, "Firm-Level Productivity and

Management Influence: A Comparison of U.S. and Japanese Automobile Producers" (Stanford University, December 1989, forthcoming).

18. *Scale and Scope,* pp. 622–24.

19. *Corporate Commonwealth,* p. 251.

20. Charles P. Kindleberger, "Foreword," in David B. Audretsch and Michael P. Claudon, eds., *The Internationalization of U.S. Markets* (New York: New York University Press, 1989), pp. xv–xvii.

21. Lewis Namier, *Avenues to History* (London: H. Hamilton, 1952), p. 1.

22. Modern R&D has proved relevant to some rather unlikely and historically labor-intensive industries. For a striking example, see David L. Huff and Lewis Brazelton, "A Tanning Industry for Texas," *Texas Business Review* (August 1990).

23. In a valuable survey much in the spirit of the present essay, David Osborne and Doug Ross ("Catching the Third Wave," *Washington Post,* July 22, 1990, p. 13), summarize industrial policy activities in the states as follows: "

• Forty-four states now fund applied-research centers and/or grants

• Forty-five states help businesses commercialize new technologies or apply state-of-the-art technologies to their manufacturing process

• Thirty-five states offer innovation capital of some kind—seed capital, venture capital or product development grants

• Forty-four states use their leverage to strengthen their capital markets by stimulating more private venture capital investments, small business loans and the like

• Forty-seven states have passed education reform measures to provide the skilled workforces necessary to compete in a global economy

• Forty-seven states have created new training programs to improve the skills of those already in the workforce.

24. A good deal of evidence justifying temperate optimism is contained in three recent books: Galbraith, *Balancing Acts,* Richard Rosencrance, *American's Economic Resurgence* (New York: Harper and Row, 1990); and Losman and Liang, *American Industry.*

25. Robert Lawrence Kuhn, ed., *Handbook for Creative and Innovative Managers* (New York: McGraw-Hill, 1988).

26. Mark and Levine, *Research Institutes,* p. 177

27. The phrase "magnificent image" is from Alexis de Tocqueville, *Democracy in America* (New York: Vintage, 1954), 2: 178. See also Gunnar

Myrdal, *An American Dilemma* (New York: Harper: 1949), p. 21. Also, a less sympathetic observer, Jean-Paul Sartre, "Americans and Their Myths," *The Nation* 165 (October 18, 1947): 402–3: "Americanism is not merely a myth that clever propaganda stuffs into people's heads, but something every American continually re-invents in his gropings. It is at one and the same time a great external reality rising up at the entrance of the port of New York across from the Statue of Liberty, and the daily product of anxious liberties."

3

Plan for Transition to a Market Economy in the Soviet Union: The Five-Hundred-Day Mandate

Gennedy Filshin

Editor's Note: *Considering the rapidly changing and uncertain political and economic environment in the former Soviet Union, it is important to recognize the precise time frame when this chapter was written—the summer of 1990 in preparation for the conference held at the beginning of August 1990. In December 1990, amidst a conservative resurgence in the Soviet Union the New York Times reported a public confrontation between Filshin and Gorbachev over economic matters. Subsequent events prior to the abortive coup in August forced Filshin from office. Now that Russia and other nations that comprised the former Soviet Union are struggling with free markets, it is fascinating to realize that this chapter, now seemingly quite tame, was viewed as quite radical just two years ago.*

By the second half of 1989, the economic crisis in the Soviet Union had acquired the traits of stagflation. Inflation growth had reached 15 to 20 percent, and, simultaneously, the recession in the production sphere deepened. Ineffective government response will result in the breakdown of the financial system, hyperinflation, and the stoppage of a great number of enterprises due to the disintegration of the business infrastructure.

The goal of economic reform is to create a self-developing economy. Therefore, it is necessary to implement reform quickly. There is support among a group of scholars and specialists to put this detailed plan into concrete practice.

The all-inclusive, radical nature of this reform guarantees its success. The time for gradual transition is past: The Hungarian and Yugoslavian experiences demonstrate the futility of partial reform. Only the swift pace, large scope, and radical nature of this proposal will lead to the desired results.

Having learned from the socioeconomic crises in the Soviet Union (1922–24) and elsewhere (United States—1929–32; Germany, France, and Japan—1947–49), it is necessary to take into account the unique features of today's economic situation in the Soviet Union. Most notably:

- the pervasiveness of state ownership of property and a lack of market ties/attitudes

- a significant pent-up demand for consumer goods

- hypertrophic growth of the leading subsectors of industry, defense, and investing

- an undeveloped infrastructure and a shortage of economic-legal (business) education opportunities

- a low quality of life

Taken together, these problems force the country to resort to radical economic reform. In short, the commodity-cash balance can be restored by the sale of a portion of the state's holdings, as well as by altering budget and credit policies. The state must refuse to support failing enterprises in order to set the stage for deep structural changes. Commodity and financial reserves will ensure transition to market (literally free) prices and a common rate of exchange. A sustenance level of consumer goods will be guaranteed to each citizen. Tax reform will lay the groundwork for this widespread degovernmentalization investment. Over the course of the transformational period—five hundred days—the details of regulating the economy will be mastered.

The goals of the "500 Day" Plan are:

- macroeconomic stabilization

- creation of a regulated market

- structural rebuilding of the economy

This plan provides for four relatively independent stages, each of which is unique in its aims and the scale of its reforms.

STAGE 1: THE PREPARATORY STAGE (DAYS 1–100)

The official announcement of the reform program will occur on Day 1, along with the beginning of an advertising campaign.

The equality before the law of all legal entities (*res judicatae,* enterprises) and citizens (including foreign citizens) will be declared, in any business dealings except activities prohibited by law.

A portion of each citizen's living quarters and land will be given over to the citizen as private property.

The process of breaking up the state's holdings will be outlined, including the requisite shift to short-term leasing.

Guarantees regarding property rights affecting legal entities and citizens will be announced; this will include all types of property, including the means of production, land, and dwellings, with certain state-owned properties declared exempt.

It will be advisable to announce the upcoming tax reform in advance, indeed, on the very first day.

The media will elucidate the plan's aims and outline the resulting benefits to the population. It will also be necessary to stress the "price" to be "paid" by society during the intermediate stages of the reform (inevitably, inflation and unemployment); the economic experiences of the United States, postwar Europe, and modern-day Poland, Hungary, and Bulgaria will also be noted.

Days 1–100 will include an evaluation of holdings in several main areas:

1. An expert appraisal (utilizing data from the incomplete reevaluation) of the basic production reserves by economic area and region

2. An appraisal of the holdings not devoted to manufacturing, primarily living accommodations (differentiated according to comfort and level of upkeep)

3. Selection of a method by which land values will be determined

4. An appraisal of the holdings of social organizations

5. Taking stock of the gold reserves

6. An appraisal of deposits held in foreign banks and property held abroad (including the property of both pubic organizations and individuals)

7. An examination of yet-to-be-completed industrial construction

8. A more precise definition of the amount and disposition of strategic reserves

9. Reserves of certain types of state property will be made public and appraised, most important in the fields of transportation and trucking, military holdings, and a portion of basic reserves not related to manufacturing (noninhabitable premises, administrative buildings, etc.)

Additionally, the scope of the government's domestic and foreign indebtedness will be accurately determined, as will the size and scope of the monetary supply, the balance of payments, the balance of trade, the balance of income and expenditure on the part of the citizens, and the size and scope of credit resources. Only with this information base will it be possible to select a course of action for radical economic reform. The abolition of subsidies and grants to enterprises will be announced, and the new relationship between enterprises and the state will be explained.

Day 20 will mark the beginning of the process of degovernmentalization. In order to demonstrate to the population the direct link between radical reform and its interests, this degovernmentalization will begin with the symbolic sale of a portion of the housing and land resources of the country (either for a token price or to be given, without cost, to pensioners and families in need), specifically,

- dwellings held by cooperatives (without compensation, with the right to sell the apartment in the future)

- apartments in block-houses built between 1950 and 1960 and other apartments with a similar level of comfort and state of deterioration (for a token price ranging from 200 to 1,000 rubles)

- the transfer of lots from .15 to .4 hectares to members of collective farms and other collective organizations, in accordance with local conditions (possibly for a small payment)

- the buyout of plots of land held by members of garden cooperatives (with a size of .6 hectares) for a token amount (200–300 rubles) (The purchase prices of the larger lots in resort and urban areas will increase progressively, and it will be necessary to limit [.1–.2] the size of the lot obtained under such favorable terms.)

Simultaneously, restrictions prohibiting tenants from purchasing the remaining housing resources must be abolished; such purchases will occur at full price, taking into account the condition of the living quarters. Those who utilize lots will be afforded the possibility of purchasing the land for a realistic price, given restrictions on the total area of the plot (with the local situation again being taken into account).

At the same time, the sale of small and medium-sized businesses will begin, notably in the following spheres: automobile transportation, retail, service, establishments catering to the public (tourism, hotel industry), contract work, construction firms, nonprofit state cooperatives, subsidiary forms of major industrial enterprises, food production and other light industry, the construction materials industry, the wood-processing industry, the printing industry, other industries with less than three hundred employees, and a large percentage of supply enterprises.

In order to stimulate the degovernmentalization process, small and medium-sized businesses must be given tax credit, and other advantages; all obstacles to foreign investment in this sphere must be removed. The transition to free pricing in those areas of the economy not controlled by the state might also serve as an incentive. (In order to restrain price hikes, it is possible to require mandatory price rise notification twenty to forty days prior to the proposed hike, as well as to freeze prices for the first 1–2 months after the sale of a business, implying that noncontrolled pricing will be the norm for the entire economy during the later stages of these reforms.)

During this primary stage, other methods of degovernmentalization will also be utilized. Starting on Day 30, based on the list of as-yet-uncompleted construction projects, the sale of on-site inventory will begin at sites where work has been suspended. Starting on Day 40, there will be a sale of basic holdings and strategic reserves, as well as of the lands of bankrupt state farms and collective enterprises, and from Day 50, free sale of shares by large concerns in several branches of the economy will take place.

During this first stage, complete purchases of enterprises will occur only in small numbers; first and foremost, the groundwork must be laid for the legal and practical aspects of widespread degovernmentalization to take place during the second stage of the reform.

On Days 10–100 tax reform will be implemented, providing:

- Equal rates of taxation of profit for legal entities using a method to calculate the tax base that stresses the lowering of inflation and is antimonopolistic
  a. a progressive taxation scale, based on profit
  b. allowance for price rises only after notification of the state, one to two months prior to the proposed hike, and the payment of a fixed progressive tax if a price is increased
  c. for the implementation, by the state, of a price cap on certain types of production and strict, progressive taxes if the cap is exceeded
- Progressive taxation of individual income, using a stiffer tax scale than that applied to legal entities

- Taxation of private property (beyond a certain amount)
- An increase in the land tax rate, and the inheritance tax rate, and reduced taxation on an individual's means of livelihood
- Harsh sanctions for failure to pay taxes (300 to 500 percent fine and imprisonment), and the establishment of a tax enforcement system
- The possible increase of indirect taxes on some consumer goods, in order to draw into the budget some part of the monetary reserves of individuals and enterprises, increasing prices to a level of supply and demand

On Days 30–50 grants and subsidies to nonprofit enterprises, including collective farms and other collective enterprises, will be canceled. In order to provide legislative support at the earliest stages of these reforms, a package of legislation will be introduced over the first one hundred days, including

> banking legislation
> legislation relative to the State Bank
> legislation on companies issuing stock
> legislation regarding free enterprise
> a statute on degovernmentalization
> temporary bankruptcy statute

Changes will be introduced in the following legislation:

> the state enterprise law
> legislative charter of the Soviet Union on leasing
> legislative charter on taxation
> the property law (including an efficient system of guarantees on individual property)
> land law
> budget legislation
> legislation pertinent to housing

Organizationally, during the following stages of the reform it will be necessary to:

1. Create an institutional system to oversee the appraisal and privatization of state property (first and foremost, land holdings and housing)
2. Establish a stock exchange and equip it with the necessary hardware and telecommunications equipment
3. Organize a comprehensive system for gathering and evaluating statistical information, as well as to create a subsystem to oversee the reforms

4. Reorganize the entire system for professional education and retraining, emphasizing modern-day professions and specialties

5. Invite foreign specialists to offer expertise and to organize market oversight in accordance with the reform plan

6. Establish an office to oversee and provide forecast information relative to socioeconomic processes

During this preliminary stage, the government will work toward ensuring a minimum level of social maintenance for all citizens, including

- a baseline consumer budget, with corresponding minimum wage, pensions, and benefits
- a system of ration cards for necessary consumer goods and support for such a system
- an unemployment benefit fund
- income indexing

Finally, during the first thirty days, the country will open negotiations with the West relative to the granting of credit, subsidies on favorable terms, and the postponement of payments. A group of specialists will be sent abroad to receive training in critical areas. The gathering of material and financial reserves at the state (republic) and regional levels will be undertaken.

STAGE 2: DEGOVERNMENTALIZATION OF PROPERTY (DAYS 100–250)

The widespread sale of state property, the creation of a nongovernmental sector in the economy, and the reduction of accumulated ("postponed") monetary demand are central to this stage. To this end, it will be important to redirect the demand for consumer goods to the purchase of state holdings and land.

This program provides a variety of methods for degovernmentalization of property: individual buyout, payment in installments, leasing with eventual purchase, the sale of stock, and foreign investment.

In the following areas, enterprises will remain strictly subordinate to the government:

electric power

railway transport

major pipelines

telecommunications

defense (some parts of the military complex)

In this regard, state oversight will be retained only over export production, in accordance with long-standing international and bilateral agreements.

Enterprises in the above-cited areas will be given the right to issue stock; 51 percent of the shares, however, will be held by the state. Likewise, shareholders will be afforded favorable terms (price reductions, service privileges, etc.). A set part of the requisite funds (50–70 percent) will remain at the disposal of the enterprise.

On Days 100–120 a stock exchange will be organized (the initial sale of shares might also occur via the banking system).

- Shares will be sold to legal entities and individual citizens.

- Unsold shares will remain state property.

- On the 100th day, in order to oversee the stock holdings of the state, a General State Stock Fund will be created; optionally, several regional funds or holding banks will be created.

- The nominal value of an enterprise's stock will be allowed to exceed the assets on-hand, and the balance will remain at the disposal of the company issuing the stock.

- The bulk of income following the sale of stock will be given/calculated into the state's budget (or put into a separate account in the State Bank), with the rest remaining at the disposal of the issuing company.

Following the appraisal of construction, as-yet uncompleted projects will be suspended. They will be sold "as is," to legal entities or individual citizens, including foreign investors. Individual completed building projects, buildings, on-site inventory, and other reserves of material value at suspended construction sites will be sold first. In this regard, the amount of marketable construction materials will be substantially increased, as a result of the redirection of these materials from industrial construction.

At this point the government must strive to maximize the scope of the privatization process and attempt to create stock-issuing companies with the least possible level of governmental support; it should also aim toward the complete buyout of the basic holdings of small and medium-sized enterprises.

Likewise, the government must allow employees' collectives to lease enterprises. Essentially, such an approach can be used, over the short term, in cases when it is impossible to sell an enterprise to a legal enterprise or to individual citizens; these rental costs will be high, with an assumption of buyout of holdings (with the option of an installment plan).

Banking reform, prepared during the previous stage, will be put into practice, in order to provide stability and to curtail inflationary financing of businesses. This will include the following:

- Sanction of account funds in specialized banks, in order to keep on the books only those resources and deposits backed by actual goods or property.

- Registration and liquidation (where possible) of commitments among legal entities or among such entities and banks; nonperforming debts (primarily those of the State Agro-Industrial Bank) owed to the State Bank will be written off during the liquidation of a legal entity.

- Transition to a two-tier banking system, with the resubordination of the State Bank to the Supreme Soviet (with the latter having the right to limit the growth of the money supply), which will no longer automatically credit funds to the state.

- The State Bank will begin to serve as a reserve bank, and during this initial period (one to one and one-half years) a high reserve rate of 20 to 40 percent will be established; a system to ensure the deposits of legal entities and citizens will also be created.

- Banks currently serving as specialized banks will go commercial, and the first tier of the State Bank (offices) and the Savings Bank will be divided between them; restrictions on the creation of commercial banks, as well as interbank organizations with different bases, will be removed (excepting those restrictions established by law).

- A universalization of banking functions will take place (the right of legal entities and citizens to hold bank accounts in any bank and, where possible, to hold hard currency accounts), with banks independently setting the amounts and conditions of credit. (For the first ten to one hundred days from the reform's inception, it will be possible to set upper and lower levels of interest on credit).

- A high rate of reinvestment in the State Bank will be maintained.

- The general regulations on taxing legal entities will be extended to cover banking (with the exception of the State Bank); and banks will be granted stock issuance rights and the opportunity to give preference to shareholders.

On Days 50–130 budget reform will be completed, designed to ensure the current state budget balance, as a result of mobilization into the budget of the monetary resources of the ministries and curtailment of state expenditures in grants to nonprofit enterprises, grants to agriculture in the form of price subsidies, large-scale investment schemes, defense, and grants and privileges to public organizations.

The budget deficit will be limited by law and will be covered *only* by the issuance and open sale of state bonds bearing a high return rate and a shorter period of repayment (five to seven years). Increasing the money supply (additional printing of money) will cease. Income from the sale of shares and state property must be set into a special part of the state budget and will be transferred to the State Bank to go toward the domestic deficit.

In order to legislatively support the reform at this stage, a number of measures will be taken.

- Changes in labor legislation, unemployment assistance, and sources of financing for the employment fund will be approved by the Supreme Soviet.

- The Temporary Statute on Governmental Decrees will be altered.

- Antimonopoly legislation will be introduced.

- The regulations of the ministries, government proxies, and the central economic departments will be affirmed.

- A list of goods excluded from export will be fixed, new customs regulations will be drawn up, and by the conclusion of this stage, the practice of licensing exports will be abolished.

- A law on foreign investment in the Soviet Union and economic zones will be adopted.

- The regulations on government oversight will be passed.

At this stage, institutional support for the reform will occur.

- Transformation (liquidation, enlarging) of branches of ministries (Days 100–150) will occur.

- State arbitration will be reorganized into a system of independent courts (initially subordinate to the Supreme Soviet).

- The workings of the state planning department, state labor council, state supply department, and other central economic departments will be reviewed and reorganized.

- The tasks of labor exchange will shift to the system of employment offices, with the assurance of appropriate information ties.

On Days 100–250 the building up of material and financial reserves will continue.

STAGE 3: LAUNCHING THE MARKET MECHANISM (DAYS 250–500)

A certain readiness on the part of the economy to operate under market conditions will be a requisite indication of the start of the third stage of the reform. When the total volume of state property reaches approximately half of the pent-up monetary demand, this will be sufficient to create a greater number of market relationships and a strong tendency to restore balance in the major markets (primarily, in the consumer goods market).

The main thrust of this stage is the widespread development of the structural reconstruction of the economy using market principles. This rebuilding of the economy will result in a recession in production, first and foremost, in several critical economic spheres (fuel and energy, the chemical industry, metallurgy, machine building), and will be accompanied by the bankruptcy and closing of the least efficient enterprises in these areas. This will lead to an unemployment problem.

It will be necessary to undertake all possible measures to lessen the unemployment problem, but not to stop the process of structural change, for this will serve as the basis of future growth. The production targets and prices in these branches of the economy will be economically determined; subsequent growth will occur only with a move to technologies that save resources, and with a significantly lesser share of intermediate production. After the recession, production in these spheres will be stabilized. The labor resources that are liberated will be immediately retrained for work in other areas of the economy. The costs in coal and metal production, as well as in several other branches of industry, will rise. Within one to two years, the machine industry will increase production of consumer goods and move out of the crisis.

The state should support those areas of the economy tied to the infrastructure (transportation, communications, etc.).

The structural rebuilding of the economy will occur due to market processes. This assumes a definitive abolition of state subsidies in these areas of the economy (and of the purchase of their products) and the abrogation of state control over prices and production targets. Along with the sharp curtailment of investment in the manufacturing sphere, the demands for production of basic fuel and other raw materials will also decrease. For a short period, these branches of the economy will collaborate with one another owing to the interdependence of production. Thereafter, when reserves have been exhausted, a sharp decline in interdependence will take place, to the point where the activities of the consumer industry, the infrastructure, and the rebuilding will necessarily result. The costs to produce fuel and raw materials will increase slightly during the initial stage, and will then decline owing to the elimination of ineffective enterprises and the interdependence of production.

Additionally, the removal of price controls will not be complete; state control over manufacturing will remain in effect in areas of production allotted to the ration card system and as regards certain other prices (electric power, housing payments, public transportation, etc.). In order to compensate for the price increases, a package of social guarantees will be introduced at the conclusion of the second or at the beginning of the third stage.

1. Following the transition to market (free) pricing, if the supply of consumer goods becomes unstable, a ration card system for the distribution of a minimum sustenance level of consumer goods will be introduced, with this bulk distribution occurring by state decree (including the necessary resources to meet this decree, calculated relative to the wealth of the various branches of the economy).

2. With the beginning of the transition to free market pricing, income indexing will be introduced. Greatest protection against price rises will be provided to benefits and pensions that provide a basic level of sustenance (with possible reference to the average salary).

3. Programs supporting selected social groups will be implemented: single senior citizens and the disabled; homes for seniors; children's homes; subsidies to refugees and immigrants; free food; aid to the homeless; dietary supplements and child nutrition.

To implement these programs, an evaluation and partial nationalization of the property of the major social organizations will be carried out.

Greatest emphasis should be given to the natural guarantees (cost-free services, ration card system, etc.) and not to the monetary guarantees. Indexing must be severe, in order to forestall the development of hyperinflation. Thus, the main burden of these reforms will fall on the middle and well-to-do sectors of the population rather than on the poor (as is usually the case in stabilization programs offered by the IMF).

STAGE 4: STABILIZATION (DAYS 400–500)

One of two factors will serve as a criterion for moving to this stage: either a slowdown in the fall of production in the fuel or raw materials sphere of the economy, the achievement of the lowest point of the crisis, or, if the development of the structural crisis is delayed, the arrival of a fixed date, say, Day 400, to allow for the proposal of the governmental stabilization programs and to finish the program with good results. Such positive results would be the substantial growth in the production of consumer goods, reduction in the prices of consumer goods, an environment conducive to economic growth and market activity, and the earning of money according to results, not labor expenditures.

The specific thrusts of the stabilization programs will be worked out over the course of the reforms. The primary aims of these programs are: the abolishment of inequality; economic methods of price regulation, primarily for consumer goods; and realignment of special-purpose social programs.

The material, financial, and hard currency resources to carry out stabilization must be accumulated, partially, over the course of the reform; in part, they should be released and redistributed during the structural crisis; available currency resources and aid from international organizations and foreign countries might also be sought.

4

Hungarian Transformation: Challenge for Innovation

Janos Vecsenyi

Hungary has plans for a radical innovation of its economy. The former socialist system stifled innovation. This stifling of innovation was assumed to be due to the centrally planned economic system. Today it is clear that the centralized political system was just as responsible. The interface between the political and economic systems is thus a crucial point of analysis for studying Hungarian changes.

The present changes are innovative solutions for transforming the totalitarian political system into a democratic multiparty system and for reducing the government's role in business life, thus providing more room for market competition. This change is expected to stimulate business and innovation.

This chapter describes the transition process in Hungary from a bureaucratic system to a market economy. The major point is that in the past decades the socialist system was only reformed, while now the whole political-economic system is being eradicated. The change of the attitude of people is a necessary element of economic development in Hungary.

THE ERA OF TRANSITION

Hungary is in a state of transition. The old "socialist" system is still prevailing while the new one has not yet taken shape. The old one-party system has already disintegrated, while the actors of the multiparty system are still new to the game. Ownership is still a reflection of the old economic system, since 85 percent of the companies are state-owned. Nevertheless, the private economy prospers with a steady increase in the number of small businesses.

Hungary is facing a tremendous challenge. The old political and economic systems could not boast of such achievements in economic development, standard of living, and political freedom. By the end of the 1980s people had lost interest in the political and economic structure of the so-called socialism. An experiment has failed.

Free elections were enforced and a new democratic political system started to operate in 1990. Although reforms have continuously changed the economic system by introducing a "regulated market" economy, real market economy still does not exist. Figure 4.1 shows a road map for the transition process.

Figure 4.1. The Process of Transition

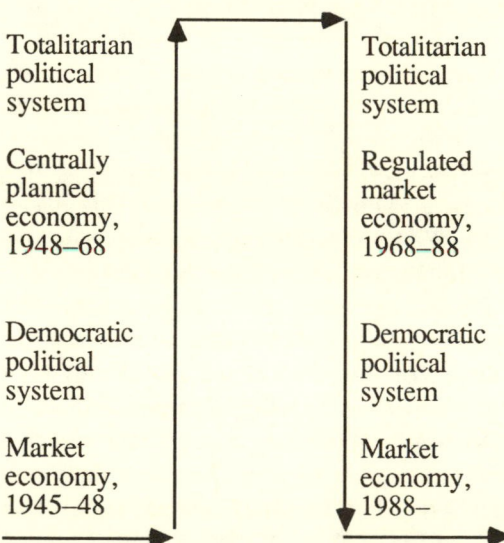

The transformation of the political and economic systems implies innovation in itself. There is no political or economic model that fits the former Eastern Bloc. New solutions are needed: New combinations evolve from the old systems and the newly adopted elements of foreign countries. Changing the large, socioeconomic bureaucratic system is expected to considerably influence the firms' innovations and, as a result, economic development as well.

These changes have been due to efforts spanning several decades. In recent times numerous attempts have been made to improve economic development and to weaken political dictatorship. It appeared for a long time that the reform of the economic system, that is, decreasing centralization of economic management, would suffice for society's development. Recently, it has become clear that economic performance cannot be improved solely by reforms of the economic system, but by the complete change of the economic system based on total political change. In other words, a modified central planning system cannot substitute for the market, although the real driving force of economic progress is the market. A change to a market economy cannot be implemented without replacing the one-party totalitarian political system. The understanding of the insights about the nature of change has been evolving during several decades.

THE WAY TO A MARKET ECONOMY

In Hungary, transition has been going on for more than forty years. The transition process started with reforming the coordination of the economic system.

According to Kornai (1986), there are two pure types of means for accomplishing coordination of the interchange between individuals or organizations in the economic system: *bureaucratic coordination,* which is a vertical, hierarchically empowered relationship between the coordinating and coordinated individuals and organizations; and *market coordination*, which is a horizontal, economically equal relationship. In bureaucratic coordination the transactions are not necessarily monetized, but if they are the subordinated individual or organization is financially dependent on the superior. The bureaucracy is active in the allocation of resources and the redistribution of income. In its pure form market coordination takes place at prices based on an agreement between a buyer and a seller who are equal from a legal point of view.

Up until 1948, Hungary was a market economy with a fully developed agriculture and industry, just surviving after the Second World War. Then, under Soviet pressure, a one-party totalitarian dictatorship hallmarked by the names of Stalin in the Soviet Union and Rakosi in Hungary replaced the multiparty democratic political system. The market economy was eliminated and a centrally planned economy was introduced with direct bureaucratic management.

During the forty years between 1948 and 1988, many efforts were made to reform the socialist system. There was an unsuccessful attempt at a radical change in the political system in 1956. Following the defeated revolution in 1956, changes affected only the economic system, with reforms having no influence on state ownership or bureaucratic control over the centralization and reallocation of the incomes of the firms.

The most influential reform was implemented in 1968. The economic development slowed down and the reform wing of the Communist party leadership could initiate a series of reforms in the economic system and get approval for implementing the New Economic Mechanism.

In the New Economic Mechanism the previous practice of prescribing for companies from what, how much, and from whom to produce was abandoned. Direct interventions were replaced by economic regulators: price policy and price control; financial policy of the state-budgetary revenues and outlays; enterprise profit through income and other taxes; regulation of personal income (wages); credit policy; foreign trade policy; and investment policy. The managers of state-owned companies were afforded greater autonomy in organizing production and framing their strategy and investment plans. To realize these plans, however, managers continued to depend on the decisions of the central bureaucratic organs, since more than 80 percent of the net income went to the state budget, which was then reallocated by governmental organs.

The New Economic Mechanism eliminated the centrally planned economic system, but could not create a real market economy (Antal 1979).

The decentralization of economic control was not accompanied by a change in the centralized function of the political system. The totalitarian political system, as revealed later, was the fundamental reason that the elimination of central planning was not achieved.

The oil crisis of the 1970s and the delayed, slow reaction to change of the economic structure and energy consumption aggravated the economic situation of the country, which could be balanced only by obtaining ever increasing credits. In 1980 the debts of the country amounted to $10.0 billion U.S. ($1,000 U.S. per capita).

The serious economic situation called for new economic management. The reform movement gained new momentum in 1978 with growing concern for the country's deteriorating trade positions. Reforms were aimed at improving the efficiency of Hungarian industry in order to increase exports, especially to the West. At the end of the 1970s the need for increasing the innovations of firms became crucial. The lack of competitive products and high potential technologies focused attention on innovation research.

INNOVATION RESEARCH

J. Schumpeter (1934) was the first researcher to recognize the importance of innovation in economics. Since then the meaning and significance of innovation have largely changed. A great wave of innovation research can be noted from the mid-1970s up to the mid-1980s (Mansfield 1968, 1975; Mensh 1975, 1978; Graham and Senge 1982; Ray 1980; Haustein and Maier 1979; Freeman 1979; Maier and Robinson 1982; Drucker 1985). Flourishing of the theme was supposed to be associated with the wave. According to Kondratieff's theory and Schumpeter's explanation, there is a correlation among economic development cycles, innovation, and the investments implementing innovation.

Politicians and experts regarded the 1970s as the descending branch of the Kondratieff cycle, and predicted the nadir of decline by the mid-1980s. An intensive search was undertaken to define what conditions would be the most inspiring for the appearance of "basic innovation"—a term used by Mensh (1975)—and to find the new driving force for economic development after the spread of steam energy, railway, automobilism, and electricity.

At the end of the 1970s innovation was discussed frequently in Hungary.[1] It was viewed not only as a buzz word of the press and new field of research, but as an economic necessity.

In 1979, a new study was started to explore the social and economic factors influencing innovation (Vecsenyi 1981a, 1981b). The political system was also investigated. The intention was to seek the lack of creativity and innovation of the companies not primarily within the management and organization of the enterprises, but in their socioeconomic environment.

The study pointed out that a centralized mechanism of economic control makes the functioning of innovation processes difficult. This difficulty could, first of all, be ascribed to the fact that firms were extremely dependent on state administration. The basis of this dependency was that the government diverted the produced income from the companies. The companies poor in capital were not capable of financing the developments and so they had to depend on the benevolence of the state bureaucracy in reallocation of resources. There were still no commercial banks from which business could receive loans. The decisions of the state bureaucracy were not defined by an economic but a bureaucratic rationality. It was also revealed that the innovation potential of the country did not so much depend on its R&D budget as on its allocation system.[2]

In this bureaucratic environment, the companies lost their independence and autonomous entrepreneurial spirit. They were, however, flexible in adapting to the ever changing bureaucratic rules. Consequently, less attention was paid to pursuing market opportunities, especially by companies that had only domestic markets. Creative solutions were presented by companies that were exposed to real market competition abroad (e.g., the pharmaceutical industry) (Vecsenyi 1982).

The study also highlighted the fact that, in order to simplify administrative control, the state administration concentrated the companies and established large firms. These firms were not large enough to be competitive in the international markets; in many cases, however, they were too large to adapt with sufficient flexibility to the changing market. It became clear that bureaucratic coordination persisted and was not actually replaced by market control.

By the end of the investigations it was also disclosed that the bureaucratic economic control was rooted in the political system. The centralized institutions of the political power structure resisted all attempts at innovation in the political system for fear of weakening their power position.

The research was terminated in 1982. Its radical statements were not acknowledged and innovation disappeared altogether from the agenda of research and governmental policy making.

ENTREPRENEURSHIP

According to Peter Drucker (1985), the "entrepreneurial economy" has created the largest peacetime extension in employment in American history. All these new jobs were created by small and medium-sized institutions, most of them small and medium-sized businesses, and a great many of them, if not the majority, new businesses that did not even exist twenty years ago.

The driving force of transformation in Hungary may be small and medium-sized enterprises. The 1982 law on small business ventures and the 1988 corporation law have given a great impetus to the development of private economy. Since 1982 several thousand new firms have been established. Due to insufficient statistics in this field, no exact figures are available. Based on company registration office records, about four thousand limited liability companies and joint stock companies were registered in 1989.

A bidirectional trend can be noted in the Hungarian economy. Small and medium-sized companies are partly established by private entrepreneurs, or they are founded as a result of the decentralization of large state enterprises. In concert with international experience, entrepreneurs are recruited in a similar percentage from those with a primary school education, those with a high-school degree or equivalent expertise, and university graduates (Hisrich and Vecsenyi 1990). The motives for starting new ventures are similar. These include an attempt at independence, an intention of implementing a new idea, and the hope for monetary and personal satisfaction. The majority of large state enterprises have been established by bureaucratic decisions, from the fusion of medium-sized companies. Their breakdown and privatization are underway.

Small business ventures in Hungary are extremely successful. The majority of firms achieve profits already in the first year of operation. Most of the small ventures keep on operating even after three years, not like those in Western economies, where this ratio is around 75 percent.

What accounts for the successful operation of Hungarian small ventures? The reasons can be found both in the environment of the firms and within them. The success of the ventures depends on three factors: (1) a shortage of products and services, (2) the lack of competition, and (3) the business flair of entrepreneurs.

One of the consequences of bureaucratic coordination is shortage (Kornai 1986). In the Hungarian economy there is a lack of basic products and services. In this field entrepreneurs can easily find a market niche with purchasing power.

The size distribution of firms in Hungarian production is much more skewed in favor of large units than in developed economies. The extremely high centralization weakens or eliminates potential rivalry. The number of small and medium-sized ventures is still limited. It is still easy for the newcomer to enter the market without finding competitors in the same industry.

The excellent business flair of the entrepreneurs has played an important role in the success of small ventures. The opportunity to start new ventures opened up in 1982, when new legislation allowed formation of private ventures. In this initial period only the most daring people took the risk. They were the quickest to recognize the business opportunities, and adapted to the changing environment. The host of entrepreneurs are still to come. Fifty to eighty thousand entrepreneurs can be expected to appear in the next twenty years in an entrepreneur-supportive environment. This rather optimistic forecast assumes that 10 to 15 percent of employees will become entrepreneurs in ten to fifteen years.

Along with an increasing number of entrepreneurs the risk of failure also increases, because shortage is expected to disappear and the number of competitors is growing. Market competition overvalues entrepreneurial expertise and flair. This latter can possibly not be taught, but a part of business knowledge can be. The role of business and management education is important in providing the knowledge necessary for business in a market economy (Fogel 1990).

ELIMINATION OF BUREAUCRACY

Unfortunately, no improvement in economic results was noted in the 1980s. Moreover, debts more than doubled during the last ten years, reaching $21.6 billion U.S. without economic development. In the meantime bureaucratic coordination has gradually weakened. Direct bureaucratic control has been replaced step by step by indirect control. Reform efforts accelerated in the 1980s.

For changing the roles and power structures of the large-scale bureaucracy in Hungary, three major directions were defined: (1) the development of the private economy, (2) the reduction of the role of the government, and (3) reintegration into the world economy. The major measures taken during the last five years for developing a real market economy are illustrated in Table 4.1.

Table 4.1. Measures for Developing a Real Market Economy

Development of the private economy
    New law of business association
    Law protecting investors
    Privatization of state-owned firms
    Encouragement of small and medium-sized business

Reduction of the government's role
    New bankruptcy law
    Two-tier competitive banking system
    Value-added, personal tax system
    Bond and stock market
    Elimination of discrete wage regulation

Reintegration into world economy
    Liberalization of foreign trade
    Import liberalization
    Decentralization of foreign exchange operations
    Enhancement of technological development

The development of the private economy is based on the acceptance of the need for market competition. Market competition is stimulated by increasing the number of rival firms. Real market competition requires firms to be dependent upon their market competitiveness rather than meeting government demands. To promote private business, measures were taken for establishing new private ventures and privatizing state-owned firms.

The Corporation (Business Associations) Law created six types of enterprise ownership: unlimited partnership, deposit partnership, limited company, business union, joint enterprise, the limited liability company, and the joint stock company. The law was aimed at enabling an easy, unhindered flow and reallocation of capital in the economy. All citizens were allowed to form joint companies and economic associations at will. This law, implemented in 1989, offered new legal forms for entrepreneurs starting their business activity based on the Small Business Act of 1982.

For facilitating direct investment of foreign capital in Hungary and for protecting foreign investors against nationalization or expropriation of investment, a Foreign Investment Law was issued in 1989. Tax benefits were given to foreign investors to encourage foreigners to transfer technology to Hungary.

For decreasing the proportion of state-owned enterprises, the Business Transformation Law offered a new way of ownership transformation of companies. New rules were provided for the transformation of state-owned companies into business associations declaring simultaneously the principle of general (legal) succession. Furthermore, it provided methods for the transformation of a company into another type of firm, including mergers and splitting. Supporting the privatization of large state-owned enterprises,[3] the State Property Agency was formed in early 1990.

A new accounting system was also introduced to develop mutually acceptable accounting and bookkeeping practices. The basic principles of the bookkeeping methods and contents of the balance sheet follow the rules of the generally accepted accounting principles of Western countries (Borda 1990).

A new infrastructure is being created for encouraging the formation of small and medium-sized businesses. Special small business development and enterprise development funds were established by using foreign funds and donations. Small business incubators and enterprise centers have been set up.

In order to reduce the role of the government in the economy, several steps have been taken during the last couple of years. New institutions were formed to reduce the enforced vertical relations between the central bureaucratic organizations and the business units. These new institutions included bankruptcy law, a competitive banking system, a personal and value-added tax system, and a bond and stock market.

A two-tier banking system was implemented, which limited its Central Bank to those functions normally associated with Central Banks in the West (credit policy, exchange controls, issuance of banknotes, etc.). The lending function was transferred to newly established commercial banks that could, within limits, compete with one another for business.

In 1986 bankruptcy law facilitated the diminishing of government interventions by allowing for the liquidation of failing enterprises, although the government is still extremely reluctant to close down inefficient factories.

A new tax reform was adopted in 1988, creating three new tax systems: a general turnover (value-added) tax, a personal income tax, and a venture tax. The major purpose of introducing value-added tax was to reduce direct government interventions by subsidizing special firms and activities. Principally, the value-added tax has created a neutral situation for all business entities.

The bond and stock market was created and the stock exchange started to operate in the summer of 1990. Economists and policy makers accepted the fact that for building the market economy, creating a capital market is essential and this is not viable without a stock exchange (Young 1989).

The liberalization of the workforce market was supported by eliminating discrete wage regulation. This has stopped the regulation of wages.

The reintegration into the world economy is the third direction in developing the market economy in Hungary. Foreign trade is nothing new in Hungary, since over 50 percent of the national products were exported. Almost all export-import transactions were supervised by the state administration and foreign trade was a state monopoly. To achieve a real reintegration into the world economy, this bureaucratic control needs to be eliminated. Along this line the following measures have been taken: liberalization of foreign trade, important liberalization, decentralization of foreign exchange operations, and enhancement of technological development. The scope of bureaucratic control gradually narrowed as a result of the appearance and strengthening of the various political forces.

BUILDING SOMETHING NEW

A turning point came in 1988–90, first of all in political life. The single party monopolizing the physical as well as state power declined so dramatically that conditions ripened in 1989 for introducing a multiparty system. At the free elections of spring 1990, six of the initial fifty-two parties were represented in parliament, giving way to political pluralism. Each of these parties considers market control as their guiding principle.

Figure 4.1 shows the way taken by the country since 1945. Diversion does not disappear without a trade. Hungary's institutions are going to persist for a long time in the everyday life of the society and the economy.

The transition continues in Hungary today. In the political system the one-party dictatorship is being replaced by a multiparty democracy. The dominance of state-owned companies is being substituted by the majority of small and medium-sized companies. Bureaucratic coordination is giving way to market coordination.

The road to hell is paved with good intentions, while the way to a market economy with question marks. What should be the role of the state and companies in this transformation? The model of which country should be adopted? What should be the pace of change? There is no one best answer to these questions, since nobody has taken this way before.

The role of the state in the economy differs greatly in the various countries. In the case of the Japanese and the South Asian "tigers," the role of the state administration is rather significant not only in formulating economic policy and regulations but also in influencing the behavior of large enterprises. At first economic development was initiated and supported separately by the governments of the individual countries. From the mid-1980s onward the European Economic Community developed joint programs like Heureka. In addition, they cooperate in improving general business conditions, such as the creation of the united European market from 1992. Government interference in the United States seems to be minimal; economic development is the responsibility of companies and entrepreneurs. The government intervenes mainly by monetary means and assists by providing infrastructural services.

In the Hungarian economy the government traditionally played a dominant role. The change in the political system has affected this dominance. The ongoing political fights make the future uncertain. Although declaring decentralization for the state administration, the representatives of the ruling power grant a greater role to the government than do the opposition parties. This particularly comes through in the privatization process. The new state administration wishes to privatize under strong state supervision. The opposition would ascribe a greater role to the stock exchange opened in June 1990 in Budapest as well as to internal and external private capital.

There is strong disagreement about the pace of change. Political transformation has occurred relatively rapidly, within a period of two years. The most important steps of economic transformation would include the decentralization and privatization of state companies, which would mean a radical change. It has still not been decided how quickly this can be implemented. The more cautious government officials think in terms of a slow, step-by-step process under their supervision. The radical wing of the opposition would support a fast, more spontaneous switch lasting for one or two years. This shock therapy would lead, on the one hand, to a mass of bankruptcies and unemployment, while on the other, to the strengthening of viable firms and the establishment of new small and medium-sized businesses. The prolonged transformation would delay economic vitalization but would, provisionally, diminish social conflicts.

Foreign investments are also disputed. The last two years General Electric gained a majority position in the biggest Hungarian company, Tungsram, investing $150 million. General Motors is investing $150 million in Raba Works in heavy vehicles spare parts manufacturing. Suzuki is implementing a large project of $100 million on assembling passenger cars. These are the big investments but there are plenty of small foreign companies forming joint ventures with Hungarians (Hisrich et al. 1990; Wolfe and Poor 1990). Are they correct business partners or would they like to occupy the country using working capital instead of an army? The worries about capitalization are rooted in the nationalism and the previous bad experiences of the country during the last seventy years.

In this altered environment the new economic system has created an atmosphere promoting the innovations of enterprises. New companies are founded, old state companies are transformed into private firms. What is needed so badly now is investigation of the innovative and creative management of companies (Kozmetsky 1988).

CONCLUSIONS

Political and economic transformation is going to produce considerable changes in the society in the years to come.

Challenging vistas are opened up before certain social strata. Tens of thousands of people are going to become entrepreneurs, they are going to establish factories and open restaurants or boutiques. Five to 10 percent of them might make it big.

Besides the entrepreneurs, a new layer of managers is emerging. They are skillful, smart, and aggressive. Acquiring an MBA degree from the International Management Center or from other business schools in Hungary or abroad, they also gain business knowledge. They make incomes far above the average.

Parallel to economic prosperity, the number of victims is not going to be low. Enterprises and whole branches of industry are going to go bankrupt. Tens and hundreds of thousands are becoming unemployed. If "entrepreneurial economy" does not emerge in due time, unemployment may persist. Poverty may give rise to discontent, leading to social conflicts and emigration.

The country is animated with the spirit of the gold rush. There is an anticipation of an ideal free-enterprise system from the last century, where the murderous laws of fighting or profit are valid, and where the best become rich and the weakest fail. Today many believe that they have a chance to get wealthy, while others are losing their hopes to rise.

We are living in an age of hope and uncertainty. The transformation of the whole political system is not sufficient for the economic development. Changes in the mindset and the attitude of the people are also necessary.

NOTES

1. At that time the following story was often cited: On January 15, 1979, the *New York Times* that P. Peter an his team invented the walking hatching machine at MIT. The following day, this report was refuted by Pravda in Moscow. According to them, this equipment had already been invented by Ivan Ivanovich in 1959. Due to its military applications, the results had not been published. In the middle of March 1979, a letter of the French industrialists appeared in *Le Monde*, in which they voiced their protest against the dumping of Japanese hatching machines. In May, September, and October 1979 conferences and lectures on innovation were held in Budapest.

2. This is well illustrated by the case of purchasing an imported product license for the company, when the approval of at least twelve governmental offices were required. This slowed down the process of innovation and, in many cases, strongly distorted the initial market strategy.

3. In 1988, 84.5 percent of the companies were state-owned, 14.0 percent were cooperatives and 1.5 percent in private possession.

REFERENCES

Antal, L. 1979. Development—with some digression. The Hungarian economic mechanism in the seventies. *Acta Oecon.* 23 (3–4): 257–73.

Borda, M. 1990. Changing role of accounting in Hungary. Working paper, International Management Center, Budapest.

Drucker, P. 1985. *Innovation and entrepreneurship*. New York: Harper and Row.

Fogel, D. 1990. Management education in Central and Eastern Europe and the Soviet Union. *Journal of Management Education* 9 (3): 14–20.

Freeman, G. 1979. The determinants of innovation. *Futures* 3.

Graham, A. K., and P. M. Senge. 1982. A long-waves in innovation: Theory, evidence, and implications. In *Innovation policy and company strategy,* ed. H. Mairer and J. Robinson. IIASA Collaborative Proceedings series, Laxenburg, Austria.

Haustein, H. D., and H. Maier. 1979. Basic improvement and pseudo innovations and their impact on efficiency. Working paper, IIASA, Laxenburg, Austria.

Hisrich, R., and J. Vecsenyi. 1990. Entrepreneurship and the Hungarian economic transformation. *Leadership and Organizational Development Journal.*

Hisrich, R., A. Gross, and J. Vecsenyi. 1990. Decentralization—a case of corporate revitalization and renewal in a planned economy. Paper presented at the Esomar conference, Madrid.

Kornai, J. 1986. The Hungarian reform process: Visions, hopes, and literature. *Journal of Economic Literature* (December 24): 687–713.

Kozmetsky, G. 1988. Why new directions for research in creative and innovative management? In *New directions in creative and innovative management*, ed. Y. Ijiri and R. L. Kuhn. Cambridge, Mass.: Ballinger.

Maier, H., and J. Robinson, eds. 1982. *Innovation policy and company strategy.* IIASA Collaborative Proceedings series, Laxenburg.

Mansfield, E. 1968. *The economics of technological change.* New York: W. W. Norton.

Mansfield, E., and S. Wagner. 1975. Organizational and strategic factors associated with probabilities of success in industrial R&D. *Journal of Business* 2: 179–98.

Mensh, G. 1975. *Das technologische Patt.* Frankfurt am Main: Umschau Verlag.

_____. 1978. 1984: A new push of basic innovation? *Research Policy* 2.

Ray, G. F. 1980. Innovation as the source of long term economic growth. *Long Range Planning* (April).

Vecsenyi, J. 1981a. The INNTEAM project (in Hungarian). *Magyar Tudomany* 4.

_____. 1981b. An innovation policy analysis in Hungary. Paper presented at the IIASA workshop on "Innovation Management," Laxenburg.

_____. 1982. Organizational aspects of large scale technological innovation programs: A case study of innovation in the Hungarian pharmaceutical industry. In *Innovation policy and company strategy*, ed. H. Maier and J. Robinson. IIASA Collaborative Proceedings series, Laxenburg.

Wolfe, J., and J. Poor. 1990. A socioeconomic note on Hungary in 1990. Working paper. International Management Center, Budapest.

Young, D. 1989. Developing securities markets in a socialist country: The case of Hungary. *Journal of International Markets* (Winter).

5

China's Reform

Dyong Kong

Upgrading China's ability to generate creativity and innovation and to make use of the opportunities created by the new technological revolution will be priority tasks in the next decade. New scientific and technological achievements will motivate socioeconomic development; new products and production technologies, and better management and organization will bring about improved working efficiency and more profits.

Technology and the results of scientific researchers were kept out of the economy for more than three decades in China. In the late 1970s, China started adjusting its development strategy, and in 1978 the central authorities proposed an economic development program focusing on profits, quality, coordinated development, and stable economic growth. In 1982, a general guideline for the development of science and technology was proposed by central authorities: "Science and technology should be oriented to economic construction, the latter should rely on science and technology."

But the old systems, structures, and mechanisms presented insurmountable roadblocks to the flexibility and fast action needed for innovation. So, the only way forward for China is to reform. A new State Innovation Management System (SIMS) has emerged gradually over the last decade, especially after the promulgation of the document on "the Reforming of the Science and Technology Management System" in 1985.

THE STATE INNOVATION MANAGEMENT SYSTEM (SIMS)

China's innovation management system can be divided into two levels of hierarchy: a macrolevel and a microlevel. SIMS is on the macrolevel, and science and technology institutes, and enterprises belong to the microlevel. The government will play a very important role in macrolevel regulation, while enterprises and R&D institutes will be enlivened on the microlevel. Since the founding of the People's Republic of China, there has been a continuing debate about the role of the central government in technological innovation management. As the result of this debate, several great swings between centralization and decentralization happened in the last four decades. This kind of swing may be inescapable, but its amplitude can be minimized into an acceptable range with the help of SIMS.

SIMS can be considered as a self-adaptive control system. It is shown in the Figure 5.1.

Figure 5.1. A Self-Adaptive Control System

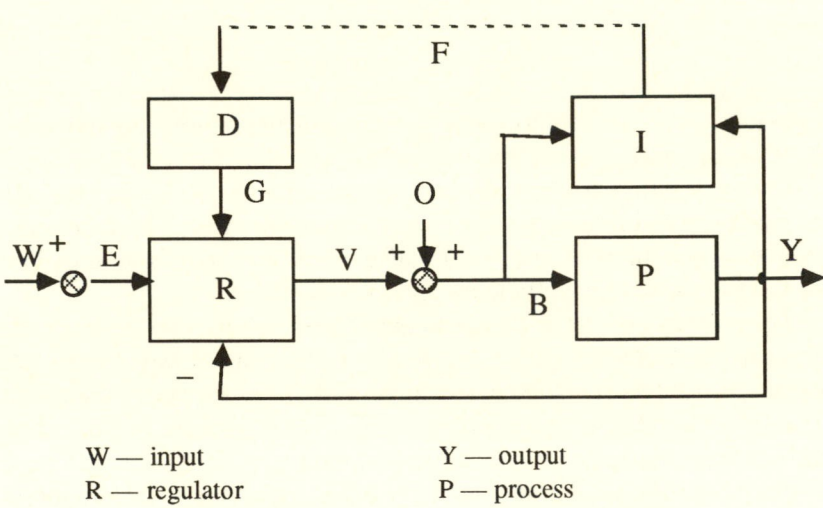

W — input   Y — output
R — regulator   P — process
I — system identification   D — decision making
V — regulations   O — input to the process from
                                       the outside world

A self-adaptive system can identify the changes of parameters of the process, then through decision making and regulation produce a set of regulations to adapt the process. The system leaves many unanswered questions: what kind of decisions should be made by the central government, and what kind of decisions the central government should not make; what the central government should regulate, and what should not be regulated by the central government; what parameters should be identified on the macrolevel, and what parameters the government need not identify.

STRATEGIC IDEAS

Science and technology can be divided into three levels of hierarchy. First, high and new technologies are used to upgrade the level of traditional technologies; most of the GNP relies on this kind of technology. Second, high-tech is the hope of future prosperity, but it is a long-term venture and China is still a developing country. Hence high-tech does not receive full financial support but adequate funds. Third, basic research, the source of creation and innovation, is supported constantly.

In terms of these three levels of hierarchy, five national programs have been proposed within the last several years.

Tackling Key Projects Program. This program selects scientific and technological research projects that will have significant economic benefits for the national economy, and the state concentrates all efforts from different fields to tackle them. It is not only urgently needed for national economic construction, but also for the rapid development of science and technology. This program belongs to the first level of hierarchy.

High-Tech Program. Seven fields are identified as the major task of this program: information technology, biotechnology, new materials, space technology, laser Technology, automation technology, and new energy. This program belongs to the second level of hierarchy.

Torch Program. The objective of this program is to develop high-technology and related industries. This program is a concrete measure to promote the commercialization, industrialization, and internationalization of the country's high-technology industries. This program belongs to the second level of hierarchy.

The Spark Program. Invigorating village and township enterprises and promoting rural economic development through the application of science and technology are the goals of the Spark program. This program belongs to the first level of hierarchy.

Basic Research Program. This program is still in draft form. It will play an important role in science and technology development. It belongs to the third level of hierarchy.

The relations between the three levels of hierarchy and the five programs are shown in Figure 5.2.

Figure 5.2. Hierarchy and Programs

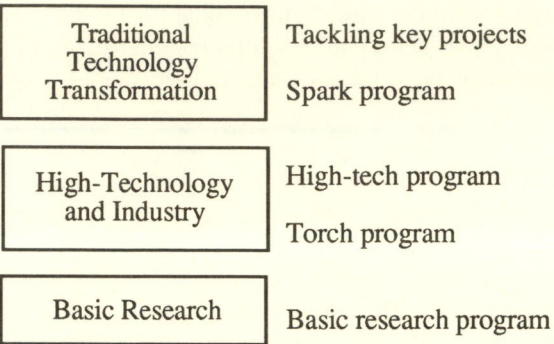

Traditional Technology Transformation	Tackling key projects Spark program
High-Technology and Industry	High-tech program Torch program
Basic Research	Basic research program

THE DIRECT SIMS

The government has direct influence on national technological innovation. The central government and the congress work together to draw up and promulgate legislation and administrative measures to encourage domestic competition and ensure that inefficiency is not subsidized.

The government allocates financial resources to soft science researchers, in order to discover the obstacles in the mechanisms for technological innovation, and allocates financial resources to promote technological innovation and to facilitate all steps in this process, including R&D, market analysis, business planning, financing, production, and sales.

The government devotes special attention to reducing the per unit consumption of capital, energy, and raw materials; improving quality and productivity to achieve world standards and participate in global markets; and controlling environment pollution.

The central authorities have initiated several programs to promote the application of research results and to support the development of technological innovation in different levels of technology, different sectors, and different industries. The Spark program, for example, was initiated by the State Science and Technology Commission of China, and the Bumper Harvest program by the Ministry of Agriculture; both programs were aimed at rural development. The former program is intended to enliven the rural small and medium-sized enterprises, and the latter is to promote the spread of agricultural technology. These programs are very successful. For example, one-half million scientists and technicians have been drawn into the countryside over the past five years. They promote the boom in rural industry, which has seen an annual growth rate as high as 30 percent over the past five years. Largely owing to their help, 61,000 new small and medium-size rural enterprises were established in 1986 and 1987. By the end of 1988, the annual production from the rural industry was $106.4 billion, larger than the total output from agriculture, and 80 million farmers turned to industrial work in their hometowns. Over the past four years 10 million young farmers have been trained in one or more specialized courses conducted as part of the overall science and technology popularization drive. According to the statistics of the Bumper Harvest program, owing to the use of new technologies, the value of crops and livestock increased in 1989 by $1.7 billion.

The Torch program was initiated by the State Science and Technology Commission, and the aims of this program between 1988 and 1990 were as follows:

- To set up two thousand high-tech and new technology enterprises and inspire them to cooperate with large and small firms.

- To develop two thousand high-tech and new technology products, 30 percent of them for export.

- To train more than twenty thousand business administrators in technology and world marketing for high-tech enterprises.

- To attract one hundred thousand scientists from higher learning institutions and research institutes to work with these enterprises.

- To set up fifty technology service centers in large and coastal areas to provide supervision and services such as helping local enterprises to collect funds and promote sales.

The Torch program was launched in August 1988. Since then more than two thousand high- and new technology enterprises have been set up in China, with total sales of $552 million and exports of $56 million.

Changing the one channel of funding, the central government, into diverse channels has been encouraged. In recent years, China has raised funds through various channels, such as enterprises, local governments, and banks. The China Industrial and Commercial Bank, for example, granted $1.41 billion for scientific and technological development between 1984 and 1989.

In 1985, a venture capital corporation—the first of its kind in China—was established to stimulate new and high-tech enterprises in their pioneering stages.

The patent system, introduced in 1985, encouraged invention and protected knowledge as property. China has also taken other measures, such as setting up a fund for patent development. Patent projects in state and local plans have been given preferential treatment in loans and taxes.

The government also encourages cooperation between research institutes, educational organization, and designing institutions on the one hand and production units on the other, and on strengthening the enterprises' capability for technology absorption and development. Collectives and individuals may set up their own research or technical service organizations.

Over the past few years, the benefit of more than a thousand technical achievements from institutes under the National Defense Science and Technology Commission have been transferred to over six hundred enterprises.

Maximum priority is given to education, with emphasis on the education required to enable the population to participate effectively in the creation and continuous improvement of successful and competitive production activities.

To promote technological innovation, many Chinese professionals have been sent abroad to study production technologies and management. And many foreign experts have been invited to China for training.

The Chinese Youth League (CYL) has come up with a project to encourage more rural youngsters to study the use of science and technology in agricultural production. In July 1988 the central committee of the CYL and the State Science and Technology Commission formed a group of rural youngsters who would spread the word about new advances in the field of agricultural scientific research. More and more rural youth will now be trained to spread information about advances in agricultural technology. Efforts should be centered on the cultivation of high-yield crops, which require little investment.

Both the Spark program and Bumper Harvest program have special training projects.

Unnecessary organizations and formalities are being reduced. Several years ago, some people wanted to open an enterprise, and almost three hundred stamps from different organizations had been put on their application form, but the result was still negative. This kind of bureaucracy is seldom seen in the past few years, because of the reform.

THE INDIRECT SIMS

The government has an indirect influence on national technological innovation.

Since the last decade, a great debate on the two models of technological innovation has been taking place. One model takes research and development of new ideas as important, going through the process of research and development, manufacturing, trial sales, and modification, and finally getting a firm foothold in the market. The second involves the selection and application of foreign technology appropriate to the local condition.

Restricted by a paucity of funds for scientific research, China is paying closer attention to pursuing and absorbing advanced technology. The second model, laying stress on the application of technology, is more suitable for China's first level of hierarchy of technology. The first model is suitable for the second and third levels of hierarchy of technology.

Under the open-door policy, technology innovation is quite different in China.

- Innovation based on foreign scientific and technological achievement aims at manufacturing new products for special needs.

- Export-oriented innovation pays attention to exploiting gaps in the world market.

- Innovation based on the advantages of technological research in certain fields lays stress on joint management and investment.

- The establishment of enterprise groups has boosted the enthusiasm for technological innovation on a large scale, focusing on the substitution of imports and nationalization of spares.

Indigenous ability is a precondition of international cooperation and self-reliance is also regarded as pivotal.

The open policy introduced in 1978 has improved the investment environment. By the end of 1989, foreign-funded enterprises numbered 21,766, absorbing $15.5 billion in overseas investment. Foreign trade increased to $111.6 billion in 1989, of which exports accounted for 47 percent. Investment in the improvement of traditional industries went up from $4.1 billion in 1981 to $20.8 billion in 1988.

The government has provided legislation and regulations for foreign investment, patents, and technology transfer that encourage and facilitate the importation and assimilation of foreign technology.

Since China's first new technology industry development zone, Shengzhen Science and Industry Park, was set up by the Chinese Academy of Sciences in 1985, around thirty high-tech development zones have been established in coastal areas and industrial cities. More than two thousand high-tech enterprises employing fifty thousand workers operate in these zones. In 1989, the total sales of these firms reached $550 million and their foreign exchange earnings totaled $56 million.

A total of 140 universities and research institutes have set up new and high-tech firms in the Beijing New Technology Development Zone. And over

3,300 scientists from the Chinese Academy of Sciences have started 154 new technology companies.

The Chinese government is giving preferential support to the development of these zones. Favorable financial, tax, foreign trade, and customs treatments have been worked out.

In order to facilitate foreign travel by Chinese businesspeople and technicians, procedures for personnel in the Beijing high-tech zone to travel abroad have been greatly simplified by the local government.

There are now thirty two foreign and joint enterprises operating in the Beijing zone and fourteen in the Shangshai zone.

China plans to create four thousand new high-tech enterprises employing three hundred thousand workers and five thousand new high-tech products with sales totaling $4.2 billion by the mid-1990s.

At the national level, traditional infrastructure support needed to create a hospitable climate for entrepreneurs should be expanded. These may include tax incentives; access to cheap finance; improved infrastructure of transport and communications; and management support and advice.

These kinds of climate are created especially in new and high-tech zones. Some zones have set up various incubators or new technology service centers.

Science and technology fairs, technical service centers, and technology shops are the major sales outlets for technical products. In 1989, more than 260,000 technical contracts were concluded with a total value of $1.7 billion. Technical marketing has become a pivotal area for the transfer of technology.

CONCLUSIONS

In the past decade, China has experienced great changes. Economy, science and technology, and society have progressed quickly. Innovation has played a vivid role. The most important factor is the enthusiasm of the whole nation excited by the progress in the last decade.

China's reform is just beginning and many challenges will be tackled in the future. Reform will be deepened, and the open door policy will be continued.

REFERENCES

Charnes, A., and W. W. Cooper. 1984. *Creative and innovative management*. Cambridge, Mass.: Ballinger.

Co-chairmen's summary of recommendations, Third Beijing International Conference for Science and Technology Policy.

Kuhn, Robert L. 1988. *Handbook for creative and innovative management.* New York: McGraw-Hill.

Lunstedt, S. B., and E. W. Colglazier, Jr. 1982. *Managing innovation.* Elmsford, N.Y.: Pergamon.

Lunstedt, S. B., and T. H. Moss. 1989. *Managing innovation and change.* IIASA. Kluwer.

Zhaoxiang, Xu. Innovation vital to developing nations. Paper presented at the Third Beijing International Conference for Science and Technology Policy.

6

Management of Change in a Large Japanese Monopoly

Hidesada Toriyama

A state monopoly, given its nature, has no need to be creative. Moreover, such a monopoly tends to become a concatenation of outside suppliers, trade unions, government officials, legislators, and other vested interest groups, which resist any efforts at organizational reform. Thus, reform from within is unlikely to occur. The only tool available to effect organizational change is, in that case, public opinion—the responses of customers. This means that the public relations department has an extremely critical role to play in bringing about reform.

In a business that is a state monopoly there is little hope for something like a creative approach to management. It is difficult to elevate and sustain morale among employees. Such a company is not likely to be tuned in to its customers. With legions of managers spread over a slew of offices, doing well in whatever managers do, there is not likely to be even one really aggressive outfit. The managers do not understand what it is about a business that makes it work. They do not get inside it. They see only the surface, the form, and that is all they work toward. So, in the end, they will fail to act like a company. They will come up with all kinds of managerial philosophies and adopt new forms of administration, but in spite of all that newness, things will not quite work out. The failures are attributed to individuals. Some things do go well here and there, and those are always courtesy of the company's upper echelons.

Is it too much to ask of the company doomed to being a monopoly or state enterprise that it be efficient, creative, or dynamic? Or would that be a contradiction in terms? The point is that when outstanding top management tried to inject that element of vigor into one such company, it ultimately had to go through a process of self-destruction and self-transformation. The rest of this chapter will focus on Nippon Telegraph and Telephone Corporation (NTT), the telecommunications monopoly in Japan.

THE REASONING BEHIND THE MONOPOLY

A telecommunications system is the nervous system of a nation. Since telecommunications are a critical part of a nation's industrial capacity, governments often take the initiative in developing a phone network as part of a modernization program. In light of the need to maintain standardization for the millions of telephones and components that comprise the system, to offer universal and fair service, and to achieve economies of scale and avoid overlapping investments, the decision may be made to have the telecommunications service a publicly operated, publicly held monopoly. That was the case in Japan.

In Japan, the monopolistic nature of this common carrier functioned effectively in terms of developing a fully formed system. Long-term infrastructural expansion programs were coordinated with the government's long-term economic plans. To fit efficiently in with a period of rapid urbanization and industrialization, the expansion began in major cities and spread outward to the countryside. The development of the necessary technologies for this was included in ultra-long-range planning, which called for borrowing technology from advanced nations, assimilating it, putting it into use, and ironing out the fine points of implementation. The implementation phase was to be carried out by cooperative research with designated corporations, where there would be optimal contracts to order work from these companies. Research on communications technology would proceed under a severe inspection system. High quality and low costs were to be ensured by careful quality control and standardization.

THE ILLUSION OF MANAGERIAL AUTONOMY

In 1952, the Japanese government changed the administration of its telecommunications business from a government agency into that of an independent public corporation. Under a new law, the business was to be guided by public service and efficiency, in the interest of achieving universal and equal service. But rather than being run by government planning, it was to be run as an independent business. The organization of the new corporation happened to fall during a period of a more active labor movement, and its structure was, in a sense, part of the government effort to clamp down on the rights of public servants to strike, engage in collective bargaining, or organize unions. The company's budget was to be a part of the national budget, and be decided annually by the Diet. Changes in fees would require changes in the law. Any new services would require the permission of the Minister of Posts and Telecommunications. The president and vice-president were both to be nominated by the prime minister. In short, government regulation was brought to bear on every aspect of the company.

Being based on a special law, the company had the status of a special juristic person so that its range of operations could be totally circumscribed by the law. While according to the letter of the law the corporation had independent management, it had to act according to legal prescriptions. The reality was that all authority was vested in the regulating agencies that granted permits and licenses, while the managerial staff had only responsibility. The regulating agencies had the authority without the responsibility.

Founded under a special law from the start, all the company's actions were fundamentally limited by that law. It was a creature of principles, regulations, and no freedom. Its formation presupposed outside regulation would be brought to bear before it took action. Nonetheless, under the mistaken impression that the company had managerial autonomy, management pounded that idea into its employees' heads and established, for instance, company policies of giving customer service top priority. The reality gap led to much dissatisfaction and frustration.

THE ORGANIZATION UNDER CENTRALIZED AUTHORITY

The fundamental service that a telecommunications company can offer is phone service and not much else. The equipment that creates the service and the necessary labor are needed in equal distribution nationwide. The simple fact that the entire nation is its service area means that the company has to have a huge organization. Since the company has an organization focused on offering one product in large quantities, there is no need for forming different strategies for competing in different markets, the way most companies that offer either a range of products or services do.

The division of labor within the organization becomes dividing up the component processes that go into that one service, and specializing in them.

Planning in this type of corporation can be completely centralized. In fact, it is easier and cheaper if it is so controlled. Equipment specifications can be set; centralized procurement is a given; and the resources required by local operations can all be provided from headquarters. New facilities can be planned at the head office, with construction handled by the local offices. Procedures can follow centrally determined work standards, and to maintain the set types of service, other practices would be prohibited. But the "universal and equal" dictum bars the company from offering different services in different regions, or services that match the peculiarities of certain regions.

PATHOLOGY 1: TECHNOLOGICAL DETERMINISM

When looking at a telecommunications carrier as a sociotechnical system, the first thing that comes to mind about that system is the importance of the equipment and technology. It would seem that by just putting together a bunch of switching equipment, phones, and circuits, the service could follow automatically. If the subscriber uses the equipment, then the service has been provided. Services that depend on human effort, like directory assistance, are relegated to the periphery. Employees wind up servicing that vast collection of equipment, or being stuck with menial jobs such as processing subscriber applications or collecting fees.

The only parts of the company that really call for people to exercise any creativity are the planning department and the R&D department. There is practically nothing like the sales activities found in a normal corporation; "traffic sales" encouraging people to make more phone calls are about all there is along those lines. As business cycles are seen to have a significant influence on telephone volume, such sales are not taken very seriously.

Aside from these general operational characteristics, since the most important thing for the company was building up its infrastructure, the chief issue for it was finding ways to build its facilities at the lowest possible cost. All corporate activities were centered around facilitating construction, expansion, and upgrading of the physical plant. The biggest problem was that things like automating exchanges and introducing new technologies involved technical training for employees and reassignments for them. That made cooperation from the labor unions absolutely critical. Instead of setting rates in terms of their cost, they were set in terms of how to provide funds for construction costs. Conditions for using services, moreover, were determined according to the limitations imposed by the technology of the equipment. Nobody thought of starting from subscriber needs in planning services.

The idea of "The Onward March of Technology" had an almost autonomous, magical power in the company. Doing anything to obstruct or slow down the introduction of new technologies, or improve them for that matter, was out. Any new invention or service that R&D came up with just had to be put to use. The subscribers were simply supposed to accept the fruits of R&D with gratitude. If they did not accept something and its sales were poor, the problem would be chalked up to ignorant subscribers or inadequate efforts on the part of the sales department. The mystic force of "The Onward March of Technology" in effect acquired incontrovertible authority in a sort of pseudo-Marxist way: Social factors were seen as subservient to technology.

PATHOLOGY 2: BUDGETS OVER BALANCE SHEETS

In a modern nation, the budget is, in essence, the mechanism that fixes a ceiling on government spending. That is to say, the authority to spend extends to the budgeted amount. The upshot is that a government agency or company can spend what is budgeted without worrying about income. The guiding principles would be the opposite to those in a normal company in a capitalist society, which is supposed to make more money than it spends. Since a government company cannot spend any money that has not been authorized, the important thing is to present an unobjectionable budget to the Diet and get it passed.

For this, consistency would be key. Any significant discrepancies between predicted and actual expenditures would have to be hushed up. The company would have to claim that since last year's projections and performance were in agreement, this year's budget was right, too. So it would become second nature to cobble together believable-looking budgets and fabricate business achievements.

The whole process, from preparation of the budget to review by supervisory authority, review by the party, review by the Ministry of Finance, and finally on to the Diet, took one year—and by that time, the *next* budget had to be in the works. A company under the government's budgetary wing would sweat over writing up its budget. By contrast, closing the books at the end of the accounting year would just be a matter of filling in the blanks.

A company with accounting practices like this will not act like a normal company, in which the balance sheet for the year determines its next actions. A company that is in the government budget ceases to be a business per se and becomes simply a budget-implementing organization.

PATHOLOGY 3: GOVERNMENT CODDLING

According to the law, if this public corporation were to have more income than expenditures, the difference was to be saved internally, and if there was ever a shortfall it would treat it as an internal loss. That was specified in the interest of implanting the operating basis of a business concern in the corporation. Not having its budget incorporated with other national budget items was supposed to make it an efficiently managed, independent, and profitable organization.

But since there was no market competition and the corporation's main interest was in building the physical plant, there was an immediate inclination to raise rates whenever it ran into the red or did not have enough capital for construction.

In fact, the terms of the law did not bring about more efficient management. Since spending power grew out of the budget, budgeting officers were valued for their ability to write budgets that called for a great deal of money and manpower. Their concern was to convince the Ministry of Finance, without managing to balance income and outflow, that all expenditures were necessary. Naturally, expenditures would tend to rise faster than receipts—and nobody thought that particularly odd. So, within the company, managerial skills became a matter of how much money could be extracted from the budget.

PATHOLOGY 4: DELIBERATE STALLING
IN DECISION MAKING

One distinctive feature of a modern bureaucracy is that the authority and responsibilities that those working in it carry are clearly delimited. When a given process is divided into its component functions, and an organization built around this way of doing business, if any of these functions stop, then the expected results will not materialize. This is fine for "programmed jobs" that fall in the usual pattern, but if the organization hits an "unprogrammed job," work may stop in mid-stream. Even knowing that this problem cannot be resolved without the cooperation of all the employees, when confronted with a situation like this they will withdraw into their little shell of Japanese habits. Out of fear of being stuck with responsibility for doing anything new or because it is too much trouble, sometimes managers knowingly and intentionally decide not to make a decision.

PATHOLOGY 5: IGNORING THE CUSTOMER

Another part of the rationale behind modern bureaucracies is standardization, that is, standardizing the way work is done, and making the organization so that anybody can pick up any job and carry it out. This also involves standardizing products or services, in the interest of maintaining quality. But if this is taken too far, the mere idea of making specific accommodations for individual customers would be out of the question. That is particularly the case for a cooperation expected to provide universal and fair service, approved by a regulating agency, at uniform prices.

If a customer asked for anything outside the standard range of services, an employee's first response would be rejection. For anything new, the user would always be a ringing "No!" After all, if you do something to satisfy one customer and another customer comes along with a similar request, what would happen? If another employee said "no" to this request, might not there be trouble? The safest thing is to say "no" no matter what. They seem to have missed the whole point of a business—giving the customers what they want. Instead of trying to figure out how to meet the customer's request, their idea was that anything not part of the predetermined package was out. Moreover, the scattered complaints of consumers, a feeble group, were nothing before the influential combination of trade unions, regulating agencies, and upper management within the company. Those on the inside and those with power came first. The customer came last.

PATHOLOGY 6: AVERSION TO STREAMLINING AND REDUCING COSTS

The company was virtually never able to implement policies that would lead to firings, staff reductions, or increased workloads—all policies obviously inimical to union interests—out of fear of angering the labor unions that management needed to appease. On the surface, at the macrolevel, production was increasing due to cooperation on introducing new technologies and large annual increases in telephone equipment construction. Looking beneath the surface to individual workplaces, however, would reveal that proposals that would result in greater work efficiency were not welcome, as they would complicate labor relations.

So managers who actually wanted to do the job right quickly would give up their efforts to improve the system, and the company would muddle along the same as it always had, with a dispirited management. All policies to eliminate waste and increase efficiency were lumped together under the heading of "streamlining," and that streamlining meant dismissals was denied across the boards. Management came to have an inverted sense of values: They viewed streamlining as a negative.

Similarly, since the unions asserted that all efforts to reduce expenditures were ways of increasing workloads, cost cutting also acquired a negative connotation among managers at the workplace level.

PATHOLOGY 7: AN ASSORTMENT

- Promotion of technology for its own sake. Disregard for ease of use.

- Promotion of technology beyond levels justified by utility.

- Less regard for evaluations coming from outside the company than for those coming from within. Also, demand for positive internal evaluations.

- An attitude that if the equipment is okay and the service is okay, the customers will come.

- Making good equipment expensive. The pursuit of quality without regard for price is the usual attitude. There is always a lack of ideas for ways of building good things cheaply.

- An inward-looking, job-oriented, insular company. Little commerce with the outside world.

- Little sense of involvement, an onlooker's or critic's attitude. No sense of basically being engaged in things. No trial-and-error approaches allowed, thus no sense of adventure.

- Caring more about appearances than content.

- Expecting to be legally and morally responsible for failures, employees always tended to find excuses, to think defensively. No room for failure.

THE TRUTH COMES OUT

After thirty years in business as a state monopoly, NTT finally achieved its goals of providing telephone service to everyone who wanted it, immediately, and supplying nationwide automatic service with immediate connections.

Beginning in the late 1970s, when it had met these goals, the company had problems. With the oil embargo of 1973, the country fell into the worst recession since World War II. In fiscal 1974, the company suffered its first major deficit. A rate increase in 1976 led to a surge in complaints about bills. The company met increasingly concrete, repeated demands from industry to open up the use of circuits. The company had anticipated none of these problems.

What was crucial was that the problems ran so deeply and so broadly that there was no way to cope with each of them individually. Take, for example, the complaints about rates. It was the lack of a billing system giving detailed report on usage that touched off customer complaints. While the company was busy expanding its physical plant, it had failed to institute a software system that would generate detailed bills. Since the company lacked close contact with its customers, moreover, its response to complaints was also unsatisfactory; that only exacerbated the situation.

Changes in the business environment called into question the role and responsibilities of the company's monopoly of domestic telecommunications and its nature as a public corporation. First of all, the technological revolution in communications and computing tended to link telecommunications and computer processing, and the line between broadcasting and telecommunications was growing unclear. This trend went along with increasingly diverse and intense demands on existing technology. A number of companies were also trying to enter the telecommunications field. Those movements were behind the opening of circuits and removal of restrictions on terminal equipment to be used.

Second, the communications and information technology in Japan was increasing in relative importance internationally, as Japan's economic power grew. In international affairs, deepening interdependencies among nations took this technological revolution toward information and communication services using international networks, for which a monopoly system guided by government policy is impractical.

Third, while the service is invisible in itself, advances in technology could make the service in a monopolistically run market seem like a massive, Byzantine machine. Customers cut off from a company hidden behind closed doors of government lose confidence in the company.

THE PUBLIC RELATIONS (PR) DEPARTMENT:
A STRATEGIC TOOL FOR ORGANIZATIONAL REFORM

The management of state monopolies enjoys a certain amount of slack, compared to its private sector counterpart, in that it does not need to worry as much about efficiency. And because of the raft of regulations that govern it, it is not even clear what the management's responsibilities are. So, management and the unions, the regulating authorities, Diet members, suppliers, and even some of the customers would all make opportunistic demands of the company. As long as each received what it wanted, it figured everything was fine. There was a confluence of vested interests, between the state monopoly and special interest groups.

There was no quick-fix that would revamp the existing organization and put the structure of a proper business in its place. Employee attitudes would have to change, and that would take time. Something would have to be done to excise the influence of vested interests. Necessary legal reforms would also take time. So the idea came up of internal reform, within the existing framework, and before any of these things could happen. It would still take a 180 degree change in attitudes among the staff. That is where the PR department came in.

Words are the most potent weapon. To reverse the value system of NTT's three hundred thousand employees, the idea of "real-world sensibility" would have to be drilled into their heads. Maybe the best way to do it would be to walk around the workplace, saying it over and over again. Another way might be through the magic of the media, which would put this message in front of their faces. Otherwise, management would have to say the same thing hundreds of times to effect change.

Why was it important to turn everybody's way of thinking around? Take, for example, the term "public service." Letting costs go through the roof, or just doing things that the staff wanted to do, could be justified in the name of this type of service. To fill its function fairly, the company would need a sound financial footing, and spreading the idea that financial soundness and public-oriented service were not mutually exclusive would take some time.

Also, this was one company that did not recognize the existence of customers as such. These people would be called "subscribers" or "users." Efforts aimed at getting the staff to substitute the word "customer" would encounter some psychological resistance.

Under Japan's life-long employment system, people hardly ever change jobs. Once people graduate and find a job, they often stay in the same company until they retire. Managerial positions are for the most part filled in-house, not from outside. Therefore, new employees adapt to a specific corporate culture or system. The result is the endless reproduction of people with homogeneous values.

Given this typical Japanese corporate climate, it is extremely rare for reforms to be brought about from within a corporation. To restructure the management of this troubled state monopoly, the government sent in a highly experienced manager from heavy industry to head the management team. That was a highly unusual move in Japan, but the management transfusion proved highly successful. The new chief executive, from time to time, told his staff how absurd, how peculiar their ways of doing business were, compared with normal business practices. And he did not just preach: He was a concrete, practical example.

The new CEO gave the company concrete, simple targets: to make income grow more than expenditures, to prepare monthly settlements by the middle of the next month, and not to hide facts from the rest of the world. These practices seem quite ordinary and simple, but for people who had never tried them before, achieving the goals was tough, both mentally and physically. In addition, since these concrete and familiar targets had no grand system of theory or ideology behind them, those who were accustomed to a seamless ideology found no value in them. They regarded these targets as low level. Many did not work seriously toward these goals. They defiantly clung to their belief that their way of thinking was superior, setting a higher value on theory than on practice.

But a theory not put into practice is meaningless, even harmful. The meaning of theory is understood only when it is practiced. Therefore, the new chief executive at first gave people only simple targets and did not explain why they needed such targets. After all, people who cannot complete simple tasks cannot understand difficult theories.

Changing from a monopolistic to a competitive environment means a total change in ways of doing business. Employees need to get accustomed to the change gradually. They cannot handle a sudden about-face. The PR department, then, was also responsible for helping employees adjust to gradual changes, to putting new ways into practice. That was the core of in-house PR activities.

DIALOGUE WITH THE CUSTOMER

For a state monopoly, the idea of having a real-world conversation was not a part of doing business at all. The PR department had always engaged in exchange of messages, and not in dialogues. Efforts were made to make the company more approachable for customers and to create a more outgoing attitude from within. Thus, the founding principle of the PR department became: "to give the facts, as is."

Customer representative councils, manned by community representatives, were formed for each exchange to pass along orders, complaints, and criticisms. A committee was formed in the interest of quickly resolving in-house complaints and criticisms, with a target of one-month response times.

It was vital to fix in the minds of everybody in the company that gripes should be taken care of. The complaints-processing committee would deliberate on all matters brought to its attention. Despite the objection that things that could not be handled identically nationwide would be problematic, the committee recommended that if something could be done, it should be done. The same set of rules could be read so that it encouraged doing things for the customers, or so that it encouraged making work easier within the company (or so the work did not need to be done at all).

THOROUGH DISCLOSURE

Naturally, the mass media tactic did encounter some employee resistance. Many people thought that the PR person's job was to make sure nothing bad about the company got out. Informing the outside world of the truth about the company was intended to make substantive changes in the company itself, but this is one of those things that is easier said than done. This amazing policy of publishing the truth, warts and all, did in fact lead to a steady improvement in the company's image as reflected in the media over the course of one year.

Even though the company was inefficient and for the real world, ineffective, it was tied to special interests. In particular, those working there saw it as the basis of their livelihoods, so there was little room to hope for self-reform that might endanger their existence. In normal companies, management provides the leadership for reform, but in a company with the special privileges of a state enterprise or monopoly, the management is pretty much the same as the rest of the staff, and its greatest interest is in maintaining the status quo.

Public opinion and news reports end up being the sole stimulants for change in these businesses. If there is not a free press, then there is no chance of things changing. Even though the media may be guilty of making a number of mistakes, naturally the free exchange of opinions is the right thing in the long run. Covering its collective ears to criticism from outside showed how afraid the company was. It would not listen to its own employees or to its customers, but when assailed by newspapers, television, and radio, management started thinking "maybe we should do something about that."

ABOLISHING PRIVILEGES: INTRODUCING THE ELEMENT OF COMPETITION

Usually, organizations that serve as public services enjoy a variety of privileges. Take the rate-approval system, for instance. The fact that the government approves certain rates means that the government underwrites a certain pricing guarantee. Take the regulation requiring that each subscriber's main telephone be company-provided, or take all the regulations on the use of circuits. From the standpoint of the subscriber, these restrictions maintain the company's privileges, but from the company's point of view, it seems like unavoidable regulations forced on it by the national government. They were not following the regulations because they wanted to, they claimed. Yet the idea of doing away with regulations caused anxiety. What if the company could not sell its telephone sets anymore, for instance? What if its revenues dropped? And so it took a foot-dragging approach to deregulation.

The decision to eliminate its privileges by its own hand and expose it to as much competition as possible gave the company a shot in the arm. It was important for people to feel that at least some parts of the company were ready to withstand competition.

REDEFINITION OF THE MARKET AND
SELF-TRANSFORMATION

A protected company cannot be expected to keep up its energy level for a long time. If it loses all its best managers, it will be no better off than before, and this has happened enough already. So the company has to stay receptive to feedback from the outside world. Obviously, the best way is to expose itself to the forces of the marketplace.

Changes in the market and advances in compute technology had made the opening up of circuit access and competition inescapable. Those actually judging the applications for use of the circuits had a keen sense that deregulation was unavoidable. Legal regulations could not hold back technical innovations or actual demand. Even though these simple facts were staring everyone in the face, nobody could recognize them. Nobody within the monopoly ever asked themselves why they were allowed to be a monopoly. Nobody asked to what extent the company could justify its own existence, and to what extent it relied on others. There would have to be top management with a clear awareness of the issues for the company's self-transformation. And it could not simply be thought of as preaching; it had to be presented as objective facts.

As a result, the company proposed to the government that the telecommunications industry be liberalized, competitive elements introduced, and monopolies eliminated, and at the same time the company be privatized. At first, the company selfishly tried simply to wrest managerial autonomy from the government, but finally recognized that it could not have autonomy by maintaining its monopoly. The urge to turn the public corporation into a normal corporation came from within the company, not from the regulating authorities. The company sued for its self-transformation in the halls of government, and the resolution itself gave the company a jump-start.

The privatization process, which was conducted within a governmental framework, was an interesting case in itself. It turned into a war with the special-interest groups that surrounded the company. But what it finally achieved was not its ultimate goals, but a start toward them. These goals are to foster a creative, invigorated company that responds to external conditions, and then to encourage more competition in the marketplace, and reflect that heightened competition in the company's own structure.

Individuals can stand up to the forces of market competition. If the products and services offered on the market are expensive and shoddy, they lose out. But such individuals cannot stand irresponsible comments or criticisms of themselves—the lack of a service-oriented mentality, the high wages, the short working hours, and the low quality plaguing it. People without managerial responsibility flaunt their authority insufferably, issuing random directives. This much at least is certain: People want to be their own masters. Corporate structure that does not satisfy that demand squelches individual creativity. The organization will be drained of life, so no matter what managerial studies or sciences the company subscribes to, it will not be able to motivate people for long. Trust will disappear. The company that does not face competition in the market will not make any effort to provide the best service, and if it does not face criticism under a free press, it will not improve itself.

Comments on Dynamic Change in Diverse Political and Economic Environments

Dennis Schorr

The chapters in this section point out the importance of approaching questions about innovation from both external and internal levels of analysis. An external level of analysis includes those variables that operate outside an individual organization, namely, economy or societywide variables. National technology policies, government regulation, and macroeconomic policies are examples of external factors that influence innovation. Kong's and Vecsenyi's chapters focus on these sorts of issues.

An internal level of analysis refers to those variables found within an individual organization. Strategic, organizational, and operational factors are examples of internal variables that affect innovation. Mensch's chapter examines some important internal variables, such as discrepancies in perceptions among managers within a company.

Up until this point, much of the research on innovation has focused on either an external or internal perspective. Increasingly, however, there is a need for integration across both levels of analysis. Toriyama's chapter, in particular, examines innovation at NTT from both perspectives. For example, he discusses the relationship between government regulation and internal organizational pathologies, as well as the relationship between changes in government regulation and changes in organizational and management practices. In thinking about the appropriate level of analysis and the possibilities of integrating ideas across perspectives, is useful to consider common issues that cut across both external and internal points of view.

One set of issues that is common to both perspectives relates to the management of change. At both levels of analysis, questions can be posed about the speed at which changes should be made and whether change should take place at once or in a more gradual, incremental fashion. Different societies have followed different paths along these dimensions. China has pursued incremental changes over more than a decade. By contrast, Germany and Poland have followed a more rapid, discontinuous set of changes during the past year or two. Vecsenyi points out that Hungary had pursued incremental transformations over a long period of time, with more discontinuous changes in the past few years.

These same issues are mirrored at the individual organization level. For example, should a company bring about changes through major organizational restructuring or through more gradual developments in processes, systems, and people? The literature on revolutionary versus incremental changes in organizations addresses these kinds of questions.

Obviously, the speed at which external change takes place has implications for the pace of change inside individual organizations. For example, the revolutionary changes in Germany's economy have made it necessary for firms to pursue major, discontinuous changes in order to survive in the new environment. Questions regarding the similarities and differences of change dynamics at both the societal and organizational levels remain to be answered.

Another set of issues that cuts across both levels relates to the relevant model for bringing about innovation. Vecsenyi raises the question of which model Hungary should pursue as it changes. Should it use the model of the United States, Japan, Korea, Finland, or some other country?

Similarly, individual firms search for models for innovation. The plethora of articles that have been written about 3M reflects the interest that managers have in looking at other organizations for models as they struggle to make their own organizations more innovative.

On what basis should a relevant model be selected? Are the criteria for selecting a model similar at the societal and organization levels? These and similar questions are fruitful areas for additional investigation.

Another common set of issues that cuts across the external and internal levels of analysis relates to the differentiation and integration of economic activities. At the firm level, much has been written about how tasks should be grouped into organization subunits and how activities should then be coordinated across the subunits. At the societal level, much has been written about the parallel question of how economic activities should be divided in individual companies and how coordination should be achieved among companies. For example, how should the activities of vendors and manufacturers or manufacturers and distributors be coordinated? At each level of analysis, both market and hierarchical mechanisms are operative.

Exchanges within firms have traditionally been viewed as governed by hierarchical mechanisms. However, quasi-market mechanisms are also operative within companies. In fact, attempts have been made to simulate market mechanisms within firms to encourage innovation, for example, through the use of internal corporate ventures or autonomous subsidiaries.

Exchanges between firms have traditionally been viewed as governed by market mechanisms in capitalist countries. Quasi-hierarchical relationships between firms, however, may be an effective way of stimulating innovation. For example, the relationship between Japanese automobile manufacturers and their vendors can be characterized as quasi-hierarchical. Automobile manufacturers, such as Toyota, have long-term relationships with a small number of suppliers and develop very close working contacts with them (Keiretsu). In fact, they even share personnel and collaborate on the development of new designs. In an extensive research project on the automobile industry, Kim Clark of Harvard University has found that these types of relationships with suppliers provide Japanese car makers with significant sources of advantage in lead time and costs over their American and European competitors.

The increasing popularity of strategic alliances or partnerships between organizations points to the importance of alternative governance mechanisms for fostering innovation. Whereas interorganizational partnerships have been widely used in Japan for some time, they have been tried with much more hesitation in the United States and Europe. Despite this hesitancy, the concept of network organizations, consisting of significant relationships between related companies, has been receiving increasing attention. The recent agreement between IBM and Siemens to develop jointly a new generation of semiconductors is an example of the increasing use of interorganizational partnerships.

Under what conditions does it make sense to form these types of interorganizational relationships? Although research in this area is just beginning, there is a great deal of speculation that partnerships may be an important way of promoting innovation, particularly in rapidly changing industries like computers or semiconductors.

In looking for a common framework that integrates the external and internal perspectives of innovation, international research seems like an especially promising avenue for further investigation. The chapters in Part 2 point out that there is quite a bit of variation among countries in the structure of economic activities between and within firms. Studying these variations should help both organizations and societies with diverse environments to promote innovation more effectively.

Part III

Restructuring Large-Scale Bureaucracies for Creativity and Innovation

7

Creativity and Innovation in Large Organizations

Paul A. Schumann, Jr.

Large organizations are traditionally noninnovative. Yet there is nothing in largeness that prohibits creativity and innovation. It is possible to balance both creativity and productivity in a large organization. A methodology to accomplish this goal will be described in this chapter.

Creativity and productivity are two important characteristics of organizations. The amount of each varies over the organization's lifecycle. It is useful to consider the evolution of organizations by mapping their history into a creativity/productivity matrix. In general, paths in the creativity/productivity matrix can be related to four primary managerial styles:

- Autocracy
- Bureaucracy
- Intrapreneurship
- Teleocracy

CREATIVITY AND PRODUCTIVITY

Creativity and productivity are important attributes of a person, a group of people, or an organization. The balance and focus of an organization on these two attributes determine what an organization can accomplish. Typically, at various stages in the life of an organization or person, there is a natural focus on one or the other.

Creativity has its roots in the Indo-European word *ker*, which means "to grow." The English word "create" came from this root by way of the Greek *khorus*, meaning youth, and the Latin *Ceres*, the Roman goddess of youth. The Latin words *creare*, "to bring forth," and *crescere*, "to spring forth," were the precedents for "create." Creativity has the connotation of growth associated with it. A creative organization is able to bring new, growing things into existence.

Productivity, on the other hand, comes from the Indo-European word *deuk*, which means "to lead." The Latin word *ducere* also means "to lead." Words like "duct" and "educate" come from this root. A duct leads something along. To educate is to lead to knowledge, not fill minds up. The roots and current definition of productivity imply for an organization the ability to lead something through bringing it forth or forward. When applied to creativity, a productive organization leads the ideas through some steps; that is, it produces something.

Creativity is the driving force of an organization. It causes growth to occur. Without creativity, there can be no productivity. Productivity results from the exploitation of the creativity of an organization. The creativity of an organization does not have to totally exist within the organization, however. An organization's productivity can be built on others' creativity as a base or through injection for creativity at any point in the productivity process. But an organization has to have some lead of internal creativity or it will stagnate and die.

Creativity and productivity can be displayed in a simple matrix (see Figure 7.1), with creativity as the driving force. With this simple perspective, typical lifecycles of organizations can be examined.

START OF BUSINESS

An organization usually starts with some level of creativity and low productivity (see Figure 7.2). It is generally an idea, collection of ideas, or pursuit of direction that characterizes a small, start-up organization. The process of development of the organization is characterized by the search for the idea or collection of ideas that will make a business. The formation of the ideas is driven by interaction with the marketplace (customers, technology, and competition). Quite often, autocracy is an effective management system. The organization is small; the ideas being tested can reside in the mind of one individual. That individual can look at the issues of the marketplace and the business, and can develop the vision. People join the autocrat because they can share the vision.

Figure 7.1. Creativity/Productivity Matrix

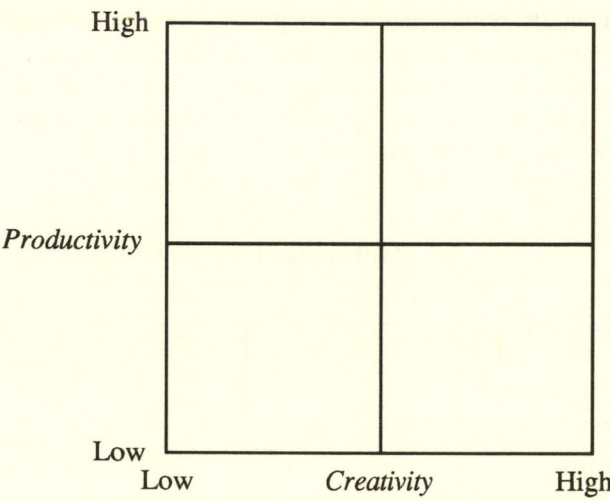

Figure 7.2. A Start-Up Business

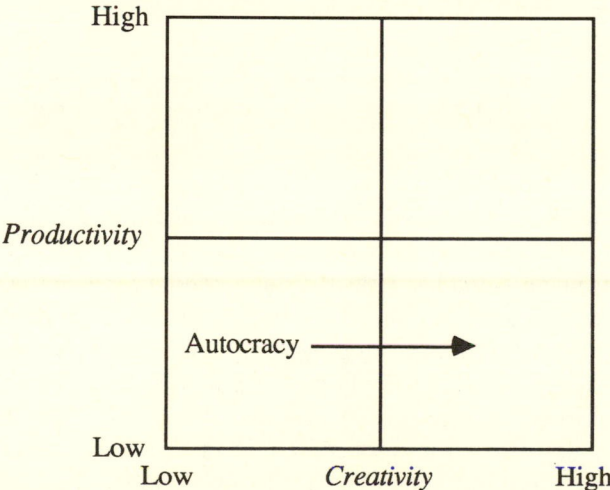

MATURATION OF A BUSINESS

When the set of ideas that define the business have been developed, the next step is to improve productivity to capitalize on the ideas (see Figure 7.3). This is a process of routinization usually carried out by a bureaucracy. The organization grows too large and the issues too complex for any one individual to handle. Rules, regulations, procedures, policies, and beliefs are established. During the canonization of the beliefs, a value set is formed and the corporate culture takes shape. It is the bureaucracy that makes decisions. The system decides like some great mechanism. The gears turn ever and ever more efficiently, grinding out product after product.

Figure 7.3. Maturation of a Business

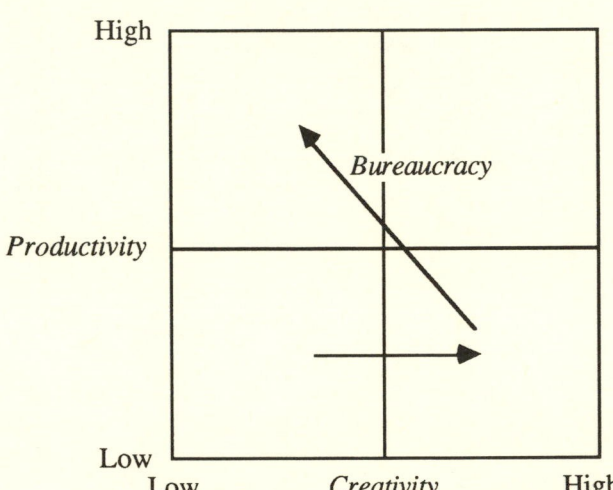

Unfortunately, the process of routinization takes the creativity out of an organization. It is easy to convince people during this stage that turning the crank again is better—and less risky—than searching for a new set of ideas.

Bureaucracies are not inherently bad. They have created large and successful companies that have employed millions of workers, and produced products useful to society. The only problem with bureaucracies is that they have been built with no mechanisms to stop their growth. Every problem that occurs, every deviation from procedure—in fact, creativity—is fixed. The organization is modified not to let that happen again. The bureaucracy is intolerant of error, even if driven by attempts at creative change.

STAGNATION

An unfortunate direct effect of bureaucracies designed to maximize productivity, now typified by concern over the quarterly bottom line, is stagnation (see Figure 7.4). Stagnation occurs because there is not enough creativity to fuel productivity, and productivity falls.

Figure 7.4. Stagnation

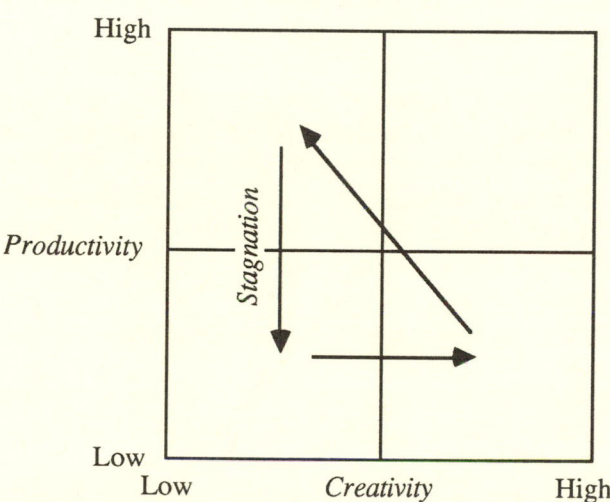

Large organizations have three optional strategies to follow: stagnation, venturing, or revitalization. Diverse organizations can consider all three in different business areas.

Stagnation is a viable strategy if it is clearly recognized by the business, and if it consciously acts in concert with the strategy. Money can be made off a declining business.

Typical large, and therefore previously or currently successful, organizations tend to avoid the stagnation path. The machine is programmed for growth, so it generally opts for venturing.

VENTURING

Venturing,[1] whether internal or external, is an attempt for at least part of the organization to return to the past. It may not be the same business area or technology, but it is an attempt to recapture the creativity remembered by the organization.

Treatment of external venturing, acquisitions, and collaborative ventures is beyond the scope of this chapter. It is clear that all of these attempts have the same general principle underlying them—to improve the creativity of the organization, usually at the cost of a temporary setback in productivity.

Internal venturing (see Figure 7.5),[2] internal entrepreneurship, or intrapreneurship, was a management system developed in the 1970s and 1980s in the United States to respond to the growing feeling among the successful large companies formed by bureaucracies of the 1950s and 1960s. These same organizations were founded by autocracies in the 1930s and 1940s.

In internal venturing, the idea was to instill an entrepreneurial value in the organization that would foster the development of independent business units (IBUs or "skunkworks") within the organization. Because the business area was limited and risks small, new ideas could be tried out, rules broken, and more creative freedom given people.

These IBUs were generally successful at developing a specific product or market, but in most cases, the bureaucracy quickly took over. Further, subsequent attempts at venturing were hindered or stopped even more quickly than the first. The system had been immunized by the first infection and quickly responded to the second.

Figure 7.5. Internal Venturing

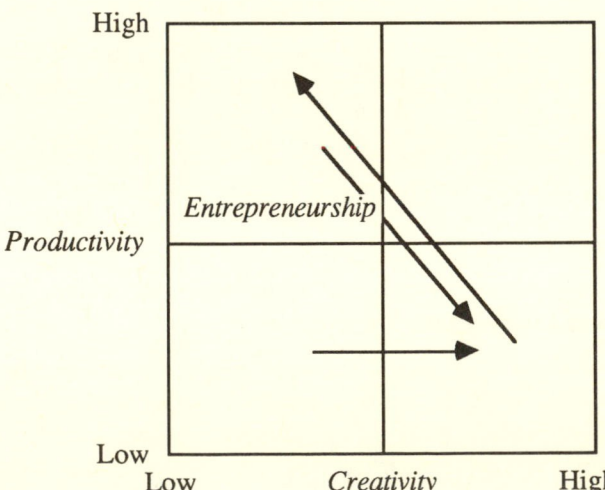

In general, intrapreneurship, as a management strategy, has been unsuccessful in making long-term, significant changes in an organization. Quickly, the creativity is reduced and productivity emphasized. This is not to say that it has not been a successful business strategy. Billions of dollars of revenues have been generated by the IBUs, such as IBM's PC.

TELEOCRACY

Effective major corporate restructuring leading to a revitalized organization requires an increase in creativity, while maintaining or regaining lost productivity, if any. The management system that seems to be appropriate to this transformation is teleocracy,[3] or management by shared purpose (see Figure 7.6).

Figure 7.6. Teleocracy

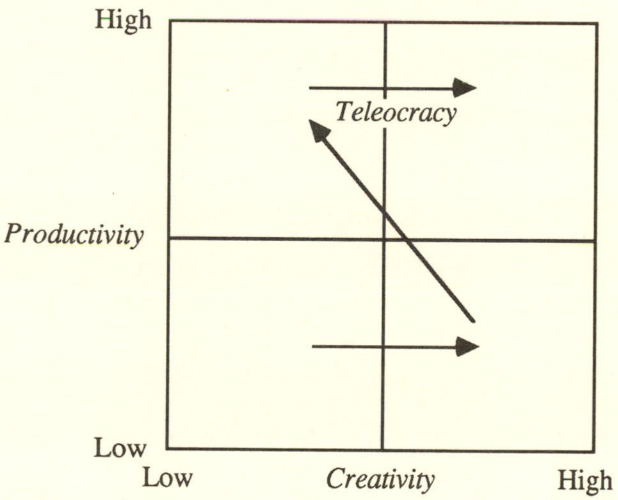

There are four key elements of teleocracy:

- *Purpose created through a vision.* A vision is a desired state to be achieved sometime in the future. It is a target that can be held up and strived for. The vision provides the organization and therefore the people with distinctiveness. It describes how the organization relates to the larger environment. It must be shared by all members of the organization. A vision ennobles people.

- *Results established by missions, goals, and objectives.* This is the organizational and measurement system that defines what is worth achieving. It is the glue for the structure that provides the hierarchy of purpose. Once the goals and objectives are established, skills and tools can be developed to enable the people in the organization to accomplish them.

- *Activities developed by plans and programs.* In a teleocracy, individuals are given a great deal of freedom. If the vision is shared and measurements established, the activities of individuals need not be directed. The people are empowered to use their creativity and productivity.

- *Problem solving and decision making.* The role of managers in a teleocracy is to monitor the activities against the vision, goals, and objectives, and correct course as necessary. Managers coach and mentor, rather than direct. The role of managers is to encourage the empowered employees to utilize their creativity and productivity to make the vision a reality.

ORGANIZATIONAL CULTURE

A key ingredient in the success of a teleocracy is to have the organizational culture aligned with the vision, goals, and objectives.[4] The primary factor to consider in the organizational culture is the values. The values of the organization, and the people in the organization, determine what will gain attention. Values direct, not always at the conscious level, the outcome of millions of incremental decisions that are made daily by the members of an organization. Values determine who will rise in the organization. They are important to decisions about markets, products, and projects. Values are the bedrock of the culture.

Three elements are important in reinforcing the values: rites and rituals, heroes and heroines, and the informal communications network.

Rites and rituals are the formal and informal processes and procedures by which the values are canonized. The values are continuously reinforced by the policies, practices, rules, regulations, standards, and the informal method by which things get done.

Heroes and heroines are the people who personify the values. They make the values real to the members of the organization. These are the people who are held in high esteem by the organization. The heroes and heroines are the ones who have gotten the recognition, accolades, publicity, promotions, awards, and salary increases.

The informal communications network is the manner in which the values are perpetuated and strengthened. Each member of an organization has two jobs. The official job is the one defined by the formal structure. The second, and sometimes more important job, is that defined by the informal network. Information is passed much more quickly through informal channels. Values are reinforced by stories that are passed around the informal network. Actions of individuals within the organization that are value-rich are passed around. Some stories in strong culture organizations have been known to be repeated for years.

In a strong culture, there is an alignment of values, heroes and heroines, rites and rituals, and the stories passed along by the informal communications network. Strong culture organizations are more likely to be successful. They are efficient, take less time turning ideas into innovations, have high role, and require little day-to-day direction. Strong cultures are not easily changed; they resist change and are susceptible to attacks from outside their line of sight.

A culturally astute manager assures that all the policies, practices, standards, promotions, and awards are reviewed against the values desired in the organization, and passes on the stories of the heroes' and heroines' actions.

The challenge of a teleocratic management system in these turbulent times is to create a strong corporate culture with flexibility. The culture must be able to change as the environment around the organization shifts. This can be accomplished in a teleocracy because it is driven by a common purpose that has been generated by the people in the organization.

Individuals change faster than institutions.[5] This is historically why revolutions occur and why institutions always seem to be "behind the times." Individuals are better able than institutions—if ennobled, enabled, empowered, and encouraged—to keep in touch with the forces and requirements of the market (technology, competitors, and customers). And, they are enmeshed in and part of the environmental driving forces. It is an organic system. Bureaucracies are more mechanical and unable to grow through creativity; they cannot transform themselves. Autocracy and intrapreneurship, while having the ability to change, are generally unable to cope with the complexities.[6]

CULTURAL TRANSFORMATION

Generally, the values of an organization are not in line with the newly established vision, objectives, and goals of the teleocracy. A transformation of the organization culture is therefore required. This is accomplished by determination of the values needed and an assessment of the current values.

The difference determines the character of the transformation program. In general, it is important to build on current programs, not destroy everything. Then, put a program in place that emphasizes the current values needed for the future, deemphasizes those values no longer needed, and creates new values desired.

The cultural change program should be implemented incrementally, staged with quality evident at each checkpoint. It should be strategically focused, but be able to demonstrate early results. And, it should have an early, highly visible, successful first step or pilot.

It is imperative that the values required by the organization be used in the implementation of the transformation. This is a common cause for failure. A market-driven value program that does not consider the market for the program, the employees, is not going to be very successful.

The transformation must, of course, support the strategic business objectives. It is important to keep in mind at all times that the culture is the enabler of the business.

Since most large organizations are already too bureaucratic, the program must add no bureaucracy, even though it is tempting to add controls and measures.

Other factors to consider are cost, experiential learning, and time frame. The transformation program must be affordable. It must provide some way of learning through experience; the program must include some mechanism for sharing experiences. And, the backers of the transformation must have patience and persistence. Time frames for transformations vary, and it is never clear when one starts or ends, but a five-year target is fairly common.

CULTURAL TRANSFORMATION EXAMPLE

The objective of this organizational culture transformation was to create a more technically vital organization, one in which the technical people in the organization viewed themselves as professionals. The values identified for professionalism are shown in Table 7.1. In this case, few, if any, of the values were held by the organization of over two thousand professionals, although studies of the people in the organization indicated that many of the people wanted these values and were frustrated.

Figure 7.7 indicates the tasks necessary to develop a transformation program. For each of the values desired, actions must be taken to reinforce those values through rites and rituals, heroes and heroines, and the cultural network.

In this example, the result was a six-year integrated program that successfully changed the culture of the organization. Once viewed as a not very vital member of the larger parent organization, it is now one of the organization's leading sites.

Table 7.1. Cultural Values for Professionalism

- Initiative for self-development
- Vision of technical direction
- Technical leadership
- Creativity and innovation
- Technical breadth with technical depth (multiple levels of expertise)
- Technical communication
- Environmental awareness (internal and external)
- Teamwork

Figure 7.7. Cultural Change Actions Matrix

Professional Values	Cultural Elements		
	Hero/ Heroine	Rite/ Ritual	Informal Network
Initiative			
Vision			
Leadership			
Creativity and innovation			
Intellectual property			
Expertise			
Communication			
Environmental awareness			
Teamwork			

MARKET-DRIVEN

The focus of the entire transformation—including the vision, goals, objectives, and the supporting organizational culture—must be the market. The entire process must be market-driven.

The principles of being market-driven are very simple, fundamentally sound, and very powerful. To be market-driven, you must understand the markets, commit to leadership in the markets you choose to serve, execute with excellence across your organization, and make your customer the final arbiter (see Figure 7.8). The combination and successful implementation of these principles will result in satisfied customers.

Figure 7.8. Market-Driven Principles

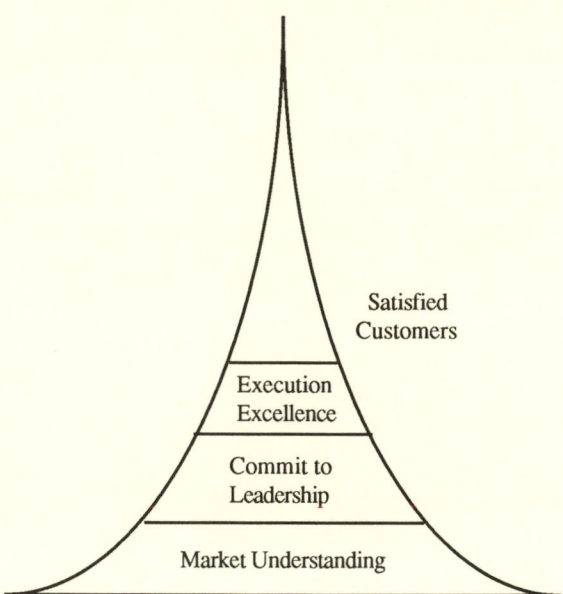

A market consists of three components: pull, push, and clash (see Figure 7.9). The pull of the market comes from current customers, and known and unknown potential customers. Market push comes from the technology—direct technology, supportive technology, and enabling technology. The clash in the marketplace comes from competitors—direct, indirect, and structural.

A systematic search through these elements of the market will identify the innovation opportunity. Ideally, it would be preferable to pinpoint an area where customers want innovation, where the technology has the potential to provide it, and where there is little competition. To understand the market, then, is to develop a description of the innovation opportunity.

A shared vision is the enabling force that can drive an organization (Figure 7.10). If this vision encompasses the commitment to leadership and embraces innovation, it can be used to develop the innovation strategy that results from the innovation opportunity developed through understanding the markets. It is through the previously described management style, "teleocracy," that the vision can be established in large organizations that have developed through bureaucracy.

Figure 7.9. Market Components

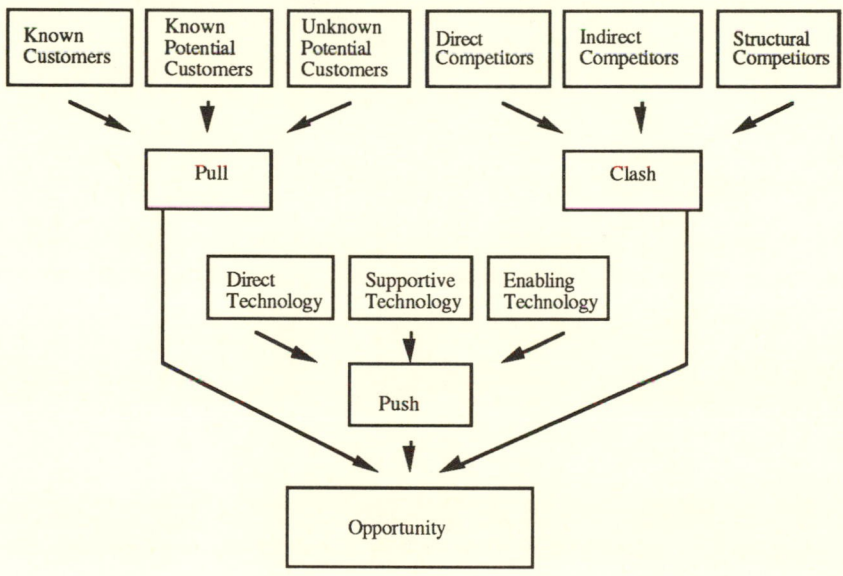

Often it is in the establishment of the vision that organizations lose sight of the customers. They get caught up in their own perspectives, and grind their own axes instead of clearly seeing the market opportunity and responding to it. It is here that the image of the lone wolf inventor or entrepreneur flourishes.

After committing to leadership, the projects must be executed with excellence to gain the leadership desired—and to have a satisfied customer. Three innovation program elements must be considered: projects, resources, and culture. The first step is to take an inventory of each of these elements and match the results to the innovation strategy. The difference is the innovation gap. This gap determines what needs change.

Figure 7.10. Innovation by Design

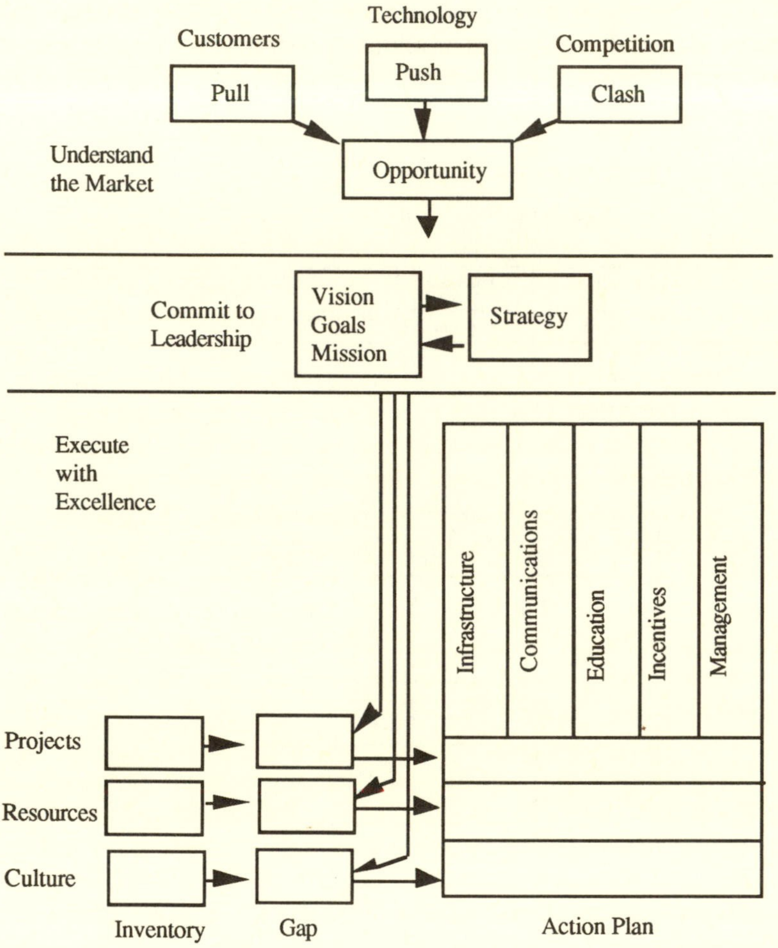

It is important to consider all three elements. Changes to the projects without accompanying changes to resources and culture will surely fail. Managers often believe that merely changing the projects will produce the desired innovation, but changes to resources must accompany changes in the project mix. Then, to assure the effectiveness of the project and resource change, the organizational culture must be changed, too. A time scale is implicit in these efforts: It is easier and faster to change the project mix than it is the resources. And, it is easier and faster to change the resources than it is the culture. But, all these efforts must be started simultaneously.

Making the customer the final arbiter means, in the context of innovation, keeping the customer in mind at all times during the innovation process. Whenever it may not be clear which direction to take, always opt for the customer's position. It is often useful to define innovation in terms of the customers.

INNOVATION BY DESIGN

What has been outlined is a procedure for innovating purposefully, for Innovation by Design. It combines the best of current knowledge on the subject of innovation and provides a methodology to look for and exploit opportunities for innovation.

A problem that a successful innovation strategy must solve is how to communicate effectively about innovation throughout the organization. It would be helpful if this method of communication broke down stereotypical thinking patterns, if it put innovation into a new context so old methods of thinking could not be used and private issues could not surface. These results can be accomplished with AIM, the applied innovation matrix, which is an integral part of Innovation by Design. The AIM map is composed of nine types of innovation (see Figure 7.11). Along one axis is the nature of the innovation—product, process, and procedure (see Table 7.2). The other axis of the matrix shows the class of the innovation—incremental, distinctive, and breakthrough (see Table 7.3).

When AIM is used in conjunction with Innovation by Design (see Figure 7.12), it is a powerful tool for understanding innovation and focusing the organization's innovation efforts. With it, the market can be tested to see what type of innovation strategy has the highest potential for success. AIM can be used to assess current innovation capabilities and to focus the organization's innovative capability in the right direction, thereby improving productivity.

There is a direct relationship between Innovation by Design and being market-driven, as shown in Table 7.4. Innovation by Design is a procedure for implementing a market-driven strategy. At the same time, Innovation by Design establishes a methodology to implement cultural and resource change, integrating a teleocratic management system.

Figure 7.11. Applied Innovation Matrix

	Class		
Nature	Incremental	Distinctive	Breakthrough
Product			
Process			
Procedure			

Table 7.2. Nature of Innovation

Product:	The goods or services offered to the customer or user for payment or other recompense.
Process:	The means used to produce goods or provide services.
Procedures:	The way in which the products and/or processes are integrated into the operations of the organization.

Innovation by Design has great value in developing a creative and productive organization that will sustain itself by continuous change. Innovation by Design can be used to identify true innovation needs, and future opportunities and threats. It can help in the process of conceiving and developing new products, processes, and procedures. Innovation by Design is valuable in establishing communication across organizational boundaries. It is helpful in communicating innovative concepts clearly and effectively. Through Innovation by Design, innovation can be fostered at all levels in all parts of the organization. In addition, the innovation thus fostered will be focused on the market opportunity. Finally, total quality can be improved.

For it is only through innovation that total quality management can be realized.

Table 7.3. Class of Innovation

Breakthrough:	An innovation based on a fundamentally different approach than presently being used. Allows one to perform a task that could not be performed at present, or perform a present task in a markedly improved manner. Typically serves as a foundation for a number of distinctive innovations.
Distinctive:	An innovation that significantly improves performance and/or profitability. Typically serves as a foundation for a number of incremental innovations.
Incremental:	An innovation that provides small improvement in performance and profitability. Allows goods or services to be produced faster, cheaper, better, more reliably.

CONCLUSIONS

Organizations go through lifecycles. Bureaucracy has created many successful, large organizations. These organizations have commercialized products and services that have added to the life of the organization and its balance of trade. They employ many people. To save these bureaucracies from extinction—and the dislocations that would result—it is necessary to revitalize them. Becoming market-driven, employing teleocratic management systems, and using Innovation by Design methodologies will revitalize them. These principles will allow large bureaucracies to transform themselves into innovative, vital, and productive organizations.

Figure 7.12. Innovation by Design Procedure

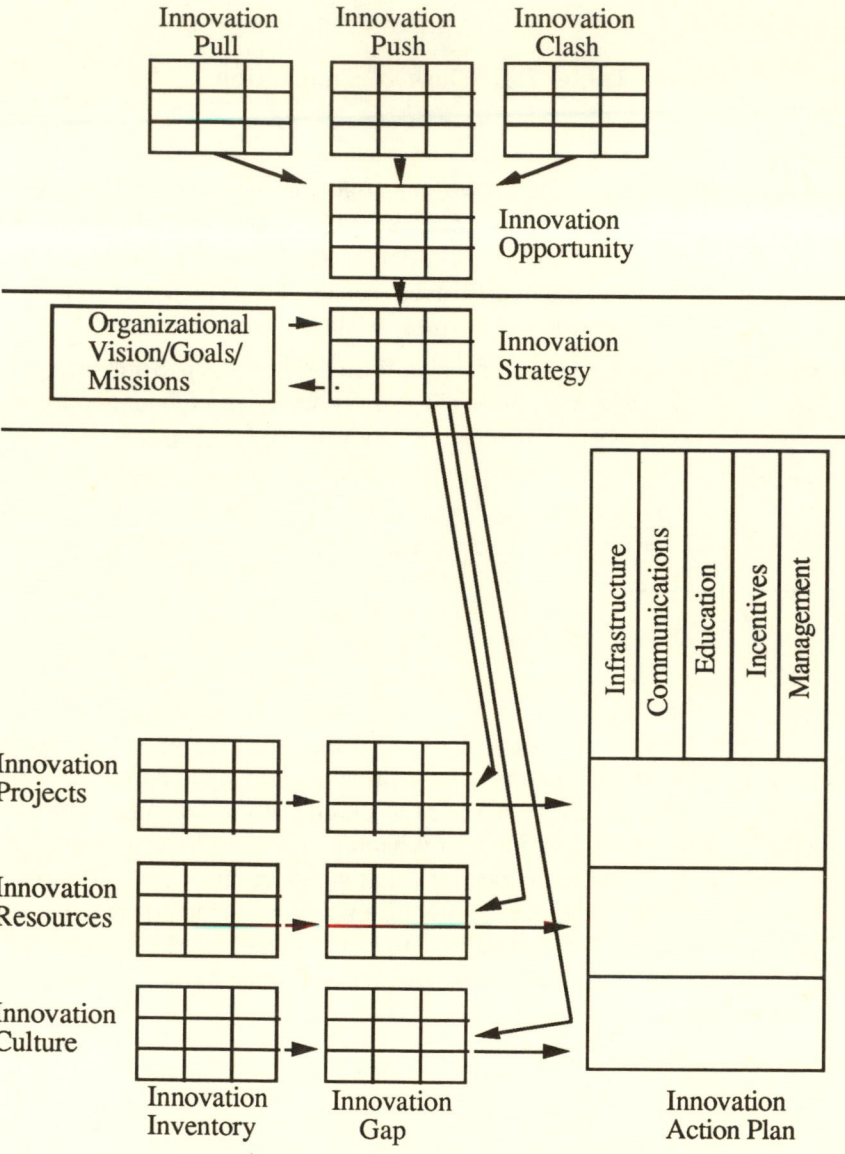

Table 7.4. Relationship between Market-Driven and IBD

Market-Driven Principles	IBD Features
Understand the markets	• Determine market pull for innovation (innovation pull) • Understand the potential innovation capability of the technical area (innovation push) • Identify innovation strategy of competition (innovation clash)
Commit to leadership	• Determine innovation strategy that meets innovation opportunities, which is probable within technical area and which produces leadership position. • Ennoble people through innovation vision
Execute with excellence	• Create an organizational culture that enables, empowers, and encourages individuals to be creative and productive • Focus innovative activities toward accomplishing innovation objectives
Make customer final arbiter	• Delight customer by producing timely, innovative solution at lowest costs • Consider customer at all stages • Understand customer's market

NOTES

I gratefully acknowledge John Vanston and Donna Prestwood (Technology Futures, Inc.) and Margaret Lehning (Tracking Trends, Inc.) in the development of the concepts presented herein.

1. James W. Dean, Jr., *Deciding to Innovate* (Cambridge, Mass.: Ballinger, 1987); T. J. Allen, *Managing the Flow of Technology* (Cambridge, Mass.: MIT Press, 1984); George Freedman, *The Pursuit of Innovation* (Amacom, 1988).

2. Gifford Pinchot, *Intrapreneuring* (New York: Harper & Row, 1985); Peter F. Drucker, *Innovation and Entrepreneurship* (New York: Harper & Row, 1985).

3. Lou Mobley and Kate McKeown, *Beyond IBM* (New York: McGraw Hill, 1989); Rosabeth Moss Kanter, *The Change Masters* (New York: Simon & Schuster, 1984); Rosabeth Moss Kanter, *When Giants Learn to Dance* (New York: Simon & Schuster, 1990).

4. Terence E. Deal and Allan A. Kennedy, *Corporate Cultures* (Reading, Mass.: Addison-Wesley, 1982); Keith D. Wilcock, *The Corporate Tribe* (Warren Books, 1984); Alan L. Wilkins, *Developing Corporate Character* (San Francisco: Jossey-Bass, 1989); Craig R. Hickman and Michael A. Silva, *Creating Excellence* (New American Library, 1984).

5. David Pearce Snyder and Gregg Edwards, *Future Forces* (American Society of Association Executives, 1984); Robert Theobold, *The Rapids of Change* (Knowledge Systems, 1987).

6. Tom Peters, *Thriving on Chaos* (New York: Knopf, 1988).

8

How to Make Entrepreneurship Work in Established Companies

*Eric G. Glamholtz and
Yvonne Randie*

For millennia, the dinosaur ruled the world. This creature was large, slow-moving, and cold-blooded—characteristics that made it perfectly adapted to the environment in which it lived. As the environment changed, however, the very characteristics that helped ensure its survival eventually led to its extinction.

While dinosaurs died out some 30 million years ago, we are currently witnessing the demise of another type of large, slow-moving organism: the corporate dinosaur. The once great and powerful organizational dinosaurs such as General Motors, U.S. Steel, Bank of America, Wicks Corporation, and Chrysler have all been sent reeling by environmental change. Other companies such as Kodak and IBM, which once dominated their markets, are now experiencing difficulties in adapting to environmental change.

As the environment changed, the dinosaurs could not adapt to meet the new demands that were placed upon them. They died out and were replaced by animals that were smaller, smarter, and more fast-moving. Similarly, we are witnessing the demise of the corporate dinosaurs and the birth of a new breed of companies that is better adapted to the changing economic environment. These companies, like Apple Computer, Mrs. Field's Cookies, Lotus Corporation, Domino's Pizza, and Federal Express, are all characterized by an ability to move quickly to take advantage of new business opportunities. These dynamic, entrepreneurial-oriented organizations have thrived while older, more established companies have struggled.

Fortunately for the established companies, companies with dinosaur tendencies can learn to behave more entrepreneurially and thus increase their chances of survival. To be successful, these companies must "mimic" or simulate the behavior of the new breed of entrepreneurships: They must learn to create new businesses within their existing structures. This is not often an easy process since those who promote entrepreneurship in established companies are often met with resistance. Further, even if the new venture is established and achieves success, there appears to be a tendency for the parent to try to destroy or "devour" the thriving offspring. The parent organization begins to feel threatened by the success of its offspring and, accordingly, takes steps to curtail its growth or even destroy it. We call this the "Medea Syndrome."[1]

The process of changing from or avoiding becoming a dinosaur, then, is one that presents an organization with a number of challenges. If a firm is to survive and continue thriving in the current economic environment, however, it is a necessity.

WHY IS ENTREPRENEURSHIP NEEDED IN ESTABLISHED COMPANIES?

Unfortunately, it appears that once an organization reaches a certain size (perhaps as early as $100 to $500 million in annual revenues), it begins to stagnate and lose sight of those factors that made it successful in the first place. Companies are founded on innovation and creativity—creating a product or service that people want. As a firm grows, however, it tends to become self-congratulatory and somewhat complacent. Its personnel come to believe that the company can live indefinitely off its initial success. These firms are the corporate dinosaurs. As evidenced by the number of once successful companies that have deteriorated or failed in recent years, this is not a very adaptive strategy for today's environment.

The key to survival for today's established organizations appears to be recreating the entrepreneurial spirit that may have been lost as the organization grew. In other words, the corporate dinosaur must transform itself into a faster-moving, sleeker animal. Management must learn how to promote new business development within the confines of the existing organization. This process has been termed "intrapreneurship" to distinguish it from the classic process of entrepreneurship.

In brief, as used here, intrapreneurship refers to the process of creating a new business within an existing business. In contrast, entrepreneurship is the process of creating a new business per se. The entrepreneur creates a new business as a separate, stand-alone entity, while the intrapreneur creates a new business within or as an adjunct to an existing business. Federal Express, Mrs. Field's Cookies, and Apple Computer were all entrepreneurships, while IBM's celebrated PC division was an intrapreneurial venture. Both required *entrepreneurially oriented behavior.*

LACK OF INTRAPRENEURSHIP

To become more intrapreneurial, a large organization must overcome a number of problems related to the tendency to continue operating as if the environment was stable and as if the demand for existing products or services will continue indefinitely. It needs to examine the degree to which it promotes intrapreneurship throughout the entire company as well as within its various divisions. There are some common symptoms of an organization's inability to become intrapreneurial. Taken together, these symptoms can be viewed as a set of "organizational aging pains." These corporate aging pains are presented in Table 8.1 and are discussed below.

One symptom relates to the emphasis in the strategic planning process on form rather than substance. In an effort to satisfy bottom line requirements, operating units tend to create strategic plans that focus on numbers rather than key issues. The goal of the strategic planning process is to create a document that makes the unit "look good" on paper, rather than focusing attention on areas that will increase the long-term viability of the operating unit. The focus is short-term, rather than on creating a vision for the operating unit's future. Further, since the plan emphasizes numbers, it may not provide the direction that employees need in working toward achieving goals consistent with maintaining the firm's success.

This limits the ability of the operating unit to become intrapreneurial because the operating unit focuses on what it is rather than what it can become. It tends to view itself only in terms of how it contributes to the functioning of the existing company rather than how it can develop into a "business" that emphasizes creativity and innovation.

Another symptom of "aging pains" is that in established organizations, the strategic planning process tends to be concentrated in the hands of senior management. They decide what the future goals of the company will be and what the role of the various operating units will be in achieving these goals. This can be done either blatantly or subtly. In some firms, senior management clearly presents its goals in a formalized corporate strategic plan. In other firms, senior management allows the operating units' management to set their own goals, but makes it very clear that there are some goals they will not support. In either case, the operating unit's management is limited by the plan set forth by senior management. They have relatively little autonomy and this leads to frustration.

Table 8.1. Symptoms of a Lack of Intrapreneurship

1. Strategic planning tends to emphasize form rather than substance.
2. Middle-level operating unit managers feel frustrated by their inability to play a more active role in the strategic planning process.
3. There is a lack of understanding about the strategic direction of the operating unit, and this affects the daily operating decisions that are made.
4. Difficulties are experienced when implementing strategic plans.
5. There is a lack of coordination and integration among the different functions (i.e., marketing, manufacturing, engineering, etc.) in this operating unit—"We are all rowing as hard as we can, but in different directions."
6. There is resistance to new ideas and innovation in the operating unit.
7. People are unwilling to take risks within the operating unit.
8. The operating unit is incapable of moving quickly to take advantage of market opportunities.
9. Managers in the operating unit tend to think as technical or functional specialists rather than as general business managers.
10. The operating unit has grown in sales revenue but not in profit.

This practice of setting a unit's direction leads to ineffective strategic planning since those who are setting the direction for the operating unit are too far removed from the actual functioning of the unit to plan effectively for its future. Senior management, because it is not involved in the day-to-day operations of the operating unit, cannot adequately assess the capabilities of its employees nor the ability of the unit to grow into a profitable independent operating unit.

It will be difficult for a unit operating under such conditions to become intrapreneurial because its management has little control over how the capabilities of its employees can be used in creating and marketing new products or services. Instead, employees capabilities must be used in the service of meeting the goals set for the company as a whole. The unit is valued only in terms of its ability to meet the needs of the company, rather than in terms of its ability to plan and meet its own future goals.

A third symptom is that employees perceive that the operating unit lacks direction. Members of the operating unit do not understand where the operating unit is headed or how it fits in with the overall plan of the organization. Employees may complain that they "feel they have no purpose" or that "there is no unifying purpose for the operating unit." They may believe that even senior management does not know what the future of the unit should be. This results, in part, from the tendency for senior management of established firms to make the majority of decisions regarding the unit's goals. It also results from inadequate communication between senior management and the operating unit's management as well as between the operating unit's management and lower level employees. The result is a tendency to focus on the day-to-day operations of the unit, rather than how the decisions made and jobs performed today will affect the long-term viability and success of the unit.

As a result of the three problems described above, the strategic plan created for these units becomes difficult to implement since it may have little or no bearing on what the unit actually does. It becomes a "paper product," rather than a document that can guide the actions of employees toward achieving the goals of the unit and the organization at large. Rather than change the planning process so that it comports with reality, units continue operating as they have done in the past and ignore the plan.

The lack of a clearly articulated and realistic strategic plan contributes to a lack of coordination and integration among functions within the operating unit. This creates a situation in which employees and various functional areas do whatever is best for themselves, not what is best for the entire unit. The business unit may eventually become a group of isolated entities fighting for power. Further, the isolation among units may result in duplication of effort or the tendency for tasks to remain uncompleted because individuals or functional areas view them as "someone else's responsibility."

To promote intrapreneurship successfully, the unit needs to work together toward a series of common goals. Without such teamwork, any efforts at new business creation are doomed to fail.

Another major symptom of a lack of intrapreneurship is resistance to new ideas. The tendency for employees to suffer from inertia within large companies greatly detracts from the ability to become intrapreneurial. There will always be some resistance to change, particularly in situations in which people have been operating a certain way for a long time. Intrapreneurship, however, depends on the ability of people to learn to think creatively in order to develop new products or new ways of employing old products. In many large organizations, the culture emphasizes doing things in the "traditional" fashion. In order to become intrapreneurial, the culture has to be changed so that the development of new ideas is valued, not devalued.

In large organizations, partly because of how profit is viewed, there is an inability or unwillingness on the part of employees to be risk takers. The "game" is played to minimize risks, rather than to take risks in the hope of getting a "big hit." This leads employees to cling to the "standard ways of operating" that have proven successful in the past and that are, therefore, "safe." The problem is that unless individuals and operating units are encouraged to take risks, there will be little change in the organization and it will stagnate. Intrapreneurship cannot occur unless the culture of the organization encourages risk taking.

Another symptom of an inability to be intrapreneurial is that the business unit, recognizing market opportunities, is unable to move quickly enough to take advantage of them. This results, in part, from the political games that units in large companies must play to acquire the resources they need for new product development and from the red tape that they must contend with. It also results from the emphasis on short-term goals to achieve the bottom line emphasized by the accounting system. The unit tends to focus on the "way it's been done" and so is slow to move when a new opportunity presents itself.

Another symptom that signals an inability to be intrapreneurial is that managers think of themselves as technical or functional specialists, rather than as managers. In other words, they devote a great deal of attention to their technical specialties, such as marketing, engineering, or manufacturing, rather than to the overall management of operations. These "hands-on" managers spend a great deal of time actually doing a specific task, rather than supervising others. Their behavior becomes symbolic; there is only one way to do a task, and the "boss" knows what it is. A spirit of innovation can hardly be fostered in such an environment. Instead, the operating unit tends to carry on much as it always has, with the manager serving as technical leader. In brief, many people with the title of manager tend to behave as technical specialists rather than as true managers.

If a number of the above symptoms are present, one final symptom may emerge. In some instances, the unit's sales (whether to customers or in the form of transactions to other units) will continue to increase while profits remain flat or actually decline.

In a significant number of cases, the decline in profits results from the tendency to stress meeting short-term numbers rather than setting and meeting long-term goals. Operating units and the people within them become like "rats in a maze." All that matters is that they meet the numbers that the company sets for them. This leads to wasted time, effort, and money.

To assist managers in measuring the extent to which their operating units suffer from the problems described above, we have developed the self-scoring questionnaire shown in Figure 8.1. Responses to the questionnaire are entered on a Likert-type five-point scale with descriptors ranging from "to a very great extent" to "to a very slight extent." By placing check marks in the appropriate columns, respondents indicate the extent to which they feel each of the ten symptoms is characteristic of their operating unit.

Figure 8.1. Corporate Aging Pains Questionnaire

Name: Firm:
Position/Title: Date:

To what extent do each of the following describe your organization? Place a check mark in the appropriate column.

Question	To a very great extent	To a great extent	To some extent	To a slight extent	To a very slight extent
1. Strategic planning tends to emphasize form rather than substance.	____	____	____	____	____
2. Middle-level operating unit managers feel frustrated by their inability to play a more active role in the strategic planning process.	____	____	____	____	____
3. There is a lack of understanding about the strategic direction of this operating unit, and this affects the daily operating decisions that are made.	____	____	____	____	____
4. Difficulties are experienced when implementing strategic plans.	____	____	____	____	____

Figure 8.1 (continued)

5. There is a lack of coordination and integration among the different organizational units— "We are all rowing as hard as we can, but in different directions."   ____   ____   ____   ____   ____

6. There is resistance to new ideas and innovation within this operating unit.   ____   ____   ____   ____   ____

7. People are unwilling to take risks within this operating unit.   ____   ____   ____   ____   ____

8. The organization is incapable of moving quickly to take advantage of market opportunities.   ____   ____   ____   ____   ____

9. Managers are technical or functional specialists rather than general business managers.   ____   ____   ____   ____   ____

10. The company has grown in sales revenue but not in profits.   ____   ____   ____   ____   ____

Scoring

A. Add the total number of responses in each column.   ____   ____   ____   ____   ____

B. Multiply the number on line "A" by the number of line "B" and record the result on line "C."   5   4   3   2   1

C. Result of line "A" times line "B."   ____   ____   ____   ____   ____

D. Add up the numbers across line "C" and place the result here.   _____

Once the questionnaire has been completed, the number of check marks in each column is totaled and recorded on line A. Each item on line A is then multiplied by the corresponding weight on line B, and the total is recorded on line C.

The next step is to determine the sum of the number on line C. This total represents the extent to which the operating unit is suffering from an inability to become intrapreneurial. It can range from 10, which is the lowest possible or most favorable score, to 50, which is the highest possible or most unfavorable score.

Drawing on our research concerning the degree of seriousness of problems indicated by different scores on this questionnaire, we have worked out the color coding scheme shown in Table 8.2. A more detailed interpretation of score ranges follows.

Table 8.2. Interpretation of Questionnaire Scores

Score Range	Color	Interpretation
10–14	Green	Everything is okay
15–19	Yellow	Some things to watch
20–29	Orange	Some areas need attention
30-39	Red	Some very significant problems
40–50	Purple	A potential turnaround situation

A "green" score represents an operating unit that is fairly intrapreneurial. It suggests that the unit operates as a "business within a business," fostering a spirit of innovation and creativity.

A "yellow" score indicates that the operating unit tends to be intrapreneurial, but there are some areas of concern. It is like a person with slightly elevated blood pressure. It is not alarmingly high and does not require medication, but the person is told to restrict salt intake and start an exercise program in an effort to bring it under control.

An "orange" score indicates that some problems require attention. They may not be too serious yet, but action should be taken to reduce the likelihood that inertia will cause it to eventually fail.

A "red" score is a clear warning of present or impending problems with regard to being intrapreneurial. Immediate action is required.

A "purple" score indicates an impending crisis situation. The operation unit is not behaving entrepreneurially and may be exposing itself to a great risk of failure if its product or service becomes obsolete.

If an operating unit's score exceeds 20, a more in-depth analysis to identify problems and develop recommendations for future action is probably required. Such a score may be a signal that the unit needs some assistance in developing and maintaining an "intrapreneurial" spirit. Failure to pay attention to a score of this magnitude can eventually lead to failure.

It is a difficult process to promote innovation in a large, relatively stable organization. The first step, however, is understanding how entrepreneurships (where creativity and new business development are the norm) differ from many large, publicly held organizations (where a great deal of inertia may exist). The next step is to find a way to incorporate the positive aspects of an entrepreneurship into strategies and practices of the larger organization.

To help established organizations learn to be more intrapreneurial, we have been doing research on two kinds of companies: relatively small entrepreneurial organizations, and larger, established companies. In entrepreneurial companies, we have been trying to identify the distinctive aspects of what entrepreneurial companies do well. In established companies, we have tried to identify the barriers to entrepreneurship. We have also looked for examples of established organizations that have been successful with intrapreneurial efforts to learn what they do well, and determine whether it can be adapted to other organizations.

DIFFERENCES BETWEEN ENTREPRENEURSHIP AND ESTABLISHED COMPANIES

To become more intrapreneurial, established organizations must change how they behave with respect to five key variables: profit, compensation, motivation, politics, and accounting systems. In brief, established companies must learn to mimic or simulate what successful entrepreneurships do with respect to these five key variables if they are to become more entrepreneurial themselves. A comparison of how these variables are treated or managed in an entrepreneurship versus a large, publicly held firm is presented in Table 8.3 and discussed below.

Profit

In entrepreneurships short-term profit is not of paramount interest. Owners are primarily interested in having enough to survive. The emphasis, rather than on current profit, is on getting a "big hit," a product or service that will itself contribute to the company's value. All of the company's energy and resources are focused on creating such a product or service, rather than creating a respectable "bottom line."

In established companies, and especially in large, publicly held companies, current profit is everything. This type of company must answer to its shareholders and they expect a profit. The best strategy for a company to use in managing its stockholders is to avoid getting a big hit because a big hit will result in greater profits for one year and create the expectation that the following years will have similar outcomes. It is better to have a stable profit picture than one that varies from year to year. In brief, this is very different from the orientation of an entrepreneurship.

Table 8.3. Entrepreneurship versus Established Organizations

	Entrepreneurship	Established Organizations
Profit	"We need enough to survive while we're trying to get a big hit."	"We want steadily rising earnings per share. The big hit is a problem because we don't want too much variation in earnings."
Compensation	"Compensation is based on commitment to the long term development of the company."	"Compensation is based on meeting this year's numbers."
Motivation	"Even though the company belongs to one person, we all have a lot invested in it. The big hit has rewards for all; the big bust hurts all."	"There are only a few people who have a personal stake in the company. It's *their* money."
Politics	"We all know who the leader is. We need to pull together to make the company a success."	"No one knows who really runs the show. We need to fight so that we get our piece of the pie."
Accounting Systems	"The bottom line is not that important."	"We have a Frankenstein accounting system: the way we account for things determines who wins and who loses."

Compensation

Many individuals who work in entrepreneurships do not expect to be compensated in traditional fashion. Generally speaking, these individuals are risk takers in the sense that they defer short-term rewards for the benefits they expect to receive when the firm makes its "big hit." Hence, they are committed to helping develop and refine the company's products or services because their rewards are contingent on the product or service being a success.

In the large, publicly held firm, compensation tends to be linked to how well an individual achieves the profit objectives of the company. The expectation is that compensation will be based on this year's numbers, rather than on how the contributions that the individual makes affect the longer-term company success.

Motivation

In entrepreneurships, individuals are motivated to work toward the company's success. Many people stand to benefit if the company is a success and many could lose if it fails. This is especially true when individuals defer compensation or take a pay cut in order to work for a small, growing company. Therefore, individuals who work for entrepreneurial companies are willing to work long hours at difficult tasks in order to achieve the company's goals.

Employees of large, publicly held firms do not share the commitment that those who work for entrepreneurships do. Few individuals share the burden of corporate ownership or have much to lose. Individuals are compensated for performing a specified task, often in a specified fashion, during a specified time. Individuals are not rewarded for stepping outside these boundaries so employees in large firms perform their jobs in eight hours and then go home. Further, creativity is often not valued because it violates the prescribed norms of the organization.

Politics

Leadership in entrepreneurships is well defined. The owner ultimately runs the company, but there tends to be a great deal of teamwork. All employees tend to share, in some way, responsibility for company decisions. They often come to feel like a "family." Politics plays a minor role, since there are a limited number of people trying to satisfy their needs and these people tend to be committed to a unified goal: making the company a success.

In established companies, especially in large, publicly held organizations, there is some ambiguity as to who actually makes decisions and how they are made. Individuals and areas tend to have their own goals and these are not always consistent with those of the company as a whole. An "us versus them" feeling often develops between individuals and functional areas and these factions tend to invest a great deal of energy in fighting over how the organization's resources should be divided. Competition rather than cooperation between individuals and areas tends to be the norm.

Accounting Systems

Given that profits are not emphasized in entrepreneurships, it follows that accounting systems are not valued. These systems are often neglected since there is little concern for the bottom line. In entrepreneurships, time is better spent on developing and producing the product than on managing an accounting system.

Accounting systems in established companies, and especially in large, publicly held firms, on the other hand, sometimes take on lives of their own. In some companies, in fact, the accounting system rules the lives of employees and divisions. The "Frankenstein" accounting systems of these firms are monsters created to tell the company what it wants to hear as well as to send subtle messages to division managers as to which divisions are currently in the most favorable position with the company's leadership.

HOW TO CREATE/MAINTAIN ENTREPRENEURSHIP IN ESTABLISHED COMPANIES

Given the problems discussed above, what, specifically, can companies do to create or maintain entrepreneurship within the boundaries of a large, established firm? There are six key areas of concern in which changes need to be made to foster intrapreneurship. These include organizational structure, planning, managerial skills, control, leadership style, and culture. A comparison of how each of these areas is usually conceptualized in large, established firms with how it should be conceptualized to promote intrapreneurship is presented in Table 8.4 and discussed below.

Organizational Structure

To become more intrapreneurial, large, established firms must make the transition from a functional to a divisionalized structure. The problem with the functionalized structure is that it promotes "tunnel-vision," so that individuals are interested only in their particular area, whether it is marketing, sales, manufacturing, or research and development. In a functional structure, coordination is a problem that is dealt with by creating strict policies and procedures, by increasing the amount of red tape. The reliance on red tape to coordinate efforts reduces the operating unit's flexibility and the likelihood that it can move quickly to take advantage of market opportunities. This structure also fosters the tendency for managers to be technical specialists in some areas rather than general managers promoting the development of new ideas and coordinating the efforts of others to achieve the goals set for them.

Table 8.4. Nonintrapreneurial versus Intrapreneurial Firms

		Nonintrapreneurial	Intrapreneurial
1.	Organizational Structure	Functional	Divisionalized plans
2.	Planning	Top-down planning	Divisionalized plans
3.	Managerial Skills	Functional specialist managers	Entrepreneurial managers
4.	Control	Centralized control	Semiautonomous control
5.	Leadership Style	Benevolent, autocratic, consultative, participative	Positive, laissez-faire
6.	Culture	"What are the rules?"	"You are responsible for your own destiny. Get the job done."

A divisional structure, on the other hand, increases the likelihood that intrapreneurship can be maintained or created because each division is responsible for a particular product or service. The managers of these areas must be true general managers since they are responsible for all aspects of producing a particular product or service: the sales, the manufacturing, the research and development. They can no longer be technical specialists or their areas will suffer. This suggests that when a firm decides to replace the functional structure with a divisionalized one, it must also replace its technical specialists with general managers. To accomplish this successfully, firms must either provide training to existing managers or go outside the firm and hire a general manager.

The major problem with replacing the functional structure with a divisionalized one that the latter is often more costly because the firm loses the economy of scale that it possesses when it needs only one marketing department, one production department, and one research and development department. The benefits of the divisionalized structure in terms of providing the firm with the ability to remain competitive in a changing environment, however, often outweigh the cost.

Planning

In many large companies, planning is traditionally done by senior management and is filtered down to the rest of the company. The philosophy is that senior management knows what is best for the company and that only they can decide what the future direction of the company should be. They establish the goals for the various areas of the company and act as the unifying force for their efforts. The intent is to band the company together toward the achievement of a common goal that is set by senior management.

In companies that promote intrapreneurship, each division creates its strategic plan and manages its own budget. While all divisions are ultimately responsible to the company at large, they are given a great deal of freedom in setting their own direction. The philosophy in these companies is that no employees know better what can be achieved than those who are directly involved. The company expects each division to be profitable, but it does little to intervene in its activities.

Managerial Skills

In a firm that is organized along functional lines, managers tend to be technical specialists or experts in some area. This creates the tendency for managers to be "doers" rather than true managers since they often are (and are expected to be) the technical gurus of their areas. They may spend so much time actually doing a job that they have little time to "manage." Managers who are too hands-on greatly reduce the motivation of their subordinates to achieve their own goals and to be creative. Further, they may assume so much responsibility in their areas that they do not delegate tasks that should be delegated and may feel overburdened while their subordinates come to believe that their managers do not trust them.

Managers who operate in a divisionalized structure that promotes intrapreneurship must be general managers. They do not need to be specialists in any one area, but instead must find ways of motivating people who work in a wide variety of areas to achieve their own goals and to work together. These managers must act like coaches: They do not actually play the game, but coordinate the efforts of their personnel who occupy a variety of specialist positions so that together, they can "win the game" (achieve the operating unit's goals). In this regard, these managers must also help the group develop a game plan, a strategic plan that outlines the unit's future goals and how they will be accomplished.

Control

As a result of the problems of coordination inherent in the functional structure, large, nonintrapreneurial companies tend to have control centralized in senior management. Since senior management sets the goals for the organization, they also adopt the role of controlling the behavior of their employees and areas so that they are constantly working toward the achievement of these goals. They tend to emphasize the achievement of the bottom line, and rewards are based on the ability of individuals and areas to produce the desired end.

In intrapreneurial companies, each operating unit or product division is responsible for monitoring its own performance. They are held accountable for achieving their goals, which should be congruent with those of the company as a whole, but they are given the freedom to do so as they see fit. Senior management believes that each area knows how best to motivate its employees to achieve the goals it sets for itself and, therefore, allows each area to design its own control system.

Leadership Style

Since senior management is responsible for planning and control throughout the company in nonintrapreneurial firms, it follows that they must adopt a leadership style that is fairly directive. In most of these firms, managers adopt either a benevolent autocratic, consultative, or participative style. The benevolent autocratic style, the most directive of the three, involves managers telling their subordinates what to do, but emphasizing that it is what is best for them. The consultative style involves telling subordinates what course of action is being considered and asking for their input, while managers who adopt the participative style ask subordinates to help define the problem and possible courses of action and then they make the final decision. All three styles allow managers to retain a certain amount of control over decisions of the firm and its employees. Using any of the three styles allows senior management to set the firm's course and provide employees with enough direction so that they will follow it.

In firms that encourage entrepreneurial behavior, managers tend to adopt a very nondirective style. The most effective style under these conditions is a positive laissez-faire style in which the manager gives subordinates a great deal of freedom in both setting goals and how they are achieved. There is a great deal of trust between these managers and their subordinates. The philosophy is that employees know what they are supposed to do so they will do it with little direction. This affords subordinates a great deal of creativity in accomplishing their goals and may result in innovative products, production processes, or procedures that increase the unit's efficiency.

Culture

Employees of nonintrapreneurial firms look to senior management for the direction they need to accomplish their jobs. The culture stresses rules, and it is the employee's responsibility to determine what the rules are and then to follow them. There are, in fact, sanctions against rule violations.

The culture of intrapreneurial companies stresses that employees are responsible for their own destinies. They, in essence, create their own futures within the parameters of the company and operating unit and have the freedom to do so. This provides employees with the freedom to experiment and do things they cannot in more structured settings.

BECOMING MORE INTRAPRENEURIAL

Given the differences listed above and the potential for decline inherent in organizations that continue to operate as dinosaurs, what steps can a company take to become more intrapreneurial? There are four areas of concern: management skills, corporate culture, planning, and compensation.

Management Skills

Intrapreneurial managers are different from those who typically assume management roles in large, established firms. Managers in larger firms tend to be functional specialists, rather than general managers who develop the vision for their area's future. Companies that seek to become more intrapreneurial, then, must train their managers to be more entrepreneurial. Reward systems must be created to support entrepreneurial behavior.

Corporate Culture

The culture of a large organization that desires to become more intrapreneurial must be managed so that it encourages and reinforces entrepreneurial behavior. Rather than supporting "standard ways of operating" and rewarding individuals for playing by the rules, the culture must be changed so that mavericks who violate rules in the service of improving the company are heroes. Further, it is important that the culture emphasizes trying to "hit a home run" rather than just "getting on base." In other words, the culture should emphasize risk taking in the hopes of creating new products or services that can benefit the company in the future rather than playing it "safe" by continuing to operate in a traditional fashion.

Another important piece of an intrapreneurial culture is an emphasis on people. To become more intrapreneurial, a company must teach its managers how to promote organizational commitment and motivate employees to achieve the organization's goals while at the same time giving them the freedom to be creative. In a sense, the culture must break down the barriers between work and play so that employees gain intrinsic reward (in the form of pleasure from actually doing work) rather than just extrinsic rewards (in the form of pay).

Planning

In companies striving to become more intrapreneurial, managers must be taught to avoid creating plans that are more form than substance. Managers of operating units need to be given the freedom to set their own directions and they need to begin thinking like entrepreneurs in planning their futures. Since they are closest to the markets they serve, they need to learn how to critically assess their own position in the market, their competitive strengths and weaknesses, and what they can do to be more effective in the future. In this regard, the company needs to promote the notion that numbers are not the only thing that matters (the Frankenstein accounting system needs to be replaced), but it is what the numbers represent in terms of the long-term goals of the company that matters.

Compensation

The compensation system must be modified so that entrepreneurial behavior is rewarded, rather than just rewarding those who play by the rules. Some systems in which employees share in "big hits" will motivate them to work toward achieving them.

CONCLUSIONS

This chapter has examined the need for entrepreneurially oriented behavior in established companies. The bottom line is that to survive in today's changing economic environment, organizations must learn how to create "business within existing businesses;" that is, to behave more entrepreneurially. This can best be accomplished through allowing divisions that specialize in certain areas the freedom to experiment, promoting a culture that emphasizes a big hit, creating compensation systems that reward individual and group creativity, and implementing an accounting system that emphasizes business development rather than the bottom line.

A company's executive leadership can be instrumental in making the needed changes. The first step that a CEO can take is to perform an organizational audit of the strengths and limitations of the company in terms of its entrepreneurial capabilities. The lens used to perform the audit should be that presented in this chapter. Once the audit has been completed, the next step is to develop some action programs for improving the company's entrepreneurial capabilities. This will typically involve some sort of intrapreneurial planning exercise and possibly a management development program designed to help managers make the transition from technical specialists to more entrepreneurially oriented general managers.

Once the plans have been implemented, it will be important to monitor the firm's progress toward creating and maintaining intrepreneurship. There will probably be some resistance to the changes that will need to be made. Organizations that fail to make these changes, however, will be placing themselves at a disadvantage in today's rapidly changing business environment. They will, like the dinosaurs, find themselves unable to compete effectively and may, therefore, run the risk of extinction.

NOTE

1. Medea, a sorceress in Greek mythology and Jason's (the leader of the Argonauts) wife, killed her children in revenge for Jason's infidelity.

9

Reassessing Human Resources in Large-Scale Bureaucracies

Helen M. Moye

To address the issue of reassessing human resources in large-scale bureaucracies, it is important to consider three major elements: (1) business and human resource trends, (2) the present and ideal future state, and (3) human resource success requirements.

Large-scale bureaucratic organizations are operating in a business and economic climate that is tumultuous and tension-ridden. To remain competitive in global markets, organizations must grow leaner, cut costs, create new technology, improve quality, and generally operate more effectively and efficiently. At the same time, these organizations must respond to the human condition by developing more open, trusting, flexible, collaborative, communicative, people-oriented cultures and environments for a changing workforce—changing in terms of age, gender, race, and ethnicity.

Bureaucratic organizations today have been described as dinosaurs incapable of responding to a rapidly changing world. To confront the future, these organizations will need to become swifter, more innovative, and more creative, particularly regarding human resources.

The apparent gap between the present and future states of organizations, as well as business and human resource trends, will require continual reassessment of human resources in every facet of the organization, including structures, staffing, skill levels, systems, and strategies. More important, these conditions will provide a framework or context for identifying and discussing human resource success requirements for the future, such as changes in beliefs, values, and behaviors of the leadership/followership in large-scale organizations.

BUSINESS TRENDS

The integration of Europe, the collapse of communism, and worldwide information network capabilities are a few reasons for the rapid increase in worldwide competition, which in turn has led to the need for major large-scale organizational change. For instance, during the 1980s, over half of the Fortune 500 companies restructured, merged, were acquired, or were downsized. Total employment in these companies was reduced by 2.8 million. Middle managers were particularly hard hit. Both leadership and followership have been and will be affected by these changes.

Also, large organizations are moving from economies of scale to niche marketing, which requires fast-to-market low-cost, low-volume products and services. These organizations also face pressures for value-added services, quality products, and quality performance.

In addition, telecommunications, particularly fiber optics, have vastly increased our ability to communicate quickly and on a massive scale. Thanks to this new technology, we have the ability to carry eight thousand conversations on a fiber optic cable compared to forty-eight conversations for a copper wire. In December 1988, the first fiber optic cable across the Atlantic went into service, with capabilities of carrying forty thousand calls simultaneously, making worldwide information networking an increasing reality.

AN ACCELERATED RATE OF CHANGE

Perhaps one of the most dramatic trends affecting large bureaucratic organizations is the accelerated rate of change. Some would say the "ground is moving as we speak." In less than thirty years, the world has moved from conventional power to nuclear power, from the piston age to the jet age, from earth travel to space travel. In less than two years, we have moved from military power to economic power. More recently we have seen whole world orders move from communism to democracy. Technology brings its own set of changing requirements to the workplace. For instance, it is estimated that 50 percent of all jobs today did not exist twenty years ago and that 75 percent of those still working in the year 2000 will need retraining. What has been familiar to us—technology, politics, education, bureaucratic organizations, leadership/followership—is being overtaken by a new and unpredictable culture. In many instances, we are facing the unknown with no precedents. Because of these rapid changes, Alan Toffler's words from *Future Shock* seem especially meaningful since, as he suggests, the accelerated rate of change creates perishability of facts, difficulty of forecasting with accuracy, and an urgent need to avoid rigidity and enhance flexibility. Even as the ground moves rapidly, organizations will at the same time be required to undergo major strategic reorganizations that will demand changes in products, services, markets, organizational structures, and, more important, human resources.

In rapidly changing environments, people often react to change by asking questions about advancements, salary, future with institutions, self-perceptions, informal and formal influences, status, amount of work, importance of work, working hours, and relationships. Based on the answers they receive, people may resist the change, causing a drop in quality, efficiency, output, and morale.

WORKFORCE DIVERSITY

Diversification of the workforce represents another important trend:

- By the year 2000, 61 percent of all women will be members of the workforce, and nearly half of the workforce will be female.

- 57 percent of net new entrants into the workforce this decade will be minorities or immigrants.

- By the year 2000, one in three Americans will be nonwhite.

In addition, day by day as a society America is growing older. By the year 2000, half of all Americans will be over forty-five and one in three Americans will be sixty-five or older. The American Association of Retired Persons (AARP) presently has 30 million members, more than any organization except the Catholic Church. By the year 2015, half of the U.S. population will be eligible to join (*Money*, October 1988). Additionally, more single parents, openly gay men and women, and people with disabilities will be part of the workforce. According to Rosalyn Taylor O'Neale, manager of Digital Equipment Corporation, diverse groups will bring values and norms, as well as knowledge, skills, and talents, to organizations, which are by and large unequipped or inadequately prepared. The industrial society was a man's world, but the information society is everybody's world—with one caveat: They must be educated. The majority of jobs in the next decade will require some college education. Presently, 23 million Americans are functionally illiterate, and the number is growing by some 2.5 million per year. The high school drop-out rate is approximately 850,000 per year. By the year 2010, there may be a shortage of 450,000 engineering and other technical graduates. Alan Toffler predicts that there could be 10 million jobs for every one million people with the skills to perform them. Some say we are reaching an age of noninterchangeable human resources, with major changes in employee bargaining power, recruiting, hiring, employee loyalty, employee efforts, and retention.

Another trend with consequences for large-scale organizations is the slowing of population growth. The number of twenty- to twenty-nine-year-olds—the typical age for recruitment by businesses—will decline from 41 million (1980) to 3 million by the year 2000.

In terms of organizational structures, large companies are "delayering" and downsizing. According to Peter Drucker, many companies will have half the levels and one-third the managers by the twenty-first century. Organizational structures, systems, and human resources must continually align and realign in order to accommodate these changes while accomplishing organizational goals and objectives. Staffing must become more flexible and responsive, by increasing part-time and contract employees, thus increasing the security of the "core" workforce. In terms of compensation, there may need to be a shift from the traditional emphasis on tenure and position to pay-for-performance or pay-for-competence. Pay for performance is described as "organizationally controlled" while pay-for-competence is described as "individually controlled." Training and development may become more important than career development, since continual training and development may be required to just "keep up."

SUCCESS REQUIREMENTS—
LEADERSHIP/FOLLOWERSHIP

Business and human resource trends, along with the present and ideal future state of large bureaucracies, make the identification and discussion of human resource success requirements important, particularly in terms of leadership/followership. These boundaries will need to be permeable, so that roles are interchanged as needed. For instance, everyone in the organization, whether a part of the leadership or followership, may be required to get extraordinary results from people over whom they have no direct control. Power must be viewed as infinite and interchangeable, with the thought that there is enough for everyone, and that the exercise of power depends on project and purpose rather than where one sits in the organization. There must be a sense of self-control rather than control of others, with employees understanding that no matter where they sit in the organization they can make a difference.

There also must be an understanding of the power of cooperation. Many times in large organizations, maintenance and linear thinking and acting have been the paradigm rather than creativity and innovation. Whole-brain thinking, therefore—operating comfortably from both analytical and creative bases—will be required. Also, both leadership and followership will need to understand both how things get done (process) and what things get done (content).

VALUES

In terms of values in large-scale bureaucracies of the future, the major requirement is 100 percent truth. Employees in large organizations must become masters of information rather than disinformation, since it is difficult to make quick, sound decisions without honest information. Employees in large organizations need to say in public what they many times say in private, thus bringing issues out into the open.

People also need to have the ability to say to themselves that "what I believed yesterday may not be true today." Developing such a nonabsolutist belief system requires (in John Bridges' terms) "letting go of the good 'ole days" and living with periods of confusion, ambiguity, and even distress. But, happily, this often leads to new beginnings, new ideas, new actions, and new states of mind.

In a rapidly changing world, there must be some acceptance and belief that most of the same paths have been taken. And as Peter Vaill of George Washington University might say, there must be tolerance for swimming in white waters permanently. Described another way, risk taking must become a permanent condition.

To handle organization in a changing environment, an important requirement is to embrace paradox, or at least handle the anxiety that paradoxes create such as the struggle between the forces of wanting change and avoiding it (stability versus change); the forces of maintenance and the forces of transformation (managing versus leading); the forces of evolution and the forces of revolution; and the forces of caution and the forces of courage.

Courage seems to be a requirement in creating and handling the future, particularly in large-scale bureaucracies. This might require changing the definition of bureaucracy from the concept of "they are responsible" to "I am responsible for personal acts." Each time we act, it is a living example of how we want things to be. The organization and the associated dilemmas are our own creations.

In large-scale organizations, change must be viewed as a natural phenomenon rather than an aberration, and there must be understanding that the threat, as well as resistance to change, may be real or even natural depending on the change.

The negative connotation associated with political skill must change to one of positiveness. Positive political skills as described by Lynn Hirsch, an organizational consultant, are the ability to manage the hopes, fears, and aspirations of others. Given such a definition, attitudes about politics may take on new meanings, which in turn may cause people to develop "new" and more positive political behaviors.

A metanoic mindset is used to describe organizations where people operate from the viewpoint that individually and collectively they can create the future and shape their destiny. This is in line with consultant Dudley Lynch's thinking that there's no "out there" out there—we create it.

According to Rosabeth Moss Kanter, a learning attitude is a clear necessity for swimming in new streams, exploring uncharted waters, seeking synergies, and discovering the benefits of strategic alliances. In future successful organizations, constant learning must be the norm, which means major challenges in training and development.

Presently many employees in large bureaucracies believe that management does not care about them, but "it" takes care of them. A stronger success value might be "we care about each other." We have total responsibility for the organization's purposes, goals, objectives, successes, and failures. From a management perspective, the shift might be toward "I care about you, I may even love you, but I do not have responsibility for your total care."

The comfort of sameness is generally the norm. In a rapidly changing, diverse workforce, however, the capacity to value differences is required. Also, the development of skills and favorable ways of behaving and interacting with people from different cultures and ethnic groups is required.

Based on a business and human resource trends and the gap in present and desired future states of large-scale organizations, human resource success will depend on organizations' ability to change/modify beliefs, values, and behaviors, establishing the context for their remaining competitive and creating desirable futures.

10

Innovation in Large NASA R&D Programs

Humboldt C. Mandell, Jr.

NASA has been forced, under a budget approximately one-third that of the Apollo era, to extend program lengths, resulting in a compounding of inefficiencies that result from conducting programs at an off-optimum pace. Program sizes have also been reduced, which has caused NASA to operate at off-optimum capacity, further increasing costs and lowering efficiencies of operation. Programs have been divided to ensure productive work for the existing institution, in some cases into inefficient work packages. Oversight of NASA programs has increased to the point where some routine design decisions have been legislated by Congress, resulting in further program inefficiencies as NASA has worked to accommodate legal requirements in the designs.

NASA has long recognized that, as an agency, it is a high cost producer, and has taken a number of steps to determine where economies might be achieved. Studies have identified many of the causes of high costs to be primarily culturally driven, but have also pointed out ways to emulate lower cost cultures that have been successful in high-technology ventures. Understanding the causes of high cost, however, is a much easier task than taking positive steps to reduce costs. In any culture, particularly a successful one like NASA, change will take place more slowly than might be desired; resistance to change is always present, and must be dealt with. Environmental inhibitors to change, such as congressional oversight requirements, may not be within the realm of feasibility to change, which can completely preclude some types of change.

At this time of beginning the largest undertaking in its history, the Space Exploration Initiative, NASA is facing a number of challenges. First, the need to change, including the threats faced, must become obvious to all leadership; which of the existing practices, processes, and tools should be changed need to be identified; change processes need to be designed and implemented; and in the intervening time, for programs just being initiated, strong gatekeeping mechanisms must be put in place to preclude undesirable cultural practices from being implemented by default. Whether or not costly external constraints can be modified or removed is problematic, but conscious efforts must be made to identify them and to inform the external decision makers of their effects.

BACKGROUND

Since the end of the Apollo program in the early 1970s, the National Aeronautics and Space Administration (NASA) has experienced budget reductions, in real dollar terms, of as much as two-thirds of the peaks experienced in the mid-1960s (Figure 10.1). Today's budgets are approaching half of Apollo levels, as NASA operates the space shuttle, develops the space station, and prepares for the largest NASA program ever, the Space Exploration Initiative (SEI), announced by President Bush on July 20, 1989. NASA manpower, although reduced, still remains almost 70 percent of the peak levels of 1967. All NASA installations created during the Apollo era and previously still remain; in addition, one has been added: the Space Station Program Management facility at Reston, Virginia.

NASA cost research has revealed a productivity decline of approximately 3.5 percent annually compounded from the Apollo era to the present. Because of the budgetary constraints, development program lengths have increased to a decade or longer (the Apollo lunar landing took place approximately eight years after President Kennedy's announcement, which included the development of an entire new agency to do the job). The increased program length has given rise almost to a cultural expectation that all new programs will take at least a decade to perform. In a study completed in late 1989,[1] NASA recently estimated that it might take until the year 2016 to send a human to Mars. After the completion of the study, Vice President Quayle, speaking for President Bush, told NASA in an address before the American Astronomical Society that "We've got to figure out how to reduce the time from idea to realization from decades to a few years."[2]

Figure 10.1. Total NASA Budget

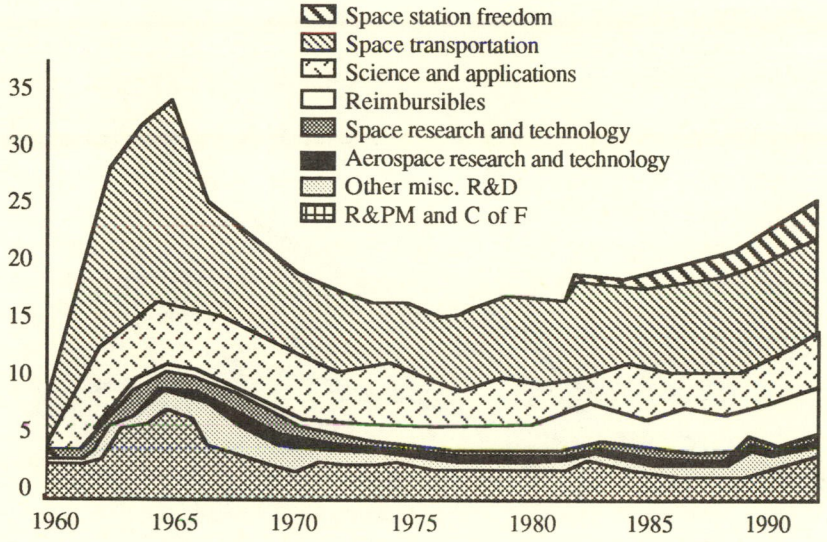

THE IMPORTANCE OF CULTURAL CHANGE
TO FUTURE NASA PROGRAMS

Using current NASA acquisition and development practices, estimates of cost for a manned Mars landing have been approximately $200 billion (1991 dollars) through the initial landing. Under any reasonable scenario of budgetary availability, assuming that the existing NASA programs are funded at current levels, budget availability would preclude a manned Mars landing much before the end of the first decade of the next century (Figure 10.2), despite the fact that, unlike the Apollo program, many of the needed facilities and technologies exist today.

Figure 10.2 also demonstrates very graphically the effects of increased program length on program costs; the cumulative Apollo program funding profile, less current NASA programs, is displayed for comparison. While the onset of resources was much faster in the Apollo program than is forecast in the president's FY1991 budgetary submission, the cumulative available dollars are comparable only through the very early years of the twenty-first century, possibly illustrating the need for shorter program development times to maintain congressional funding support and momentum for the program.

Figure 10.2. Effect of Program Cost on Landing Date

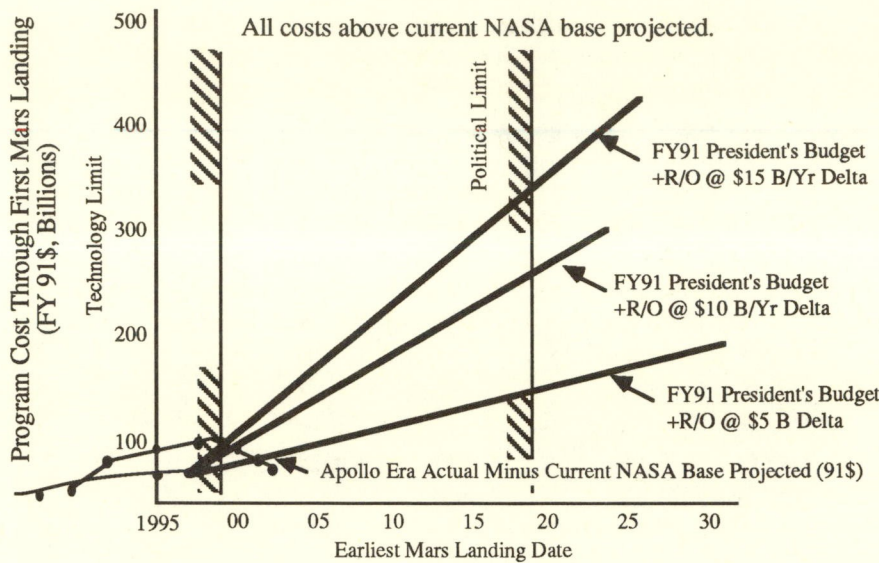

The effects of various levels of cultural change are illustrated in Figure 10.3. While change to the levels of aircraft development programs may not be feasible in the current NASA environment, the large influence of even modest changes is very evident. Under a $5 billion increase in current NASA funding levels, for example, Mars landing dates can be moved forward by an entire decade by only a 30 percent improvement in the nonlinear culture variable.

It should also be noted here that just the demonstration of the ability to achieve earlier meaningful program milestones can have a positive influence on the national political resource allocation process, and can result in more available resources for the new initiative. Thus, cultural change, by producing early achievable milestones within a fixed budget, might actually increase the budget availability, resulting in still earlier milestones.

As will be described more fully below, NASA cost research has also shown that the major contributor to program cost is the way of doing business of the managing organizations.[3] Thus, all other things being equal, theoretically large cost reductions are available within the manned spacecraft development industry. Care must be taken with this conclusion, because the change required to effect the cost reductions may be environmentally constrained, outside the purview of the agency (e.g., legislative requirements).

Figure 10.3. Effect of Culture Change on Nominal $200 B SEI Architecture

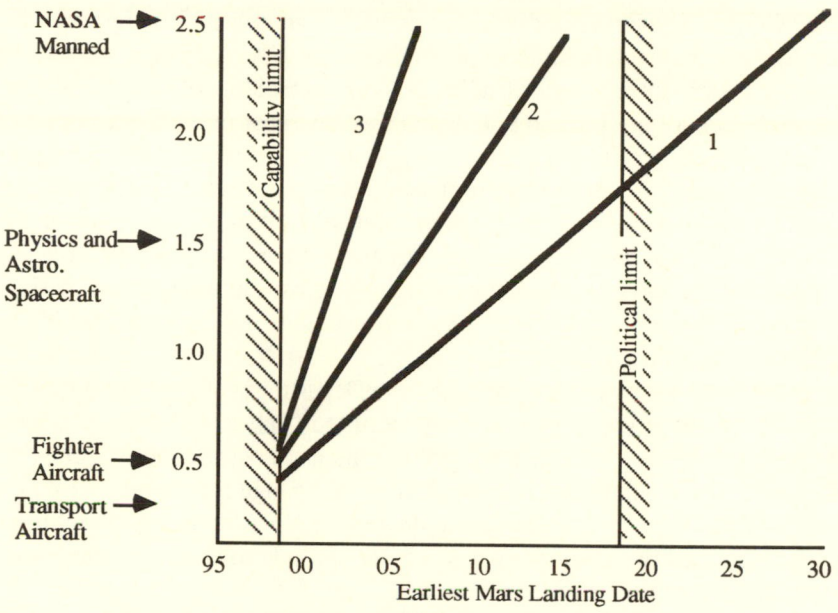

1. 1991 President's Budget w/Runout @ $5 B Delta (above NASA Base)
2. 1991 President's Budget w/Runout @ $10 B Delta
3. 1991 President's Budget w/Runout @ $15 B/Yr Delta

NASA EFFORTS TO REDUCE DEVELOPMENT COSTS

Since before the initiation of the space shuttle program, NASA has conducted research into the causes of high costs and feasible solutions to problems producing them. After each major program, NASA has documented lessons learned; and before the start of each major manned program, studies have been made of other programs, both within and outside NASA, to identify potentially better ways of doing business. Yet the simple knowledge of problems and ways of making improvements are not sufficient to produce change. Change has always occurred, of course, but in few cases has it been calculated and planned to produce a specific lower cost outcome. This will be further illustrated below.

Prior to the beginning of the space shuttle program, NASA performed an extensive study of successful and unsuccessful aerospace programs throughout the nation. Programs studied included several commercial aircraft, the C-5A transport, the Navy AWACS, the SR-71 "Blackbird," the X-15, F-14, Polaris/Poseidon, B-52, B-58, the F-111 program, and others.

Later, when the successes of the YF-16 program were realized, NASA visited General Dynamics to discuss how that program had been developed at costs far less than would have been predicted by NASA experience. All of these studies produced similar findings of the ingredients of successful low-cost, high-technology programs (Table 10.1). Almost universal acceptance was given by successful program managers to the principles, indicating the desirability of cleaner government/private sector interfaces; stating realistic requirements and not changing them; stating requirements only for the performance of the hardware, and not for how to achieve that performance; the need for the use of demonstrated technologies; the importance of short development schedules; and the maximum use of the competition of the marketplace to reduce costs.

In subsequent studies performed by the Department of Defense under the streamlining initiative, similar findings resulted (Table 10.2). Other studies have reached the same conclusions, making them almost a modern cliché.

The need for change and the objectives of change are therefore known. Each program will have its unique requirements. For example, the Apollo program required two manned spacecraft and a stable of earth-to-orbit launch vehicles to accomplish the first manned lunar landing. Around a small core of research facilities, NASA constructed facilities and management structures to conform to the lunar program work breakdown structure, which resulted in a very successful program management process, one that has been heralded in management literature, and that has endured, with some modification, to the present time. The missing ingredient for the design of the management structure for the Space Exploration Initiative is a knowledge of the content and makeup of the program. Studies are underway to define these program attributes.

CULTURAL SIGNATURES: THE DYNAMIC BEHAVIOR OF PROGRAMS

In its ongoing research into the causes of high costs and cost growth, NASA has made some significant discoveries, which are pertinent to the introduction of change into government organizations. It should be noted here that NASA in the 1970s and 1980s was an ideal laboratory for organizational studies, and many were performed. A characteristic of the organization that has proven to be valuable is its static personnel makeup. Once one of the youngest organizations in government, with an average age of under forty, retirements were few and turnover rate was extremely low for almost two decades. Cultural studies in this environment did not have to deal with any extraneous variables that might have been introduced by a changing workforce.

Table 10.1. Management Design Objectives

- The ingredients of successful low-cost, high-technology programs are well known and universally recommended by successful program managers interviewed
  - Use government only to define requirements
  - Keep requirements fixed: Once requirements are stated, only relax them; never add new ones
  - Place product responsibility n a competitive private sector
  - Specify end results (performance) of products, not how to achieve the results
  - Minimize government involvement (small program offices)
  - Ensure that all technologies are proven prior to the end of competition
  - Utilize the private sector reporting system: Reduce or eliminate specific government reports
  - Do not start program until cost estimates and budget availability match
  - Minimize or eliminate government-imposed changes
  - Reduce development time: Any program development can be accomplished in three to four years once uncertainties are resolved
  - Force people off development programs when development is complete
  - Incentivize the contractor to keep costs low (as opposed to CPAF, CPFF of NASA)
  - Use geographic proximity of contractor organizations when possible
  - Use the major prime contractor as the integrating contractor
- Collectively, these describe the true "skunk works" approach to management
- Several successful programs have resulted from these practices
- These lessons should be the guidelines for program management design
- To achieve them in NASA, cultural change will be necessary

In developing models to simulate the time distribution of program costs, three program behaviors were noted, which have occurred in virtually all NASA manned spacecraft and launch vehicle development programs. First, cost growth has followed predictable patterns: Program costs generally rise in time more slowly than planned, because NASA has usually not received funding from Congress at the rate planned in the first few years of a program. This has introduced early delays and planning inefficiencies, particularly in the space shuttle and space station programs.

Table 10.2. Streamlining Initiative

Key Elements

- System level requirements specified in terms of mission performance
- Industry involvement in draft request for proposal
- Only specifications called out in contract are imposed, others (e.g., lower tier) are for guidance only
- Specifications are tailored for the job at hand
- Specifications already used for off-the-shelf hardware become the contract requirement
- Management requirements are for results wanted, not how-to-manage; contractors' existing management systems used
- Challenge every requirement

Second, programs have generally encountered development problems near their peak funding years, which has caused schedule growths, which in turn tend to hold program funding at peak levels for two or three years past the point predicted in early planning.

Third, schedule growths have tended to be very predictable, with the average of all NASA manned programs growing (from inception to first operational flight) by an average of 1.56. (The space shuttle schedule grew by a factor of 1.52.)

These three phenomena are all influenced by the way in which NASA interacts with Congress and the Office of Management and Budget (OMB). Program funding requirements submitted by NASA at the outset of a program are usually not fully supported by the administration or Congress. But in the two years between submission of requirements and the passage of an appropriations bill, little feedback has been available to NASA on which to base program replanning. Thus, the usual occurrence is for NASA to be "surprised" by funding reductions, resulting in turbulence at the outset of programs as NASA and its contractors work to cope with restructuring the programs to fit available funding. In the space station program particularly, this restructuring has been very expensive for U.S. taxpayers.

Understanding these culturally characteristic dynamic program trends should empower NASA to recognize the repeatability of the phenomena and to avoid the costliness associated with early program turbulence, as well as to plan for the timing of required program funding reserves.

THE NASA EQUIPMENT SPECIFICATION COST EFFECT STUDY OF 1976

Midway through the development of the space shuttle, as NASA worked to control program costs,[4] a study was performed to determine the ingredients of NASA program development costs, what about the way NASA managed was affecting development and production costs.[5] From the "lessons learned" studies (above), it was surmised that such requirements as safety, maintainability, parts certification programs, environmental tests, parts traceability, failure reporting, and configuration control were large "cost drivers." While the study did find positive correlations with all of these causes, a large residual error remained in the regression analyses; changes in the specification levels did not explain all cost differences between manned and unmanned space programs, military, and commercial programs. "Organizational work habits do not readily change completely as a result of imposing a different specification level," the study found. Residual costs were found to be attributable only to the "organizational manner of doing business," or culture.

Because the shuttle program was already producing flight hardware at that time, the implementation of changes would not have been practical or even cost-effective. Therefore, the full significance of the study results were not to be explored further until the advent of the space station program, which began at the Johnson Space Center in 1981.

THE SPACE STATION DEVELOPMENT PROGRAM: A CASE STUDY IN CULTURAL CHANGE

From the outset, the small development group at the Johnson Space Center had hoped to make the space station program a model of low cost development. Advisory groups in the early 1980s had warned NASA that low development costs would be the key to political support for the program. At one time, a group chaired by a former NASA administrator had cautioned the space station management that if program costs exceeded $1 billion (1981 dollars), political support would be lost. Later, as more congressional input was received, that figure was raised to $8 billion (1984 dollars). (Current runout estimates are now in excess of $20 billion [real-year] dollars.)

Low-cost development approaches, following the paths indicated by the "lessons learned" studies, began in earnest in 1982 at Johnson Space Center.

But the small development group at the Johnson Space Center was soon replaced by a larger, multicenter development working group, operating in an isolated area near NASA headquarters in Washington. Because of the way the group was formed, with representatives from virtually all of NASA's installations, the then-current agency culture was created in microcosm. And because most of those making up the group came from highly successful development programs around the agency, few were motivated by any desire to make changes in the ways in which the agency developed spacecraft.

The primary motivation was to seize the opportunity of the moment to provide the nation with a magnificent new space capability. Cost, although a point of constant discussion and debate, was to become secondary to objectives such as rejuvenating the development skills of the NASA civil service workforce, which had not undertaken a major new manned development for some fifteen years (since the start of the space shuttle program). And so some of the opportunity to change to a lower-cost development process was to be left for a later generation of development.

Some successes were achieved. In every request for proposals (RFP) issued by NASA for the four work packages of the space station program, cost-saving innovation was called for. But, once again, the objective was compromised in the method of execution.

The government acquisition process, as represented in the Federal Acquisition Regulations (FAR), is intended to be the epitome of fairness, with several levels of checks and balances built in to ensure that all proposers play on a level field. Proposals are evaluated by a Source Evaluation Board, composed of highly qualified, usually senior, specialists representing every skill and discipline required in the acquisition.

In the case of the space station acquisition, some dozen specialists were chosen from each center to comprise the SEB. At the Johnson Space Center, responsible for only a portion of the spacecraft development (despite the fact that the entire acquisition represented a much smaller undertaking than the just completed Space Shuttle Orbiter development) a board was assembled from representatives of the Engineering, Operations, Safety Reliability and Quality Assurance, and Administrative Directorates, plus senior program managers, themselves chosen from the same directorates or from the management of the space shuttle program. The credentials of the board were superb, each member a specialist, each a product of the then-existing NASA development culture. In those pre-Challenger days, NASA was riding high on a series of successful space shuttle launches, an agency without peer in government, whose successes reinforced its management practices and deterred any detractors. Why, then, should it change anything?

Into this forum, which epitomized virtually every element of the existing culture, came two major proposals for the development program. In these proposals were the obligatory responses to the RFP requirement for innovation. But every cost-saving innovation requires, almost by definition, that some or all of the proposed tasks be performed with less manpower than the same tasks on previous programs.

For example, one proposer suggested that he could perform the logistics planning tasks with approximately 10 percent of the manpower that was then being used for similar tasks in the space shuttle program. "Fine," said the board. "Real innovation." Except for the member of the board representing the logistics discipline: "Foul!" said he. "It can't be done; the proposal is not credible." And so it went for all of the disciplines represented around the board table. Members all recognized the value of innovation, and were relatively comfortable with innovating outside their own area of responsibility; but they all felt some degree of threat when they saw how that innovation was to affect the staffing.

In a selection process, which in the final analysis, and despite all efforts to remove subjectivity, remains subjective, it takes not too much threat to board members' area of responsibility to make them think twice about the credibility of any proposed changes to the existing culture.

Thus, the proposer with the greatest cost-saving innovations is sure to create the largest doubts as to credibility. Had it not been for the constant reminding of the board chairman, the most creatively innovative proposer could easily have lost the competition, which held innovation as a major competitive factor.

A good innovation has to produce cost savings; to produce cost savings, innovation has to involve performing tasks with fewer people; to perform tasks with fewer people is to take more management risk of being able to do the job, and to take more risk of not being accepted by the existing culture. To be good, innovation must be perceived by some (or all) in the existing culture as bad. This is a true paradox, culturally driven, and one that NASA has learned from the space station acquisition process. With apologies to Jerry Harvey, author of *The Abilene Paradox*, we shall call this The Houston Paradox, since it was observed here.

CONSULTANTS: ANOTHER DETERRENT TO CHANGE

Like all government agencies, and most large private sector corporations, NASA needs and uses consultants where temporary access to high skill levels warrants their use. During the early days of the space station program, much was made of the need for implementing a program management structure that would accommodate all of the constraints on the program. The agency's desire to rejuvenate the development skills of its civil service workforce has already been mentioned. Because of the long drought in agency development funding, new programs coming only every decade or longer, every NASA center and installation felt a need to participate, lest it be another decade before its next program came along. And then there were the congressional delegations of all states and districts containing a NASA installation, each demanding a fair share for that installation, often regardless of how much engineering or economic sense it might make to divide the work to accommodate their desires.

NASA responded by commissioning General Sam Phillips, former Apollo program manager, distinguished by his military career as well as his NASA accomplishments. No one in NASA would have questioned the wisdom of bringing Phillips in to resolve, in an objective way, the management dilemmas of the agency.

Phillips and his group worked very hard to mitigate the compromises that had already been made to the program, some for reasons of politics. His solution was very analogous to that of King Solomon, who resolved a dispute over a child by threatening to divide the child in half, until the true mother intervened. Unfortunately, there was no true mother to intervene in this case, and the Phillips commission recommended dividing the development of the space station among four NASA centers, and along boundaries that later proved to be very difficult to produce. An additional, brand new, costly NASA installation was created to manage the program.

The accommodation had been made, despite its well-recognized adverse effects on program cost. But the experience base of those on the Phillips commission had, in fact been in another era of NASA, during the mid-1960s when resource and budget constraints were all but unknown. Had the commission been involved in highly budgetary constrained programs, would their solution have been so costly? One could make an argument that a manager will solve problems based on personal experience, and that, realizing the extreme cost constraints to be imposed on the space station development, the appointment of a consultant team, most of whom had not developed a base of experience under those conditions, in retrospect, was a mistake. But we shall never know if the Phillips solution was indeed the least expensive possible, considering all constraints.

CULTURE AND RESISTANCE TO CHANGE

Culture, the learned behavior patterns of organizations, discriminates among civilizations, nations, and organizations at any level; thus, organizations that produce steel are far different from those that fabricate steel into spacecraft. Processes and policies designed for one may not be at all applicable to the other. Solutions to economic problems designed for one culture could cause major problems in another.[6]

Successful organizational change is a highly complex, difficult undertaking. The experiences of the American automobile and aircraft industries, as they strive to meet foreign competition, contain many examples of successful and unsuccessful cultural change, which can provide some guidance for NASA. A common element in all changes is the need for a shared recognition throughout the organization that some reason for change, some threat, exists.

Once that recognition exists, a designed process must be undertaken very deliberately, a process that will involve identification of what needs to be changed, on what schedule, and what resources will be required to accomplish it.[7] But, as illustrated in the space station example, all change will meet with some degree of resistance. Often, overcoming that resistance requires major commitment on the part of the organization.

ENVIRONMENTAL OBSTRUCTIONS TO THE CHANGE PROCESS

It is not enough to recognize the need for change. It is not even enough to put a change process in place. A change program with even the best of intentions must recognize that certain constraints will exist outside of the capability of the organization. And so it is with NASA.

NASA has at least seven stakeholders who must agree to any change. There are six oversight committees in Congress. And there is the National Space Council, chaired by the vice-president, representing the administration. And there are, of course, the individual congressmen representing the districts of the various NASA installations. Any successful change design must begin with acceptance of the goals and plans by all clients in a position to inhibit the change.

A SUMMARY OF CHALLENGES

It would seem almost superfluous to observe that the first thing an organization must do to implement change is to recognize the need to change. As it begins the process of implementing potentially the largest space initiative in history, NASA finds itself very preoccupied with flying the space shuttle and developing the space station. It is not always easy for NASA management to recognize and analyze threats that might drive the need for change, and with the fast pace of ongoing programs, even harder to find the resources to implement change. In any noncompetitive environment, such as that enjoyed by many public sector organizations, the need for change is much more obscure than it might be in the highly competitive private sector. The first and most critical challenge is then to recognize the need.

The second challenge is to identify what needs to be changed. NASA is now heavily involved in strategic planning to help identify potential change areas. But an across-the-board change process, not directed at the more critical areas, could rapidly consume change resources, and not resolve problems with the highest leverage on the future. With the advent of the Space Exploration Initiative, it is highly important that change be focused on reducing the development time and costs of planetary exploration hardware. In planning this new initiative, NASA has the advantage of knowing, from the "lessons learned" studies, the directions to take for cultural change. When the attributes of the initiative are better defined, a nearly complete picture should emerge of the ingredients and directions of the change process.

It may be necessary, in order to build a consensus for, and to plan the change, to place considerable emphasis on "education" of all key players, to show where the greatest needs exist, and to assist in the prioritization process of the change activities. This burden will inevitably fall on staff people who are trusted by the leadership of the organization.

The third challenge is to plan the change, recognizing a hierarchy of needs, utilizing knowledge of the cultural behavior of the organization, and involving the right people in the change process. It has been shown in a number of instances that the change process is greatly enhanced by a team of internal and external change agents; failures have resulted from an incomplete understanding of the organizational culture, and full participation by key members of the organization is essential.[8] In the instance of the NASA Space Exploration Initiative, the involvement of senior NASA managers, who are consumed by their day-to-day responsibilities in the space shuttle and space programs, as well as the many other programs of the agency, will require a major commitment on the part of each individual involved.

The fourth set of challenges are those presented by the external environment. One decision that must be made early is that of which externalities should be influenced. In its Space Exploration Initiative, for example, NASA will have to decide whether or not to try to influence the way in which it interacts with congressional oversight groups. One very attractive alternative to program budgeting, which would obviate some of the problems associated with the early program turbulence described above, would be to obtain from the Congress multiyear funding for the initiative. NASA must decide whether the benefits of such funding would outweigh the effort required to obtain it, as well as the risks involved.

In addition, NASA has the advantage of having learned the dynamic behavior of the program-planning environment. Tools based on this knowledge will prove valuable to the avoidance of future problems, in this case, in providing stability to the early program planning, scheduling, and funding processes, and creating a climate of trust between NASA and its stakeholders.

A final challenge, which may be somewhat unique to NASA in its current situation, is the need to implement change into a major new program, while at the same time planning and executing the program. There are both opportunities and difficulties associated with this.

The opportunities are predicated on the fact that no structure exists for the new program; thus, anything that is created can be created in the image of the desired change. The difficulty is implementing the change quickly, and putting in place mechanisms that will preclude the intervention of parts of the old culture that might not be desirable in the new environment. To do this, NASA must implement a system of gatekeepers, to ensure that whatever is brought into the program fits within the scope and plan of the desired change. Thus, some mechanism to avoid placing this initiative in predicaments faced by the early space station program is imperative, as well as a mechanism for controlling the influx of well-meaning, but culturally laden people from throughout the aerospace community, until they are needed, if indeed they are.

CONCLUSIONS

Introducing cultural change into the public sector brings a special set of challenges; chief among them is the absence of competition which drives most private sector change.[9] Management, at least within NASA, is preoccupied with doing the currently defined jobs as well as possible. The main challenge in the introduction of change, beneficial though it might be, can be the creation of an awareness of the benefits.

At this time in the evolution of NASA, with the advent of perhaps the largest exploration program in the history of the world, change of some sort is mandatory, whether it be the simple addition of more people to the existing workforce to perform the job in the same cultural manner as previous programs, whether it be the changing of ways of doing business to do the new initiative with the existing workforce, or more likely, something in between.

NASA has an advantage in planning the change, however. Through experience and the study and analysis of other successful cultures, NASA has the understanding of the direction that successful change should take. The ingredients of successful low-cost, high-technology programs are well known today.

But change should be planned, as a conscious part of designing the program, to provide the most efficient possible utilization of national resources. It is not at all easy for an agency like NASA to identify what best satisfies national objectives, those that are superordinate to those of our own space program. Therefore, all clients and stakeholders must be involved in the agenda setting for any change to a federal agency, and preferably from the outset, as participants, with ownership in the superordinate goals.

Often overlooked is that the NASA of today is not the NASA of the Apollo exploration period. The Apollo program started with a clean sheet of paper, and a major federal agency was literally built around that program. Now the nation enjoys the existence of that aging institution, built to take man to the moon the first time. It is an open question in some quarters whether or not the current NASA is where the management of the Space Exploration Initiative should reside. Whether or not the existing NASA is any more a national asset to be used in the implementation of man's greatest exploration is a decision that today is very much in NASA's hands.

But the decision will be made not by how fervently NASA wishes to manage the initiative, but rather by how NASA demonstrates to its stakeholders aggressive leadership in the introduction of change to the national space exploration process.

NOTES

1. National Aeronautics and Space Administration, "Report of the 90-Day Study on Human Exploration of the Moon and Mars," Washington D.C., November 1989.

2. Notice to NASA, *Aviation Week and Space Technology* (January 15, 1990).

3. RCA Price Systems Division, "Equipment Specification Cost Study," phase 2, final report, NASA Contract NAS 9-14427, November 30, 1976.

4. The development costs of the space shuttle were very close (within 10 percent or less) to congressional cost commitments made to NASA at the outset of the program in 1981, making it one of the more successful NASA programs from the standpoint of cost control. The Orbiter spacecraft project actually cost less than the congressional commitment.

5. RCA Price Systems Division, "Cost Study."

6. H. C. Mandell, *Planning to Manage the Space Station Program* (Houston, Tex.: NASA Johnson Space Center, 1987).

7. See R. Blake and J. S. Mouton, "The Introduction of Change in Industrial Organizations," *Scientific Methods* (January 1962).

8. N. Gluckstern and R. Packard, "The Internal-External Change Agent Team," *Journal of applied Behavioral Science* 13 (1): 41.

9. A survey of the extensive literature of organizational change in the public sector will not be attempted here. The interested reader should see Edward J. Giblin, "Organization Development: Public Sector Theory and Practice," *Public Personnel Management* 5 (2) (March–April 1976): 112–19; and W. B. Eddy, "Beyond Behavioralism?" *Public Personal Review* 31 (July 1970): 169–75. These sources describe the fundamental differences between organizational change in the public and private sectors.

11

Introducing Creativity in Educational Bureaucracies

Arie Y. Lewin

Much of the literature suggests that large firms and state bureaucracies are inertia bound and impervious to change even under the most conducive conditions (Stinchcombe 1965; Aldrich 1979). Miller and Friesen (1980) and Tushman and Romanelli (1985) point out, however, that significant changes in organizational structure are much more likely to appear in times of crisis and with changes in top management. Anecdotally it appears that recent organizational transformations of such companies as Allied Corporation, Apple Computer, General Electric, and Dupont closely reflect the incumbency and individual properties of their respective CEOs: Edward Hennessy, John Scully, Jack Welch, and Edgar Woolard (Lewin and Stephens 1990). The transformation of Georgia Institute of Technology is a further illustration, in this case involving a major public university, that a CEO can shape an organization according to a personal strategic vision and preferences.

Although it is too early to judge the long-term organizational effectiveness outcomes at Georgia Tech (e.g., in terms of creativity and innovation of academic programs and research) the enormity of the changes speak for themselves. So far in this volume, we have not discussed the extent to which the individual properties of the CEO are a critical factor in organization design and strategy. The remarks that follow are intended to insert the person and the personal attributes of the leader into the discussion of organization redesign and change. Figure 11.1 (from Lewin and Stephens 1990) summarizes the model linking individual properties of the CEO to organization design and change.

John Patrick Crecine seems a paradigmatic high need for achievement individual. Such individuals spend a great deal of time thinking about "how to do things better." They are not interested in rewards in and of themselves, but on the basis of the recognition of achievement that rewards represent. High achievement individuals will have a strategic vision and tend to articulate a viable strategic direction. Such individuals set attainable yet challenging goals and their organizations will be characterized by highly formalized strategic planning, goal setting, and reward and appraisal systems. It is clear that Crecine has imbued Georgia Tech with his academic strategic vision and that a new form of academic strategic planning has been implemented.

Locus of control (Rotter 1966) may be another individual property characteristic of Crecine. Locus of control captures the extent to which individuals believe that they can control their fate, or conversely, the extent to which they believe that luck, environment, and other externalities determine their personal outcomes. Individuals with internal loci of control (internals) are likely to be proactive in controlling circumstances while externals are likely to be fatalistic.

Overall, internal CEOs can be expected to redesign their organizations so as to minimize environmental constraints and allow for maximal personal impact. One of the most obvious means for controlling the environment and affecting the organization is strategic planning. To articulate a strategic vision and to undertake formal planning imply the belief that the environment is tractable, and that strategic choice can prevail over determinism (Child 1972; Hrebiniak and Joyce 1985). Therefore CEOs with internal loci of control are expected to believe in strategy, espouse strategy, and implement viable strategic planning processes. In order to garner the information necessary to support strategic planning, internal locus of control CEOs can be expected to implement monitoring of the environment and to set up concomitant boundary spanning structures and staffs. It is clear that the Georgia Tech transformation was guided by an academic strategic vision, a viable strategy, and planning processes that were articulated, directed, and implemented by Crecine.

In a sense Georgia Tech "lucked out" when it chose Crecine as its president. It could be argued that he would have imprinted his academic vision on any research university that chose him as president. While the contextual and implementation details would vary it is reasonable to assume that the fundamental vision and strategy would remain the same. Lewin and Stephens (1990) note that CEO background and demographics—career

Figure 11.1. The CEO as a Determinant of Organization Design

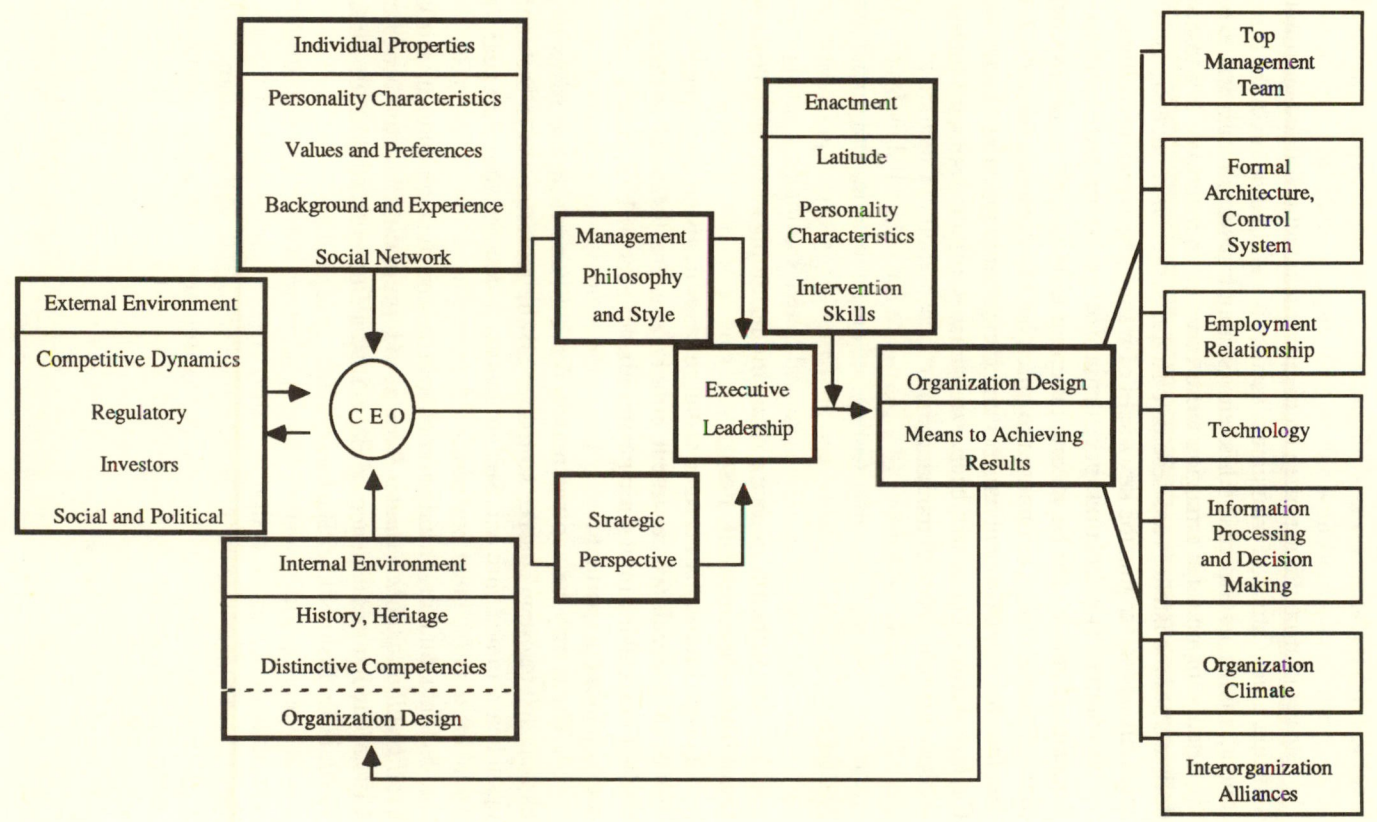

histories and social network—influence strategy, the composition of the top management team, and how the organization is managed. In the case of Crecine the case could be made that his prior experiences at the University of Michigan and Carnegie Mellon as well as his formal education have been crucial in the evolution of his views about research universities—the importance of nurturing and institutionalizing interdisciplinary programs, defining new constellations of fields of inquiry, and teaching and conducting research at the frontier of knowledge by building on existing distinctive competencies. The creation at Georgia Tech of three new colleges—the College of Sciences, the College of Computing, and the Ivan Allen College of Management, Policy and International Affairs—illustrates that philosophy. The first two colleges build on existing strength at Georgia Tech and the Ivan College represents a synthesis of interdisciplinary social science and professional education embodying many ideas rooted in Crecine's intellectual and administrative experience (e.g., Institute for Public Policy Studies at the University of Michigan; dean, College of the Humanities and Social Science at Carnegie Mellon University; and provost, Carnegie Mellon University).

Successful implementation is central to redesigning the organization as a means to implementing strategy. Lewin and Stephens (1990) discuss CEO enactment of organization design in terms of several factors—latitude for action, personality characteristics, and intervention skills. Although we have few details to address enactment, it is known that the board of regents has backed the leadership of Crecine and his new vision for Georgia Tech, thus providing one important basis of latitude. Also historically new leaders are accorded greater latitude early in their term and Crecine acted with alacrity to exploit that transient basis of latitude. Most important, he benefited from the latitude associated with his ability to obtain additional resources for Georgia Tech from the University of Georgia system. Finally clarity of vision, intellectual stimulation, and persistence are important elements of successful enactment of change (Bass 1985). These properties are identifiable with Crecine and may further explain the rapid implementation of change at Georgia Tech.

Leadership and the individual properties of the leader are critical determinants of organization redesign and change. The transformation of Georgia Tech is one more instance demonstrating the potential of this argument, which in recent years has not been in vogue as the old traditional theories of leadership lost favor.

REFERENCES

Aldrich, H. 1979. *Organizations and environment.* Englewood Cliffs, N.J.: Prentice-Hall.

Bass, B. M. 1985. *Leadership and performance beyond expectations.* New York: Free Press.

Child, J. 1972. Organizational structure, environment, and performance: The role of strategic choice. *Sociology,* 6, 1-22.

Hrebiniak, L., and W. Joyce. 1985. Organizational adaptation: Strategic choice and environmental determinism. *Administrative Science Quarterly* 30: 336–49.

Lewin, A. Y., and C. U. Stephens. 1990. Individual properties of the CEO as determinants of organization design: An integrated model and implications for upper-echelons theory. Fuqua School of Business Working Paper.

Miller, D., and P. Friesen. 1980. Archetypes of organizational transition. *Administrative Science Quarterly* 25: 268–99.

Robinson, J. P., and P. R. Shaver. 1973. *Measures of social psychological attitudes.* Ann Arbor, Mich.: Institute for Social Research.

Rotter, J. B. 1966. Generalized expectancies for internal versus external control of reinforcement. *Psychological Monographs* 80.

Stinchombe, A. L. 1965. Social structure and organizations. In *Handbook of Organizations,* ed. J. G. March. Chicago: Rand-McNally.

Tushman, M. L. and E. Romanelli. 1985. Organizational evolution: A metamorphosis model of convergence and reorientation. In *Research in Organizational Behavior,* ed. L. L. Cummings and B. M. Staw. Greenwich, Conn.: JAI Press.

12

Continuous Quality Improvement in Health-Care Services

Bertram S. Brown,
Susan F. Lefkowitz, and
J. D. Aguera-Areas

The industrialization of medicine—its great transformation from a professional cottage industry to a business commodity ethos—makes the advent of the quality era inevitable. The health care industry is poised to move from its traditional focus on quality assurance to a forward-thinking embrace of continuous quality improvement techniques. The health-care industry, long self-analyzing using methods that retrospectively review any unusual or untoward event, is ready to accept the all-encompassing approach of ongoing assessment and implementation quality used in manufacturing. Whereas quality assurance as currently practiced in health care tends to focus on correcting problems in patient care quality after the fact, particularly problems with individual practitioners, continuous quality improvement emphasizes finding opportunities to improve quality by changing systems as well as the behavior of individuals. It is this approach to contemporaneous assessment of entire systems that is of urgent importance to the health-care industry.

This chapter reviews current thinking on the definition of quality in health-care services, a topic of ongoing discussion, and attempts to clarify the difference between traditional quality assurance and contemporary continuous quality improvement. It surveys activities and organizations involved in the field, including the recent report from the Institute of Medicine.

There exists a window of opportunity for an institution of higher education to begin immediately to develop a full graduate program at the masters and doctoral levels, in the application of continuous quality improvement techniques to the health-care industry. The following activities and plans are necessary to develop such a program:

1. An appropriate advisory panel should be convened.

2. A senior professional should be engaged as project director to develop the program.

3. The directions of the Joint Commission on the Accreditation of Health Care Facilities must be monitored carefully, along with other key organizations in the field.

4. The university or institution must begin to build a reputation in the field by offering introductory seminars to health-care executives.

5. A marketing survey should be conducted in the area, as well as a survey of academic medical centers, nursing schools, and large hospital networks nationwide.

6. The program strategy should be incremental, building from short, noncredit courses to the full doctorate and should explore the possibilities of joint efforts with existing consulting firms.

All of health care's major players are placing quality at the top of their priorities, each for different reasons:

*   For hospitals, *ambulatory surgical centers and other patient care sites*, quality is the goal of patient care and a competitive advantage that will differentiate them in a high-competition market;

*   For Physicians, *nurses, and other professionals* quality is the goal of medical practice and the standard by which they will be measured by peers, patients, regulators, and malpractice attorneys;

*   For major employers, insurance companies, *and managed care networks*, quality is the primary criterion for selecting doctors and hospitals when price is not a factor; and

*   For government regulators *and health advocacy groups*, quality is the means of protecting the public welfare and responding to voter *and consumer* blocks. (Coile 1990, emphasis added).

The findings and conclusions of the recently completed Institute of Medicine (IOM) study of Medicare quality assurance assert that significant problems exist in quality of care and in our present approaches to quality assurance. "The problems are sufficient to justify a major redirection for quality assurance in this country and, in particular, a more comprehensive strategy for Medicare" (Lohr 1990).

The stage is set to focus on the quality of health care to an extent far more intensive than ever before. The industrialization of medicine makes the quality era an inevitable major new component. The industry has long attended to the assurance of quality through established practices like peer review, but now is moving beyond in an attempt to define and measure health services outcomes. Further, it is clearly an emerging interest in the application of continuous quality improvement techniques to the provision of health care.

Whether quality is absolute or in the eye of the beholder, it is clearly the most desired, yet elusive, factor in the ongoing assessment of the value of health-care expenditures. As more attention is paid to the national burden of health-care costs, and as many of the cost containment efforts of the mid-1980s fail to produce significant savings, questions inevitably arise about what is purchased with the American health care dollar. Physicians, consumers, insurers, and regulators alike are seeking ways to identify what is good care, what is worth the cost, how to guarantee that it is provided, and how to *buy right*. Managed care programs are now using quality as a marketing tool. The regulators, insurers, and purchasers of health care have a more fundamental responsibility to quality: They must determine whether the care that they purchase really exists and, if it does, if it is totally appropriate or even fraudulent. Here we are not dealing with effectiveness or appropriateness so much as outright abusive medical behavior directed at the utilization of medical technology for fee-raising purposes rather than for apt medical care itself.

QUALITY: WHAT IS IT?

It is said that quality, like pornography, is easy to recognize and hard to define. After extensive discussion about the essential dimensions of the definition of quality, the Institute of Medicine study produced the following definition: "Quality of Care is the degree to which health services or individuals and populations increase the likelihood of desired health outcomes and are consistent with current professional knowledge." This definition is similar to that of Donabedian (1988b): "quality consists in the ability to achieve desirable objectives using legitimate means . . . the objective specified is an achievable state of health."

Caper (1988) identified three components of quality: (1) efficacy or outcome; (2) appropriateness; and (3) caring as manifested by patient satisfaction. He acknowledged the difficulties in measuring each of these, and joined many in the field who are stymied by the lack of standards against which to gauge health care. The 1990 IOM definition is broader. This wide perspective reflects the current trend toward using large data sets to assess the value of all service provided.

These definitions, however, do not address the economic impact of quality improvement. Implicit in this concept is the assumption that improvement in quality, in the long run, lowers costs. Experience from industry bears out this inference; it is less costly to do something well, once, than to redo, repair, or replace the item produced. As yet, there is little empirical proof that the improvement of quality in health-care services lowers costs. Although economic benefits logically follow, there is a growing demand for proof. Consumers, third-party payers, and regulators are all applying pressure for the highest quality health care at the lowest possible cost; in fact, perceived quality is becoming the most valuable commodity in the purchase of health-care services in an increasingly competitive environment.

QUALITY ASSURANCE

Medicine, as a self-reviewing profession, has well-honed processes for finding and analyzing unacceptable care. Virtually every site where health-care services are provided has some form of quality assurance. Effective quality assurance builds confidence and faith in the quality of the health care provided and is not an end in itself (Lohr 1990). It is a process that deals with exceptions. Events or results that fall outside the realm of acceptable are reviewed and analyzed on a case-by-case basis in a cycle that identifies problems, devises long-term solutions, and monitors to avoid reoccurrence. It is a process best suited to the identification of specific poor performers although, in some cases, it can provide the means to address and improve the average level of overall care provided.

Lohr (1990) lists four major purposes for a quality assurance program:

- to identify providers of unacceptable care with the intention of preventing them from doing or third-party payers from reimbursing such services
- to identify providers of unacceptable care with the intention of improving such practices and increasing the quality of services

- to increase the average level of care delivered by a given group of providers and to prevent the degradation of existing acceptable levels of care

- to motivate providers to ever higher levels of services

The traditional model of providing quality assurance has evolved over more than twenty years in the Donabedian (1966, 1980, 1982, 1984, 1988a, 1988b, 1988c) model of structure-process-outcome. This model requires the assessment of (1) the capacity (structure) universally present in any health-care setting (physical facilities, governance, licensure, ownership); (2) what is done to the patients (process) by individual practitioners, groups, or entire systems; and (3) the end results (outcomes). Assessments of quality are, therefore, based on the premise that structure, process, and outcome are interrelated and that the level of quality can be inferred from the provision of these three elements.

Donabedian (1988b) admits that little is known about the relationship between structure and process, and that assessment of quality in this manner is valid only to the extent the basic premise is verifiable. Nonetheless, the body of work called quality assurance has developed from this basic concept with extensive attention paid to explicit measurement demands in an attempt to quantify standards while acknowledging that different service sites (i.e., hospitals, long-term care facilities, offices, etc.) may require different measures. Quality assurance programs internal to an organization, and even those accrediting bodies that are external, function best in identifying and addressing problems that fall outside the norm. Lohr (1990) acknowledge that such programs are not likely to identify systematic problems, improve the average performance of providers, or offer help in aspiring to overall higher levels of quality because they concentrate on events that fall outside the norm. At the lower end of the curve we are dealing not only with poor, incompetent, or inept performers, but we may be dealing with outright malicious, fraudulent, and antisocial behavior. Clearly this does not add to quality and has a very complex relation to the quality issues discussed above. In fact, because health-care providers and organizations desire not to be considered fraudulent they tend to resist oversight of any sort. This makes it easier for those who are fraudulent to get away with it.

CONTINUOUS QUALITY IMPROVEMENT

Continuous quality improvement, total quality management (TQM), organizationwide quality improvement, and other methods of ongoing review and revision in the processes and results of production have had a successful history in industry, particularly in Japan (Ishikawa 1985). The techniques developed by Deming and Juran, now chronicled in the popular press, combine statistical analysis of the elements of processes with organizational structures that motivate all levels of employees. This combination, when supported at the highest managerial levels of an organization, creates a powerful, effective method to address the production of quality, at the lowest possible cost, on an ongoing basis.

Because quality improvement techniques rely on lines of accountability in an organization, health-care organizations are well suited, assuming that the top leadership is committed to the process.

Lohr (1990) outlines eight key aspects of continuous quality improvement as it applies to health care:

1. Emphasis is on external customers or recipients of care. All that is done is done for the benefit of the patient.

2. All that underlies the benefit to the patient, for example, facilities, equipment, providers, support staff, and organizational policies, must be involved in a relentless, systematic, and cooperative effort to improve care.

3. The PDCA cycle (planning, doing, checking, and acting), makes it possible for all to apply continuous improvement methods to daily work with responsiveness to patients' needs.

4. The work of individuals and departments is recognized as interdependent. Internally, many departments are each others' *suppliers* and *customers*.

5. Emphasis is placed on systems and processes, and organizations are seen as interrelated networks.

6. The opinions of both customers and employees are continually incorporated into the program of review and improvement.

7. Commitment at the highest levels of an organization is crucial. Successful implementation of continuous quality improvement methods requires a change in the corporate culture that must be sanctioned and supported.

8. The process uses practical analysis tools such as flowcharts, line graphs, decision matrices, Pareto analyses and scatter diagrams, which have been adapted from decades of use in industrial quality control.

There are some similarities between continuous quality improvement methods and traditional quality assurance, particularly in their approaches to information as the link between process and outcomes, and in the general focus on outcomes, per se. Although the continuous quality improvement approach is consistent with traditional quality assurance methods, it is far broader and differs in several significant ways.

Continuous quality improvement emphasizes the views of patients and other participants and encourages the analysis of systems from that perspective. It addresses the quality of average services provided, intending to improve them constantly regardless of the level of current performance (even if it is quite high). It focuses on the interrelationship of departments and the effect of improved cooperation on service. Traditional quality assurance primarily addresses the outliers, exceptions to acceptable care, with less attention paid to the average level of care. Traditional quality assurance has a proven history of success in identifying and rectifying specific clinical problems, a function to which continuous quality improvement may not be as well suited. However, it does not, for the most part, focus on the interrelatedness of care providers or the systems of an institution.

Of primary significance are the differences in assignment of accountability between the two methods. Traditional quality assurance vests accountability in the leadership of an organization. Continuous quality improvement emphasizes the personal responsibility of each employee in contributing to constant betterment even though the ultimate accountability rests at the very top.

THE PHYSICIAN FACTOR

Merry (1990b) identifies the conundrum of physician participation in the introduction of continuous quality improvement techniques. On the one hand, because physicians historically have a quasi-independent role in health-care facilities and are accountable to each other as professionals, they are accustomed to and accepting of structured review of individual cases. On the other hand, the same quasi-independence and self-accountability is resistant to the management inherent in continuous quality improvement methods. Merry further points out that "the traditional way of doing medical quality review has . . . been blind to what has been known in industry for decades: that quality is the end result of a complex interaction of people and support systems." Controlled studies performed to identify ways to induce physicians to change their practice patterns, however, showed that education and information alone had no significant effect (Schroeder et al. 1984). Merry offers many suggestions on how these techniques can be acceptably introduced to physicians, but much work remains to be done in this key area. It is universally agreed that physicians are a critical element in the health-care system and that, for continuous quality improvement methods to be effective, everyone must play by the same rules.

THE NURSE FACTOR

There is a need to focus on the vital role of the nurse in quality assurance issues. While physicians may be the dominant professionals in health care, there are other professionals who have quality assurance approaches that need to be taken into account. Their contribution to quality assurance or total quality management is another area to research.

UTILIZATION REVIEW, UTILIZATION MANAGEMENT, CASE MANAGEMENT, RISK MANAGEMENT, AND MALPRACTICE

The field of quality assurance has in its developmental history certain elements that have been in existence for several years. The field of utilization review (UR) began with committees of physicians (peers—hence the term "peer review") within hospitals reviewing admission, treatments, procedures, charges, and outcomes of health care in that facility. This function then moved to groups outside the hospital carrying out this function—peer review organizations (PROs). The function was carried out to assure that quality care was received by the clients of the payer groups, particularly Medicare. Eventually this process was expanded to involve Medicaid and now includes all private insurance and other payer groups. There are presently two thousand utilization review companies that carry out this function. The field of UR develops guidelines, screens, and profiles of what is and what is not permissible care and the procedures covered by a given health contract or insurance policy. The results are brought to the attention of health-care providers. Denial of payment because the care is outside the scope of the contract, or because it is excessive or inappropriate, is a dynamic and contentious issue between the providers and payers.

UR then led to the next development, utilization management (UM). UM is directed at informing the provider in advance what is permitted, and then monitoring the actual provision of the resources during the course of the illness. These include processes such as precertification or preadmission review, concurrent review during the course of care, and a whole range of UR management approaches. This led eventually to the discovery that the largest economic costs come from a few difficult, high-risk cases. Managing and working with these complex cases has led to the third evolution, the field of case management.

CM is the process by which the outside reviewing body monitors the physician and hospital as to provision of care. The case manager hones in on the difficult costly cases, and helps in the planning of home care, surgical procedures, and special medications, facilitating and approving rehabilitation aspects of health care. There is a complex unresolved tension in the boundary between the CM functions and the provision of care. It is not always clear when CM is advisory and consultative, and when it is directive. This is not only a power issue, but a liability issue. If things go wrong, do you sue the doctor or the case manager? In the course of UR, UC, and CM, information becomes available as to when there may be malpractice exposure.

Risk management is traditionally represented as the hospital's facility for dealing with malpractice suits; however, its true role is also preventive. It should provide positive feedback for the improvement of hospital care, and therefore, the personnel, resources, and databases necessary for its implementation overlap those typically designated for the use of quality assurance. Thus a new Joint Commission standard has been developed to merge quality assurance with the preventive component of risk management. The aims of these two departments are not, of course, entirely parallel, and some institutions have raised concerns that legal materials gathered during a case investigation would require attorney-client protection. The integration would lessen the redundancy inherent in the previous arrangement, however, as well as optimize the use of otherwise limited resources.

The field of malpractice, the improper treatment of culpable neglect of a patient by a physician, has developed a clear mandate that only when harm is done can a specific situation become a litigious case. UR, UM, and CM have enormous potential for the quality assurance process. What is common to UR, UM, CM, and malpractice is what is known as the current thrust in health care—outcome measures and outcome studies.

The final common denominator of all these facts of QA is a question: Does intervention make a difference in the outcome that counts—the health status of the individual? This has become the current cusp of the wave, leading edge of QA research and activity—outcome measures and outcome studies.

FRAUD AND ABUSE

A key dimension of the quality assurance field can be assessed by understanding the bills processed by organizations such as insurance companies that provide funds to hospitals, physicians, and other health-care providers. These bills are generally called claims. Physicians, health practitioners and organizations that fraudulently bill for services never rendered, purposefully misdiagnose to increase the funds they receive, or organize themselves for the purpose of enrichment and financing, clearly do not have quality of care as a major goal.

The field of fraud and abuse is an enormous one. The Federal Trade Commission (FTC) has estimated that at least $15 billion is involved. Others such as Leonard Abrahamson of the U.S. Health Care and Bert Browne estimate that approximately 10 to 15 percent, or $50 billion, of the $600 billion dollars spent yearly for health care in the United States, is either outright fraudulent or abusive. The payer structure in the United States consists predominantly of Medicare and Medicaid through the federal and state government, $140 billion; Blue Cross-Blue Shield, with approximately $200 billion or 40 percent of the hospital market; and perhaps $150 billion for the commercial insurance industry. All these organizations have in common a desire to weed out fraudulent and abusive practices. The department of HHS, which administers Medicare and Medicaid through HCFA, is critically important. There, the inspector general has a statutory responsibility to weed out fraud and abuse. Within Blue Cross-Blue Shield the seventy-four independent programs have recently been ordered to upgrade their audit units into full fraud and abuse programs; all commercial insurance companies have programs identifying fraudulent and abusive practices. They vary from primitive to sophisticated.

The era of computers and management of information through computerized billing creates the potential for abusive practices as well as their identification by practice profiling and other techniques. AQ paradigms, computer profiles, and the like have the ability to deal with quality problems as well as economic and financial issues. Emerging modes of information analysis will permit new ways to uncover both poor care and outright fraud and abuse. This is an unexplored major research area.

Clearly the fraud and abuse issue raises not only the contemporary aspect of ethics—who should receive what care, and when and how to prolong life—but actualizes at the other end the most classical issue of ethics such as cheating and stealing. There are moral, humanistic, and philosophical dimensions to the quality of care issues yet to be explored. The impact of regulatory cost containment strategies on quality is now being studied. One such issue is explored in a recent article (Burda 1990), showing that disease-related groups (DRGs) have not reduced the quality of care but have led to earlier discharges.

Some authorities feel that the practice of medicine should not be linked to financial gain through ownership of the structural elements of health care. The issue of kickbacks has been in medicine for a long time but there is a whole set of laws around safehaven and other such legal devices that may be relevant to quality concerns. There are new quality issues to be researched: Is quality improved when the physician also owns the laboratory or imaging center or is it decreased? Should there be separate quality control over the x-ray laboratory and other facilities when they are owned by a physician group?

When can the hospital own its home care facilities or nursing home? At which point does the promotion of competition by the FTC make sense and when does it not? These questions can enrich a research agenda on the interface of policy and regulatory controls and quality of health care.

THE CURRENT STATE OF AFFAIRS

In 1987, the John A. Hartford Foundation funded a program to explore the application of continuous quality improvement techniques to the health-care industry. This program, dubbed the National Demonstration Project (NDP), is headed by Donald M. Berwick, M.D., Harvard University Health Plan, Paul Batalan, M.D., Hospital Corporation of America, and A. Blanton Godfrey, Ph.D., Juran Institute, Inc. According to their own literature, the first phase of the NDP combined twenty-one health-care organizations with experienced quality experts from industry. The intent of this marriage was to determine if modern techniques could address specific problems in health-care settings. The results were encouraging.

The project then offered introductory seminars that granted CMEs and attempted to interest institutional leaders in continuous quality improvement techniques. Due to the success and interest built in the first courses, they have expanded their roster to include subsequent courses in how-to take these methods from the classroom to the institution.

The American Medical Review Research Center, founded in 1985, identifies itself in its literature as advancing the science and art of quality evaluation and medical review with the ultimate goal of effective operational quality and cost evaluation programs. Its activities are designed to create a dynamic link among all quality evaluation efforts of individual providers, physicians, allied health professionals, academic medical institutions, health organizations and agencies, business and industry, peer review organizations, consumers, and public and private payer organizations. Many of its recent efforts have begun to address the development of the medical practice standards essential for the clinical application of continuous quality improvement techniques.

Several major consulting organizations have attempted to build practices in the continuous quality improvement field. SRI (formerly Stanford Research Institute) tried and, deciding they were ahead of the curve, dropped the effort. One of the largest international accounting firms, Coopers and Lybrand, has had a team devoted exclusively to quality improvement consulting for several years. Although the firm recognizes the enormous potential, it has found marketing of the service difficult. A local data analysis firm has begun to compile and offer large sets of clinical statistics for use in development of outcome standards. As these databases become available, previously impossible measures of quality will emerge. At this writing, at least two other major firms are developing solid consulting resources.

In its *Agenda for Change*, the Joint Commission on the Accreditation of Healthcare Organizations (JCAHO) issued a call for all health-care providers to focus on the results of their efforts. This dictum originally intended to improve assessment of outcomes on the entire industry by 1991; the earliest expected date now is 1994. There is much debate at present as to the viability of this edict. Some schools of thought contend that neither JCAHO nor the science of measurement is ready to apply such crucial judgment to the products of the health-care industry. Those who think that JCAHO will successfully move ahead to delineate industrywide standards expect continuous quality improvement to be mandated. Those who see the change as precipitous and premature often acknowledge the value of the technique but do not expect universal application. JCAHO considers the development of clinical indicators and revision of its standards and survey process as a way to help health-care organizations in the transition from quality assurance to quality improvement (Schyve and Prevost 1990).

Most recently, the Institute of Medicine of the National Academy of Sciences issued a report in response to the charge of Congress to design a strategy for quality review and assurance in Medicare. This report is certain to redirect the focus of quality of care for the foreseeable future. To address the shortcomings in quality of care identified, the traditional mode of retrospective review will have to change. The report makes a strong case for a more integrated approach to provision of quality of care and describes the continuous quality improvement method as a plausible means to that end. The IOM recognizes that there may, at present, be insufficient research and data on which to base the changes, and that a trained professional corps will be needed. The report recommends that establishment of academic programs be an early congressional priority since there is clearly an inadequate number of professionals (Lohr 1990). The IOM suggests that academic programs provide an extended period of study, that they build on existing programs in related fields, and that resources will be needed to develop appropriate curricula.

Internationally, because the United States is considered a front-runner in the areas of quality assurance and quality improvement in health care, many countries are seeking help. Australia, the Netherlands, Belgium, and Saudi Arabia have all begun to explore application of American quality assurance methods to varying degrees. This has begun with close ties to the American Joint Commission for the Accreditation of Healthcare Organizations.

The Department of Defense (DoD) has had a specific quality assurance project since 1985, the Civilian External Peer Review Program (CEPRP), managed by the Forensic Medical Advisory Service, Inc., a firm in Rockville, Maryland. A medical advisory panel representing specialty societies helped to write criteria and standards for specific surgical and medical cases. Abstracted data are compared with computer algorithms created from the medical standards and criteria. Those cases failing the algorithm are reviewed by a physician peer review panel. The program, which now reviews more than a one hundred thousand cases yearly, has moved into the emergency room and mental health areas.

At the present time there is a near crisis in the Veterans Administration. Its internal quality assurance program is no longer considered adequate and they are exploring how to deal with the quality assurance products that they have. They may move toward the Civilian External Peer Review Program or other modalities, but quite clearly the federal government in its own domain has been dealing with this quality assurance issue, specifically the DoD and VA, which together comprise 350 hospitals, 22 million people, and a $40 billion budget.

Two major health-care institutions, George Washington University Medical Center and the Fairfax Hospital System, have begun to incorporate the philosophy into their management. GW has a full-blown program guided by Healthcare Corporation of America and intends to develop a division of education within the medical center to teach every employee. All new employees will be required to attend five full days of training in quality improvement methods in their first three months of employment. The university currently has one doctoral student specializing in quality improvement in health care and is also considering a full graduate level program offering a doctoral degree.

Fairfax has engaged several consultants to shepherd them through the process. They have taken the key leaders of each part of the system on a retreat in Florida to introduce continuous quality improvement concepts and to gain their support. They are now moving on to involve all the board members within the system.

GENERAL OPPORTUNITIES

The intentions of JCAHO will determine the richness of this field for development of education and business opportunities. If, in fact, hospitals will be held to assessment of outcomes within the next few years, the potential is enormous. Further, quality improvement techniques are clearly suited to all sources of health-care services, not merely hospitals. Managed care systems, outpatient clinics, ambulatory surgical centers, physicians' offices, dentists' offices, home health services, and extended care facilities are potential sites for these methods.

There will be many players in the field, however, because the cost of entry is low. Some of the newcomers will be from industries like aerospace, where diversification is essential and quality control processes are already sophisticated. 3M is currently marketing education and consulting programs in this discipline directly to hospitals.

In the next ten years, people trained in the application of industrial quality assessment methods to health care will be in great demand. As the Joint Commission and other regulators require such programs and as consumers, insurers, and managed care providers increasingly question the quality of services purchased for their dollars, the few people educated in the field will be rare commodities. An acknowledged demand has already developed within insurance companies and managed care programs, which currently need more people than are available to direct assessment and control of quality.

Educational Opportunities

At the noncredit level, every health-care institution will need mid-level and senior people trained in methods of improving quality. Only those institutions affiliated with universities will have an in-house source (assuming the foresight to have developed one); all others will have to buy the training elsewhere. There will be a rapidly growing market for noncredit programs tailored to boards of directors, medical executive staff, nursing executive staff, and other senior people. Similarly, as the field of quality assurance changes, those currently certified will have to be brought into the new ways of thinking. To tap into the first group, up-to-the-minute information on the industry will be essential; to reach the second, a recognized presence in the field will be needed.

As the industry truly moves toward a focus on quality, the demand for graduate degrees will be indisputable. Both master level and doctoral programs will be sought and such graduates will remain a rare commodity for some time as the field mushrooms in importance within health care. The dearth of trained personnel will make these highly transferable skills particularly appealing to those seeking routes to advancement within health care.

Since continuous quality improvement necessitates a change in corporate and organizational culture, and because total commitment from the most senior management is essential, another market exists in selling the concepts to executive medical staffs, boards, and executive management. As Harvard has found, the subsequent demand for more in-depth information speaks to the efficacy of such introductory programs. The key, of course, is to have enough faculty depth to provide at least the inference that there is more beyond the introductory level.

Research Opportunities

There is a growing call for sound information to guide the first forays into the measurement of quality. Regardless of the urgency driven by JCAHO, scholars in the field recognize the dearth of such research to date. Most research has focused on definitions of quality care in specific diagnoses; research into quality improvement, particularly its relationship to costs, is minimal at best. The IOM study lists dozens of potential research areas, both basic and applied. Some examples are:

- how to change the habits and practices of physicians, nurses, and other caregivers
- increasing knowledge about the links between the process of care and outcome of care
- definition of needed data and databases and their best use; how to validate their accuracy
- explanations for the variations, appropriateness, and effectiveness of care
- developing adequate measures for specific care processes
- assessment of medical technologies as they relate to the process of care
- development of outcome measures incorporating severity of illness considerations
- most effective ways for health-care institutions to shift to continuous quality improvement methods
- how to demonstrate the added value of quality improvement techniques to the outside world
- how health care differs from other industries to which continuous quality improvement has been applied
- how to incorporate new approaches to quality into the health-care regulatory process.

Clearly, undertaking studies of this type requires a credible, established capacity and an appropriate laboratory.

Consulting Opportunities

The most fertile opportunity in this entire field is the business of helping institutions move to continuous quality improvement. It is a long, painstaking process that can best be done with outside help. Should the JCAHO edict come to fruition, every health-care provider will need some sort of guidance. The key to attracting this business, since the field is already appealing to many people, is to get into it as soon as possible, even if only on a trial basis. The potential market extends beyond hospitals to managed care organizations, the Department of Defense, the Veterans Administration, private clinical providers, and many others.

REFERENCES

Banta, H. D., and B. R. Luce. 1983. Assessing the cost-effectiveness of prevention. *Journal of Comm. Health* 9: 145–65.

Begner, M., R. M. Kaplan, and J. E. Ware. 1987. Evaluating health measures. *Journal of Chronic Diseases* (supp. 1): 23S–26S.

Berwick, D. M. 1989a. Health services research and quality of care: Assignments for the 1990s. *Med Care* 27: 763–71.

_____. 1989b. Continuous improvement as an ideal in health care. *New England Journal of Medicine* 320: 53–56.

Brook, R. H., and C. J. Kamberg. 1987. General health status measures and outcome measurements: A commentary on measuring functional status. Proceedings of the Advances in Health Assessment Conference. *Journal of Chronic Diseases* (supp. 1): 131S–136S.

Brook, R. H., and J. B. Kosecoff. 1988. Competition and quality. *Health Affairs* 7: 160–61.

Brown, B. 1969. The profession of hospital administration. *South Hospitals*.

Brown, C. R., and H. S. Uhl. 1970. Mandatory medical education: Sense or nonsense?" *JAMA* 213: 1660–68.

Brown, R. E., S. H. Sheingold, and B. R. Luce. 1989. *Options for using practice guidelines in reducing the volume of medically unnecessary services*. Washington, D.C.: Batelle Human Affairs Research Centers.

Burda, D. 1990. Rand study says care hasn't worsened under PPS. *Modern Healthcare* 20 (42) (October 22): 4.

Caper, P. 1988. Defining quality in medical care. *Health Affairs* 7: 49–61.

Chassin, M. R., et al. 1987. Does inappropriate use explain geographic variations in the use of health care services? A study of three procedures." *JAMA* 258: 2533–37.

Chassin, M. R., J. Kosecoff, and R. Dubois. *Value-managed health care purchasing. An employer's guidebook series,* vol 2, *Health care quality assessment.* Chicago: Midwest Business Group on Health.

Clearly, P.D., and B. J. McNail. 1988. Patient satisfaction as an indicator of quality of care. *Inquiry* 25: 25–36.

Coile, Russell C., Jr. 1990. *The new medicine: Reshaping medical practice and health care management* Rockville, MD.: Aspen Publishers.

Conn, R. B., R. D. Aller, and G. D. Lundberg. 1985. Identifying costs of medical care. An essential step in allocating resources. *JAMA* 253: 1586–89.

Couch, N. P., N. L. Tilney, and F. D. Moore. 1978. The cost of misadventures in colonic surgery. A model for the analysis of adverse outcomes in standard procedures. *American Journal of Surgery* 135: 641–46.

Council on Medical Service. 1988. Guidelines for quality assurance. *JAMA* 259: 2572–73.

Coward, V. S. 1989 Health fraud's toll: lost hopes, misspent billions. *JAMA* (22) (June 10): 3229–30.

Craddick, J. W., and B. S. Bader. 1983. *Medical management analysis: A systematic approach to quality assurance and risk management.* Auburn, Calif.: J. W. Craddick.

Davies, D. M., and J. E. Ware. 1988. Involving consumers in quality assessment. *Health Affairs* 7: 33–48.

Davis, D., et al. 1984. The impact of CME: A mythologic review of the continuing medical education literature. *Evaluation and the Health Professions* 7: 251–84.

Deming, W. E. 1986. *Out of crisis.* Cambridge: Massachusetts Institute of Technology Press.

Division of National Cost Estimates, Office of the Actuary, Health Care Financing Administration. 1987. National health expenditures, 1986–2000. *Health Care Finance. Review* 8 (4): 1–36.

Donabedian, A. 1966. Evaluating the quality of medical care. *Milkbank Mem. Fund Q.* 44: 166–203.

_____. 1981. Using decision analysis to formulate process criteria for quality assessment. *Inquiry* 18: 102–19.

_____. 1980, 1982, 1984. *Explorations in quality assessment and monitoring.* Vol. 1–3. Ann Arbor, Mich.: Health Administration Press.

_____. 1988a. Quality assessment and assurance: Unity of purpose, diversity of means." *Inquiry* 25: 173–92.

_____. 1988b. The quality of care. How can it be assessed?" *JAMA* 260: 1743–48.

_____. 1988c. Monitoring: The eyes and ears of healthcare." *Health Progress* 69: 39–43.

Drummond, M., and A. Maynard. 1988. Efficiency in the national health service: Lessons from abroad. *Health Policy* 9: 59–74.

Dubois, R. W. and R. H. Brook. 1988. Preventable deaths; Who, how often, and why?" *Ann. Intern Med.* 1909: 582–89.

Eddy, D. M. and J. Billing. 1988. The quality of medical evidence. *Health Affairs*, 7: 19–32.

Eisenberg, J. M. 1986. *Doctors' Decisions and the Cost of Medical Care.* Ann Arbor, Mich.: Health Administration Press Perspectives.

Ellwood, P. 1988. Outcomes management. A technology of patient experience. *New England Journal of Medicine* 318: 1549–56.

Enthoven, A. 1988. Managed competition: An agenda for action. *Health Affairs* 7: 25–47.

Fauman, M. A. 1990. Monitoring the quality of psychiatric care. *Psychiatric. Clin. North Am.* 13: 73–88.

Fink, A., E. M. Yano, and R. M. Brook. 1989. The condition of the literature on differences in hospital mortality. *Med. Care* 27: 315–36.

Finkler, S. A. 1982. The distinction between cost and charges. *Ann. Intern Medicine* 96: 102–09.

Fisher, J. H., II. 1989. Fraud and abuse in health care joint ventures. *Indiana Medicine* (April): 298–301.

GAO (General Accounting Office). 1988. *Medicare: Improving quality of care assessment and assurance.* Washington, D.C.: General Accounting Office.

Garvin, D. A. 1986. A note on quality: The views of Deming, Juran, and Crosby. Harvard Business School Note, pub. no. 9-687-011, Cambridge: Harvard College.

_____. 1988. *Managing quality. The strategy and competitive edge.* New York, NY: The Free Press.

Gaynes, M. J. 1989. Civil monetary penalties law: Mistakes could be (very) costly. *Texas Med.* 85 (May): 85–6.

Gerbert, B., et al. 1988. Agreement among physician assessment methods: Searching for the truth among fallible methods. *Med. Care*, 26: 519–35.

Ginsburg, P. and F. Hammons. Competition and the quality of care: The importance of information. *Inquiry* 25: 108–14.

Grassi, L. C. 1988. Life, money, quality: The impact of regionalization on perinatal/neonatal intensive care. *Neonat. Network* (February): 53–9.

Greenfield, S. 1988. The challenges and opportunities that quality assurance raises for technology assessment. In *Report of a Forum of the Council on Health Care Technology*, ed. K. N. Lohr and R. A. Rettig. Washington, D.C.: National Academy Press, 131–41.

Guncheon, K. F. 1982. Tracking computer fraud. Blue Cross plans girl to battle illegal claims. *Hospitals* (October 1): 106-9.

Hall, M. A. 1988. Making sense of referral fee statues. *J. Health Pol. Polic. Law.*

Hannan, E. L., et al. 1989. A methodology for targeting hospital cases for quality of care record reviews. *American Journal of Public Health* 79: 430–36.

Havighurst, C. C., and N. M. King. 1983. Private credentialing of health care personnel: An antitrust perspective. *Am. J. Law Med.* 9: 131–201.

HCFA. 1989. Technical notes. Peer review organization data summary (May 1989). Baltimore, Md.: Office of Peer Review, Health Standards, and Quality Bureau, Health Care Financing Administration.

Heinen, L., J. A. Gorski, and W. Roe. 1988. Quality of care research and projects in progress. *Health Affairs* 7: 145–50.

Hendershot, G. E. 1988. Health status and medical care utilization. *Health Affairs* 7: 114–21.

Hetherington, R. W. 1982. Quality assurance and organizational effectiveness in hospitals. *Health Serv. Res.* 17: 185–201.

Himelstein, D. U., S. Woolhandler, and D. H. Bor. 1988. Will cost effectiveness analysis worsen the cost effectiveness of health care? *Int. J. Health Serv.* 18: 1–9.

Hyman, D. A. and J. V. Williamson. 1989. Sounding board. Fraud and abuse: Setting the limits on physicians' entrepreneurship. *New England Journal of Medicine* 320 (10) (May 11): 1275–78.

Iglehart, J. K. 1988. Competition and the pursuit of quality: A conversation with Walter McClure. *Health Affairs* 7: 79–90.

Ishikawa, K. 1985. *What is total quality control? The Japanese way.* Englewood Cliffs, N.J.: Prentice-Hall.

Jenks, S. F., et al. 1988. Interpreting hospital mortality data. The role of clinical risk adjustment. *JAMA* 260: 3611–16.

Joint Commission (Joint Commission on Accreditation of Healthcare Organizations). 1988. *Field review evaluation form: Proposed principles of organizational and management effectiveness.* Chicago: Joint Commission on Accreditation of Healthcare Organizations.

Juran, J. M., F. M. Gyrna, and R. S. Bingham. 1988. *Quality control handbook.* 4th ed. Manchester, Mo.: McGraw-Hill.

Kanouse, D. E., et al. 1987. *Changing medical practice through technology assessment: An evaluation of the NIH consensus development program.* Santa Monica, Calif.: RAND.

Kaplan, B. 1988. Development and acceptance of medical information systems: An historical overview. *J. Health Hum. Res. Adm.* (Summer): 9–29.

King, B. 1989. *Hoshin planning: The developmental approach*. Methuen, Mass.: GOAL/QPC.

King, S. S. 1985. Impact of competition and cost containment on the university hospital. *Am. J. Cardiol.* 56: 27C–31C.

Kusserow, R. 1988. An interview with DHHS' Richard Kusserow: Weeding out fraud, waste, and abuse in health care. *Nurs. Econ.* 6 (6) (November–December): 287–90.

Landfeld, C. S. and L. Goldman. 1989. The autopsy in quality assurance: history, current status, and future directions. *Qual. Rev. Bull.* 15: 42–8.

Larson, E., L. F. Oram, and E. Hedrick. 1988. Nosocomial infection rates as an indicator of quality. *Med. Care* 26: 676–84.

Lehmann, R. 1989. Joint commission forum: Forum on clinical indicator development: A discussion of the use and development of indicators. *Qual. Rev. Bull.* 15: 223–27.

Lohr, K. N., ed. 1990. *Medicare. A strategy for quality assurance*. Vol. 1. Washington, D.C.: National Academy Press.

Lohr, K. N. and R. H. Brook. 1984. Quality assurance in medicine. *Am. Behav. Sci.* 27: 583-607.

Lohr, K. N., et al. 1985. *Impact of Medicare prospective payment on the quality of medical care: A research agenda*. Santa Monica, Calif.: RAND.

Lohr, K. N., K. D. Yordy, and S. O. Thier. 1988. Current issues in quality of care. *Health Affairs* 7: 5–18.

Longo, D. R., K. R. Ciccone, and J. T. Lord. 1989. *Integrated quality assessment. A model for concurrent review*. Chicago, Ill.: American Hospital Association.

Mayer, W., et al. 1988. A first report of the Department of Defense external civilian peer review of medical care. *JAMA* 260: 2690–93.

MBGH (Midwest Business Group on Health). 1989. *Value-managed health care purchasing: An employers guidebook series*. Chicago, Ill.: MBGH.

McCourt, A. E. 1987. Implementation of nursing diagnoses through integration with quality assurance. *Nurs. Clin. North Am.* 22: 899–904.

McLaughin, C. G., W. K. Zellers, and L. D. Brown. 1989. Health care coalitions: Characteristics, activities, and prospects. *Inquiry* 26: 72–83.

McDue, J. D., ed. 1989. *The medical cost containment crisis*. Ann Arbor, Mich.: Health Administration Press.

Merry, M. D. 1990a. Total quality management meets health care: Threat or opportunity? Opening address. American College of Physician Executive Annual Conference, San Antonio, Texas, May 16.

_____. 1990b. Total quality management for physicians: Translating the new paradigm. *QRB* 16: 101–05.

Meyer, C. M. 1988. How to recognize a kickback and avoid unwitting entanglement in the inspector general's net. *Col. Med.* (September 15): 370–71.

Meyer, H. 1989. Peer review's limits visible once again. *AMA News* (May 5): 1, 9–12.

Mizuno, S. 1988. *Managing for quality: The seven new QC tools.* Cambridge, Mass.: Productivity Press.

Moloney, T. W. and D. E. Rogers. 1989. Medical technology—A different view of the contentious debate over costs. *New England Journal of Medicine* 301: 1413–19.

Munoz, E., R. Soldano, A. Laughlin, I. B. Margolis, and L. Wise. 1986. Source of admission and cost: public hospitals face financial risk. *Am. J. Public Health* 76: 696–97.

Nelson, E. C. and D. M. Berwick. 1989. The measurement of health status in clinical practice. *Med. Care* (March supp.) S77–S90.

Neuhauser, D. 1971. *The relationship between administration activities and hospital performance.* Chicago: University of Chicago Center for Health Administrative Studies.

O'Leary, D. Quality assessment: Moving from theory to practice. *J. Am. Med. Soc.* 260: 1760.

ORD (Office of Research and Demonstrations). 1988. *Status report, research and demonstrations in health care financing.* Baltimore, Md.: Health Care Financing Administration.

Palmer, R. H. 1988. The challenges and prospects for quality assessment and assurance in ambulatory care. *Inquiry* 25: 119–31.

Paterson, M. L. 1988. The challenge to technology assessment: An industry viewpoint. In *Quality of care and technology assessment*, eds. K. N. Lohr and R. A. Rettig. Washington, D.C.: National Academy Press.

Paul-Shaheen, P., J. D. Clark, and D. Williams. 1987. Small area analysis: A review and analysis of the North American literature. *J. Health Pol. Law* 12: 741–809.

Payne, S. M. C. 1987. Identifying and managing inappropriate hospital utilizations: A policy synthesis. *Health Serv. Res.* 22: 709–69.

Pryor, D. B., et al. 1985. Clinical data bases: Accomplishments and unrealized potential. *Med. Care* 23: 623–47.

Read, J. L., R. J. Quin, and M. A. Hoefer. 1987. Measuring overall health: An evaluation of three important approaches. *J. Chronic Dis.* (supp. 1) 40: 7S–22S.

Rhee, S. O. 1983. Organizational determinants of medical care quality: A review of the literature. In *Organization and change in health care quality assurance*, eds. R. D. Luke, J. C. Krueger, and R. E. Modrow. Rockville, Md.: Aspen Systems Corporation, 127–46.

Richardson, F. M. 1972. Peer review of medical care. *Med. Care*, 10: 29–39.

Rocky, B. N. 1988. Practicing profiling. *Journal*, 54 (11) (November): 817–18.

Roper, W. L., and F. M. Hackbarth. 1988. Commentary: HCFA's agenda for promoting high-quality care. *Health Affairs* 7: 91–8.

Roper, W. L., et al. 1988. Effectiveness in health care. An initiative to evaluate and improve medical practice. *New England Journal of Medicine* 319: 1197–1202.

Ross, L. L., et al. 1989. Risk adjustment in claims-based research: The search for efficient approaches. *J. Clin. Epidemiol.*, 42: 1193–1206.

Schaffer, W. A., et al., Falsification of clinical credentials by physicians applying for ambulatory-staff privileges. *New England Journal of Medicine*.

Schieber, G. J. and J.P. Poullier. 1988. International health spending and utilization trends. *Health affairs* 7: 105–12.

Schroeder, S. A. 1987. Strategies for reducing medical costs by changing physician's behavior. *Int. J. Tech. Assess. Health Care* 3: 39–50.

Schroeder, S. A., et al. 1984. The failure of physician education as a cost containment strategy. Report of a perspective controlled trial at a university hospital. *JAMA* 252: 225–30.

Schwartz, W. B. 1987. The inevitable failure of current cost-containment strategies. *JAMA* 257: 220–24.

Schyve, P. M. and J. A. Prevost. 1990. From quality assurance to quality improvement. *Psychiatric. Clin. North Am.* 13: 61–71.

Steele, K., et al. 1981. Iatrogenic illness on a general medical service at a university hospital. *New England Journal of Medicine* 304: 638–41.

Steinwachs, D. M., J. P. Weiner, and S. Shapiro. Management information systems and quality. In *Providing quality care: The challenge to clinicians*, eds. N. Goldfield and D. D. Nash. Philadelphia: American College of Physicians.

Tarlov, A. R., J. E. Ware, S. Greenfield, E. C. Nelson, E. Perrin, and M. Zubkoff. 1989. The medical outcome study. An application of methods for monitoring the results of medical care. *JAMA* 262: 925–30.

Vladeck, B. C., E. J. Goodwin, L. P. Myers, and M. Sinisi. 1988. Consumers and hospitals: The HCFA 'death list'. *Health Affairs* 7: 122–25.

Warner, K. E., T. M. Wickizer, R. A. Wolfe, J. E. Schildroth, and M. H. Samuelson. 1988. Economic implications of workplace health promotion programs: Review of the literature. *J. Occup. Med.* 30: 106–12.

Weisman, C. S., et al. 1989. Practice changing in response to the malpractice litigation climate: Results of a Maryland physician survey. *Med. Care* 27: 16–24.

Wennberg, J. E., J. P. Bunker, and B. Barnes. 1980. The need for assessing the outcome of common medical practices. *Ann Rev. Public Health* 1: 277–95.

Williamson, J. W. 1986. Future policy directions for quality assurance: Lessons from the health accounting experience. *Inquiry* 25: 67–77.

Wilson, C. K. 1986. Strategies for monitoring the cost and quality of care. *J. Nurs. Qual. Assur.* 1: 55-65.

Zook, C. J., and F. D. Moore. 1980. High cost users of medical care. *New England Journal of Medicine*, 302: 996–1002.

13

Sustaining Excellence in the Twenty-First Century: A Vision and Strategies for the University of California's Administration

Richard N. Katz and
Richard P. West

Since 1988, the University of California Office of the President (UCOP) has considered establishing new campuses as a means of maintaining the university's historical enrollment commitments to the people of California. To support the overall planning efforts, the university's Site Selection Task Force established the New Campus Administrative Support and Ancillary Services Planning Group (task group) in April 1990.

In fulfilling one element of its charge, the task group submits for consideration a new version of administration. This vision is based on the task group's belief that the twenty-first century will place striking new demands on and offer unprecedented opportunities to UC's administration. The task group recognizes that the complexity, competitive climate (for faculty, funds, students), demographic upheaval, and event-driven character of the coming century require innovative organizational, technological, and operational solutions. The need to meet sharply increasing enrollment demand will accentuate this requirement.

The new vision of administration identifies a number of critical directions in the administrative and ancillary services. In addition, a number of strategies are suggested that will enable the administrative leadership of new UC campuses to influence campus culture in ways that leverage the organization's research, instructional, and public service mission.

Universities can no longer be characterized as "amiable, anarchic, self-correcting collectives of scholars with a small contingent of dignified caretakers at the unavoidable business edge"[1] Existing and planned University of California campuses will be large and complex organizations at the turn of the century. This complexity will be amplified by the increasing enrollment demands on the university, by the changing demographic makeup of the State of California, and by the increasing need to respond quickly to unexpected opportunities and events. Universities will be forced to compete increasingly for world-class faculty and funds to attract premier students and to fulfill the expectations of their constituencies.

UC is committed to fulfilling its teaching, research, and public service mission in world-class fashion. To create and sustain its leadership position in higher education, the university depends increasingly on its academic strategy, faculty and business acumen, and vision. This chapter proposes a new organizational vision for UC campuses in the twenty-first century and identifies a number of strategies required to achieve the vision.

A number of assumptions are made. First, it is assumed that outstanding administrative leadership can leverage a university's academic strategy by fostering a service-oriented culture to attract and retain faculty and program funds. Similarly, an administrative focus on timeliness, quality, and service can reduce the administrative demands on faculty permitting productivity gains in core areas of the university's mission. Third, it is assumed that the service and economic demands facing higher education institutions in the twenty-first century cannot be satisfied through the incremental addition of resources; significant changes must be made.

A number of recent events and trends support the assumed need for fundamental change. First, administration and support costs amount to approximately 30 percent of public education institutional expenditures.[2] These costs are the growth rate leaders in higher education owing to their labor-intensive cost structures.[3] The increased complexity faced by universities, posed by increasing regulation (e.g., environmental sponsored projects), anticipated rapid enrollment growth, and other factors, is increasing the volume and complexity of administrative transactions required. At the same time, tight budgets and increased public scrutiny and accountability constrain the ability to increase resources, principally staff, at the margin.[4]

While administrative service providers run harder to meet these increasing demands, the task group concludes that we are facing a time when the external environment is adding complexities to our world faster than we can implement improvements at the margin to offset them. Unabated, the evolving gap between transactions and labor inputs carries at least three major risks: erosion of service quality; loss of financial and administrative control; and diversion of resources from academic to administrative activities.

All of these risks, as argued above, threaten to undermine the university's mission. The strategies proposed are optimized for working smarter (and harder). See Figure 13.1.

Figure 13.1. Compound Growth in Selected Transactions and Staff Since 1980

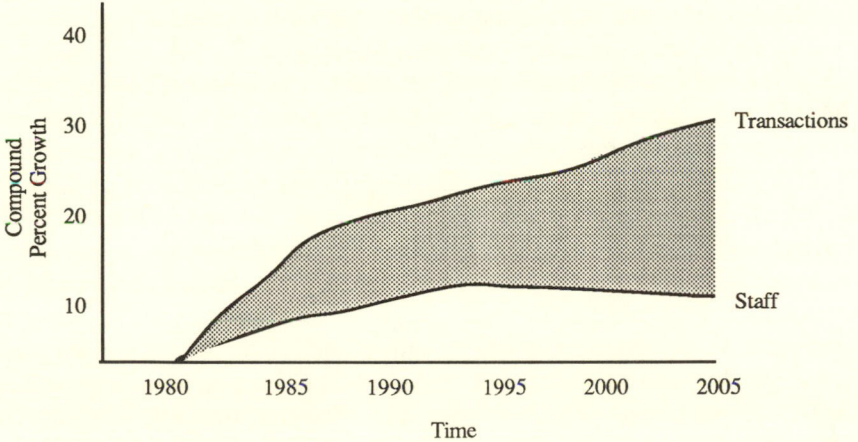

Note: Qualitative inference from selected readings

Two additional trends reinforce the conclusion that planners of new UC campuses must organize their efforts around a new vision of administration. The preceding discussion describes the increasing dichotomy between administrative demands and resources. This discussion focuses on the administrative environment in what physicists and engineers refer to as its steady state. More and more, the university has been subject to unanticipated extranormal impositions and opportunities at an increasingly regular rate. Such "shocks" are typically financial (e.g., Proposition. 13, Proposition. 111, budget crisis), but can be regulatory (e.g., CEQA, Clean Air Act, IRC Section 89), natural (e.g., earthquake, water shortage, waste disposal), programmatic (e.g., Superconducting Supercollider, Human Genome Project), or other (e.g., union elections).

While such shocks to the university's operations have always occurred, their frequency has increased. These shocks divert already scarce administrative resources, particularly senior management, and create additional risk. New administrative cultures, organizations, and control systems must be configured to respond rapidly to unplanned crises and opportunities.

The final trend adds additional urgency to the call for fundamental change. As traditionally labor-intensive organizations, universities are particularly sensitive to demographic change. Demographic trends are precipitating sweeping changes throughout California. Within this planning horizon, trends in population migration, birth rates, aging, and death rates will combine to reshape the composition of the university's workforce and student body. Labor shortages, in particular, will underscore the need for a new administrative vision and supporting strategies.[5]

The California labor market will be shaped by the aging of the population, the in-migration of unprecedented numbers of both highly educated and illiterate foreign nationals, and the continued entry of women into all levels of the workforce. These trends will reinforce the need for university programs that support historically underrepresented classes of employees. New programs must also be developed to leverage the strengths of an increasingly diverse workforce. Shortages of entry-level workers are likely, while an increasingly healthy older work group is likely to remain in the workforce beyond today's customary retirement age.[6] The student population will reflect these demographic trends. Student facilities and support services must be planned in the context of this increasing diversity. English will be a second language for a significant number of UC students. While adult education is not a part of UC's core educational mission, older students will be increasingly commonplace as higher skill levels are sought in the labor market.

A higher percentage of small businesses will be owned and operated by women and minorities. State and extramural funding will continue to reinforce the policy objective of ensuring that women and minority business owners receive an equitable slice of the pie. Innovative programs and systems to support this policy objective will be needed.

A SERVICE-ORIENTED ADMINISTRATIVE CULTURE

For administrative and ancillary services to realize their full positive impact, they must be organized around service. Because many ancillary services compete for university business, these activities are often well equipped with the skills and tools needed to deliver quality service. The more classical business services of the university (e.g., accounting, personnel, etc.) are often organized around an internal control model and only incidentally around service. As controls are implemented increasingly through information systems, the value added by administrative units should be their ability to leverage faculty time and productivity through improvements in service.

Currently, the administration's ability to provide optimal service is constrained by two interdependent tendencies: high employee specialization and a complex procedural environment. The resolution of administrative concerns often requires departmental administrators to contact numerous service providers in a time-consuming search for expertise. The high levels of technical specialization imbedded in current operations exacerbate this requirement. The trend toward specialization creates organizational biases that favor long-time departmental personnel whose chief strengths lie in the extensive historical knowledge of key players. A system of reciprocal favors drives a significant amount of administrative behavior. These exception-based favors generally slow the flow of campus administrative transactions, except for those who "play the system."

The current procedural environment, which requires multiple approvals of transactions (salary actions, expenditures), is highly dependent on paper and forms, resulting in tremendous amounts of institutional waiting time. Long waits for service are unproductive and create negative perceptions about service providers.

To shift the orientation of the administrative units toward service, it should be recognized formally that the faculty, students, chancellor, alumnae, governmental authorities, and other administrative units are the "constituents" of the administration. In particular, administrative systems and operations should be integrated and optimized from the viewpoint of the academic department administrator. Too often, departmental administrators face a maze of conflicting procedural requirements, forms, and apparent obstructions from unintegrated administrative units. Multiple approval requirements for commonplace personnel, purchasing, or other transactions cause substantial delays and miscommunications resulting in a high frustration level among campus "constituents." Significantly, not all of these control-based administrative impositions reduce financial risk. Some, on occasion, generate actions by end users to circumvent both the impositions and the controls.

The implementation of information technologies and approaches will go far in promoting service to the campus. Many information technologies, properly implemented, have been shown to improve the quality of service, while lowering costs at the same time. New intelligent voice processing systems, for example, are becoming an increasingly commonplace element in the administrative landscape. Within this planning horizon, systems such as voicemail and automatic call distribution will be ubiquitous. As in data communications, the increased benefit in the area of these new voice technologies will be realized in the data management function. The need for standards will be essential. Future campus administrative leaders should seek to define and manage one consistent voice system interface across administrative functions and ancillary services. Emphasis in training should be placed on call management strategies that optimize ease of use and problem resolution.

Another promising information technology is the capability to authorize transactions electronically. Such a capability can eliminate significant processing time by eliminating the need to route and manage forms throughout the campus.

Most service providers argue that the keys to creating a service culture are to "get close to the customer," and to reward employees for service-enhancing efforts. The new vision of administration, to be described, is an organizational model and capability that is configured to get service providers and consumers closer together. A number of supporting strategies are offered as means of enabling leaders to sustain a service culture.

REAL PRODUCTIVITY GAINS WILL REQUIRE SUBSTANTIAL CHANGE

In addition to the need to create and sustain a service-oriented culture, the trends identified and the resulting dilemma suggest the need for a major institutionally supported commitment to increasing administrative productivity at the University of California. In support of the university's institution, research, and public service mission, the institution's administrative leadership must craft a productivity-enhancing vision that promotes:

- excellent leadership and management across all organizational levels

- the creation of mechanisms to stimulate ideas and generate a continuous stream of leadership

- an administrative infrastructure that will support competent management and allow early detection of problems and opportunities

As in the case of the service environment, administrative productivity at the University of California is constrained by: (1) a complex (and occasionally conflicting) policy environment; (2) a reliance on paper and forms to mediate and document transactions; (3) technical, organizational, and other barriers separating central administrative units and departments; and

(4) a dependence on unintegrated batch central systems. The productivity leakages from this closed system are self-evident. The layering of administrative policies and procedures creates additional work and complexity. This complexity is mitigated, in part, by additions of staff, local systems, and forms. To maintain administrative control, additional administrative approvals are required. This pattern of administrative response degrades productivity by:

- necessitating the creation and management of duplicate data to meet information and decision-support needs

- creating unnecessary data reconciliation activities to maintain the integrity of institutional and departmental data

- increasing waiting times by relying on forms to facilitate an approval process (transit time)

- increasing necessary, but unproductive, filing and retrieval activities

- necessitating regular, periodic error checking due to batch processing requirements (limited error checking at entry point)

As productivity continues to degrade the marginal additions of new policies, staff, forms, and controls become self-perpetuating. Only with the application of fundamentally different information technology, and human resources and operational strategies to support a new organizational vision, can real gains in productivity be achieved. See Table 13.1.

Current administrative and ancillary services are configured in a bureaucratic fashion. A bureaucracy is an authority system that governs transactions under ambiguous conditions by creating employment contacts.[7] Close monitoring of employee performance is central to the governance of bureaucracies.[8] Because of their dependence on close monitoring of employee performance, bureaucratic organizations respond to complexity by adding layers to the organization in order to preserve relatively narrow spans of control. The successive layering of reporting levels impairs and slows the flow of information and actions through vertical chains of command. Information flows across organizations can be incomplete or, in some cases, nonexistent. Universities, as information-intensive enterprises, are particularly dependent on prompt and accurate information exchanges. Communication failures degrade productivity, increase errors, and jeopardize service delivery.

In addition, university bureaucracies—which are particularly labor-intensive—are highly subject to both "cost disease" and "growth force." The cost disease stems from the inevitable rise in unit support costs as student-faculty ratios are held constant. The growth force "drives up budgets even faster than cost-rise because of program additions and reluctance to reallocate money from old programs."[9]

Table 13.1. A Bureaucracy versus a Network Organization

Existing Environment (Bureaucratic)	Proposed Vision (Network)
Central administration is focus	Department is focus
Reliance on policy, procedure	Guidelines and accountabilities
Specific and narrow delegations of authority at high institutional level	Delegations at lowest competent level
Labor is specialized	Emphasis on generalists
Rewards for individual performance	Rewards for team performance
Fragmented central services	Integration of operations
Answer shopping	One-step shopping
Small span of control	Large span of control
Deep hierarchy	Shallow hierarchy (flat)
Focus on function optimization	Focus on system optimization
Civil service culture	Service culture
Rewards for working hard	Rewards for achieving defined objectives
Merit pay for professionals	Merit pay for all (where possible)

To meet the increasing demands posed by external events, transaction creep, and changing demographic conditions, new campus planners are offered for consideration an alternative vision to the existing bureaucratic model. Already in place in many private corporations, this vision can be referred to as the "network" organization.

The network model views the organization as an information system and recognizes that key information flows across the lines of traditional hierarchies. The network model is described in many ways. Business consultant Tom Peters discusses "flattening the organization," while Lehigh University President Peter Likins argues for "managing less."

The network organization eliminates levels of hierarchy by empowering managers and staffs with greater authority and span of control. The more charismatic leadership styles enabled by a smaller control span are replaced, in part, by controls embedded within information systems. Responsibility and authority, in network organizations, are delegated to the lowest competent level. In the UC framework, decision-making authority would reside in the departments for most day-to-day operations.

To succeed, the network organization depends on a sophisticated information infrastructure and outstanding personnel programs.

Another major element of network organizations is the substantial reliance of such organizations on outsourcing as a competitive and cost containment strategy. In the extreme case, enterprises have become "hollow"; that is, have contracted for most of the operational activities such as manufacturing, marketing, and so on. In the higher education context, administrative leaders need to develop a model to support outsourcing decisions in a systematic fashion.

The network model is an organizational vision and form that is optimized for flexibility, speed, and service. In this vision, the administration of new UC campuses will need to be comprised of sophisticated problem solvers who have easy access to their "customers" and the authority to act. Where multilayer hierarchies can diffuse accountability for decisions and actions and retard the flow of critical information and decisions, network organizations eliminate layers of hierarchy through the use of sophisticated information technologies and control processes. In this vision, central administration provides general administrative leadership by undertaking "strategic thinking" and by developing policies and guidelines for the conduct of campus business. Emphasis in this new environment is on control and accountability, not on procedure.

For the network organization to succeed, the personnel programs of the campus must recognize explicitly the need for talent at the lowest decision-making level. These programs must be configured to recruit, develop, and reward departmentally based employees. Employee training is a key element of the empowerment process. The empowering of the individual is best accomplished by the central administration's aggressive management of an organizational culture that stresses collaboration, merit pay, and management by objectives.

Another attribute of the network organization is the relative geographic independence of administrative units. Traditionally, campus administrative functions are clustered together as a means of achieving organizational integrity through geographic proximity. As in the case of vertically organized corporations, organizations of this character can foster the growth of the segregated fiefdoms that while self-optimizing, are typically suboptimal from the institutional perspective.

In addition to providing the information-processing capabilities needed by a twenty-first century campus, the network organization enables campus leaders to develop and foster a service culture. By establishing departments as the centers of administrative operations, effort is directed at enhancing productivity at service points where the administrative and academic environments intersect. The active management of the service culture, through enabling strategies described below, can leverage both the academic strategy and faculty time in direct support of the university's mission.

To enable the network vision of the administrative organization of the university, a number of strategies must be employed. Elements of the strategic environment that precondition the successful adoption of this vision include:

- an information technology strategy

- institutional business partnerships

- operational integration

- a human resources strategy

INFORMATION TECHNOLOGY STRATEGY

One strategy that is central to the achievement of the university's productivity goals and that preconditions the establishment of a network organization is an information technology strategy. In order to shift the locus of administrative activity to the departmental level, where services are typically consumed, departmental administrative staff require easy access to central campus administrative choices. To create this access, an information technology strategy is proposed. This strategy has four major elements:

- access to all appropriate central administrative systems via networks

- distributed online transaction processing capabilities with a common interface between departments and central systems
- integration of appropriate central systems
- deployment of paper-reducing technologies where cost-effective

An idealized evolutionary path that represents the implementation of this strategy is reflected in Figure 13.2.

Central to the overall information technology is the development and management of the campus local area network (LAN). Universal access to the LAN by administrative (departmental and central) employees, students, faculty, vendors, and others will help define the future administrative landscape.

The need for widespread access to high-volume transaction processing administrative systems dictates a major emphasis on campus network development as a necessary element of infrastructure. In this planning horizon, the size of administrative systems, the introduction of remote multimedia access, and the pricing trends in hardware, software, and cable suggest a commitment to campuswide use of fiber optics. Distribution of fiber optic cable should be planned to every administrative workstation, dormitory, and student service facility. In addition, campus access to external networks to promote cost-effective relations with schools, vendors, and other UC computing resources will be essential.

The second element of the information technology strategy suggests commitments to and investments in online transaction processing capabilities. Online transaction processing across administrative systems can lower the costs of administration by eliminating redundant recordkeeping. In cases where data in central batch systems is not current, departments turn to stand-alone systems to meet their information needs between central processing cycles. This leads to duplicate entry of information between central processing cycles, which adds measurably to campus productivity losses. In addition, disparate central information systems require specialization among departmental staff due to differences in the systems' technical design and approaches. A unified and consistent view of the central administration would not require the conversion of existing systems, and would increase productivity by lowering unit training costs and permitting the evolution of departmental generalists (empowerment).

The next logical element of this strategy is the integration of appropriate systems. Comprehensive enrollment management, an essential element of the university's competitive and service strategies, can be enabled once admissions, financial aid, class enrollment, and other systems are integrated. The integration of these systems with those of other higher education segments and schools may enable further improvements in productivity and service delivery. Integration of information systems will reduce further the volume of transactions by eliminating redundancies and reconciliations while increasing the quality of institutional data.

The fourth element of the information technology strategy is the deployment of new paper-reducing technologies. Paper-based transactions continue to account for nearly 50 percent of administrative transactions. More important, they account for nearly 80 percent of the clerical effort. Transactions requiring paper can be performed by only one person at a time, adding considerable time and transit expense to administrative activities at the expense of service. The implementation of electronic authorizations, imaging, and electronic data interchange (EDI) will make significant productivity improvements possible.

The implementation of the information technology strategy will enable the elimination of organizational levels by delivering ubiquitous access among interdependent staff, departments, and supervisors. The organizational spans of control can be increased by empowering staff to perform more transactions

Figure 13.2. Implementation of an Information Technology Strategy

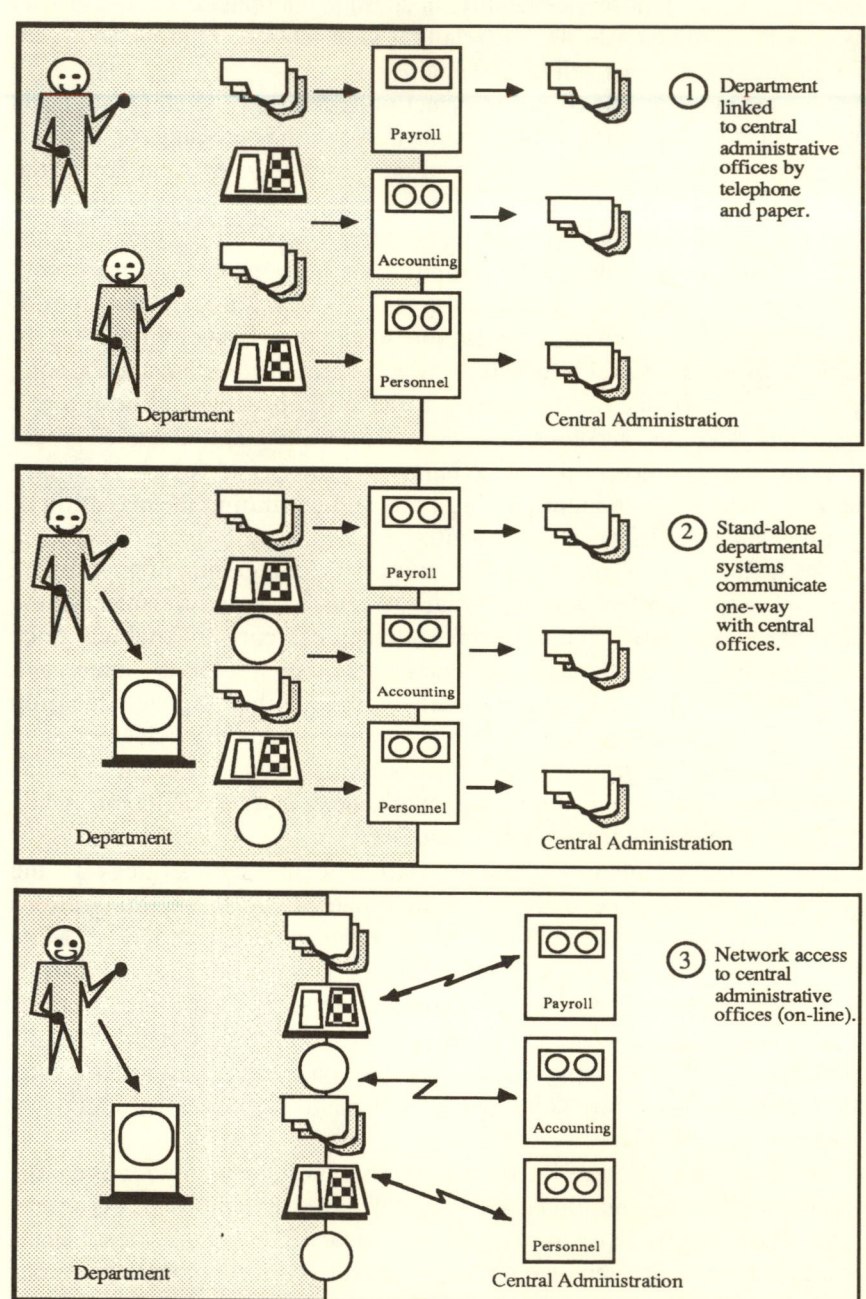

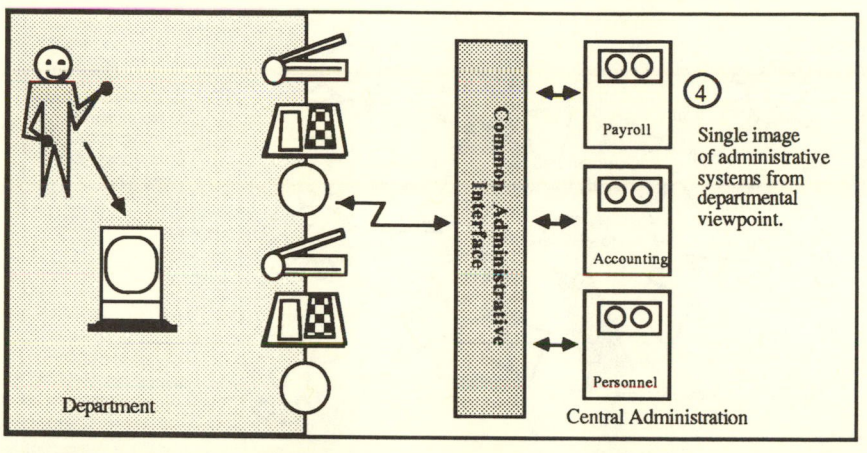

④ Single image of administrative systems from departmental viewpoint.

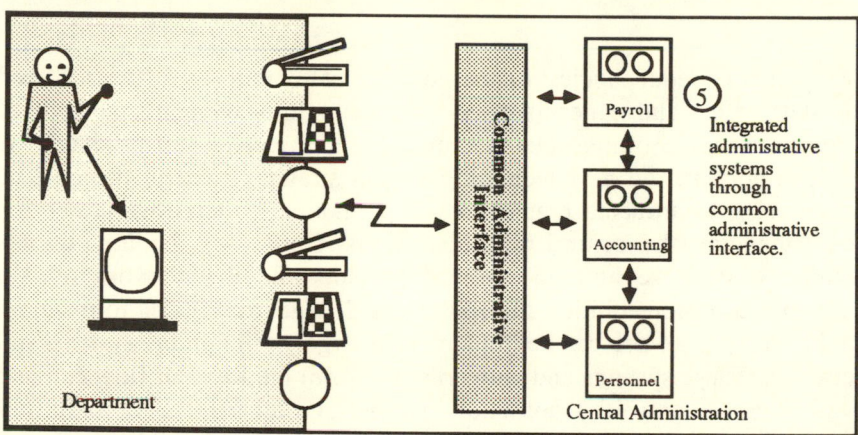

⑤ Integrated administrative systems through common administrative interface.

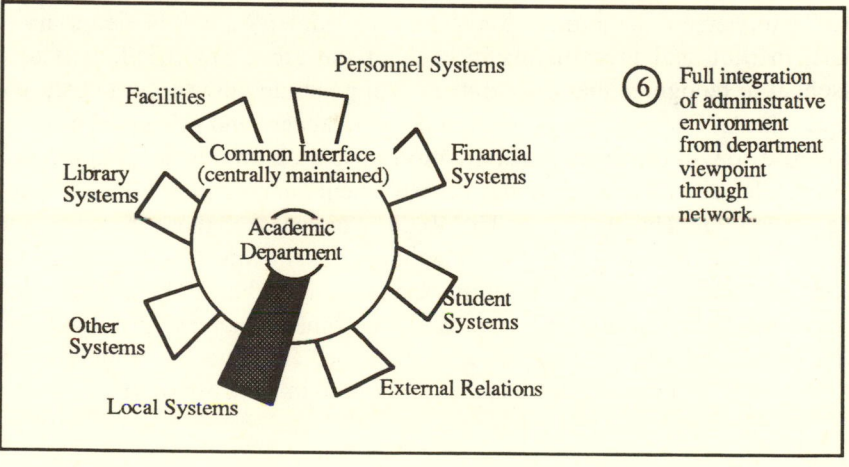

⑥ Full integration of administrative environment from department viewpoint through network.

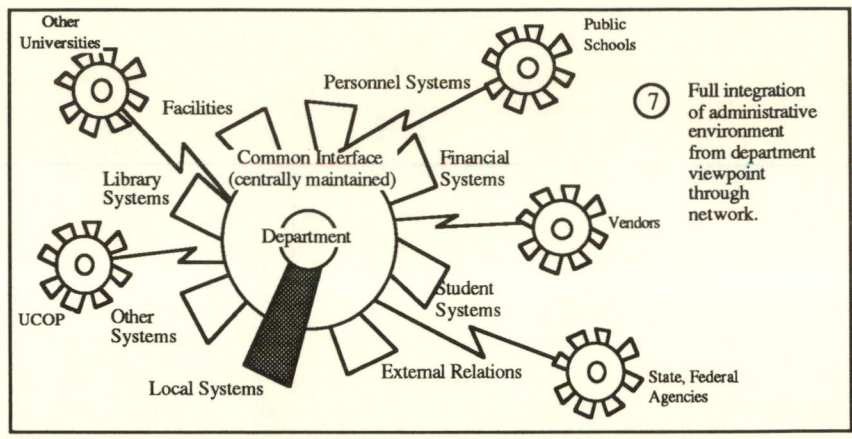

by eliminating redundancies. Improved data quality reduces further the need for staff effort and supervisory intervention. Improvements in activity throughput reduce timing-related complaints to the benefit of productivity. Most important, the new technologies and strategy achieve the goal of empowering departmental employees and promoting service while preserving and enhancing the central administrations' control of the institution's resources. Because both the central systems and the network remain institutional responsibilities, the controls and standards needed to maintain quality and reduce risk can be implemented largely through the systems and networks. These systems and networks will form the locus of financial and administrative controls. Transaction histories and other forms of audit trail should be maintained in machine-readable form wherever possible.

To implement the information technology strategy it will be necessary to make institutional investments in each of the areas identified. It is also essential to recognize that this strategy will generate new support costs and requirements. For example, improved network access and price/performance of hardware will diminish the contention for computing cycles and the unit cost of administrative computing. Improvements in software will occur, but at a generally much slower rate. The ubiquity of access to these resources and the complexity of new mixed media technologies, however, will enhance the need for standards and the difficulty of maintaining them. The organization and administration of institutional data will become an increasingly significant area of administrative concern and expense. Information management professionals will become increasingly important in this environment.

While the unit cost of hardware maintenance will decrease due to ongoing manufacturing improvements and shorter technology lifecycles, total costs in this area will rise significantly. The cost of maintaining the university's software environment is likely to rise significantly. New funding strategies must be developed to support these anticipated requirements.

Similarly, while advances in end user interfaces will reduce individual training costs, overall administrative requirements in the training area will rise.

Administrative leaders must concentrate attention on managing the economic and technical lives of the campus technology base. The rapid obsolescence of hardware and software will create significant heterogeneity in the technology base and will exacerbate the maintenance and training requirements.

INSTITUTIONAL BUSINESS PARTNERSHIPS

Another activity that supports the goals of maximizing flexibility to handle rapid campus growth and meet the demands of unplanned events is the strategic management of UC's business partnerships. The elements of the strategy in this area of activity include a systematic approach to producing or acquiring goods and services and strategic alliances.

Increasingly, as a means of controlling costs and achieving maximum management flexibility, organizations are looking to third parties to supply many administrative services previously operating in-house. Universities are becoming increasingly aware of this opportunity.

Outsourcing administrative services is particularly important as a potential element of the initiation strategy for new UC campuses. New campus planners need to develop an analytic model for making outsourcing decisions on a systematic basis. One model, developed by UC Berkeley economist Oliver Williamson, identifies a framework for making the outsourcing decision based on transaction costs.[10] In this model, frequently occurring and nonspecific activities, such as fleet services, reprographics, and others, should be outsourced. Activities that are unique to the university, such as employee relations, should be operated in-house. Infrequently performed tasks of a somewhat specific nature might be performed by a vendor operating under a sole source agreement. (See Table 13.2.) Executive recruiting might be such an activity.

A considerable shift toward reliance on outsourcing will underscore the need for strong on-campus contract administration skills. Strategies for recruiting and developing outstanding contract administrators are needed.

Outsourcing is a particularly important enabler of the network organizational vision because the judicious use of third-parties supports increased spans of control by leveraging staff. Fewer managers are needed to administer third-party contracts than to manage operations directly. While the decision to outsource should remain the responsibility of operating management, institutional guidelines should be established and monitored to ensure that economic analyses are performed regularly. Due to personnel considerations, it is considerably easier to import a service performed initially by vendors than to privatize an activity performed in-house.

Figure 13.3. Asset/Service/Activity Matrix

		Asset/Service/Activity Characteristics		
		Nonspecific	Mixed	Idiosyncratic
Frequency	Occasional	Use Commercial Provider	Contracts	Contracts
	Recurrent	Use Commercial Provider	Joint Ventures Affiliation Agreements, etc.	Perform Internally

The ability to create and operate an administrative environment that relies more heavily on outsourcing will be enhanced by strategic alliances with vendors, other universities, schools, and others. These alliances will be enabled by new technologies such as EDI and by access to external networks. Owing to its size, purchasing power, and faculty, the University of California has long been an attractive business partner. Strategies should be developed to leverage this strong competitive position.

A strategy for creating partnerships with private firms could include joint studies, such as those currently employed with IBM and Digital. These studies often exchange university expertise and technology for financial support and grants of equipment.

In administrative areas that indicate a fair level of specificity and a high degree of activity recurrence, decision makers should contemplate new bilateral relations, such as joint ventures, with vendors. Technology can be used in this area to create university-specific advantages in key service areas. For example, a joint venture with Hertz for automobile renting might include online access to Hertz reservation systems and electronic billing through EDI.

Connectivity to external systems may also create additional purchasing power by creating the potential for integrated purchasing collectives.

OPERATIONAL INTEGRATION

Another essential strategy to support the network organization and service culture is operational integration. New information technology will enable future campus leaders to optimize multifunctional clusters of interrelated activities (e.g., financial aid, registration, housing). In addition, to design administrative and ancillary service operations that optimize for quality, throughput, and flexibility without sacrificing standards and controls, individual and organizational responsibilities require clarification and standardization at all levels. Interdependencies among administrative units should be identified (payroll, personnel, accounting, information systems) and the linkage between units should be strengthened. Strategies that foster such linkages might include ongoing cross-functional teams; physical siting strategies; team oriented reward systems; encouragement of cross-functional transfer career development; and others. Well-integrated cross-functional units are considered to be highly effective information processors and disseminators.

Operations should be configured to create a unified view of services from the departmental viewpoint. Again, this requirement will be satisfied, in part, by developing standard user interfaces in information systems. Such standardization must be accompanied by ongoing efforts to eliminate redundancies and to create and implement campuswide performance standards.

Standards and controls must be articulated at all levels of the campus. The capability for periodic and ongoing assessments of service against established criteria and benchmarks should be a planned element of the administrative and ancillary services infrastructure.

One specific operational strategy that fosters both productivity and service is referred to as fast-cycle capabilities. Fast cycle processing is an organizational capability and a level of performance that management shapes and builds into the organization's operating system and the attitudes of its employees. Fast-cycle capability optimizes organizational activities across the dimension of time by designing and enforcing organizations that perform without bottlenecks, delays, and errors.

Fast-cycle organizations are highly integrated systems in which operational units are linked. They make the main flow of operations visible and comprehensible to all employees and compensate, to a large extent, on the basis of group success. The systemic nature of the organization is reinforced in the operations and systems architecture.

In the context of existing UC organizations, increasing use is made of multifunctional teams to collapse time requirements in projects. Such teams assimilate the specialized functional knowledge of team members and incorporate and reconcile cross-functional perspectives at the stage of project definition and design. In fast-cycle organizations multifunctional teams are used for everyday work at all levels, not just for special projects. Reward systems are configured to recognize team results.

Fast cycle organizations emphasize breadth of knowledge among their employees and use time as the critical performance measure. Responsibility for actions is placed as far down in the organization as possible. The organization charts of fast-cycle organizations resemble closely a system flow chart with arrows and feedback loops indicating the actual paths of decisions and work.

HUMAN RESOURCES STRATEGY

To achieve maximum flexibility, the administration of new UC campuses will need to be comprised of sophisticated problem solvers who have easy access to their "customers" and the authority to act. Multilayer hierarchies can diffuse accountability for decisions and actions and retard the throughput of critical information and decisions.

New network technology will make it possible to flatten the future campus administrative organization. Central administration, in this vision, provides general administrative leadership by developing policies and guidelines for the administrative conduct of business. Emphasis in this new environment is on control and accountability, not on procedure.

In addition to relying on information technology, partnership strategies, and operational integration, campus leadership must develop human resources strategies and programs to reinforce service norms and maintain productivity. Key enabling elements of a strategic human resources strategy include:

- accountability systems

- organization design

- staff and management development

- reward systems

The accountability system includes the campus's policies, controls, procedures, delegations, and evaluation systems. Productivity is degraded, in part, by the accretion of unnecessary tasks. Such accretion occurs for many reasons, such as the organization's tendency "to institute procedures to correct new problems without going back periodically and asking how the set of procedures may be pruned."[11] The continual layering of new procedures to address new problems will in time degrade productivity. Administrative leaders must monitor and manage the accountability systems and align these systems with the campus's service and control objectives. In spite of the fact that new information technology will enable many service improvements while enhancing controls, hard tradeoff decisions will continue to be needed. Building bigger mousetraps to catch smaller mice will, over time, undermine the network organization and service culture.

A second element of this strategy is organizational design. Network organizations should be designed to reflect the following:

- increased dependence on generalists

- uniformity of job descriptions, by function, across departments;

- deeper delegations of authority

- formal recognition of nonfunction specific teams as organizational entities

- explicit and participative succession planning.

While human resources professionals may provide technical support to these activities, responsibilities for organizational design is a line management and, in particular, cabinet-level responsibility.

The oversight and refinement of programs and controls in these six areas will provide the organizational energy needed to maintain the benefits of the network form and service culture.

While not synonymous, employee development and training are essential to enable the continual delegation of responsibility to the lowest competent level (empowerment). As new programs, systems, and initiatives are pursued, training costs must be anticipated and resources identified. Untrained employees cannot be empowered. The orientation of employees should not be constrained by function and should anticipate functional interdependencies and employee participation in cross-functional workgroups.

Reward systems are key elements of any strategic human resources strategy. In the network organizational model, rewards must recognize:

- level of accountability

- attainment of defined objectives

- contribution to team efforts
- quality of services delivered

Formal reward systems, where possible, should be merit pay-based. In addition, most studies indicate a strong correlation between motivation and nonpecuniary rewards. Informal recognition programs should be established at all organizational levels. Rewards need to be tied closely to the evaluation system and to the institutional service and productivity goals and set within the network framework. Criteria for rewarding performance might include the following:

- Suggested/developed a system or process that improved the quality, service, and/or productivity of work.

- Suggested/developed a work simplification system or process.

- Developed a creative solution to meet the needs of a client or department.

- Increased job knowledge by voluntarily participating in cross-training.

- Exhibited tact and diplomacy in dealing with faculty, staff, or outside community on a sensitive issue beyond normal scope of job.

- Made a difficult decision using sound judgment and reasoning and carefully weighing alternatives.

- Consistently promoting teamwork by help and cooperation outside of requirements.[12]

NOTES

1. George Keller, *Academic Strategy: The Management Revolution in Higher Education* (Baltimore: Johns Hopkins University Press, 1983), pp. viii–ix.

2. Arthur M. Hauptman, "Why are College Charges Increasing?: Looking into Various Explanations" (Working draft to College Board, 1989).

3. *Digest of Educational Statistics,* 1988.

4. Peter Likins, "In an Era of Tight Budgets and Public Criticism, Colleges Must Rethink their Goals and Priorities," *Chronicle of Higher Education,* (May 1990).

5. Gilbert Fuchsberg, "Many Businesses Responding too Slowly to Rapid Work Force Shifts," *Wall Street Journal,* July 13, 1990.

6. U.S. Department of Labor; and *Workforce 2000: Work and Workers for the 21st Century* (Hudson Institute, 1987).

7. Max Weber, "Three Types of Legitimate Rule," 1922; translated in 1953 and published in the *Berkeley Journal of Sociology*.

8. Alan Wilkens and William Ouchi, "Efficient Cultures: Exploring the Relationship between Culture and Organizational Performance," *Administrative Science Quarterly* 28 (1983): 470.

9. William F. Massy, "Productivity Improvement Strategies for College and University Administration and Support Services," a presentation to the Forum for College Financing, 1989, p. 2.

10. Oliver Williamson, *Transaction Cost Economics*.

11. Massy, *Improvement Strategies.*, p. 7.

12. Ibid., p. 25.

14

Strategic Alliances
for Japanese
Mid-Sized Firms

Robert Lawrence Kuhn

Large Japanese corporations have been making substantial investments in the United States and these investments have attracted a great deal of media attention. This chapter considers Japanese *mid-sized* firms, a neglected and misunderstood class of economic enterprise, and suggests a new approach to their required globalization.

The business world of tomorrow, with rapidly changing international markets, may favor such smaller enterprises. No longer is bigger always better; no longer does increasing size always mean increasing success. In emerging segments of many markets, consumer and industrial, medium size is a competitive advantage.[1]

MID-SIZED COMPANIES

The fact that mid-sized firms can outperform their larger rivals may come as a surprise. The conventional wisdom that always equates high market share with high ultimate profits may be flawed.

First, consider the increasing "narrowcasting" of consumer demand. The fact that contemporary consumers require extremely specific products generates a proliferation of products and services, with these trends being fueled by the enormous variety of media information (such as specialty magazines). Here medium-sized companies have more flexibility to change and shift product lines, and they do not need the immense production runs required by immense production facilities.

Second, many creative and innovative workers, managers, and production workers as well as scientists and engineers, desire closer contact with their firms' products and services. Mid-sized firms offer these valuable personnel the best employment and personal fulfillment.

But mid-sized companies can be dangerously overpowered by their large-sized rivals, especially in highly competitive markets increasingly dependent on international investments. In addition, Japanese mid-sized firms are vulnerable to the combined threat of their large customers going overseas while domestic markets are being forced open to increased competition.

Japanese mid-sized firms must develop independent, special, international investment strategies. The formation of strategic alliances—especially with similar mid-sized companies in the United States—is essential.

STRATEGIC ALLIANCES

Many Japanese companies are discovering the benefits of creating strong business relationships with U.S. corporations. Such connections between Japanese and American firms, which can be structured with great variety and innovativeness to adapt to individual circumstances, are "strategic alliances."

Strategic alliances are exceedingly important for Japanese companies today, and they will become even more so as we approach and enter the twenty-first century. Strategic alliances are formed for various reasons, such as marketing and distribution, technology development and transfer, raw materials sourcing, and manufacturing and production. Strategic alliances are especially critical for Japanese mid-sized firms that lack the depth of management to own foreign companies.

INVESTMENT OPTIONS AND ALTERNATIVES

In a *total acquisition,* the foreign company becomes a wholly owned subsidiary. Although merger and acquisition activity is typical, serious problems can arise, especially with mid-sized firms. Management incentive for the U.S. side, and management control for the Japanese side, are primary issues.

In a *majority ownership* the foreign shareholders retain some ownership but not control. This structure is often used when local managers are given ownership as incentives.

In a *minority ownership* the foreign shareholders retain control, while the legal and operating structure assures that the Japanese company will achieve its strategic objectives. This is the typical strategic alliance structure where the Japanese company has a specific business motivation for the association (such as technology transfer).

In a *joint venture* the Japanese and U.S. company form a new entity, often owned equally, with each partner contributing strengths. For example, Japanese manufacturing may be combined with U.S. marketing.

In a *corporate investment* the Japanese company makes investments in highly specific projects such as a new product class, a particular technology, one production plant, or marketing arrangements.

In a *fund investment* the Japanese company makes investments in funds that offer a portfolio of carefully targeted companies and industry areas. Participation in various companies and learning the buyout business as well as financial return is the motivation.

In a *venture capital investment* the Japanese company invests in a high-quality venture capital fund. Such a fund may make twenty or more investments in a diverse number of innovative technologies. Firms that invest in such venture capital portfolios are often looking for a "window" through which they can view critical state-of-the-art technologies important for their future success in addition to the expected high rate of financial return.

Each of the above general structures can be designed and crafted to meet the most exacting requirements of Japanese mid-sized firms. Advance planning must be both strategic and specific. Extremely thorough requirements should be established and spelled out. Managerial issues are particularly important. Careful attention to detail, *before* the investment is made, is vital.

BUILDING DOMESTIC MARKETS

After emerging in the 1980s with abundant financial resources, unprecedented in recent history, Japanese companies have been shocked by extreme volatility in the financial markets. From world domination to financial turmoil, the sudden shifts, in both directions seem, to occur with stunning surprise. The point is clear: Volatility and turbulence dominate modern economics and the only way to deal with such unrelenting uncertainty is strategic planning.

Financial resources demand optimum utilization. Resources that are underutilized are resources that erode, and Japanese companies must adapt quickly to the odd combination of financial power on the one hand and unhealthy dependency on volatile domestic markets on the other. Large Japanese corporations have begun to use international diversification as a primary strategy for survival. It is even more vital that Japanese mid-sized firms consider investment opportunities in the United States.

SERVING THE JAPANESE MARKET

We are working with a Japanese bank that is concerned about the long-term prospects of an important client, a long-established domestic manufacturer with a good name and excellent distribution channels in Japan. While the company has substantial financial resources (through real estate holdings), revenues have leveled off and profitability has been eroded severely in recent years. The bank is concerned not about its credit position, which is secure due to the real estate, but about the long-term viability of an important client.

The company's market position is slipping due, primarily, to a product line that is solid and reliable but uninteresting and unresponsive to dynamic change in its customers' desires. Dull products, even if steady, do not work in this increasingly fashion-conscious industry segment anymore. This company needs exciting, energetic products, but does not seem to be able to create them itself. Although this is a large mid-sized company whose revenues are measured in the hundreds of oku yen per year (one oku yen is 100 million yen or about $770,000 U.S. at an exchange rate of 130 yen to the dollar), it does little international marketing and hence is not energized by world competition. The result is a lack of competitive edge even in the Japanese market where more innovative companies—that is, companies that are more internationally aware and therefore more fashion-conscious—are meeting (sometimes creating) customer interest and demand.

Our solution is to find several highly innovative, mid-sized American companies whose products can be licensed for the Japan market, thereby refreshing and enlivening the Japanese company's image and approach and injecting excitement into all of its products. In some cases such an alliance may require the Japanese company to make a minority investment in the American company, such as 10 to 20 percent of the equity. Most of these smaller U. S. companies are private and entrepreneurial, run by their founders who are more often creative and less often financially secure. Oftentimes in many industries in the United States, the most creative companies are starved for capital. The reason is that the most creative people are more likely to want to work for themselves than for a large company. Thus, each U.S. company benefits greatly from this strategic alliance with Japanese companies. Not only does it obtain the capital needed for growth, but it also achieves efficient entry into an untapped large market.

Another domestic Japanese company is quite successful in its primary field and seeks entry into another industry for which it has developed interesting products. The nature of the new industry, however, requires special skills along with satisfying technical and legal requirements. One potential solution on which we are working is to form a joint venture in the U.S. with a qualified U.S. firm. The joint venture would then set up a subsidiary in Japan that could both attract a new business and subcontract those products to the Japanese partner.

Japanese Partnership with U.S. Service Companies

We are representing a mid-sized, internationally known, U.S.-based, creativity consulting company that seeks to operate in Japan. With all of its clients being among the one hundred largest U.S. corporations, this U.S. company (which also has a strong presence in Europe) seems ripe for a strategic alliance in Asia. We believe that the special appeal to potential Japanese partners in general, and perhaps the large trading companies in particular, would be their new capacity to improve the innovative performance of allied and related group companies. Such operational leverage is what makes strategic alliance successful.

Similarly, a state-of-the-art database software firm with proprietary technology that dominates one major U.S. industry is targeting other vertical technical industries. While its technology is the best in its category and its reputation for delivery is excellent, it needs financial power to secure large contracts with major corporate clients. By forming a strategic alliance with a multinational Japanese corporation, rather than by going public, this U.S. technology firm could concentrate on long-term strategies rather than short-term performance. In addition, the company can start its international business at the same time.

Since this company is highly entrepreneurial, there is concern about protecting the corporate culture in such a strategic relationship with a large Japanese firm. Our task is to structure an alliance that gives both sides what they need, securing the necessary flexibility and freedom for the U.S. company, while enabling the Japanese side to have the full exploitation of the technology as well as the appropriate financial security for its investment.

EXPANDING INTERNATIONAL MARKETS

International competitive advantage is never sure and never steady. Successful companies must remain ever vigilant, scanning the environment for both new opportunities and new threats. This is why many Japanese corporate leaders have been exploiting their organizations' financial strength as a new competitive weapon in international business. For mid-sized companies, the clearest mechanism for developing such a competitive weapon is through international strategic alliances.

International business combined with modern finance is revolutionizing contemporary commerce. No longer merely an option for expansion, foreign investments direct organizational strategies and drive enterprise structures. In today's world, international financial mechanisms and investment techniques have become powerful vehicles for corporate achievement and significant determinants of corporate success. Nowhere are such overseas investments more important than for Japanese corporations.

Japanese international investments, particularly in the United States, have become very large. Japanese leaders know that it has become essential to forge active business alliances with U.S. corporations in order to sustain and build market share. There is nothing more important for the future of Japanese industry.

Japanese Entry into U.S. Service Industries

Financial strength at home can greatly facilitate a corporation's effective and efficient market entry abroad.

A rapidly expanding Japanese industrial service company is planning entry into the United States for two reasons. First, the Japanese company seeks U.S. knowhow in order to acquire greater knowledge for developing its domestic business. Second, many of this company's Japanese clients have moved some operations to the United States and there is need to follow its larger customers.

This service industry in Japan is different from that in the United States. In Japan, the industry is unified with many diverse services being offered by the same companies (even when the companies are small), while in the United States the industry is segmented and highly specialized with most companies only offering a few of these services (even when the companies are large).

Although the advantages of structuring one large strategic alliance is simplicity for the investment bankers, such a plan would not satisfy the overall objectives of this company. Several, small strategic alliances (minority investments) work better, enabling the Japanese firm to learn the latest ideas from each of the different U.S. market segments.

The U.S. firms benefit as well but not in the same manner. Since this Japanese company services large Japanese companies in Japan, it can produce incremental business for its American partners from these same companies, which have major operations in the United States. Such business development can be more important than the cash investment.

Japanese Entry into U.S. Health-Care Industries

In a similar case, a Japanese health-care organization desires to purchase a specialized hospital in order to learn techniques for use back in Japan. Because of the public nature of health care, which involves external constituencies such as federal, state, and local government, third-party health-care insurance providers, groups of doctors, medical associations, and labor unions (for nurses and technicians), there are hard-to-control complicating factors necessary in making an institution successful. Thus it is often vital for the foreign owner of health-care services to involve local citizens prominently in ownership, management, and operations. In fact, whenever regulation and professional relationships are essential for success, local management must have a major stake in the venture. For its part, the U.S. institution achieves capital inflow, cross-cultural management ideas, international prominence, and a partner with less interest in short-term financial performance than in long-term business development. Since there would be initial reluctance to foreign ownership of a health-care organization, how the initial structure is established and presented is crucial in forming first opinions.

Low Leveraged Buyout of U.S. Companies

Here we bring together the American management of an U.S. food company with a Japanese firm that seeks a long-term presence in this specific segment of the food industry. Although this food commodity is currently not in short supply, it is anticipated that shortages will develop within five to seven years. The Japanese firm is willing to invest a much higher amount of equity than would any of the U.S. buyout funds, since the Japanese company is more concerned with strategic positioning than with returns on investment. Ultimate returns on investment will be measured ten to twenty-five years into the future.

The American company benefits in several ways. The original shareholders in this public company gain a somewhat higher price of the buyout paid by a strategic buyers in a weak financial market. Customers and clients benefit by subsequent operational efficiencies, and the management/new owners benefit by having a less leveraged balance sheet.

In another example, a mid-sized division of a large public company had languished for years. The company manufactured an industrial product that dominated the low-technology segment of the market, and hence the parent company used it as a cash cow, taking money out and never investing it back. U.S. management sought to purchase this low technology division in cooperation with a Japanese company. This Japanese company, from an allied but not competing segment of the same industry, had resisted coming to the United States because it was too small to take the gamble of establishing the necessary market presence. The great benefit of acquiring this U.S. division in partnership with U.S. managers was the U.S. division's reputation for reliability and its dominance of the channels of distribution. The Japanese company could afford to pay a premium price since they would now be able to utilize those same channels of distribution to give its own products a highly efficient entry mechanism to the U.S. market.

RESTRUCTURING TROUBLED FOREIGN SUBSIDIARIES

The Japanese economy, like the rest of the world's economy, is volatile. Industrial growth is not permanent and sudden shocks to financial markets are common. Yesterday's competitive advantage may not hold today, nor today's tomorrow. Increasing market pressures are emerging, many from other countries in Asia, in areas of prior Japanese dominance. In certain basic industries, many Japanese companies have seen that their long, steady climb upward, once seemingly unstoppable, cannot continue forever. New realities for a new world must force new strategies and new structures.

But new strategies and new structures bring new complications and new problems. In the attempt to diversify internationally, reduce dependence on the Japanese market, and participate in the global marketplace, many Japanese companies have expanded to the United States. Often such expansion has taken the form of an acquisition of a U.S. company, and not infrequently such acquisitions have run into trouble.

All too often, postacquisition business plans are not followed, sales are not achieved, costs become excessive, time is lost, money is lost. Local management does not perform well, and worse yet, sometimes does not even seem to care. A great deal of effort must be exerted by Japan to fix problems that can seem hard to define and even harder to solve.

In the great rush to promote Japanese acquisitions of U.S. companies, many U.S. investment bankers, intoxicated by abundant financial resources in Japan and lavish M&A fees for themselves, have instigated a "feeding frenzy" of M&A activity. Japanese companies were encouraged, pushed, and cajoled to buy U.S. companies by investment bankers with beautiful presentation books and fast-talking mouths. A competitive fear was instilled by these fee-obsessed deal makers, pitting one Japanese company against another.

Financial strategy was promoted far more than corporate strategy and what would happen six weeks, six months, or six years after acquisition was irrelevant. Such was the serious error of financially oriented M&A investment banking, and many Japanese companies are now paying the real price, a cost in time, effort, and aggravation as well as cash far above the original purchase price of the initial transaction. What had been sold as a "bargain" turned out not to be a bargain.

Why Foreign Acquisitions Go Wrong

There are many reasons why Japanese acquisitions of U.S. companies have developed problems. Following are five of the most important.

Buying for the Wrong Reason. It is frightening how many companies are purchased for the wrong reason. A typical case is when there is good technology but no business; the most dangerous eater of cash is excellent technology with no product or an excellent product with no market. Acquisitions are risky at best, and the more they deviate from an acquirer's current competence, whether such deviation is in product area or geographic area, the more opportunities there are for failure. An acquisition should never be motivated by a cheap price. Worse still, overseas M&A should never be done because others are doing it; the supposed prestige of an international acquisition can drown quickly in a sea of red ink.

Minimal Strategic Thinking. For too long, strategy took a back seat to finance. This distorted thinking stated that "if a company could be bought with financial efficiency (or cleverness) then it should be bought." What happened later was almost irrelevant. It is vital that detailed strategic planning precede all acquisitions, especially when they are foreign. Alternative scenarios must be considered, so that under various economic and business conditions a clear plan is developed. Investment bankers must learn to put strategic thinking ahead of financial thinking in their M&A priorities.

Excessive Spending. Managers of companies bought by foreign buyers have been preconditioned to believe that the acquiring company has "deep pockets" and that there is plenty of money to invest. In some cases, the expenditure of large amounts of capital is a psychological reaction to the acquisition itself, often as a way of asserting local independence or justifying that the acquisition was beneficial. In other cases, heavy spending is simply triggered by empire builders freed by the apparent absence of owners.

Artificial Synergy or Synergy Too Soon. Most M&A activity is motivated by the acquirer's belief that real business synergy exists. Either increasing revenues or decreasing costs or enhanced products and services are envisioned in virtually every Japanese purchase of foreign companies. Problems arise when such synergy is sought too intensely or too soon. Sometimes, what appeared to be synergistic just is not (e.g., technologies or products or marketing or manufacturing that are not compatible). On occasion, apparent synergy on the surface can be antisynergistic in reality when the attempt to generate synergy artificially creates more friction and waste. Sometimes real synergy is there but it is attempted too soon. In most M&A situations, it is vital to maintain and strengthen the current business until stability is regained.

Cross-Cultural Misunderstanding. Although there are real differences between Japanese and U.S. business methods, cross-cultural misunderstanding is more often an excuse than the real problem. It is easy to blame the clash between Japanese and U.S. management styles when in reality other, more traditional business problems are the cause. Nonetheless, there can be real cross-cultural issues. A frequent complaint of U.S. managers is that they become second-class citizens after a Japanese acquisition since their career paths are limited. Another perceived problem is the appearance of Japanese managerial "spies," apparently more interested in reporting problems back to Japan than in working as team members with U.S. peers.

In most Japanese acquisitions in the United States, virtually every post-M&A problem relates directly to management. The recruiting, training, developing, motivating, and retaining of good management should always be the primary issue in any Japanese acquisition of a foreign company, and this is especially true for mid-sized firms. The best investment bankers are sensitive to the particular requirements of mid-sized firms, particularly the intersection of strategy and management.

Case Example: The Right Price, the Wrong Question

"We thought we had gotten a bargain on a Cadillac, until we looked under the hood and found no engine." So stated the astute head of M&A for a large Japanese company when reviewing the failure of a recent U.S. acquisition made by an autonomous division that he was asked to help fix.[2] Although the acquisition price was considered excellent at about $9 million, an additional $30 million had been invested over three years with no end in sight.

The Japanese company is a well-known major manufacturer that had been acting as a representative in Japan for a low-revenue but important line of allied products produced by a relatively small U.S. company. As a result of high fluctuation in this capital spending-related, medium high-tech industry, the U.S. company was having difficulty financing its generation of products and its owners were considering a sale. The Japanese company was concerned that it might lose its supply of future equipment, or worse, that its customers in Japan might be abandoned by the new owners. A seemingly great price encouraged a strategy of 100 percent acquisition.

The primary problem was that, after the acquisition, engineers ran the company as a developmental cost center; there were no businesspeople obsessed with profit making and financial return. A large engineering group was developed and it was decided that all production would be done internally. Many problems arose as a result: The fixed overheads became very large; the price of the products escalated as highly sophisticated technical features (not necessarily needed by customers) were added; and development time was extended so that the product was late coming to market.

Our strategic solution involved a corporate combination with an industry competitor. After analyzing the industry and meeting with CEOs of every single competing company, we structured an interesting transaction where the Japanese company reduced substantially its ongoing financial exposure while assuring a continuing flow of products for its Japanese customers. The essential structure had the Japanese company sell its subsidiary to an aggressive entrepreneurial company in return for a 25 percent ownership interested in the combined company. The entrepreneurial acquirer was managed by its owners and was highly profitable; the manager-owners had built the business with their own private capital and still retained the full fervor of entrepreneurial ownership as evidenced by aggressive marketing and fierce cost containment. Although the Japanese company had to guarantee some working capital as part of the deal, the financial exposure was far less than it would have been and the business benefits were substantially better.

Thus, by reducing its ownership from 100 percent to 25 percent, the Japanese company not only reduced its risk substantially but more important increased the likelihood of achieving all of its strategic objectives. The perception that 100 percent ownership is the best way for a Japanese company to control a foreign subsidiary is almost always wrong when Japanese companies acquire U.S. mid-sized firms. The key issue is management quality and management motivation, and to enhance both we like to structure minority ownership positions for our Japanese clients combined with both strong strategic advantages and financial controls.

RESOLVING ECONOMIC CONFLICT

Japanese businesspeople, especially those who work in the United States, are incredulous to discover that American public opinion now compares the threat of Japanese acquisitions to that of the Soviet military. And since Japanese acquisitions are expanding while the Soviet military is contracting, fear of Japan is increasingly a media-hyped, all-American worry along with drugs, crime, and taxes. (Even the hit motion picture *Back to the Future II* portrayed the hero's future character as working for, and being fired, by a ruthless, heartless, humorless Japanese manager.)

The United States is not alone in its xenophobic fear of Japan; most of Asia is well ahead and much of Europe is catching up. That such reactions may be neither socially desirable nor economically sensible makes no difference: the unpleasant emotion creates its own harsh reality.

We need not rehash the wearying macroeconomic arguments of America's overspending, undersaving, and underinvesting on the one hand, and Japan's closed markets, monopolistic practices, and predatory pricing on the other. The truth is obvious but not helpful: Both are "correct" (in terms of the facts) even though both may not be "right" (in terms of each country's misunderstanding the other's culture and society). What is helpful is the simple realization that a high standard of living is the primary goal of economic development and all policies must aim to achieve it.

Like much nationalism, American thinking is simplistic and contradictory. While people complain one way with their voices, they vote the other way with their wallets. Americans like Japanese automobiles and consumer electronics, and well they should; Japanese products are innovative, appealing, made with quality, and provide excellent value. These are the natural laws of the free market. This is economic Darwinism—where the unfit perish, the fit survive, and the fittest prosper—and where the selection is made by all the people all the time. There is no central control, no higher legislation, no coercive force. As such, free-market capitalism is the purest form of democracy.

But Japan is not a monolith. Nor is it invulnerable. Severe economic problems are looming as Japan faces the 1990s. Three powerful forces are creating major dislocations in Japan's domestic environment: (1) financial instability at home, (2) international pressure for Japan to open up its home markets, and (3) the increasing competitiveness of Pacific Rim countries in product/market areas of Japan's historical dominance.

Then add to the cauldron the world's growing nationalism, a combustible mixture of ethnic aspirations and angers.

Japanese Mid-Sized Firms

The major Japanese multinationals will continue to prosper by transferring operations to other countries and becoming true world citizens. It is the smaller Japanese companies, however, which will encounter trouble, and this trouble will not be either pleasantly endured or easily fixable.

Traditionally, many small and mid-sized Japanese firms have existed as loyal subcontractors to the giant corporations, yet usually they cannot be taken along on the journey abroad. Although large Japanese corporations would prefer to continue the same intimate relationship with their suppliers that they enjoy in Japan, public opinion overseas demand local content from local companies. Consequently, for Japanese small and mid-sized firms to survive and prosper, new thinking is needed.

We have been working with a number of Japanese companies whose interests have become allied with those of U.S.-based companies of similar size.[3] The motivation in exploring a strategic alliance can differ considerably between U.S. and Japanese sides. The U.S. side may need capital infusion and manufacturing expertise. The Japanese side may need technology access and market entry. We like such differences; they make for strategic alliances that thrive and endure. Increasingly, there is a real opportunity for such strategic alliances to act as preferred supplies to large Japanese corporations operating in the United States.

Why Economics Cannot Solve Economic Problems

One might believe by reading erudite arguments that industrial prosperity is always linked to economic policy, whether U.S. trade restrictions on the one side or freer Japanese markets on the other. A cardinal mistake here—and it permeates contemporary thought—is the notion that economic solutions to industrial problems will yield business success. Macroeconomics is vital for defining and modulating the pace and proportions of the economy, but it is deficient in making individual firms prosper. It is like trying to coach a basketball team by determining the theoretically proper mix of heights, weights, and talents of players without ever teaching any of them how to dribble, pass, and shoot.

Economics dominates economic thinking. But economists do not run companies. They do not manage budgets or direct staffs. They never formulate corporate strategies and never build corporate structures. P&L, personnel, and product positioning are issues they do not face. Meeting payrolls is the work they do not do. Making enterprise run is responsibility they do not have.

Yet enterprises—for-profit businesses and not-for-profit institutions— are the components of the economy. Like cells in a body, they *are* the economy, and to treat the economy only by macroeconomics is to treat an epidemic only by statistics. Building businesses in the former, like curing people in the latter, must be addressed. To leave the economy solely in the hands of economists is to leave the sick solely in the heads of statisticians.

Central planning runs an economy in reverse. The primary functions of macroeconomic policy should be to empower microeconomic principles. The more freely individual companies can operate, the more healthy the economy will become.

Alliances Between U.S. and Japanese Mid-Sized Firms

The real battles between the United States and Japan may be between multinational corporations on one side and small and mid-sized firms on the other. As such, small and mid-sized firms in the United States and Japan are truly more allies than enemies on the economic battlefield. But neither, in today's international marketplace, can go it alone. They must forge alliances.[4]

Mid-sized firms are a critical component of modern capitalism. They are often more innovative and dynamic than their mammoth rivals, offering employees a greater sense of participation and job satisfaction. Mid-sized firms assure the efficiency of the economic sector by thwarting monopolies, and they secure the pluralism of the political sector by disrupting the hegemony between big business and big government. Indeed, today, with the collapse of socialism and its historic reliance on giant enterprises, the entire world is looking to small and mid-sized businesses to bring about the economic resuscitation of the former Eastern Bloc and lead the worldwide charge into the twenty-first century. By building strategic alliances among themselves, mid-sized firms in the United States and Japan can create a corporate strategy solution to a political-economic conflict.

New Investment Banking Thinking

The key making all of these transactions successful is a new way of investment banking thinking, an approach that promotes strategy over finance and long-term market positioning over short-term M&A fees.[5] It is much more difficult, and much less lucrative, for investment bankers to do several small deals for a client than one large one. But good investment bankers serve their clients more than themselves. Especially for mid-sized firms, who cannot afford the luxury of second chances, such new-thinking investment bankers, with proven expertise in strategic analysis and business alliances, are essential.

Japanese and U.S. companies can work together with a great variety of structures. How does a Japanese company establish the optimum relationship with an American counterpart? A new breed of investment bankers can facilitate this objective. No longer exclusively financial technicians, the best of the new investment bankers understand a company's goals and objectives and help plan appropriate strategies and policies. Then they search for the ideal corporate partners, develop an array of structural techniques, and construct various financing mechanisms to best implement these strategies and policies.

All Japanese companies doing business internationally (or planning to do such business) should understand the many facets of investment banking. Corporate leaders must appreciate these state-of-the-art financial concepts, mechanisms, and techniques in order to design, develop, and execute proper business plans, goals, and objectives.

Commitment and sensitivity as well as knowledge and creativity are required to establish the best investment opportunities and strategic alliances, and which investment bankers a company chooses will dramatically affect its level of achievement and degree of ultimate success. It is vital that mid-sized Japanese companies select the right investment bankers to represent them in the United States. Expertise with mid-sized companies is vital; what works for large companies may not work for smaller ones.

The best bankers for arranging strategic alliances for mid-sized firms should have business experience and strategic planning expertise as well as financial sophistication. They must be able to devote substantial time and effort to highly specialized requirements. To choose a very large international bank—whether American or Japanese—may not always be the right decision for small and mid-sized firms. After all, your company should always be given priority by your investment bankers, and never be shunted aside by larger requirements of larger clients.

CONCLUSIONS

Strategic alliances are often more complicated than simple acquisitions, and thus a new breed of investment banker is required to structure them. No longer is financial expertise sufficient. Strategic and even technical expertise are equally important in arranging these complex transactions. In addition, the best investment bankers are sensitive to the particular requirements of mid-sized firms, focusing on the key issues of management and motivation.

Investment bankers must put as much weight on strategic analysis as on financial structure, and be willing to invest in long-term relationships with their corporate clients as opposed to quick-hit M&A transactions. Only when the interests of investment bankers and their clients are more closely aligned for long-term success will corporate strategy play a dominant rather than subservient role in M&A transactions.

NOTES

1. See Robert L. Kuhn, *Creativity and Strategy for Mid-Sized Firms* (New York: Prentice-Hall, 1989).

2. The company featured in this case study has been disguised.

3. In general, we represent either Japanese financial institutions or trading companies in assisting corporate clients or U.S.-based companies seeking Japanese partners.

4. There may be another reason for U.S. and Japanese firms to form alliances. The New Europe, no matter all the protestations to the contrary, must begin to look inward. Self-interest will demand that Europeans resist both U.S. and Japanese business.

5. For a detailed description of investment banking "way of thinking," see *The Library of Investment Banking* (Homewood, Ill.: Dow Jones-Irwin, 1990); *The Art and Science of High-Stakes Dealmaking* (Harper Business, 1990, in English; Nikkei Business, 1990, in Japanese).

Part IV

New Technologies for Inducing and Measuring Creative and Innovative Management

15

Generating Creativity and Innovation: A Marketing Perspective
Jerry Wind

Traditionally, marketing concepts and methods have been directed at customers and prospects. With the growing importance of other stakeholders, such as suppliers, distributors, employees, various consumer groups, and government, marketing perspectives have been increasingly employed in the design of strategies and programs aimed at all stakeholders (Wind 1988). It is quite surprising, therefore, that the internal management of an organization, especially those activities aimed at increasing its creativity and innovativeness, have not taken advantage of marketing concepts and methods.

The basic premise of this chapter is that marketing perspective and the same marketing concepts and methods that develop and introduce successful new products and services can greatly enhance an organization's success in becoming more creative and innovative.

ASSESSING THE SPECIFIC CREATIVITY AND INNOVATION NEEDS OF THE ORGANIZATION

One of the major criticisms of the modern corporation is its lack of creativity and innovation. Even organizations that excel new product development activities and introduce major innovations are often conservative and noninnovative when it comes to other aspects of their business. It is quite disheartening to see innovative products and businesses fail due to lack of creative marketing, operations, financial, or human resource decisions. In fact, as the uncertainty and complexity of the competitive business environment increase, innovative strategies in all facets of the business are a must.

With the few exceptions of firms whose corporate culture and reward systems center on innovation and risk taking, most U.S. firms tend to be risk-averse. In such a climate, a first step toward becoming more innovative is to establish mechanisms for assessing the creativity and innovation needs of the organization.

Assessing the creativity and innovation needs of an organization can greatly benefit from specific marketing concepts and approaches, including the concept of market segmentation and the methods for internal marketing audit, and external competitive benchmarking and market analysis.

Market segmentation recognizes the fact that all markets are heterogeneous and that effective marketing strategy requires the identification of target market segments, assessing their needs and characteristics and using these as guidelines for the design of products and services and associated marketing programs.

In the context of making organizations more creative and innovative, it is important to assess the areas in which the organization can benefit the most from greater emphasis on creativity and innovation. Furthermore, since all organizations are heterogeneous, one cannot assume that the creativity and innovation needs of one organization automatically apply to others.

Marketing audit is "a comprehensive, systematic, independent, and periodic examination of a company's—or business unit's—marketing environment, objectives, strategies and activities. With a view of determining problem areas and opportunities and recommending a plan of action to improve the company marketing performance" (Kotler, Gregor, and Rogers 1977). Marketing audits, even though not as common as financial audits, can provide invaluable input to marketing strategy by identifying problem areas and opportunities. The process and discipline of a marketing audit can be applied to the assessment of those areas of the firm that can gain the most from enhanced creativity and innovation. Furthermore, an audit can also identify the major obstacles to the introduction of more creative and innovative processes and suggest ways of overcoming these obstacles.

Competitive benchmarking can serve both as a way of identifying what creative and innovative things competitors are doing as well as finding out for each of the areas requiring creativity and innovation who is the best. Once such a "benchmark" is identified, whether in the firm's industry or in any other industry, it is useful to study the case thoroughly to see what can be learned from the experience.

A *market analysis* of the current and expected needs, behavior, perceptions, and preferences of consumers and intermediate marketing organizations (retailers, wholesalers, and others) is critical to the firm's ability to identify areas requiring creative solutions and innovative products and services. There is no substitute to a thorough market analysis as a guide to understanding the firm's customers and prospects and their distributors, and identifying areas that can benefit from creative solutions and innovative products and services.

IDENTIFYING APPROACHES FOR THE GENERATION OF CREATIVE AND INNOVATIVE SOLUTIONS

Once the areas that can benefit from creative and innovative approaches have been identified, a key question is how to generate the needed creative and innovative solutions. To address this question, marketing (based on the experience with approaches to the generation of new product ideas) can offer both a number of key concepts and a set of methods.

The concepts/findings that marketing can offer are:

- Generation of new ideas require use of both structured and unstructured approaches.

- Idea generation should rely on both internal (the decision makers) and external (consumers, competitors, suppliers, etc.) sources.

- Idea generation should be conducted on an ongoing basis.

- The more diverse the approaches used for generating new ideas, the higher the likelihood of success.

A basic premise of this chapter is that the approaches used for the generation of new product ideas can be utilized to generate creative and innovative solutions (Wind 1982). These approaches are listed in Table 15.1.

Consumer-based approaches to the generation of new product ideas can, of course, be used as part of any consumer studies aimed at identifying areas requiring creative solutions and innovative products and services. In addition, these approaches can be used on the "internal consumers," all the organizational members who use organizational products and services. For example, the data processing department can use any of the approaches to generate new products and services ideas for its own internal corporate clients.

Table 15.1
Approaches to the Generation of New Product Ideas

| | Research Approach | |
Source	Unstructured	Structured
Consumers	Motivation research	Need/benefit segmentation
	Focused group interviews	Problem detection studies
	Consumption system analysis	Market structure analysis/Gap analysis
	Consumer complaints	Product deficiency analysis
"Experts"	Brainstorming	"Problem/opportunity" analysis
	"Synectics"	Morphological analysis
	"Suggestion box"	Growth opportunity analysis
	Independent inventors	Environmental trends analysis
		Analysis of competitive products
		Search of patents and other sources of new ideas

Since every organizational unit has its own internal clients, explicit efforts to identify their needs and problems using any of the structured and unstructured approaches listed in Table 15.1 can be of great value. In selecting the specific approaches, it is desirable to include at least one of the unstructured approaches of motivation research FGI and consumption system analysis and at least one of the four structured approaches, and to undertake an analysis of consumer complaints based on the firm's own data as well as the public complaint files of the Better Business Bureau, consumer protection agencies, and newspaper action columns.

As with the consumer-based approaches, the "expert"-based approaches are both structured and unstructured, involving both experts as individuals and as members of a group. These approaches are to a large extent, but not exclusively, marketing research-oriented.

As with the consumer-based approaches, it is suggested that the firm use at least one of the unstructured approaches of brainstorming, synectics, and independent inventors and at least one of the structured approaches and, in addition, the "suggestion box" to get broader involvement of all employees.

Among the most useful approaches to generation of new ideas are morphological analyses. These approaches question things as they are and ask why they cannot be combined, used in new ways, modified, magnified, minimized, rearranged, or reversed.

The major advantages of such approaches are that they are:

- Systematic
- Capable of encompassing a very large number of alternative new ideas
- Flexible with respect to the selection of relevant attributes
- Simple and relatively inexpensive to use

The experiences with morphological approaches when compared with the traditional brainstorming is that it can lead to the generation of a larger number of ideas and more creative/novel ideas.

In searching for new ideas for creative and innovative business solutions, it is important to focus on both short- and long-term opportunities. The latter are more difficult to assess and often require as a starting point the identification of the expected scenario five, ten, or twenty years ahead and focusing the new idea generation process on those approaches capable of identifying ideas under the conditions of the specific scenarios.

EVALUATING THE VARIOUS IDEAS AND SELECTING A STRATEGY

Employing any of the approaches outlined in Table 15.1 would lead to the generation of a large number of new ideas. These ideas have to be prioritized. As with generation of ideas, marketing concepts and methods can help evaluate the various ideas.

Evaluation of the various options should be done explicitly against *all* relevant criteria. The selection of a strategy should reflect current and expected conditions. Evaluation of the various options should include "consumer" reactions to the options.

The methods one can use to help evaluate the ideas are the analytic hierarchy process (AHP) and conjoint analysis.

The analytic hierarchy modeling and measurement process (Saaty 1977; Saaty and Boone 1990; Wind and Saaty 1980) is one of the most powerful approaches to determine the relative importance of a set of criteria. The novel aspect of this approach is that it structures any complex, multiperson, and multiperiod problem hierarchically and assists in determining the relative priority of the identifiable courses of action (typically presented as entities at the lowest level of the hierarchy). Consider, for example, the simple three-level hierarchy of environmental scenarios, objectives, and innovative new courses of action in Figure 15.1 Such a hierarchy can aid management in identifying their relevant objectives, forces them to look at the environmental scenarios most likely to affect their business decisions, stimulates their creativity in generating specific new courses of action, and facilitates the evaluation of the generated courses of action on the various criteria by taking into consideration the effect of the environmental scenarios.

The objectives of the AHP are:

1.　To decompose a complex problem into a hierarchy; each level consists of a few manageable elements and each element is, in turn, decomposed into another set of elements. The process continues down to the most specific elements of the problem, typically the specific courses of action considered, which are represented at the lowest level of the hierarchy.

2.　To establish priorities among the elements within each stratum of the hierarchy with respect to the elements (e.g., criteria) of the next higher level.

3.　To establish a single composite vendor of priorities for the entire hierarchy by yielding the relative priority of all entities at the lowest level that enables the accomplishment of the highest objective of the hierarchy.

These objectives are achieved while allowing for a group interaction among the relevant managers and the incorporation of any available data with the participants' subjective judgments. The AHP offers a procedure for conflict resolution among the participants and offers total flexibility for the participants, in both defining the hierarchy and judging its components. The AHP measurement problem is formulated into a largest eigen value problem, and the principal eigenvector with appropriate hierarchical weighing and composition leads to a unidemensional scale of the priorities of the elements in any level of the hierarchy.

The AHP is the most appropriate approach for prioritizing the various strategies for increased creativity and innovation; especially if the group that is conducting the analysis includes all the key decision makers.

Conjoint analysis (Green and Wind 1974; Green and Srinavaanan 1990) is concerned with the measurement of preferences. It is based on a "tradeoff" type (decompositional) choice model and involves the determination of weights or part-worths of a set of independent variables. Typically, the independent variables or the choice attributes are presented as "full profile" descriptors of hypothetical product offerings, each described as having different "levels" on the preselected set of factors. The specific combinations are selected by following an experimental design (typically, an orthogonal array), and the stimuli are presented as verbal, pictorial, or actual product representations. A simple additive main-effects model is commonly used to establish the relationship between ordinal dependent variables and independent variables. This model can be extended to include nonlinear and interaction terms.

Figure 15.1. Basic Decision Hierarchy

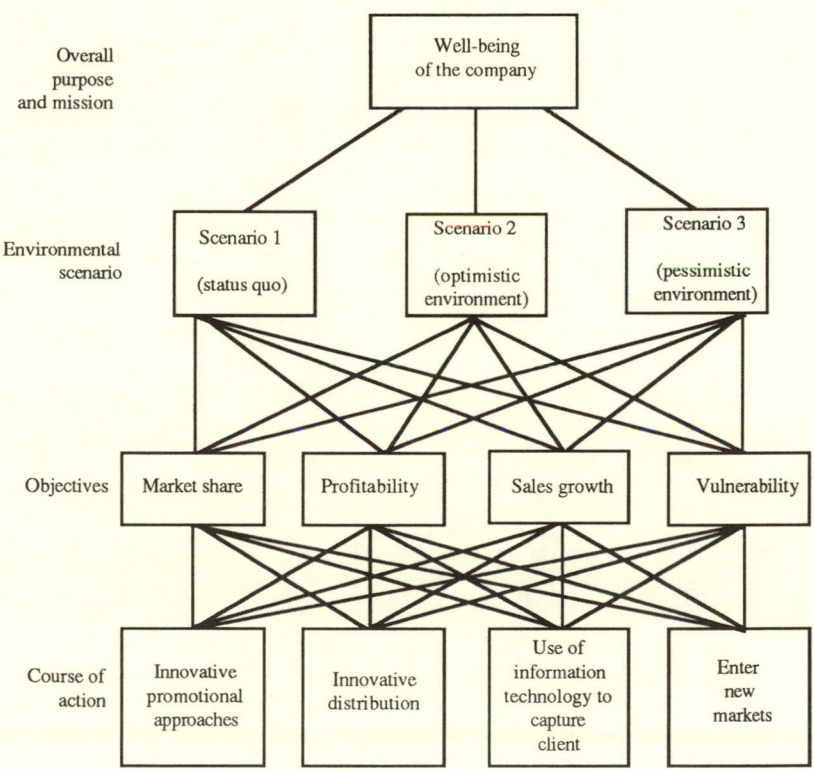

The objectives of conjoint analysis are:

1. To establish a function that relates the independent variables to the dependent variable.

2.   To examine the strength of the relationship between the dependent and independent variables (e.g., prediction of choice alternatives reflecting the respondent's tradeoff among the various alternatives).

3.   To determine the part-worths or utility scores associated with each attribute level.

4.   To determine the relative importance of each of the independent variables (factors).

The typical output of conjoint analysis programs (such as MONANOVA and LINMAP) includes:

- Part-worths (utilities) for the various attribute levels
- Relative importance weights for the attributes (factors)
- A measure of badness of fit that reflects how well the predicted rankings of choice alternatives match the rankings provided by the respondent

The results of conjoint analysis studies often are incorporated in a computer simulation or an optimization program aimed at finding the optimal solution among the attributes studied in the conjoint analysis study.

In the context of evaluating new strategies for increased creativity and innovation, conjoint analysis can be used to assess the importance potential users assign to various options. These methods can obviously be used with consumers to assess their likely reaction to the innovation the firm may offer.

DESIGNING THE IMPLEMENTATION PLAN

Having selected a strategy for enhancing the creativity and innovation of an organization, the critical question is how to assure successful implementation of the strategy.

If one uses the AHP as a process and methodology for prioritizing the options, the chances of implementation are increased significantly since the executives who participate in the process are more likely to "buy in" the process and its recommendations. Yet, even this "buy in" is not enough.

Marketing again can provide concepts and methods that can help design a plan for the implementation of the selected strategy for increasing the organizational innovation and creativity.

Successful implementation requires the development of an implementation plan. Keys to any successful implementation plan are:

- Identify those most likely to resist implementation.
- Identify the reasons for resistance.

- Establish a positioning strategy for the selected strategy—offer the target internal segments a reason for "buying" the new strategy. This reason should be consistent with the benefits they seek and their perception of the ability of the strategy to help them achieve their objectives.

- Develop a marketing program to implement the plan.

The major methods one can use in planning the implementation are those used in positioning analysis. Figure 15.2 shows some of the approaches that can be used for positioning analysis.

Figure 15.2. Positioning Analysis

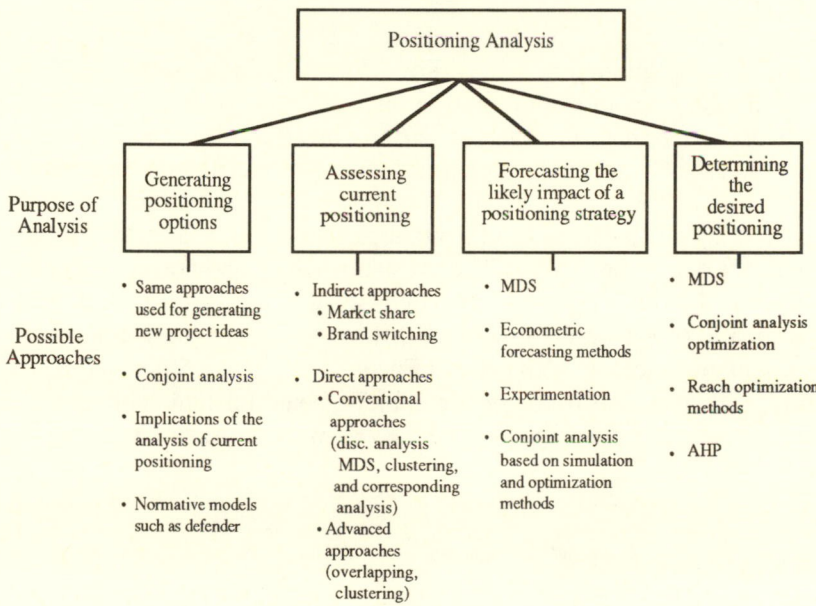

ASSURING CONTINUOUS AND EFFECTIVE EMPLOYMENT OF THE APPROACHES TO ENHANCED CREATIVITY AND INNOVATION

Even if one follows all the concepts and approaches suggested in the preceding four sections, it is not enough to assure that the organization will continue to be creative and innovative. Since management objectives should always include the long-term perspective as well, it is critically important to follow the concept of continuous monitoring and continuous improvements and innovation. The two critical concepts and their associated methods are the Japanese concept of continuous improvement and innovation and the concept and methodology of adaptive experimentation.

Given the attention given in recent years to the Japanese concept of continuous innovation and improvement, we will focus in this section on adaptive experimentation.

Adaptive experimentation is based on the concept that one cannot learn from a single strategy option (i.e., specific level of advertising, specific new distribution outlet, etc.) and that the only way of learning is by experimenting with a number of options (i.e., three levels of advertising, two different distribution outlets, etc.). By evaluating the results of the various levels of effort, management can decide what is the best strategy options to experiment with next.

This concept can and has been applied to all the strategic variables of the firm, and it is not limited to the level of effort of a single strategy option. It can be applied to any combination of variables such as advertising, salesforce, and promotion, each at various levels. This would require, of course, the use of appropriate experimental designs (such as the Latin Square design).

Following an adaptive experimentation strategy offers a better long-term performance due to the firm's ability to establish the market response function facing it and thus develop a long-term optimal strategy. This is best illustrated by the success of Anheuser-Busch in following an advertising-based adaptive experimentation strategy (Ackoff and Emshoff 1975). A second and equally important advantage of following an adaptive experimental approach is the difficulty it presents to competitors who try to monitor the firm's strategy and its impact.

CONCLUSIONS

Marketing as the boundary function of the organization can help create innovative products and services to meet the needs of the key target segments. Organizational creativity and innovation in designing products and services as well as in making any business decision can greatly benefit from marketing concepts and methods. In this context, marketing is not only a function, but also a management perspective and philosophy that offers a set of concepts and tools that can help an organization enhance its creativity and innovation.

By utilizing marketing concepts and methods to increase the organizational creativity and innovation, management has a better chance at preparing the organization for the twenty-first century. Table 15.2 lists some of the expected characteristics of the twenty-first century organization as identified in a recent study of three hundred CEOs.

Table 15.2. The Twenty-First Century Enterprise

Flatter, less hierarchical organization

Cross-functional

Global in perspective and scope of operations

Networked

Information technology-based

Customer-driven

Stakeholder-focused

Centers on value-added, quality, and time-based competition

Individually and group empowered

Innovative, entrepreneurial

Flexible learning

In particular, the concepts and approaches discussed in this chapter have focused on the establishment of an innovative learning organization. These concepts and approaches help meet the research challenges outlined by Kozmetsky in his opening chapter: the need to offer new methods and provide stimulants for rethinking, realigning, and restructuring large bureaucracies.

This rethinking along the lines of a marketing perspective is consistent with the current focus on quality, as exemplified, for example, by the increasing number of applicants to the Malcolm Baldrige Award. Quality focus stresses customer satisfaction and the establishment of extremely high-quality performance targets such as Motorola's 6 sigma or HP's 10X improvement. Such targets cannot be achieved with minor changes in current practice, but require innovative thinking and approaches. The use of marketing concepts and methods to generate, evaluate, and implement approaches to enhance the creativity and innovation of an organization can help achieve the quality goals of the organization and enhance the organization's ability to compete effectively in the turbulent business environment.

REFERENCES

Ackoff, R. L., and J. R. Emshoff. 1975, 1976. Advertising research and Anheuser-Busch, Inc.—1963–68 and 1968–74. *Sloan Management Review* 16 (Winter): 1–15.

Adams, J. L. 1974. *Conceptual blockbusting: A guide to better ideas*. San Francisco: Wilt, Freeman.

Green, Paul E., and V. Srinavaanan. 1990. Conjoint analysis in marketing: New developments with implications for research and practice. *Journal of Marketing* (October).

Green, Paul E., and Jerry Wind. 1974. New way to measure consumers' judgment. *Harvard Business Review* 53 (July–August): 197–217.

Kotler, P., W. Gregor, and W. Rogers. 1977. The marketing audit comes to age. *Sloan Management Review* 18 (Winter): 25–43.

Saaty, T. L. 1977. A scaling method for priorities in hierarchies applied to political candidacy. *Behavioral Science* (June 15): 234–81.

Saaty, T. L., and L. W. Boone. 1990. *Embracing the future*. New York: Praeger.

Wind, Jerry. 1982. *Product policy: Concepts, methods, and strategies*. Reading, Mass.: Addison-Wesley.

Wind, Jerry, and T. L. Saaty. 1980. Marketing applications of the analytic hierarchy process. *Management Science* 26 (July): 641–58.

16

A Managerial Tool for Diagnosing Structural Readiness for Breakthrough Innovations in Large Bureaucracies (Technocracies)

Gerhard O. Mensch

A STALEMATE IN TECHNOLOGY

This chapter addresses a burning issue that is currently troubling many "technology-driven businesses." "Technology-driven" denotes businesses that grow over time at the rate at which a new "technology base" gains acceptance in customer groups. Usually, innovation researchers describe the growth process of such businesses by some sigmoid (S-shaped) diffusion curve. A transition emerges when the S-curve levels off. Then the business runs into what Mensch calls a "stalemate in technology."[1] This is a lackluster situation where two driving forces are wanting. On the one hand, the driving forces of the previously rapidly diffusing technology have lost their momentum, because the technical trajectory has reached its market envelope (see Figure 16.1). On the other hand, a substitute technology may not yet exist, or has not yet been found, or is not yet being exploited with full force. What is it that usually happens in the "maturity phase"?

1. The series of product and process innovations tends to converge to mere pseudo-innovations with little driving power.

Figure 16.1. Business Growth Trajectory

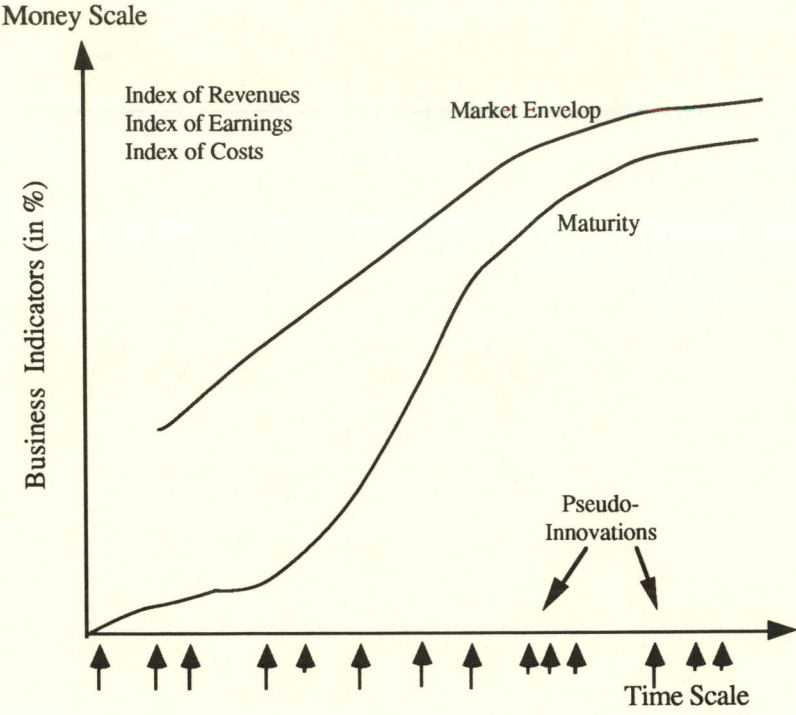

2. While technology is settling in, at least temporarily, the *limits to growth* narrow in on the firm, and managers now experience a *growth of limits* (see Figure 16.2).

3. During the settling-in phase, business leaders experience several unsettling developments characteristic of a state of limbo: (1) *earnings*, previously running high, fall as they attract rivals with lower prices and better products in niches; (2) customer reactions flatten *revenues* when straight-line projections promise accelerating order entries; and (3) *per unit costs* run away when volume of business drops below expectations (see Figure 16.3).

4. If the business field is highly concentrated, and "technocracies" exist that enjoy monopoly privileges and/or support from an omnipotent power structure or bureaucracy, than the odds are that the "technocracy" will fail to react smoothly and in time.

Rather, it will probably break at worst possible instances, creating super-damage.

But let us first go back to lessons learned from our previous research in American and Western European firms. It is simple. Even if the situation changes fundamentally, many senior managers in bureaucracies (technocracies) continue to perceive their position as superior. In a "stalemate in technology" they fail to understand the nature of the undercurrents. Consequently, they may look at minor reasons for declining income. Typically, they lament about high labor cost, high capital cost, or unfavorable exchange rates. Of course, such factors have hurt many businesses, and will continue to do so. Yet the same factors did not hurt when the business was booming and behaving as sellers' markets do "in good times." Only when the business slowed down and turned into a *buyers' market*, where buyers gained greater bargaining power, did vendors find out that they were in trouble.

Figure 16.2. The Settling-In Window

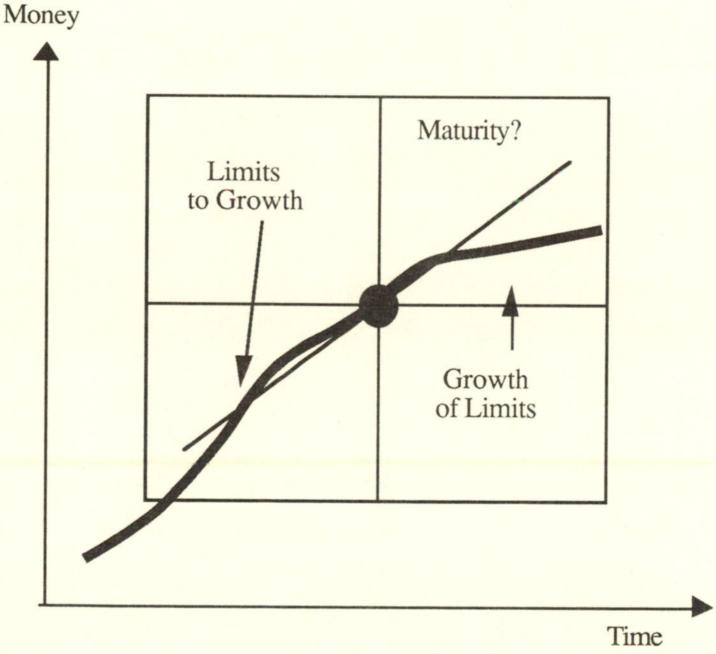

Figure 16.3. Settling-In Phase

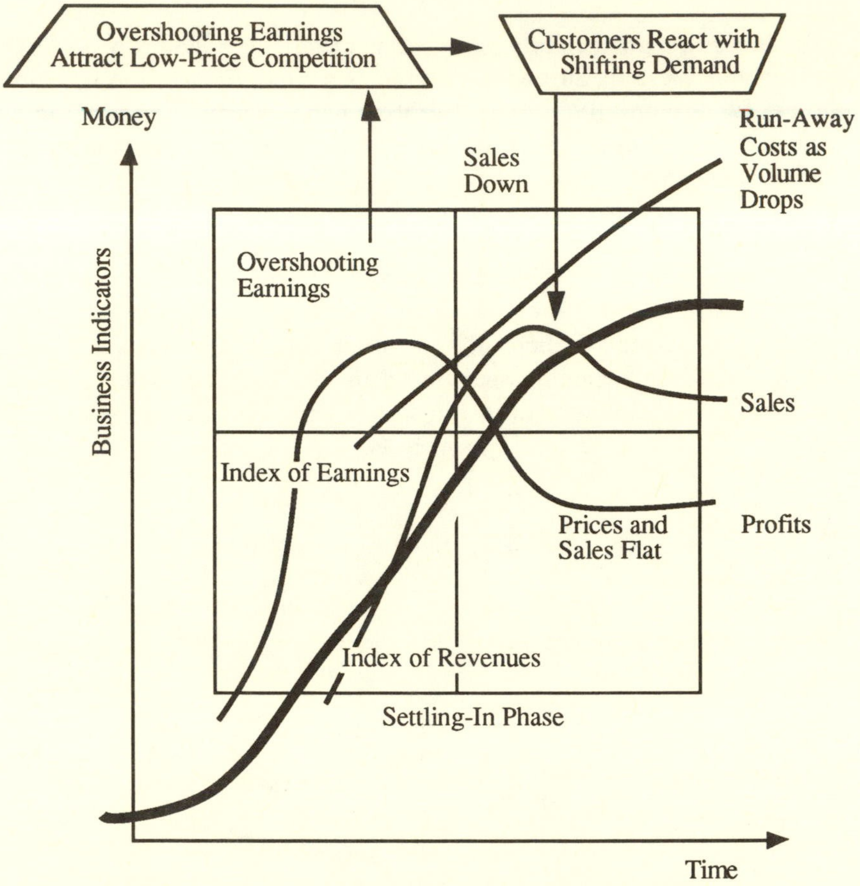

During the stalemate in technology phase, the incumbent technology is not good enough to yield continued positive power and prosperity, whereas new technology is not, or does not appear as yet, good and strong enough to another takeoff into prosperity. Hence, such stalemated businesses become structurally ready for change. If change is blocked, it may turn disruptive (breakthrough). The two scenarios (decline versus expansion) emanating from this view are depicted in Figure 16.4. The underlying strategic issues, therefore, shift from traditional product management to transformation process management. In a phase of major transition, an infusion of transformational management and new technology is needed.

Figure 16.4. Decline versus Expansion

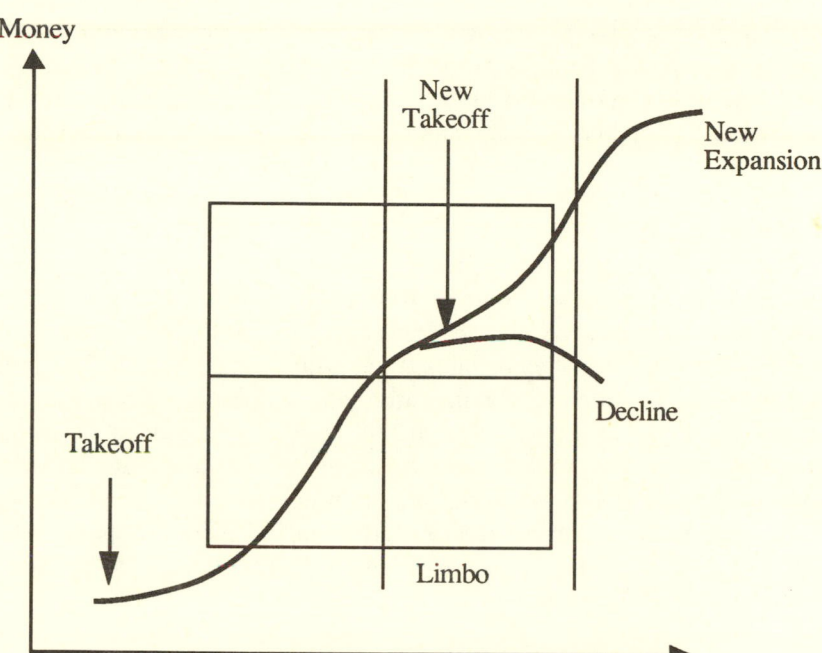

In a stalemate in technology, the radicalness of innovation is a key variable. Incremental innovations in existing lines of business are not necessarily the best choices any longer (in terms of risk and return expectations). Needed is a cutting-edge technology, and process management to implement it in the organization and in the market. The experience curve that used to fit the dynamics of the existing technology base does not necessarily give good guidance for next steps. The experience curve for systems in transition exhibits "knees," and adverse reactions of the people in charge.[2] Consequently, we must look at internal and external factors that may hinder a smooth and timely reaction. For example, Western countries have greatly benefited from the existence of capital markets as countervailing forces to excess profits, or losses, accruing in monopolies, and firms that behave as such. An efficient capital market will point fingers at inefficient firms in technology-based industries. Stock market participants will discover when a mismatch occurs between market pressures and a firm's goals or actions. They will apply the "Wall-Street Rule." First, someone will cry "Wolf!" An example is a *New York Times* article (October 28, 185) on the

Harris Corporation. In 1985, the $2.3 billion revenue firm was beset by exactly the symptoms of crises indicated in Figure 16.3. Harry Rosenthal, a security analyst at Bear, Stearns & Co., was quoted as having said that "aside from the supply and demand problems currently bedeviling the industry, Harris has other more profound problems." The press dug into the fundamentals, notably, management thinking: "They are captive to an obsolete ideology, one that holds that one company can offer all sorts of equipment to a client. The reality is that customers are choosing different equipment from various vendors."

Many technology-based businesses used to share Harris Corporation's problems. An aggressively competitive environment had redefined the market, repositioned products, and redirected technological trends, while managers stuck to old ways of thinking and doing business. Today, much has improved. In order to regain initiative, competitive advantage, and momentum, many Western corporations have developed an up-to-date understanding of the strategic implications of the stalemate situation, improved the strategy-innovation link, and prepared for major innovations Today, in the tirade of Japan, North America, and Western Europe, a rush of basic innovations is taking place. Now the challenge is to help the Former Eastern Europe to shape up.

THE TEAM APPROACH TO ORGANIZED CREATIVITY

What we have learned from our clinical research in American and West European firms is that teamwork is an essential ingredient for successful innovation and transformation. Time and time again studies of successful innovation have emphasized the need for and importance of close cooperation among members of multifunctional groups.[3] It has been noted that good teamwork is both an effectiveness and an efficiency factor. The presence of a cohesive team leads to higher goals and greater success, whereas the absence of such a team relationship is associated with project failure.

Of course, teamwork alone may not lead to successful innovation. In fact, if teamwork can be expected to lead to ends-means consensus, it may sometimes also lead to shared misperceptions, agreement on unsuitable goals, or wrong ways. Furthermore, the "not-invented-here" syndrome exemplifies cases where team consensus generates inaction in the face of external threats or opportunities. Hence, the effect of the team factor may sometimes be ambiguous. This makes it all the more imperative that we understand conditions under which team processes exert a favorable influence on innovation outcomes, and conditions under which they lead to conflict.

Despite the importance of teamwork as a critical factor impinging on innovation success, the diagnosis and resolution of conflict within teams remain little understood. The following comments made by Blair Little in a recent editorial in the *Journal of Product Innovation Management* reflect this lack of understanding:

> In spite of some promising beginnings, there is much that still needs to be learned in most new product organizations about how to work together more effectively. Perversely, the difficulties of working together are becoming greater as firms build more multifunctional teams of multi-competent groups of individuals. But the need for more effective teams gets greater as firms spend more and more on product innovation to meet tough competition and to exploit the opportunities in the new technologies. We need a better understanding what we do and don't know. We need to be more systematic about putting into practice what we do know. And we need more progress in rolling back the covers from areas where we don't know.[4]

The purpose of this chapter is to present and discuss a diagnostic tool aimed at uncovering latent and actual conflict in multifunctional groups. The insidious thing about intergroup conflict is that it is seldom explicit. "Hidden agendas" may abound. Rivalry, and even hostility, may be expressed in tacit or roundabout ways, even in an environment of apparent cooperation. How then can we diagnose and deal with intergroup conflict? Conventional "direct" approaches such as attitude surveys or observation of group dynamics may be helpful, but true progress in diagnosis and resolution of conflicts cannot be made unless the participants themselves use diagnostic tools and become "self-aware" of their own situation, of the common factors, and unless the awareness is methodologically shared.

The diagnostic devices to be discussed in this chapter are intended for self-administration. Using these simple tools, members of research and development groups and project teams in a company can learn to identify differences and similarities among themselves regarding a variety of factors pertinent to innovation success and failure in a changing environment. The managerial tool presented here helps surface the different reasons why views differ, and thus provides a way for turning aspects of the problem into aspects of the solution.

ARCHITECTURE OF THE DIAGNOSTIC INSTRUMENT

In order to obtain a functional tool, meaningful dimensions of agreement/disagreement had to be developed and evaluated against "baseline" standards of conduct. The development work was greatly enhanced by international technology transfer. We gratefully acknowledge the participation of innovation researchers from Germany (L. Scholz), France (A. Piatier), and Holland (A. Kleinknecht) who helped pretest the survey instrument that they have applied in those countries, and which we have used here to examine the innovation management practices and policies of a significant group of small, medium, and large firms operating in the Northern Ohio region. Such "baseline" data were considered to be an important prerequisite for generating meaningful policy and comparisons of corporate strategy. Comparison creates a sense of reality that is necessary for improving the chances of success of innovation projects undertaken by corporate innovation networks. In the interest of conserving space, few results of the 1983-84 pilot survey will be discussed here. Some of the demographics and findings of the research have been published[5] and are forthcoming elsewhere.

Our interest centered on detecting discrepancies between respondents' perceived pressures for innovation and their chosen innovation goals. Our working hypothesis was that some of these discrepancies can be attributed to objective barriers to innovation, others to interpersonal, interdepartmental or interfunctional differences in perceptions and priorities. The discrepancies, we maintain, can be minimized either by top-down intervention, by lateral self-management (personalized approach), or by bottom-up self-organization (group approach). At any rate, such approaches require a diagnostic in the first place.

Data were collected on two major sources of conflict in organized groups: (1) internal or external pressures for innovation; and (2) different perceptions and conflicting priorities that affect goal formation and choices among alternative means-ends relations (agendas for action). Figure 16.5 presents our correspondence model, which relates these pressure and goal variables to intervening variables indicating various barriers to innovation.

The correspondence model allows formulating testable hypotheses that, in addition, are operationalizable. Conflict in task groups arises from disagreement over ends (i.e., different goals), means (i.e., different priorities or pressures), or both. Therefore, only from a purely rational perspective would it seem reasonable to expect a tight relationship (correspondence) between innovation goals and pressures for innovation. This is the high correspondence hypothesis within the framework of neoclassical theory of the firm. For example, a high level of emphasis on "new product development" as a goal would appear to correspond with a high degree of customer-imposed pressure for product differentiation. Similarly, a strong focus on the goal of "cost containment" would be the direct response to "profit squeeze" pressures.

Figure 16.5. The Pressure-Goal-Activity Sequence and Intervening Barriers

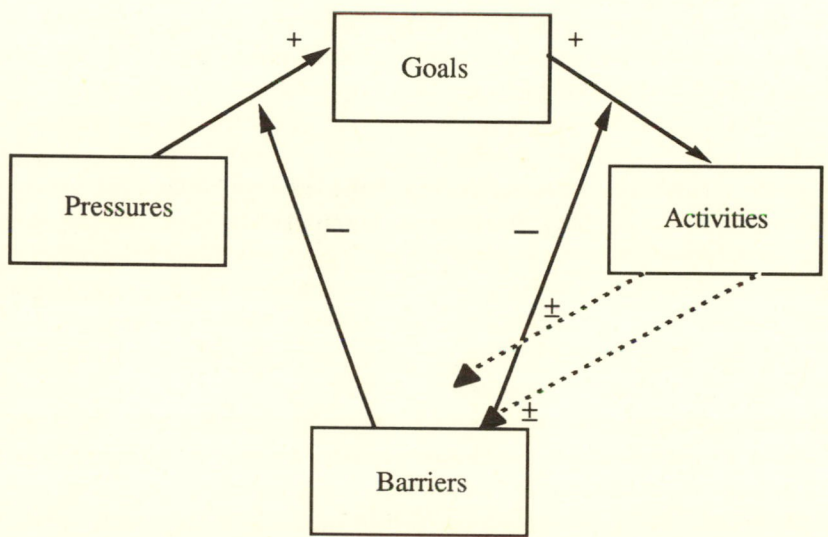

Behavior is seldom perfectly rational in general, however, and it is usually "bounded rational" (H. Simon). In the case of product innovation, which may take an average of five years from idea to implementation,[6] we should even expect to see many mismatches between pressures and goals. This is the low correspondence hypothesis. The extent of such mismatches depends partly on conduct, partly on unfavorable facts, and partly on the extent of perceived uncertainty. Partly it is symptomatic of "internal uncertainties"[7] typical of the stalemate situation when a technology-driven business runs into limits to growth and growth of limits. When the tightening of market limits puts pressure on the organization, it also generates schizophrenic (ambiguous) signals of inconsistencies at the interpersonal level, and contradictions at the corporate level. The practical question is: How can make them visible and communicable?

MEASURING PRESSURES

Pressures for innovation were measured in a two-step procedure. The first step was to define and rate pressure factors. The second step was to compress the set of factors into a relevant subset. Table 16.1 lists the respondents' rankings of twelve pressures. It can be ascertained at a glance that "labor cost" was rated as the most critical pressure by respondents, and "low price imports" as the least critical (in a relative sense). The latter point illustrates the competitive acumen of participating companies, which seem to be doing quite well in contested markets at a time when the U.S. trade deficit has surpassed the $100 billion mark.

Table 16.1. Ranking of Innovation Pressures by Perceived Intensity*

Pressure	Pressure Category	Average Intensity Score
Labor costs	Cost	3.15
New manufacturing systems	New technology	2.77
New materials/component parts	New technology	2.73
Shift in composition of demand	Product-market	2.72
Product obsolescence	Product-market	2.64
Superior rival products	Competition	2.61
Entrepreneurial needs	Human resources	2.46
Product safety	Regulation	2.37
Staff-worker involvement	Human resources	2.28
Environmental	Regulation	2.15
Shortage of skilled workers	Human resources	1.80
Low price imports	Competition	1.70

*Respondents indicated the importance of each pressure on a 6-point scale, ranging from 1 (not important) to 6 (extremely important). The scores in the rightmost column are the averages for 122 respondents.

Factor Analysis of Pressures for Innovation

Each respondent's 12 pressure scores were transformed into loadings with regard to the following four pressure factors:

$$P_1 = \text{General Management's Attitude}$$
$$P_2 = \text{Actual Profit Squeeze}$$
$$P_3 = \text{Expected Product Obsolescence}$$
$$P_4 = \text{Entry of New Technology}$$

Pressures for innovation within the responding firms appear to be related primarily to cost containment, new technology, and product and market scope. Competitive threats or regulatory actions (e.g., product safety environmental standards) appear to be less specific or weaker pressures for innovation, at least in our sample.

Data on the twelve pressures were further factor analyzed to yield a parsimonious set of "pressure factors." Four principal pressure factors, which we labeled as "general management attitude," "profit squeeze," "product obsolescence," and "new technology" pressures, emerged from this principal component analysis.

MEASURING GOALS

Goals for innovation were similarly quantified. Table 16.2 shows the respondents' goals for innovation as a long list and as a reduced list of goal dimensions. In the upper part, we have ranked them by the relative importance respondents attached to them on an aggregate basis. The data reveal that productivity of efficiency-oriented goals are dominant in our sample of companies. This would prima facie suggest a primary emphasis on developing process innovation. Of somewhat less importance are expressed goals pertaining to product innovation. Goals relating to other aspects of the innovation process, such as promoting entrepreneurship, complying with environmental requirements, or reducing energy costs were given relatively low priority by our respondents.

The set of twelve goals were also factor analyzed to achieve a reduction in dimensionality. Three principal goal factors, which we labeled "quest for new products," "regulatory compliance," and "cost containment" goals, emerged from this analysis.

ANALYZING PRESSURE-GOAL RELATIONSHIPS

Do the principal pressures correspond to the principal goals? As a visual aid, a series of scattergrams were developed. Each scattergram links a pressure factor to one of the three goals by pairwise association. Any factor not paired-up is tentatively treated as an intervening variable.

Not every pressure factor was related to every goal factor; only those pressure-goal pairs that seem meaningful on the basis of the innovation research literature were considered. Both the literature and common sense provide justification for expecting "new product" goals and "product obsolescence" pressures to be somehow connected. By contrast, any posited relationship between a "regulatory compliance" goal and a "profit squeeze" pressure would be difficult to justify a priori, in the United States, but not in Western Europe.

Table 16.2. Ranking of Innovation Goals by Perceived Importance[*]

Goal	Goal Category	Average Intensity Score
Increase in overall efficiency	Productivity/Efficiency	3.86
Increase product efficiency	Productivity/Efficiency	3.71
Reduction in material costs	Cost reduction	3.43
Creation of successor products	Product-market	3.32
Reduction of labor costs	Cost reduction	3.25
Restructuring of product mix	Product-market	2.29
Rounding out of product mix	Product-market	2.90
Inducing internal entrepreneurship	Human resources	2.74
Response to regulatory pressures (other than environmental standards)	Regulatory compliance	2.74
Compliance with environmental standards	Regulatory compliance	2.68
Energy cost savings	Cost reduction	2.64
Improvement of working conditions	Human resources	2.63

[*]Respondents indicated the importance of each pressure on a 6-point scale ranging from 1 (not important) to 6 (extremely important). The scores in the rightmost column are the averages for 123 respondents.

Factors Analysis of Innovation Goals

Each respondent's 12 goal scores were transformed into weights with regards to the following three goals:

$$G_1 = \text{Quest for New Products}$$
$$G_2 = \text{Compliance with Regulation}$$
$$G_3 = \text{Cost Containment Goals}$$

The *tightest correspondence* between any pressure and goal was observed in the pairing of x = "*general management attitude*" and y = "*compliance with regulation.*" Either a firm must comply or it must not. That fact is reflected in a relatively high correspondence between y ≡ x and a relatively low deviation e = y − x. *In all other cases the low correspondence hypothesis prevailed.* Figures 16.6 to 16.10 depict scattergrams for the most important pairings from the viewpoint of strategic innovation management.

Figure 16.6. Scattergram of "New Technology" Pressure and "Cost Containment" Goal

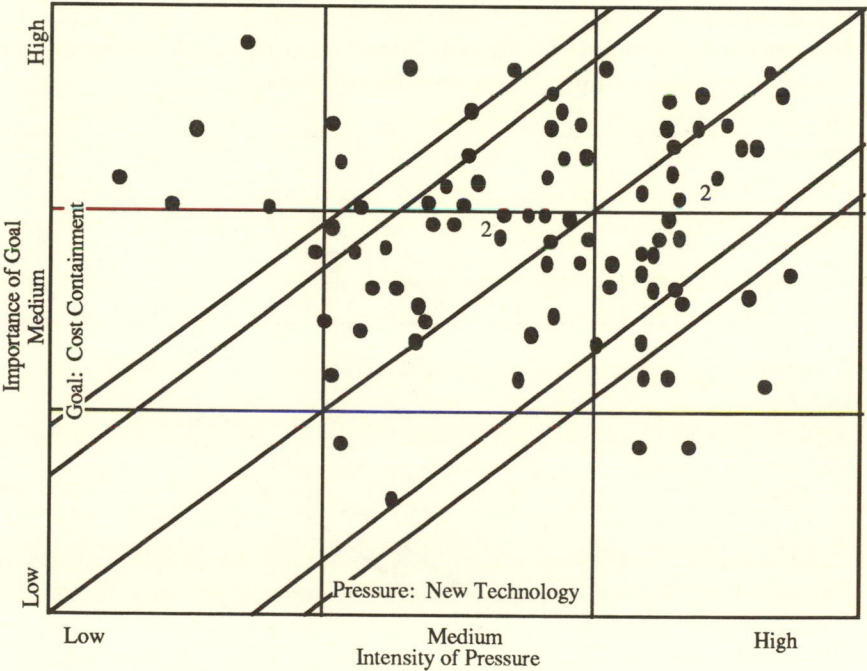

Experience in the field[8] had already prompted us not to expect a high degree of correspondence between innovation pressures and goals. In fact, we expected some mismatches. In all scattergrams, these mismatches are visible as a lack of tight correspondence between pressures and goals. The least squares trend lines fitted to the pressure-goal data has uniformly low R^2 values when we take no intervening variables into account.

The low correspondence in pairwise presentation of the data is thought-provoking. Why do corresponding pairs of pressures and goals exhibit such strong evidence of discrepancies between participating managers' opinions? Two causes may explain the congruence. One is time-related. There may be a time lag between the sensing of a pressure and the formulation of an appropriate goal that would respond to it. The second cause of mismatch includes various mediating influences. They are man-made and include hierarchical and functional position of the respondent, and other cultural, structural, and situational variables. The value of the diagnostic tool is that it provokes discussion of these discrepancies, and the facing-up to the very reasons for dissensus and delay.

Figure 16.7. Scattergram of "New Technology" Pressure and "New Products" Goal

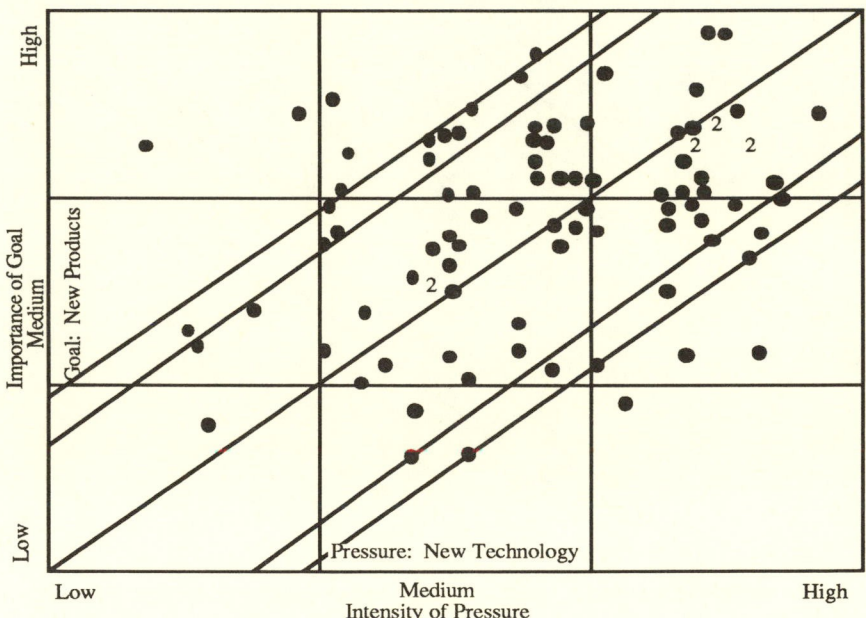

APPLICATION AS A DIAGNOSTIC TOOL

In order to operationalize the correspondence model and measurements, we distinguish company-specific scattergrams from those for all firms.

Interesting insights are achieved when data for the respondents of one individual firm with multiple respondents are overlayed on the scattergram for all companies, or for a subset of comparables. In some cases the responses of managers from the same firm are closely clustered, while in other cases they are scattered widely, indicating intraorganizational discrepancies. These are patterns of diagnostic value.

Figure 16.8. Scattergram of "Product Obsolescence" Pressure and "New Products" Goal

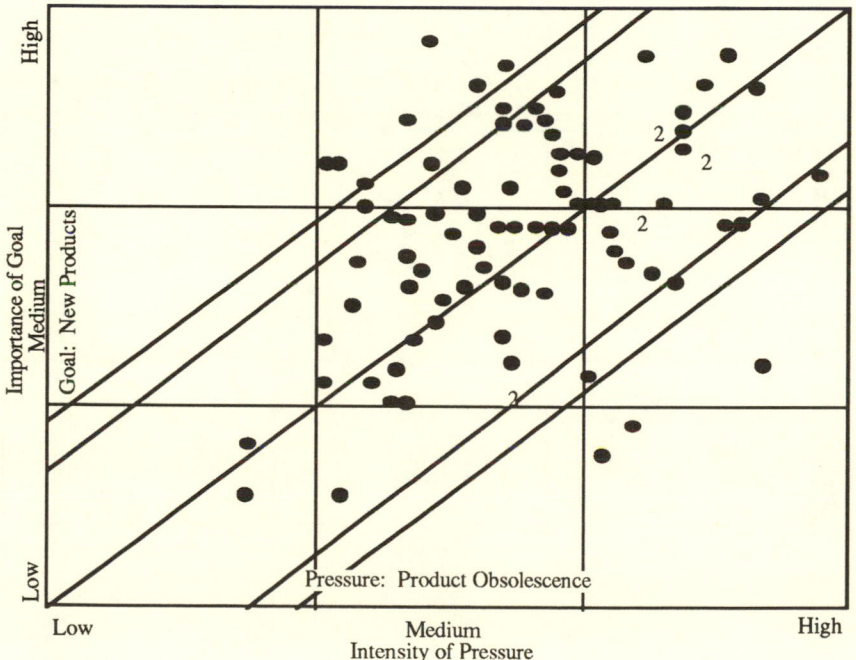

For example, consider two "outliers" in the scattergram that relates goal G_1 = Develop New Products to pressure P_4 = Entry of New Technology (see Figure 16.7).

First, consider an "outlier" in the north west corner. Dots there represent a seemingly incongruent combination of high G_1-score and low P_4-score. We have dubbed it the *"high-hope-empty-hand"* posture. In this case, the respondent is the head of development engineering at a $50 million revenue company. His mission is to generate new product prospects, a mission he highly identifies with. But what he also wants to say to his peers is this: As a liaison between R&D and production, I guess I must inform you that the specific technology promoted by R&D will probably not amount to a cost-effective new line of product. Yet I don't know how to tell you the bad news.

Figure 16.9. Scattergram of "Profit Squeeze" Pressure and "Cost Containment" Goal

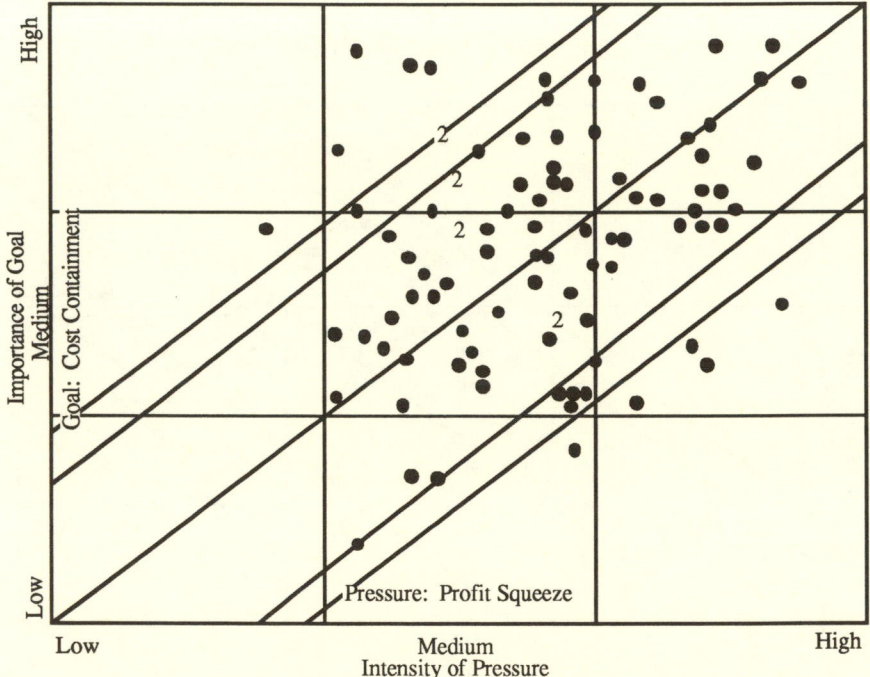

Second, consider an "outlier" at the southeast corner. Dots there represent the converse combination, namely, a low G_1-goal score and a high P_4-new technology pressure score. We have dubbed it the *"fear of flying"* combination. In this case, the respondent is the director of marketing of a $12 million revenue company. He personally believes in the great market potential of the new product technology, but he cannot assess both the true extent of technological risk, and he doubts his ability to sell to his superiors a "still somewhat uncertain project."

SELF-ADMINISTERED APPLICATION

A team of managers in a given company can use the scattergram as a clinical device for brainstorming about their situation, or position, vis-à-vis other firms in that industry. This helps in exploring, in a DELPHI-process type of discussion, the underlying reasons that determine internal agreements and critical differences among key players. To facilitate such diagnosis, we have developed transparency overlays that superimpose the scattergram of a particular company's responses over the general scattergram. This was done for every pressure-goal pair analyzed. Superimposing the transparencies then clearly indicates varying degrees of "mismatch" of a firm's executives opinions. The graphics show:

- how much the team members differ from each other vis-à-vis their perceptions of the pressure, priorities and goals

- whether one or more of the respondents occupy an "outlying" position with respect to the central tendency or "sense" of the entire group

- whether the whole group is-off base when compared to similar firms or industries

In utilizing these data, the question of most interest is probably this: Does the location of a company's respondents on these plots represent the norm or does that company's situation deviate in some way? Is the firm possibly abnormal, or positively exceptional? If the answer to these questions is the latter, then the company may want to know what the implications of an "exceptional" situation are. For example, does "exceptional" carry a truly positive connotation for this particular company? By what standard? Some firms are proud of a marginal innovation while their rivals bring a breakthrough to the market. Based on intensive analyses of data pertaining to several companies represented by multiple respondents in our survey, we have developed some tentative approaches to answering these questions.

COMMONLY OBSERVED PATTERNS OF MISMATCH

The company-specific scattergram overlays give a visual picture of where a particular company's respondents are located on the scattergram in relation to other participants in the survey. In a clinical situation, of course, it is inadvisable to make absolute judgments as to the future value of postures toward innovation. A company's revealed innovation-related set of attitudes must be seen in a "relative" light, namely, against some baseline values or benchmarks. How does a company obtain such benchmark values? There are several approaches; their respective advantages are being discussed in the emerging field of data envelop analysis pioneered by Charnes and Cooper.

Figure 16.10. Scattergram of "Profit Squeeze" Pressure and "New Products" Goal

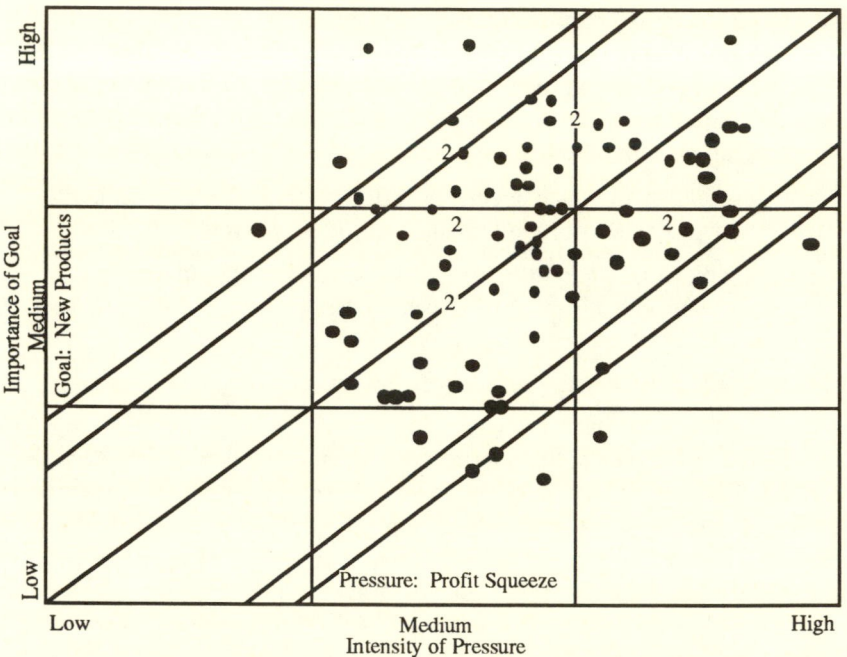

Our approach was the following: We regard the totality of survey participants as providing the data for calculating a benchmark or norm for comparison. Individual respondents can then be compared with peers from the same company, and the team pattern can be compared against the benchmark calculated for groups of firms (look-alikes), or for the whole population of firms. In fact, electing the "proper" norm for assessing a firm's present position is in itself the core of the strategic decision that needs to be made for repositioning the firm in a changing competitive environment.

Figure 16.11 depicts five types of patterns that are observed in the company specific overlays. Again, we shall explain the ideal and follow up with explaining deviations, and making observations.

In Pattern 1, the diagonal line *OC* represents the "ideal" situation. Points located on or close to this diagonal line represent high degrees of correspondence. Normally, one would expect high levels of a pressure, say P, as leading to correspondingly high levels of an appropriate goal, say G. In reality, however, such an ideal pattern is seldom obtained. Figures 16.6 to 16.10 show how dramatically responses vary. Again, we should normally find the variations to be confined to the band enclosed by lines PQ and TU or RS and VW. We can draw these lines such that they envelop all or a fraction of data points, for example 75 or 80 percent of all observations, or a subset representing the firm's strategic group in the industry.

Individual points (G, P) falling outside these bands are interesting to look at because—as exemplified above—they call for additional supervisory help and better leadership. Furthermore, when many respondents from the same company are involved, additional insight can be derived by examining the pattern formed by all their responses in relation to either the general scattergram, or in relation to more specific, strategically selected benchmarks. In fact, playing with modified benchmarks is the gist of sensitivity analysis and contingency planning.

EMPIRICAL OBSERVATIONS

Pattern 1 is characterized by proximity of three executives from the same company. With respect to the intensity each feels about pressure P and importance of the corresponding goal G, they are similar. For the three managers, this is significant information. This similitude amongst them contrasts with the obvious dissimilitude with the "mainstream." The reasons for such a divergence from the general pattern and for their proximity to one another are well worth exploring in more focused workshops on the firm's competitive posture.

An example for application are the responses of four managers from a Northern Ohio utility company. In the scattergram relating new technology pressures P_4 to the cost containment goal G_3, Figure 16.6, one person's response is on the line $G_3 = P_4$, whereas the three others are strongly onesided such that $G_3 >> P_4$. The dots representing these three responses can be found in the upper left quadrant. They indicate maximum cost consciousness and minimum regard for the emerging new technology that is currently threatening the very core of their industry. The new technology is a widely publicized prime example of innovation by invasion, yet the three managers' priorities do not reflect it. Why not? One reason is the predominant objective of this regulated company to keep rates below the threshold of severe political repercussions. The three respondents with (G_3, P_4) in the upper left corner all are district managers with staff responsibilities, notably

Figure 16.11. Company Patterns

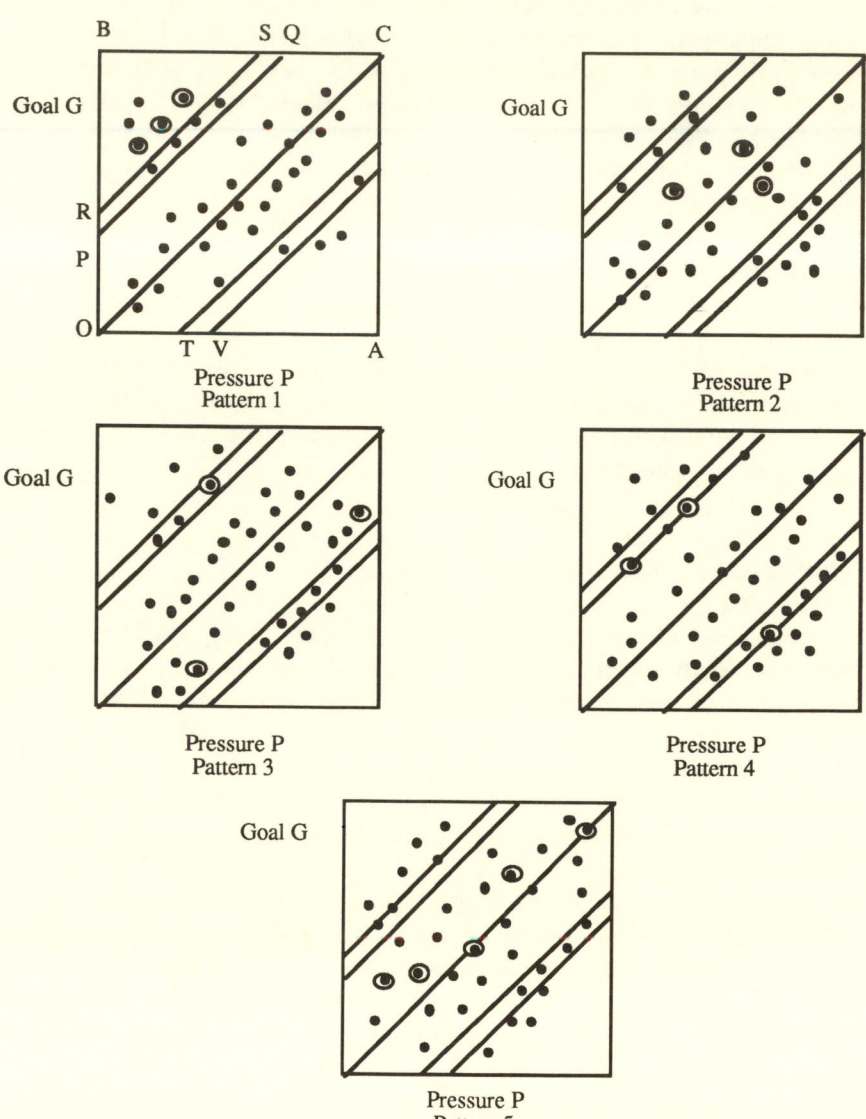

planning, whereas the manager with line responsibilities, notably operation, has a balanced view of cost cutting and new technology utilization. The revealed differences in priorities and orientation thus follow the classical pattern of functional division of labor in large organizations. Hence, this organization is in a technological stalemate, and it appears to be far from solving the concurrent problems: increasing cost-effectiveness of standard operations, and simultaneously adopting new technology that responds to changing customer habits, in a balanced way that is reflected in goal consistency and consensus about the environmental challenges as depicted by Pattern 2 in Figure 16.11.

Pattern 3 indicates a situation where two of three managers agree on either of two dimensions but are miles apart from the third on another dimension—a situation called the "tragic triangle." What it depicts is a managerial group haunted by decisiveness along two conjoint, intersecting lines of conflict. None of the potential coalitions of the managers can be stable as long as the three executives stand by their convictions, which create a double prisoners' dilemma. Only if at least two of the three will compromise on at least one of their two mismatching points of view can they reach an arrangement where two dominate the third and go on with their duties, as is depicted in Pattern 4.

Participating in our project were seven senior and junior vice-presidents of a Fortune 500 company with eighty to one hundred lines of products (depending on whom you ask). The corporation on the whole is highly profitable in terms of return on capital, although about 85 percent of revenues are generated with products five years or older. "Much older!" said those participants who argued forcefully that the company should make a concerted effort toward product innovation. In the scattergram relating pressure from product obsolescence, P_3, to the goal of creating new products, G_1, these managers scored high on G_1 but varied on P_3. They strongly disagree on the reading of the market data. The trouble is that nobody seems to know the whole picture. The heads of strategic business units know in much more depth and detail than do the respective group VPs what goes in their markets and related fields. On the other end, the senior and executive VP may have a wider picture from a bird's-eye perspective, but that means they have only superficial knowledge about any of the many markets the company serves. In their regular meetings, knowledge does not flow well. The stream of data is too intensive to be grasped, and the time and attention spans are too short for the string of messages that must be exchanged.

In addition, managers also differ greatly in admitted product obsolescence, knowing what it entails: It may mean near disaster to your career chances if your area becomes reclassified as a "dog business." Therefore, several heads of divisions responded saying $G_1 = P_3 = $ low; in other words, they maintain that there is little product obsolescence and therefore little need for product innovation. They are thus located in the southwest corner of the scattergram, whereas the corporation's top managers occupy the $G_1 = $ high spectrum in the picture. The top managers express minimum concern for innovation, and try to foster innovation in any way they see fit. At the same time, a significant subgroup of subordinate managers does not see, or admit to, product obsolescence as a pressure for innovation, thus holding on to ongoing lines of products, implying: "Pass! Let the other guy do the risk taking."

EVALUATION OF THE TOOL IN SELF-ADMINISTERED USES

How effective is the method of encouraging constructive inputs via measuring and diagnosing discrepancies? We have not made a comprehensive, formal evaluation of effectiveness gains made by participating users of the tool! Companies want us to see only the tip of the iceberg, and we respect that decision. A few example of positive results might suffice to indicate results.

In the large corporation just mentioned, the participating group of managers opted not to invite us to the in-house discussion they held after they saw the serious hierarchical, functional, and divisional discrepancies that existed. Seeing quantitative measures of disharmony on the table induced them to air their differences, clarify the underlying issues, and verbalize the implicit assumptions. We have been told by the executive VP that "our positions have somewhat converged in the process. At least we have reached a point where individuals have consistent views, while they may still have a different sense of urgency." This situation is depicted by Pattern 5 in Figure 16.11. In other words, managers now agree on the general direction the corporation should take, namely, fostering breakthrough innovations, while at the same time they tolerate great differences in pace and push for innovation across groups and divisions. In a nutshell, the degree of divisiveness before has been reduced to a regular coordination problem. "We felt dead in the water," one senior manager said. "Now we feel going again."

Another word of appreciation of results comes from the owner-manager CEO of a medium-sized company ($35 million sales). The firm owes its experience and former growth to a series of technical innovations the owner-manager made during the 1950s and 1960s in the instrument industry. As a technology-driven business, the firm developed as an example par excellence of the dynamic depicted in Figures 16.1 to 16.3, and was facing the stalemate situation depicted in Figure 16.4. The company's problem apparently was to develop or find new technology for renewed growth. However, most members of the "mature" organization felt they might never be able to live up to the standard of achievement manifest in the track record of the CEO.

As a result, participants from this company responded with high scores in regard to both profit squeeze pressure, P_2, and quest for new products, G_1. These employees' recent experience was that product development in the company showed a disappointing success rate, and they thought it was largely a financing problem. In the process, this erroneous perception was discovered and corrected through applying our tool. "Working with your material changed all that," the CEO explained to us. "There was a time my development folks always seemed to miss the mark for reasons that did not add up. If I now ask of a new product proposal: Is it real? Can we win? Is it worth it? I get solid answers."

FROM DIAGNOSIS TO THERAPY

Self-administration of a diagnostic tool often results in a therapeutic effect on the user. When a group of managers in a company agrees to use the diagnostic, they might have not only a sense of need but also a perception of cause and possible remedy.

The next step in the methodological advancement lies in controlling for the therapeutical effect: What is to be accomplished? For whom? How is it to be done?

At the time we conducted our diagnostical experiments, we found that managers who initiated the adoption of our tool were cautious not to induce resistance from colleagues. One factor of resistance clearly is the implication of "illness" if the diagnostic should indeed have any therapeutic effect. "Who needs it?" was a question we often heard; but what the question really meant was this: "Who in this world wants to admit that he needs a diagnosis as a first step toward therapy?"

In other words, once managers agreed to use the diagnostic, they were able to reduce discrepancies among themselves, and to move from "dead in the water" to problem solving and concerted action. However, they would not have even tried the diagnostic if it implied that they had behavioral deficits in, for example, problem solving or cooperation.

No such cultural barrier to admitting "corporate disease" now exists in former East European countries. There, the need for improvement in productivity, marketing, and coordination is widely recognized, and accepted. Hence, it is there that the next step will be implemented.

AN INNOVATION CLINIC IN MID-GERMANY

An innovation clinic is an institution that provides orderly therapy for business units hit by a structural crisis. Clearly, the facilities must be large enough to accommodate hundreds of men and women of all ranks and files from the same firm. While at the location of the troubled business unit the old capital stock (plant, equipment, infrastructure) has been refurbished for the new production that is to replace the old, the bureau capital (manpower system) has been prepared for the new tasks.

An innovation clinic thus provides an alternative to the sequential process of shutting down the plant, sending all employees home, renovating the buildings, relieving people, and training them for the new jobs. The alternative is a "flying start"; it is a parallel process of adjusting physical and human capital to tasks simultaneously.

To the employees, this means greater security.

To the public, this saves unemployment costs.

To the firm, this saves time, set-up costs, capital costs, transaction costs, and—last but not least—opportunity costs.

From a methodological point of view, this creates an environment where an orderly therapeutical process is applied toward the desired therapeutical effect (what, for whom, how).

From the managerial perspective, the need is there. In Eastern Europe, the fall of the Iron Curtain opened the markets to foreign competition, and also exposed each and every market's imperfection. Of course, the very collapse of the socialist system was caused by people's dissatisfaction with market conduct. Hence, all firms in all markets in Eastern Europe face a structural crisis. As the saying goes, "When it rains, it pours." For socialist firms, which were—and still are—organized as multiplant concerns ("combinants") designated to a special field of business ("industry" in the narrow sense), restructuring means facing two obstacles at the same time. First, due to overspecialization and underutilization of creative and innovative potential (in the command economy), these firms need external assistance. Second, since all plants of the firm need restructuring at the same time, these firms lack the capacity to buffer-stock. Hence, they need an external capacity for temporarily housing employees while schooling and training them for new jobs.

The Mid-German Innovation Clinic will offer the physical facilities to satisfy the need of several firms at the same time, and it will provide a complete set of value-added services to teach the "therapeutical effect" that is appropriate for customized uses of the clinic. In a nutshell: The innovation clinic can do it better, faster, and more cost-effectively.

NOTES

1. G. O. Mensch, *Stalemate in Technology: Innovations Overcome the Depression* (Cambridge, Mass.: Ballinger, 1979).

2. V. Ramanujam and G. O. Mensch, "Improving the Strategy-Innovation Link," *Journal of Product Innovation Management* 4 (3) (December 1985); G. O. Mensch, "Perspective: Get Ready for Innovation by Invasion," *Journal of Product Innovation Management* 4 (3) (December 1985).

3. See G. O. Mensch, "Innovation Management in Diversified Corporations," *Human Systems Management* 3 (1) (1982): 10–20; W. L. Shanklin and J. K. Ryans, "Organizing for High Tech Marketing," *Harvard Business Review* 62 (6) (1984): 164–71; W. E. Souder, "Organizing for Modern Technology and Innovation. A Review and Synthesis," *Technovation* 2 (1) (1983): 27–44; W. E. Souder, "Disharmony Between R&D and Marketing," *Industrial Marketing Management* 10 (1) (1981): 67–73; W. C. Fernelius and W. H. Waldo, "Role of Basic Research in Industrial Innovation," *Research Management* 23 (7) (1980): 36–40; M. Jelinek, *Institutionalizing Innovation* (New York: Praeger, 1979).

4. Blair Little, editorial, *Journal of Product Innovation Management* 1 (1984): 138.

5. See Mensch, "Innovation Management."

6. Fernelius and Waldo, "Basic Research"; G. O. Mensch, "Innovation in Smaller Companies," in *Current Innovation,* ed. B. A. Vedin (Stockholm: Almquist and Wiksell, 1980).

7. G. O. Mensch, "Innovation Management in Diversified Corporations," in *Organizing Industrial Development,* ed. W. Wolf (Berlin/New York: Springer-Verlag, 1986).

8. See Ramanujam and Mensch, "Strategy-Innovation Link"; Mensch, "Innovation Management"; "Innovation in Smaller Companies."

17

Forecasting Manpower Supply and Demand at Different Stages of Industrial Development: Strategies and Methodologies

Arnold Reisman

Forecasting the supply and demand of trained human resources is an integral part of "manpower planning." Both are done at national, regional, and institutional levels in developed and developing societies. This chapter represents a digest of some of the pertinent literature. In taxonomic fashion it discusses the issues considered relevant by the various authors. It addresses problems with the availability of data (educational statistics) that may be encountered even in the most industrialized societies and concludes with insights gained from a retrospective review of a number of manpower supply and demand forecasts made in the United States for the decade of the 1970s.

BACKGROUND

Availability, in the right mix and at the right levels, of trained human resources[1] is essential to industrial development. Industrial development can apply to a national or a regional economy. A region is considered to comprise geographical parts of one or more nation-states. However, industrial development may also imply the development of a new or emerging technology within an economy. The word "development" implies transition or change from one state to another. Each of the intermediate states of industrial development requires its characteristic mix and level of human capital—more specifically, of trained manpower. Unfortunately such training typically takes time, money, and other resources, including trained human resources. There is a feedback loop. Often such training processes can only be measured in years if not generations. Planning and implementing training programs are not trivial tasks, especially in freedom-of-choice societies. Nor is the task much easier in the centrally planned or command and control societies.

Good planning requires balancing supply with demand. Since balance is to be struck at some time in the future it is necessary to forecast both. Forecasting however, is not, by all accounts, a perfect science (Pollack-Johnson et al. 1990). Long-range forecasting is especially an art which, at best, can be aided by technology if not science per se (Martino 1983).

Rostow (1971) synthesized much factual as well as anecdotal information and produced a theory explaining the path leading toward industrialization of national and/or regional economies. The stages of economic growth as theorized by Rostow can be helpful in serving as a basis for distinguishing among the differing objectives, characteristics, and approaches to be used in manpower forecasting and planning. However, in light of the fact that most countries now have pockets of development, for purposes of this discussion, we will lump the developing societies into a single category to be distinguished from the "postindustrial" or "mass consumption" societies.

RELATIONSHIP BETWEEN MANPOWER FORECASTING AND PLANNING

There are four principal assumptions regarding the quality of knowledge pertaining to the future: certainty, risk, uncertainty, and ignorance. Irrespective of the quality of knowledge, planning must be preceded by forecasting of the future states or events. The forecasting effort required depends largely on the level of knowledge regarding the states of the future. Moreover, the techniques used may also depend on the availability and quality of historical data. For example, when certainty about the future is assumed, the forecasting effort required is trivial as there can be but one outcome to a given set of decisions. This is often true in "push" type educational systems such as compulsory elementary school education or technical training programs within the military. Under conditions of risk the outcomes are assumed to fall into a probability distribution, the shape and the parameters of which are known. Education at the secondary school level exemplifies a "push" system with fairly well-known probabilities of dropouts. Under the assumption of uncertainty, the outcomes are presumed to depend on scenarios of the future. Therefore, the forecast of outcomes given the future states of events is most valuable to the planning effort as they provide a basis for the justification of any planning decisions to be made.

The value of any manpower plan is a function of the quality of the forecast on which it is based. While this measure of a plan may be true, the value of knowledge from even the most sophisticated forecasting techniques cannot be fully realized unless, of course, the results of such forecasting techniques can be effectively applied in the manpower planning process.

The higher up one goes in the educational system ladder, the greater is the impact on graduation rates of "pull" versus "push" type forces. "Pull" type forces result from perceptions regarding current and future states of various socioeconomic factors within a society. These change. The changes can take place over time, as is currently the situation affecting U.S. dental school enrollments, or be quite abrupt. The best example of a relatively sudden change in such perceptions occurred in the United States immediately following the launching of Sputnik I by the Soviet Union.

Manpower planning has become sufficiently sophisticated that the forecasting and the planning functions have come to be recognized as integral parts, supportive of one another, in the planning process. Two recently published papers in the literature (Fildes 1979, 1985) provide an excellent review of forecasting methods in general. Some of these methods can be used to forecast the parameters needed in a manpower forecast.

However, a cautionary note is in order. The predisposition of forecasters in general is to use objective statistical techniques with time-series and other objective data (Pollack-Johnson et al. 1990). Such data may not be available at all or, as we have discovered to be the case involving practicing physicians in Nigeria and also the rate of attrition from the workforce of Ph.D.s in the United States, quality may deteriorate as the level of professional training goes up. As a rule the lesser the development of a society the lower down the "pipeline" one must reach for good-quality educational statistics. Reisman et al. (1986) indicate that even in our postindustrial society with all the government agencies and private sector institutions dedicated to capturing and/or managing educational data and statistics we still have significant data voids. These clearly are much more pronounced at the postgraduate level.

A TAXONOMY OF MANPOWER
FORECASTING AND PLANNING

Because the approaches used by the various authors writing on manpower forecasting and planning are quite disparate, it is helpful to review the entire field in terms of the universe of things considered germane within the literature. A good way to do this is through some form of a taxonomy. In a recent paper (Reisman, Song, and Ikem 1990) we presented such a taxonomy. Following is a summary of the parameters used for purposes of classifying the literature of manpower forecasting and planning methodologies:

H symbolizes the length of the planning horizon considered by the methodology. It is further subdivided into short-range (H_s), medium-range (H_m), and long-range (H_l).

L symbolizes the level of planning: national (L_n), regional (L_r), state (L_s), and institutional or company (L_i).

A symbolizes the level of professional and/or geographic aggregation or lumping: high (A_h) and low (A_l).

W symbolizes the basic approach used: objective (W_o), subjective (W_s), and mixed (W_m).

P symbolizes the purpose of the model; optimization (P_o), policy evaluation (P_e), and forecasting (P_f), where optimization models for manpower planning match the forecasted or projected manpower supply with manpower demand in an optimal fashion.

I symbolizes the assumed impetus for people movement within the system; push (I_p), pull (I_e), and mixed (I_m). Education of youngsters in a system based on compulsory education is assumed to be a push flow, because the students are "pushed" through the system. Recruitment and promotion in a workforce, on the other hand, are assumed to be pull flows. Manpower planning models sometimes contain mixed flows, part of the pipeline is push type (students in elementary schools) and part is "pull" (students graduating from doctoral programs and entering the workforce).

The six symbols *HLAWPI* with the appropriate subscripts represent the common factors used in manpower forecasting and planning models. Other factors included in some, but not all, manpower forecasting and planning models are summarized next.

F   symbolizes the fact that manpower flow feedback (closed) loops are incorporated in the model. Closed loops allow outflows to reenter a particular sector of the model.

N   symbolizes the fact that mathematical nonlinearities are allowed in the model.

M   symbolizes the fact that multiple variates are incorporated in the model. Univariate models are based on extrapolation of manpower trends, whereas multivariate models incorporate structural changes and/or environmental circumstances.

C   symbolizes the cross-sectional structure of the system at a given time. The common feature of all cross-sectional models is that historical data prior to the given time are not required by these models, whereas longitudinal models require a historical time series database.

S   symbolizes the stochastic nature of the model. If all or some of the flows (recruitment, attrition, promotion, and transfer) are controllable and deterministic, then it is not necessary to have a stochastic model. Voluntary attrition is almost always not controllable and probabilistic but promotion may indeed be controlled and deterministic.

T   symbolizes the time-dependent behavior (nonstationary) of the model.

The most general model that can be conceived using the above factors, in turn a reflection of how this field of knowledge is currently bounded, will include all of them. Such a model would therefore be symbolized by the acronym $H_h L_l A_a P_p I_i\ FNMCST$, where the general subscripts take on specific meanings. This model is conceived to explicitly consider the length of the planning horizon, the level of planning, the level of aggregation, the basic approach applied to the model, the purpose of the model, and structural considerations such as feedback loops, nonlinearities, multivariates, stochastic nature, and time-dependent behavior (nonstationary). The less complicated models are symbolized simply by deleting the symbols represented by capital letters and/or by specifying the subscripts in *HLAWPIFNMCST*. For example, a model described as having a long-range planning horizon, directed at a national level of planning, high level of aggregation, using objective methods, optimization, push flows, and having a stochastic nature would be the $H_l L_n A_h W_o P_o I_p S$ subcase of *HLAWPIFNMCST*. Should it also contain non-stationary then the model would be the $H_l L_n A_h W_o P_o I_p ST$ subcase of *HLAWPIFNMCST*. Since every model must contain some planning horizon, level of planning, level of aggregation, methodology, purpose of the model, and impetus for people movement every subcase of *HLAWPIFNMCST* must contain the symbols *HLAWPI* with the appropriate subscripts. If a particular model is applicable to all levels of *H, L,* or *A,* respectively, however, then the subscript is omitted. For example, if a model is applicable to all lengths of the planning horizon (e.g., short, medium, and long), then no subscripts appear next to *H*. The Reisman, Song, and Ikem (1990) paper reviews some of the landmark contributions to the literature of manpower forecasting and planning and uses the above taxonomic scheme to classify each of the papers reviewed.

The approach used in the above was a generalization of an earlier taxonomy of manpower forecasting and planning (Balinsky and Reisman 1973). In another paper (Reisman 1988) it is shown that this approach can also be used to delineate or to specify those models/methodologies that need to be developed for any given occasion.

MANPOWER REQUIREMENTS PLANNING IN DEVELOPING COUNTRIES

Manpower requirements of most developing countries can be met by developing local training facilities, sending indigents to train abroad, or recruiting expatriates. Foreign training and expatriates often involve expenditures of scarce foreign exchange in competition with other development projects. A recent paper (Ikem and Reisman 1990) develops a manpower planning model that coordinates physician manpower requirements of a developing country with its capacity to train such physicians along with national objectives to contain costs. That paper also presents computational results from a dynamic programming model using the best data available from Nigeria.

As stated earlier, planning for human resources is primarily concerned with matching the supply of people with the jobs available. Unlike individual career planning, human resource planning is concerned with aggregate behavior. Any modeling in this context must attempt to describe how changes take place in the system. Among other considerations, this requires specification of constraints under which the system operates. In particular, the models require that the training patterns be represented in a network flow-like diagram. As indicated earlier the literature has recorded many network-flow models dealing with national or regional human resources forecasting and planning.

Debeauvais and Psacharopoulos (1985) and Jolly and McCollough (1972) point out that there are three major steps to manpower planning:

- projecting the demand for educated manpower
- projecting the supply for educated manpower
- balancing the supply with the demand

The first two of these steps are forecasting in nature. The third step dictates policy.

Most of the manpower planning literature, concerned with single occupations, concentrates on one or two of the above steps. The Ikem and Reisman (1990) paper addressed all three issues for planning a single occupation in a developing country. Specifically, the paper develops a manpower planning model that coordinates physician requirements of a developing country with its capacity to train such personnel along with the national objectives of containing costs.

The requirements for physicians in most developing countries are often met by some combination of developing local training facilities, sending indigents to train abroad, and recruiting of expatriates.[2] Consequently, national planners and decision makers, as well as institutional administrators, must periodically grapple with questions such as how many students to admit to local institutions in any given year, how many scholarships/fellowships to award for training abroad in any given year, whether to start a new medical school in any given year, and whether to import expatriates and how many.

The model developed in Ikem (1987) and Ikem and Reisman (1990) addresses all these questions from the viewpoint of national planners or decision makers with the objective of minimizing total costs while meeting specific (per capita of population) norms for physicians.[3]

Development of the Model

The planning problem was formulated in the form of a dynamic programming (DP) problem. The objective was to meet all projected physician manpower requirements, at a minimum total cost to society, through an optimal mix of locally trained indigenous physicians, foreign-trained indigenous physicians, and expatriate physicians. The problem was viewed as being analogous to a dynamic multistage production inventory system with a positive delivery lag, the "products" being the physicians and the production facilities (or "plants") the medical schools.

A typical solution of the DP model answers the four questions cited in the preceding section. Moreover, a typical solution yields the total cost, within the planning horizon, of meeting all physician manpower requirements in an optimal manner.

Assumptions of the Model

The following assumptions were made in formulating the DP problem:

1. Training capacity once created has a long life and does not change over time.

2. Local production (of physicians) is capacity-limited.

3. Local secondary schools produce adequate talent with interest in becoming MDs.

4. It takes six (postsecondary) years to train physicians in Nigeria and in most countries. The United States and Canada are notable exceptions.

5. All demand (for physicians) will be met by training indigenous physicians locally or abroad or by importing expatriate physicians or some combination of these.

6. Inventories of indigenous physicians at the end of some period (t_1) plus the net incremental supply of indigenous physicians in the following period t are available for use any time during period t.

7. The inventory maintenance (holding) cost for the tth period is proportional to the amount of ending inventory (of trained physicians) for period t.

8. Import and overproduction costs are proportional to the number of physicians imported or overproduced.

9. The production alternatives in each period are: local production using only existing local facilities; local production using existing facilities and adding a new facility; local production using existing facilities only plus importing foreign physicians; local production using existing facilities, adding a new facility, and importing foreign products.

10. A new school opening is considered only after all existing capacity is saturated.

11. The locally produced physicians are indistinguishable from one another and from the "imports" (expatriates), the model aggregates all specialties into one.

The Immediate Contributions to Cost

The immediate contributions to cost in any one period consist of the following three components:

1. The cost of any decision as discussed above.

2. "Maintenance" costs of indigenous physicians. This is the cost to society of having a given level of indigenous physicians. It was assumed that this cost is proportional to the number of practicing indigenous physicians at the beginning of the period.

3. Import and overproduction costs.

This component of cost in a given period involves the cost of importing expatriate physicians to help meet demand and a penalty cost for having more physicians than needed.

In the case of overproduction, one may elect not to penalize overproduction at levels less than or equal to some constant β (set by policy).

Solution to the DP Formulation

Forward dynamic programming (DP) was used to solve the above formulation. Based on the "level" of indigenous physicians in any one period, the model determined the optimal number of physicians to be "produced" and/or imported in order to meet demand in the next period, given the number of schools operating and their "pipeline" inventory.

Although the above model fixated on the medical profession it is perfectly applicable to other professions such as engineering in a developing society.

DEVELOPMENT OF HUMAN CAPITAL AND ITS RELATIONSHIP TO ECONOMIC GROWTH IN A POSTINDUSTRIAL SOCIETY

In the postindustrial era, human capital is claimed (Marshall 1961) to be the most vital source of economic growth. It is developed in many ways. The most obvious is by means of formal education and research, especially higher education and organized research. In his doctoral thesis, Song (1986) developed a methodology for analyzing the contributions of higher education and research and development to economic growth. His methodology was based on economic theory of production and technical change. The methodology was then empirically tested and evaluated based on 1955 to 1983 time-series data for the U.S. economy.

PREDICTING DOCTORATE PRODUCTION IN THE UNITED STATES: SOME LESSONS FOR LONG-RANGE FORECASTERS

Ph.D.-granting programs in American universities became a focus of national concern in the post-Sputnik era. The number of doctorates granted during the 1960s exceeded the total production prior to 1960 (NCES 1982). This highly accelerated growth prompted a number of public and private organizations to look at the factors likely to affect future doctorate output in the United States. Of particular concern was evidence publicized by Cartter (1966) that the demand for teachers and researchers in higher education, industry, and government was likely to decline, possibly leading to underemployment and underutilization.

With underemployment and even unemployment as distinct possibilities, several efforts to forecast doctorate production through the year 1980 were undertaken in 1970 and 1971. Such studies were performed by government-related agencies such as the National Center for Educational Statistics (NCES) and the National Science Foundation (NSF), by private foundations such as the Commission on Human Resources and Advanced Education (CHRAE) of the Russell Sage Foundation, and by independent faculty members such as Gus Haggstrom (1970) at Berkeley. A number of these studies were summarized and discussed by Wolfe and Kidd (1971).

After reliable data on the actual results became available, it was discovered that one of the forecasts (Dean, Reisman, and Rattner 1977; hereafter referred to as DRR) was extremely accurate. Moreover, this was also true on a year-by-year basis.

It is rare to have so many concurrent forecasts of the same phenomenon for which the recency, predictability, and time horizon are all comparable. Such a similarity of conditions reduces the number of independent variables involved and makes a comparison of methodologies more meaningful (Ascher 1978). A study of the various methodologies used and the differences between them was undertaken to see what lessons might be learned.

After summarizing the methodologies of each of the studies examined and discussing some hypotheses and conclusions regarding long-range forecasting (LRF) methodology as found in the literature, the results of this analysis were presented in Pollack-Johnson et al. (1990). A number of practical suggestions for all long-range forecasters, especially those who work in the fields of education and human resource policy and planning, resulting from this retrospective review can be summarized as follows. "First and foremost is the importance of core assumptions: being aware of them, avoiding 'assumption drag' by making sure that assumptions are current, testing them when possible, reconciling them with known theory from disciplines beyond the immediate topic at hand and avoiding biases due to one's institutional affiliation."

Also of great importance is the question of possible structural changes in the system. The very form of forecasting approaches used should depend on the likelihood of the feasible levels of system stability Pollock-Johnson et al. (1990) discuss these issues at some length. They conclude by suggesting that:

> Overall, a forecasting method should be as objective as possible, as causal as it can be, and broken down in segments where appropriate. It should be as simple as is needed to model the most crucial factors, and as eclectic as possible in order to be robust and to synthesize as much information as possible.
>
> In forecasting doctorate production, or in higher education and other forms of human resource forecasting, it is especially imperative to recognize the importance of economic forces on enrollments and degree production.

NOTES

1. The classical term "manpower" will be used for the remainder of this chapter.

2. Interestingly enough, there is an analogy between the above and planning at the enterprise level in postindustrial societies. A company can always set up an in-house training course for its current employees, send some out for training at local institutions, or hire from the outside.

3. Projecting (forecasting) the demand for physicians in this case was relatively simple: a proration of population projections using the World Health Organization standards for Subsahara Africa.

REFERENCES

Ascher, W. 1978. *Forecasting: An appraisal for policy-makers and planners.* Baltimore: Johns Hopkins University Press.

Balinsky, W. L., and A. Reisman. 1973. A taxonomy of manpower-education planning models. In *Socio-Economic Planning Science,* vol. 7. Elmsford, N.Y.: Pergamon.

Cartter, A. 1966. The supply and demand of college teachers. *Journal of Human Resources* 1: 22–38.

Dean, B. V., A. Reisman, and E. Rattner. 1977. Supply and demand of teachers and supply and demand of Ph.D.s, 1971–1980. Unpublished paper, Weatherhead School of Management, Case Western Reserve University.

Debeauvais, M., and G. Psacharopoulos. 1985. Forecasting the needs for qualified manpower: Toward an evaluation. In *Forecasting skilled manpower needs: The experience of eleven countries,* ed. R. Youdi and K. Hinchliffe. UNESCO, International Institute for Educational Planning.

Federal Ministry of Health, Nigeria. *Federal Republic of Nigeria Health Profile—1984.*

Fildes, R. 1979. Quantitative forecasting—the state of the art: Extrapolative models. *Journal of Operational Research Society* 30 (8): 691–710.

_____. 1985. Quantitative forecasting—the state of the art: Econometric models. *Journal of Operational Research Society* 36 (7): 549–80.

Haggstrom, G. W. 1970. On analyzing and predicting enrollments and costs in higher education. Unpublished paper, University of California, Berkeley, Calif.

Ikem, F. M. 1987. Physician manpower planning for developed countries. Ph.D. diss., Case Western Reserve University, Cleveland, Ohio.

Ikem, F. M., and A. Reisman. 1990. An approach to planning for physician manpower requirements in developing countries using dynamic programming. *Operations Research* 38 (4) (July–August).

Jolly, R., and C. McCollough. 1972. African manpower plans: An evaluation. *International Labour Review* 106 (2–3).

Marshall, A. 1961. *The principles of economics.* 9th ed. London: Macmillan.

Martino, J. 1983. *Technological forecasting for decision making.* New York: Elsevier.

National Center for Educational Statistics (NCES). 1971. *Projections of educational statistics to 1978–80.* Washington, D. C.: U.S. Government Printing Office.

_____. 1982. *Digest of education statistics 1982.* Washington, D.C.: U.S. Government Printing Office.

National Science Foundation. 1971. 1969 and 1980 science and engineering doctorate supply and utilization, NSF 71–20. Washington, D.C.: National Science Foundation.

Pollack-Johnson, B., et al. 1990. Predicting doctorate production in the USA: Some lessons for long-range forecasters. *International Journal of Forecasting* 6 (1): 39–52.

Reisman, A. 1988. Finding research topics via a taxonomy of a field of knowledge. *Operations Research Letter* 7 (6) (December).

Reisman, A., et al. 1986. On the voids in U.S. national education statistics. *Journal of Economic and Social Measurement* 14 (4) (December).

Reisman, A., M. H. Song, and F. Ikem. 1990. A taxonomy of manpower forecasting and planning. Department of Operations Research, Case Western Reserve University, Cleveland, Ohio.

Rostow, W. W. 1971. *The stages of economic growth: A non-communist manifesto*. University Press at Cambridge.

Song, M. H. 1986. Development of human capital and its relationship with economic growth. Ph.D. diss., Case Western Reserve University, Cleveland, Ohio.

Wolfe, D., and C. V. Kidd. 1971. The future market for Ph.D.s. *Science* 173: 784–93.

18

Identifying the Scope for Creative and Innovative Management in Large Bureaucracies: An Ordinal Time Series Analysis Approach
Timothy W. Ruefli

BACKGROUND

The incidence of creative and innovative management is supported in large part by an extensive body of both anecdotal evidence and case studies (Charnes and Cooper 1986; Kuhn 1986, 1988). The trade literature is replete with examples of creative and innovative management; these are often individual entrepreneurs who have departed from the managerial norm and managed to make successes of their organizations. Only slightly less frequently these stories involve reports of whole organizations that engage in creative and innovative activities and thereby prosper. Few reports of either type are placed in the context of large bureaucratic organizations (for exceptions, see Collomb and Ponsard 1986; Kirby 1985, 1986). In all cases, there have been, however, few proposals for methodologies to investigate empirically the possible organizational scope or to measure performance impacts of management activities of a creative and innovative type.

Types of questions that might be addressed by appropriate methodologies include the following: What types of change occur in and between large bureaucratic organizations and what is the rate of these changes? Does creative and innovative management in large bureaucratic organizations necessarily yield change or are there circumstances in which creativity and innovation are needed to maintain the status quo? Are there restrictions or constraints on the range of creative and innovative activities of management in large bureaucratic organizations? This latter question is especially important because, given that large bureaucratic organizations have evolved to meet general organizational needs, it is to be expected that forces both internal and external to the organization militate against a very wide range of viable alternatives.

METHODOLOGY

Traditional Methodologies

Empirical investigation of innovative and creative management activities is hampered by serious deficiencies in traditional methodologies. These methodologies, with few exceptions, employ cardinal (absolute) data. The underlying properties of cardinal methodologies are such that longitudinal analyses, comparative analyses, and multidimensional analyses are extremely difficult, if not impracticable in most cases. Creative and innovative activity necessarily involves a dynamic context, and while performance in cardinal terms is easy to measure for a firm in isolation, it is somewhat more difficult to compute on a relative basis.

Cross-sectional studies, where a set of time periods is aggregated, predominate in cardinal analyses, in part because the commonly employed parametric statistics require subsamples larger than those found in any one time period, but mostly because cardinal longitudinal analyses are so complicated (Kimberly 1976, 1980). Analysis of cardinal data over several time periods requires that the effects of inflation, business cycles, economic shocks, and changes in accounting practices, be taken into account by indexing, detrending, and other mathematical manipulations. In spite of these difficulties there have been a limited number of longitudinal studies in the strategy area (Cool and Schendel 1988; Gray and Arliss 1985). Cardinal longitudinal analyses are especially useful in situations where isolated change is critical, such as turnarounds (Hambrick and Schecter 1983).

Ordinal Time Series Analysis

Since dealing with creative and innovative management on a static basis is contradictory to the very concept being studied, alternative approaches to the traditional cardinal analyses must be employed.

An ordinal perspective defines the world in terms of ordinal numbers (1st, 2nd, 3rd, etc.). Ordinal analysis requires a priori that a reference set of firms be defined. This reference set is necessary for the generation of ranks, but it also serves as a context within which managerial analysis can be undertaken. The ordinal metric is a weak metric; changes in firm performance that do not result in one firm overtaking another on an absolute basis are not evident in the ordinal data. In ordinal space there is no possibility of computing change statistics for an individual firm in isolation.

Ordinal time series analysis was developed at the IC^2 Institute as a methodology for examining the behavior of firms and other entities on a longitudinal basis (Ruefli 1990). The initial step in employing the methodology is to define a reference set of organizations and select performance and attribute dimensions for the analysis. Data are collected in cardinal form, but the reference set of organizations is then ranked in each year by each performance dimension. The resulting longitudinal ordinal data can then be analyzed by employing statistics developed for the purpose (Ruefli and Wilson 1987; 648–58; Ruefli 1990: chaps. 2–3).

The ordinal transformation removes the fine detail from the cardinal data and leaves only the gross relative effects. Events external to the reference set of organizations that affect all entities proportionally, are not evident in the ordinal data. Common effects of business cycles, inflation, and changes in tax or account rules are screened out. Only the significant differential effects are transmitted by the ordinal transformation. Further, analysis of the ordinal data on a longitudinal basis does not require mathematical manipulations required by traditional time series analysis to compensate for seasonality, inflation, and the like.

RANK STATISTICS

While a number of statistics have been developed for ordinal time series analysis, only two will be used here: the position statistic and the volatility statistic. The position statistic for a set of firms, S, in period t for dimension k is the average rank of the firms in S, and is defined by:

$$P(S)_{t,k} = \sum_i \frac{r_{itk}}{n} , i \in S \tag{1}$$

where $r_{i,t,k}$ is the rank of firm i in period t on dimension k, and n is the number of firms in S.

The volatility in rank shift of a set S of firms from year $t - 1$ to t is given by:

$$P(S)_{t,k} = \sum_i \frac{|r_{i\,t-1\,k} - r_{i\,t\,k}|}{n} , \quad i \in S \tag{2}$$

where the vertical lines denote the taking of the absolute value and n is the number of firms in S.

The position and volatility statistics will be employed in the ensuing empirical studies. First, however, the relation between creative and innovative behavior and ordinal performance must be established.

AN ORDINAL TIME SERIES PERSPECTIVE ON IDENTIFYING CREATIVE AND INNOVATIVE PERFORMANCE AND THE SCOPE FOR MANAGEMENT DECISION

To apply the methodology outlined above to the problem of identifying creative and innovative performance and delimiting the scope for that activity, an empirical definition of performance associated with creative and innovative management must be made. Since the selected methodology is ordinal, the definition is in these terms. The following is proposed: *Successful creative and innovative management performance with the firm as the unit of analysis is identified through a superior strategic position associated with intentional management activities that depart from the accepted norm of management behavior*. Strategic position in this case is defined as in Ruefli (1990: chap. 10); it is a better ordinal position in the sense of rank or average rank on those dimensions that are of strategic importance to the reference group of firms.

This definition has several implications. First, it rules out average behavior in terms of the reference set as being creative and innovative. Imitative behavior per se is not ruled out; individual acts of imitation may be creative and innovative, but when imitation becomes the norm, it is neither creative nor innovative. Second, because it is in ordinal terms, the definition suggests that there are threshold effects to creative and innovative management. That is, there may be creative and innovative activities that yield changes in performance on an absolute basis, but unless they cumulate to a scale whereby they yield a superior strategic position (i.e., result in a rank change), they are not recognized as such. Third, the definition does not address the problem of identifying unsuccessful creative and innovative management; it only refers to behavior that is successful. Fourth, the concept of superior position in the ordinal sense does not necessarily mean improved performance in the absolute sense. That is, superior position may mean performance that yields a decrease in a firm's absolute level of performance during a period when its reference group experienced a greater decline in absolute performance. Fifth, the definition does not require management to break with past actions to be creative and innovative. If the majority of other firms in the reference group are trying new and different strategies, a firm that holds its course and gains superior position is being creative and innovative according to the definition. Finally, note that the definition is relative to the reference group of firms, and what is superior position for one set of firms, may be inferior in position in a wider context.

CHANGE AMONG LARGE BUREAUCRATIC ORGANIZATIONS

Antecedent Studies

A major problem in studying change in large bureaucratic organizations is finding data on comparable organizations. For this study the *Fortune* list of the 500 largest U.S. mining and manufacturing firms has been selected for analysis. There have been numerous studies employing the firms in the Fortune 500 as the population of interest. It is one of the most often studied sets of firms in the management research literature, but it is rarely studied on a longitudinal basis. There have been some instances of longitudinal studies of this population. Bock (1968, 1972, 1974), Bock and Farkas (1970) and Bock, Farkas, and Weinberger (1979) studied the growth and turnover in the Fortune 500 for a twenty-year period, as did Boyle and McKenna (1970) for a smaller sample. Miller and Friesen (1982) studied the lifecycle implications of a sample of the Fortune 500—a study that was replicated with different results by Drazin and Kazanjian (1990). In his seminal study of strategy structure and economic performance Rumelt (1974, 1982), following Wrigley (1970), employed a sample of the Fortune 500.

Data and Analysis

Data for this portion of the study were drawn from a database on the Fortune 500 mining and manufacturing firms for the period 1954 to 1988. Table 18.1 gives the size range along three dimensions for the Fortune 500 in 1954 and 1985. While these are private sector organizations, albeit publicly listed, they clearly qualify as large organizations, and while no measure of the level of bureaucratization of these firms could be found, their sheer size argues in favor of a substantial degree of bureaucracy.

Table 18.1. Magnitudes of the Fortune 500

Year	Rank	Assets (thousands)	Employees	Revenue (thousands)
1954	1	$ 6,614,743	370,442	$ 9,823,526
	500	$ 12,816	300	$ 49,694
1985	1	$ 69,160,000	811,000	$ 96,371,700
	500	$ 89,846	742	$ 424,173

In the period examined, 1,265 different firms appeared in the Fortune 500, a statistic that is in itself indicative of the amount of change in this set of organizations. It can be ascertained that the Fortune 500 has turned over its membership two and one-half times in thirty-four years. For organizations of the size of those in the sample, this is a significant amount of change. To detail the pattern of change over time, we can first examine the number of firms entering the Fortune 500 on a year-to-year basis. Figure 18.1 shows the number of new firms (equals the number of departing firms) appearing in the sample each year. In this graph it can be noted that the pattern of change in the Fortune 500 is not stable.

There has, in fact, been some periodicity in the additions to the Fortune 500. From 1954 to 1955 just over forty new firms entered the list, 8 percent of the total. By 1963 this was down to just over twenty firms, or under 5 percent of the sample. However, by 1969, at the peak of a merger wave, the number of entrants had more than doubled, and 9 percent of the firms were involved. The early 1970s saw the lowest entry rates of the study period (4%), albeit with some variability. From a low in 1977, the entry rate increased until 1987–88, when it reached an all-time high of fifty-five new firms entering the Fortune 500, or 11 percent of the total.

The main implication of these entry rates is that there is considerable instability in the makeup of the largest five hundred mining and manufacturing firms in the nation. Unfortunately the definition of creative and innovative management performance given above does not permit the identification of this behavior from entry data alone. It would be expected that some of the new entrants into the Fortune 500 got there through creative and innovative means, but such behavior cannot be distinguished from, say, that of conventional managers who rode a wave of industry growth into the 500.

Figure 18.1. Number of Firms Entering or Leaving the Fortune 500 Annually, 1954–88

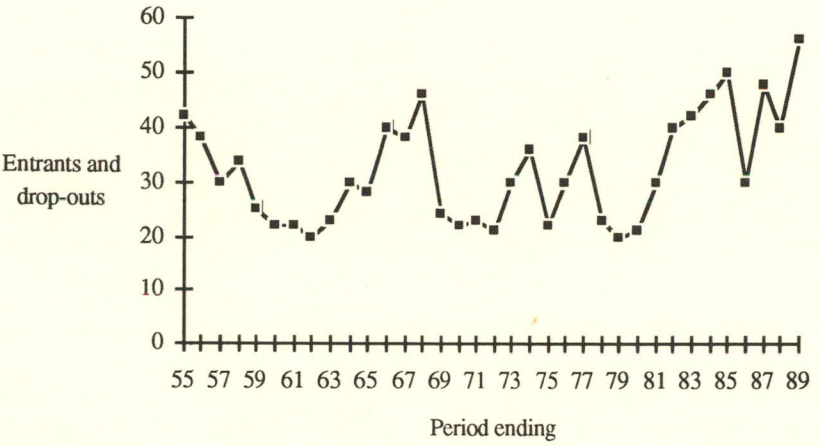

The entry rate of new firms measures the change across the boundary between the Fortune 500 and the rest of the domestic publicly held mining and manufacturing companies. To assess the amount of change within the 500, we can use rank statistics from ordinal time series analysis. Specifically, the statistic to be employed here is the volatility statistic, which measures the aggregate amount of rank shift among a set of firms from one year to the next. The dimension of interest is operating revenue, because this is the dimension along which membership in the Fortune 500 is determined. Publicly listed firms with more than 50 percent of their revenues derived from mining or manufacturing are candidates for inclusion in the largest 500.

Figure 18.2 graphs the revenue volatility for the Fortune 500 from 1954 to 1988. The pattern of average rank shifts followed the pattern of the new entrants, with a bit more exaggeration. For the nine periods following the first, volatility declined, and then sharply rose to two peaks separated by a one-period decline. A sharp decline in 1969–72 followed those peaks, and then a long rise was initiated. The last five periods of the study period saw relatively high variance in the volatility. In the last period of the study, the average firm in the 500 changed more than fifty ranks.

Figure 18.2. Volatility: Fortune 500, 1954–88

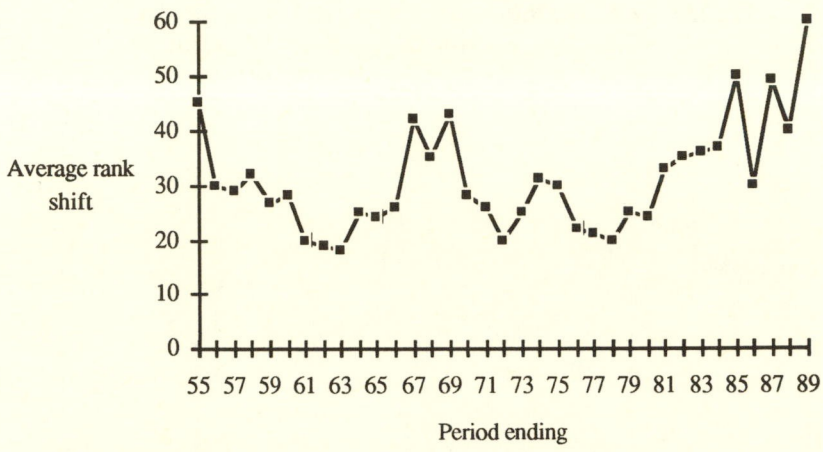

Period ending

The implication of the volatility analysis is that not only was there movement across the boundary between the five hundred largest and the rest of the mining and manufacturing firms, but that there was a considerable amount of change in rank within the largest five hundred. Again it cannot be determined with any accuracy that all changes were due to creative and innovative management. However, it does provide more evidence that change in large bureaucratic systems is not only possible, but the norm—on a within-system basis. To identify possible instances of creative and innovative management it is necessary to focus on more detailed characteristics of the firms in the sample.

CHANGE WITHIN LARGE BUREAUCRATIC SYSTEMS

Context

To provide an arena for the search for possible instances of creative and innovative behavior, events must be identified that can be, on the one hand, traced to significant management decisions, and on the other, associated with relative performance. While there are a number of alternatives in this regard, for the purposes of this study, change in diversification strategy was selected. The degree and nature of diversification are important strategic parameters of a firm. Change in these parameters could be expected to be a result of considerable management attention and to involve the efforts of a significant number of mangers to implement. In addition, the relation between diversification strategy and performance has been extensively studied.

Data and Analysis

Data for this study of within-firm change were drawn from the Fortune 500; this time the firms were a sample of the Fortune 500 in the period 1954 to 1985 identified by diversification strategy in 1949, 1959, and 1969. Specifically, the sample employed by Rumelt (1974) in his study of diversification strategy served as the basis for analysis. The set of firms is a random sample of 100 firms drawn in 1949, 1959, and 1969. The original sample totaled 246 firms; of those, 240 were used in this study. Rumelt categorized these firms by their diversification strategy and organization structure in 1949, 1959, and 1969. In Rumelt's study, firms that held a diversification strategy for at least ten years were of interest. Firms that changed strategy were not considered. Table 18.2 gives the numbers of firms that either maintained or changed their diversification strategies in each period.

Table 18.2. Numbers of Firms Maintaining or Changing Strategies

	1949–59	1959–69	1949–69
Maintained Strategy	155	115	84
Changed Strategy	85	125	156

In the period 1949 to 1959, more firms maintained their strategy from one end of the decade to the next, than changed strategies, indicating that change in the "very short run" was not the rule. In the ensuing decade, slightly more firms in the sample changed their strategy than maintained it. It was only when two consecutive decades were examined that change of was only when two consecutive decades were examined that change of strategy clearly dominated. To permit an evaluation of the worth of changing versus maintaining strategies, the ordinal position in terms of return on assets (ROA) and return on sales (ROS) of the various groups of firms were examined on a longitudinal basis. Average position for the periods 1954 to 1959, 1960 to 1969, and 1960 to 1985 was computed. No strategy classifications for the years past 1969 were available, but performance data were available to be examined for the possible persistence of the effects of strategies.

Results

It has already been indicated that the norm with respect to strategy maintenance or change varied with the time period considered. Tables 18.3 and 18.4 give an ex post justification supporting the tendency to maintain a strategy. As can be seen in the tables, firms that maintained their strategy, on average were rewarded with a better rank position in terms of both return on assets (Table 18.3) and return on sales (Table 18.4) than was achieved on average by the firms that changed strategy. This was true not only for behavior in each decade, but was also true across two decades. The best results were obtained by firms that maintained their strategies for at least twenty years.

Table 18.3. ROA Position for Maintenance or Change of Strategy

	1954–59	1960–69	1960–85
Maintained 1949–50	223	223	234
Changed 1949–59	260	265	270
Maintained 1959–69	200	218	231
Changed 1959–69	270	258	265
Maintained 1949–69	192	208	225
Changed 1949–69	261	254	260

**Table 18.4. ROS Position for Maintenance
or Change of Strategy**

	1949–59	1960–69	1960–85
Maintained 1949–50	221	211	221
Changed 1949–59	265	265	264
Maintained 1959–69	208	220	226
Changed 1959–69	270	263	268
Maintained 1949–69	200	211	221
Changed 1949–69	265	261	264

Figure 18.3 shows that the advantage in ROA position held not just on average for the decade, but also in each year 1954 to 1983. Only in 1984 did changing a strategy before 1969 yield a higher position than maintaining a position. Graphs for the other time periods for strategy maintenance and for ROS show a similar pattern, indicating that firms that changed their strategies held a position inferior to firms that maintained their strategies, except in the last three or four years of the study—long beyond the period when strategies were identified.

Broadly speaking this evidence suggests that there are some bounds on creative and innovative management in large bureaucratic organizations. Based on this broad evidence, on average, creative and innovative behavior is constrained to operating within the original diversification strategy insofar as possible. Such a dictum changes the conceptual scope, and perhaps the very idea, of what we consider to be creative and innovative behavior. Since change takes place in the Fortune 500, there is room for creativity and innovation to produce growth, but, generally speaking, the foregoing evidence indicates that this effort should have been directed largely at growth within existing markets, but should include only limited new product and markets. By implication, changes in product lines and businesses should be limited to activities whose individual and cumulative effects are such that they do not change the various business ratios (related, specialization, and vertical ratios) that define diversification strategies. These constraints generally support the advice given by Rumelt (1974), and Peters and Waterman (1982), and support the research findings of studies that are based on an assumption of organizational inertia and cite the pervasive and long-lasting effects of conditions at the founding of a firm (Eisenhardt and Schoonhoven 1990; Schein 1985; Stinchcombe 1965).

Figure 18.3. Return on Assets Position, 1954–85

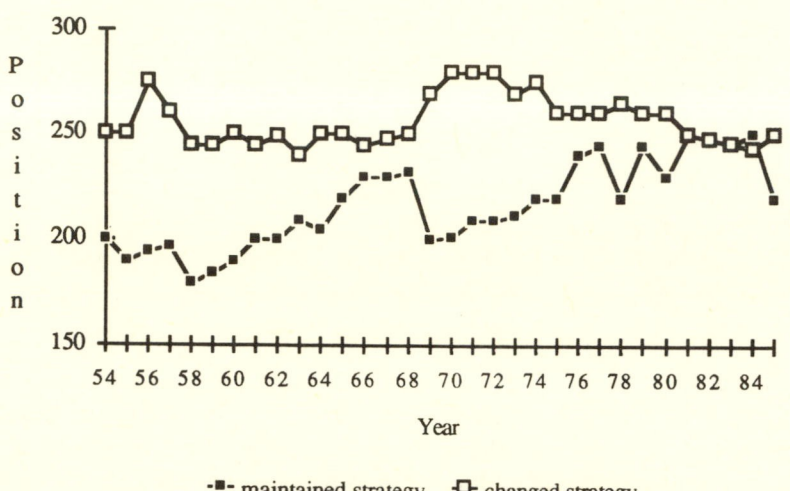

Refined Analysis

That the majority of firms changed their diversification strategy in a two decade period, while the minority that did not tended to perform at relatively better levels of returns, suggests that the thrust of creativity and innovation in these large bureaucracies may well have been directed toward keeping the balance among the ratios that define diversification strategy. This is in keeping with the definition of creative and innovative management performance proposed earlier.

The prospects for creative and innovative management are not as dim as the foregoing averages would imply. An in-depth examination of particular diversification strategies and their related performance indicates that there may be room for innovative change. Tables 18.5 and 18.6 present the ROA and ROS positions of selected diversification strategies and sequences of strategies. For the purposes of this analysis consideration will be limited to firms that held a single business strategy at some point during the study. Performance of firms that held dominant-constrained (DC—one in which there is a dominant line of business, with diversification constrained to be related to this business) and related-constrained (RC—one in which there is a series of businesses, none dominant, with diversification constrained to be related to this set of businesses) strategies for at least two decades will be included for purposes of comparison.

Table 18.5. ROA Position for Selected Strategy Sequences

	1954–59	1960–69	1960–85
SING-SING-SING	217	216	210
SING-SING-?	240	211	218
SING-SING-DV	159	125	163
?-SING-DV	220	186	232
?-SING-SING	216	200	203
SING-DC-?	200	212	243
SING-DC-DC	117	104	133
SING-RC-?	273	273	302
SING-SING-RC	191	217	226
?-SING-RC	215	158	188
DC-DC-DC	130	175	181
RC-RC-RC	157	136	161

From these tables it can be seen that there were selected changes in diversification strategy that yielded superior performance. In terms of ROA, firms that had single business strategies in 1949 but changed to a dominant-constrained strategy before 1959 and then maintained that strategy at least through 1969 outperformed by a wide margin all other strategy sequences—including those in which strategy was maintained—in all periods studied. The second-best strategy sequence was the maintenance of a related-constrained strategy for at least twenty years. The third best overall strategy sequence was generated by single business firms in 1949 that maintained that strategy until at least 1959 and then vertically integrated (DV) by 1969. Thus, several sequences in which strategy change took place had performance levels that were equivalent to those achieved by the best levels achieved by maintained strategies.

Table 18.6. ROS Position for Selected Strategy Sequences

	1954–59	1960–69	1960–85
SING-SING-SING	310	247	284
SING-SING-?	290	267	314
SING-SING-DV	202	209	265
?-SING-DV	134	106	167
?-SING-SING	294	231	281
SING-DC-?	248	239	248
SING-DC-DC	375	248	319
SING-RC-?	249	312	321
SING-SING-RC	282	238	291
?-SING-RC	218	200	231
DC-DC-DC	149	175	210
RC-RC-RC	206	179	220

With respect to ROS, Table 18.6 indicates a similar situation. Firms that had either a single business or dominant-constrained strategy in 1949 or were new entrants before 1959 (all indicated by the question mark), moved to a single business strategy in 1959 but vertically integrated by 1969, yielded performance levels for the period 1960–85 that were superior to other strategy sequences. Firms that maintained either a dominant-constrained or a related-constrained strategy from 1949 to 1969 were the next best performers. Other strategy sequences involving change of strategies performed at levels near these two latter sequences.

It might be argued that those firms that made strategy changes did so only because they were forced to by circumstance, and thus creativity and innovation did not figure into the situation. Common wisdom holds that firms change diversification strategy only under duress; the reduction in opportunities in the current market scope motivates such changes; firms that are doing well, "do not fix it, if it isn't broken." Evidence from Tables 18.5 and 18.6 refutes this contention. For example, firms that adopted the strategy sequence single-single-dominant vertical were among the better performing single business firms in 1949 and 1959, yet changed their strategy by 1969 and remained among the best performers, while firms that stuck to a single business strategy were not among the best performers. Similarly, firms that held a single business strategy in 1949 and then diversified to a dominant vertical strategy had the best position as single business firms in 1949. This contradicts the notion that firms do not change strategies unless they are in trouble, and supports the idea that these firms acted in a creative and innovative manner. On the other hand, firms that had single business strategies in 1949 and then changed to related-constrained by 1959 were, on average, in worse position in all periods than those that held their single strategy until 1959 and then changed to related-constrained. This suggests that reasons for strategy change are much more complex than conventional wisdom would have us believe.

The foregoing appears to be clear evidence of creative and innovative management. Firms made strategy changes that were definite departures from both the common wisdom and from management practice, and gained strategic position that was superior to other groups of firms in the reference set.

The statistics reported above are in terms of average positions of groups of firms over periods of time ranging from six to twenty-six years. To achieve an idea about the type of information environment for creative and innovative management it is worth inquiring whether the performance differentials were equally as clear on a shorter time scale. Figure 18.4 provides information pertinent to this question. This graph shows the annual ROA position of the six best-performing strategy sequences from 1954 to 1985. It can be clearly seen that except for selected strategies for a period of time (e.g., S-DC-DC from 1961 to 1965), performance by strategy sequence did not dominate on a consistent bias. The implication of this for management decision making is that even if managers had been tracking the positions of firms classified by strategy type, the information feedback would not necessarily have provided them with clear signals about relative performance in the long run. Strategic decisions were thus presumably being made more on instinct and inspiration than on the basis of the feedback of information on performance and rational calculation.

Implications for Scope

The results reported above imply that managers in large bureaucratic systems were able to exercise their creativity and engage in some changes of strategy that resulted in relative improvement in their performance over firms that maintained that strategy. The latter, in turn, were able to outperform the bulk of strategy changes, suggesting that, in this case, maintenance of a particular strategy had an element of creativity and innovation attached to it.

Thus there has been room in the strategic arena for managers to engage in change, but this was somewhat restricted. In terms of ROA, for example, firms had to possess either a single business, dominant-constrained, or related-constrained strategy in 1949, or be a new entrant to the Fortune 500 in order to be among the best performers in later periods. The implication here is that there is an element of history that conditions the results of creative and innovative management. Given that historical position, however, there is then room for managerial creativity to improve the firm's performance.

Figure 18.4. Annual ROA Position for Selected Strategy Sequences

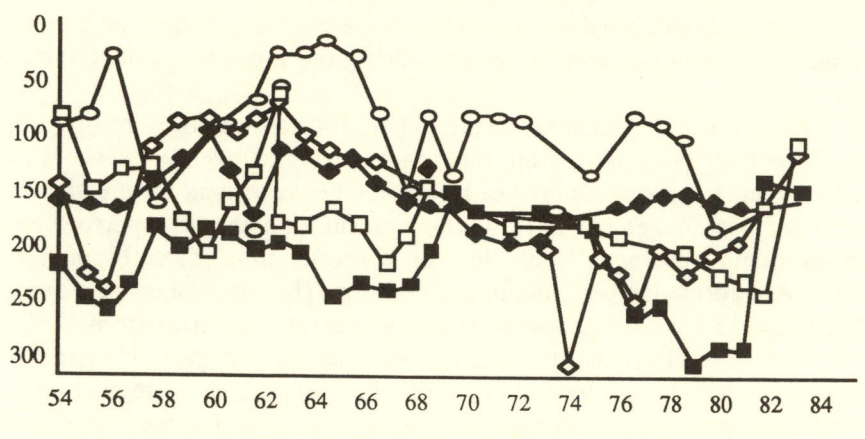

■ S-S-S □ DC-DC-DC ◆ RC-RC-RC ◇ S-S-DV ○ S-DC-DC

CONCLUSIONS

This research has attempted to place the phenomenon of creative and innovative management in large bureaucratic systems in an empirical context. To accomplish this in a reasonable fashion it was necessary to turn to a new ordinal methodology to provide the conceptual structure to support both a practicable definition of creative and innovative management performance, and a feasible computational analysis. Data from the largest U.S. mining and manufacturing firms were employed to show that at an aggregated level, there was a considerable amount of change within this group of large firms, and between this group and the rest of the industrial sector. While this did not provide direct evidence of creative and innovative performance, it did indicate that there was sufficient dynamism in these large bureaucratic systems to warrant further investigation.

Diversification strategies and their associated performance were selected for investigation, and here, at a very general level, performance evidence militated against changing strategies. A more detailed analysis revealed that there were particular sets of changes, undertaken by a small minority of firms, that suggested that not only was there room for creative and innovative management in these large firms, but that in several instances it was associated with superior performance. The findings further suggested that while creative and innovative management could be identified in terms of its performance on an ordinal basis, there were constraints on the scope of such activities and that some of these constraints on creative and innovative management were historical in nature.

As a pioneering study, the research reported above suffered from a number of limitations. First, the set of firms studied was limited to the domestic manufacturing and mining sector in the period 1954 to 1988, and there is no guarantee that the findings will generalize even to privately held manufacturing and mining firms, let alone to publicly listed or private firms in other industries, nonprofit organizations, government entities, or even other time periods. Second, the analysis was limited to a consideration of diversification strategy and does not necessarily shed light on other significant creative and innovative management decisions. Third, the definition of creative and innovative performance was made in an intransitive fashion; it runs from management activity to successful performance only. The reverse logic and the case of inferior performance are beyond the scope of the definition. Fourth, industry effects and other such influences may have had significant impacts on performance (Christensen and Montgomery 1981), but were not taken into account here. Finally, the methodology employed here requires that there be a reference group of firms available; thus this approach is not useful in the case of one-of-a-kind organizations like NASA.

It is clear that there is scope for further research in empirical studies of creative and innovative management and its associated performance. Remedying the limitations of this study should serve as a starting point for subsequent research, but should not obscure the need to develop new methodological approaches to enable continued investigation in this important area.

REFERENCES

Amit, Raphael, and Joshua Livnat. 1988. Diversification strategies, business cycles, and economic performance. *Strategic Management Journal* 9: 99–110.

Balakrishnan, S., and B. Wernerfelt. 1986. Technical change, competition, and vertical integration. *Strategic Management Journal.* 7: 347–59.

Beard, D.W., and G. G. Dess. 1981. Corporate-level strategy, business-level strategy, and firm performance. *Academy of Management Journal* 24: 663–88.

Bettis, Richard A. 1981. Performance differences in related and unrelated diversified firms. *Strategic Management Journal* 2 (October–December): 379–93.

Bettis, Richard A., and Vijay Mahajan. 1985. Risk/return performance of diversified firms. *Management Science* 31 (7) (July): 785–99.

Biggadike, Ralph. The risky business of diversification. *Harvard Business Review* 57 (3): 103–11.

Bock, B. 1968. *Statistical games and the '200 largest' industrials: 1954 and 1968. Studies in business economics.* National Industrial Conference Board.

_____. 1972. *Dialogue on concentration, oligopoly, and profits: Concepts vs. data.* New York, Conference Board.

_____. 1974. *Restructuring proposals: Measuring competition in numerical grids.* New York: Conference Board.

Bock, B., and J Farkas. 1970. *Relative growth of the "largest" manufacturing corporations, 1947-1971.* New York: Conference Board.

Bock, B., J Farkas, and D. S. Weinberger. 1979. Aggregate concentration. *Conference Board Information Bulletin* 57.

Botkin, James W. 1986. Transforming creativity into innovation: Processes, prospects, and problems. In *Frontiers in creative and innovative management,* ed. Robert L. Kuhn. Cambridge, Mass.: Ballinger Publishing Company.

Boyle, Stanley E., and Joseph P. McKenna. 1970. Size mobility of the 100 and 200 largest U. S. manufacturing corporations, 1919–1964. *Antitrust Bulletin* 15: 505–20.

Carnall, C. A. 1986. Toward a theory for the evaluation of organizational change. *Human Relations* 39: 745–66.

Caves, Richard E. 1964. *American industry: Structure, conduct, performance.* Englewood Cliffs, N.J.: Prentice-Hall.

_____. 1980. Industrial organization, corporate strategy, and structure. *Journal of Economic Literature* 18: 64–92.

Chandler, Alfred, Jr. 1962. *Strategy and structure: Chapters in the history of the American industrial enterprise*. Cambridge, Mass.: MIT Press.

Charnes, A., and W. W. Cooper, eds., 1986. *Creative and innovative management*. Cambridge, Mass.: Ballinger Publishing Company.

Christensen, H. Kurt, and C. A. Montgomery. 1981. Corporate economic performance: Diversification strategy versus market structure. *Strategic Management Journal*. (2): 327–43.

Collomb, Bertrand, and J. P. Ponsard. 1986. Creative management in mature capital intensive industries. In *Creative and Innovative Management*, eds. A. Charnes and W. W. Cooper. Cambridge, Mass.: Ballinger Publishing Company.

Cool, Karel, and D. Schendel. 1988. Performance differences among strategic group members. *Strategic Management Journal* (9): 207–23.

Daniel, Wayne W. 1978. *Applied nonparametric Statistics*. Boston: Houghton-Mifflin Company.

Drazin, R., and R. K. Kazanjian. 1990. A reanalysis of Miller and Friesen's life cycle data. *Strategic Management Journal*. 11 (4) (May–June): 319–26.

Dundas, Kenneth N. M., and Peter R. Richardson. 1982. Implementing the unrelated product strategy. *Strategic Management Journal*. (3): 287–301.

Dutton, J., and Duncan, R. B. 1987. 1987. The influence of the strategic planning process on strategic change. *Strategic Management Journal* (8): 103–16.

Edstrom, A. 1986. Leadership and strategic change. *Human Resource Management* 25 (4): 581–606.

Eisenhardt, Kathleen M., and Claudia B. Schoonhoven. 1990. Organizational growth: Linking founding team strategy, environment and growth among U.S. semiconductor ventures. *Administrative Science Quarterly*.

Galbraith, J. R. 1983. Strategy and organization planning. *Human Resource Management* 22: 63–77.

Grant, Robert M., and Azar P. Jammine. 1988. Performance differences between the Wrigley/Rumelt strategy categories. *Strategic Management Journal* (9): 333–46.

Gray, B., and S. S. Arliss. 1985. Politics and strategic change across organizational life cycles. *Academy of Management Review* (10): 707–23.

Hall, M., and L. Weiss, Firm size and profitability. *Review of Economics and Statistics* (49) (August): 319–31.

Hambrick, D., and Schecter, S. M. 1983. Turnaround strategies for mature industrial-product business units. *Academy of Management Journal* (26): 231–48.

Johnson, Gerry, and Howard Thomas. 1987. The industry context of strategy, structure and performance: The U.K. brewing industry. *Strategic Management Journal* (8): 343–61.

Jones, Gareth R., and Charles W. Hill. 1988. Transaction cost analysis of strategy-structure choice. *Strategic Management Journal* (9): 159–72.

Kimberly, J. R. 1976. Issues in the design of longitudinal organizational research. *Sociological Methods and Research* (4): 321–47.

_____. 1980. Data aggregation in organizational research: The temporal dimension. *Organization Studies* (1): 367–77.

Kirby, Michael J. L. 1985. Government, efficiency and the social market: Alternative approaches for delivering and financing social services. In *Frontiers in creative and innovative management,* ed. Robert L. Kuhn. Cambridge, Mass.: Ballinger Publishing Company.

_____. 1986. Innovation in government: Problems and possibilities. In *Creative and innovative management,* ed. A. Charnes and W. W. Cooper. Cambridge, Mass.: Ballinger Publishing Company.

Kuhn, Robert L., ed. 1986. *Frontiers in creative and innovative management.* Cambridge, Mass.: Ballinger Publishing Company.

_____. 1988 *Handbook for creative and innovative managers.* New York: McGraw-Hill Book Company.

Leontiades, M. 1980. *Strategies for diversification and change.* Boston, Mass.: Little, Brown & Company.

Lorsh, J. 1986. Managing culture: The invisible barrier to strategic change. *California Management Review* 28 (2): 95–109.

MacDonald, James M. 1984. Diversification, market growth, and concentration in U.S. manufacturing. *Southern Economic Journal.* 50 (4) (April): 1098–111.

Markham, Jesse W. 1973. Conglomerate enterprise and corporate performance. Cambridge, Mass.: Harvard University Press.

Miller, Danny, and Peter Friesen. 1982. The longitudinal analysis of organizations. *Management Science* 28 (9) (September): 1013–34.

Montgomery, C.A. 1982. The measurement of firm diversification: Some new empirical evidence. *Academy of Management Journal* 25 (2): 299–307.

Palepu, Krishna. 1985. Diversification strategy, profit performance and the entropy measure. *Strategic Management Journal* 6: 239–55.

Peters, Thomas J., and Robert H. Waterman, Jr. 1982. *In search of excellence.* New York: Harper & Row.

Pitts, Robert A. 1976. Diversification strategies and policies of large diversified firms. *Journal of Economics and Business* 28 (2): 181–88.

_____. 1977. Strategies and structures for diversification. *Academy of Management Journal* 20 (2): 197–208.

Porter, Michael E. 1980. Competitive strategy: Techniques for analyzing industries and competitors. New York: The Free Press.

Quinn, J. B. 1977. Strategic goals: Process and politics. *Sloan Management Review:* 21–37.

_____. 1978. Strategic change: Logical incrementalism. *Sloan Management Review:* 7–21.

_____. 1980a. Managing strategic change. *Sloan Management Review* 21: 3–20.

_____. 1980b. *Strategies for change: Logical incrementalism.* Irwin.

Ruefli, Timothy W. 1985. Creative and innovative management: A manifesto for academia. In *Frontiers in creative and innovative management,* ed. Robert L. Kuhn. Cambridge, Mass.: Ballinger Publishing Company.

_____, ed. 1990. Ordinal time series analysis: Methodology and applications in management strategy and policy. Westport, Conn.: Greenwood Press.

Ruefli, Timothy W., and Donde Ashmos. 1988. Diversification strategy and corporate performance: Longitudinal ratio and ordinal time series analyses. IC^2 Institute Working Paper, University of Texas.

_____. 1990. Strategy, structure and corporate performance. In *Ordinal time series analysis: Methodology and applications in management strategy and policy,* ed. Timothy W. Ruefli. Westport, Conn.: Greenwood Press.

Ruefli, Timothy W., and Rob L. Jones. 1990. Excellent companies: An ordinal time series approach. In *Ordinal time series analysis: Methodology and applications in management strategy and policy,* ed. Timothy W. Ruefli. Westport, Conn.: Greenwood Press.

Ruefli, Timothy. W. and Wilson, Chester L. 1987. Ordinal time series methodology for industry and competitive analysis. *Management Science* 33 (5) (May).

Rumelt, Richard P. 1974. *Strategy, structure and economic performance.* Boston, Mass.: Harvard University Press.

_____. 1982. "Diversification Strategy and Profitability," *Strategic Management Journal* (3): 359–69.

Salter, M. S., and W. A. Weinhold 1978. Diversification via acquisition: Creating value," *Harvard Business Review* (July-Aug.).

_____. 1979. *Diversification through acquisitions: Strategies for creating economic value.* New York: The Free Press.

Schein, E. H. 1985. *Organizational culture and leadership.* San Francisco, Calif.: Josey-Bass Publishers.

Scherer, Fredrick M. 1980. *Industrial market structure and economic performance.* Chicago, Ill.: Rand McNally.

Singh, Habir, and Cynthia A. Montgomery 1987. Corporate acquisition strategies and economic performance. *Strategic Management Journal* (8): 377–86.

Steiner, Peter O. 1977. *Mergers: Motives, effects, policies.* Ann Arbor, Mich.: University of Michigan Press.

Stinchcombe, Arthur L. 1965. Social structure and organizations. In *Handbook of Organizations,* ed. James March. Chicago, Ill.: Rand McNally & Company.

Tushman, M, L., and P. Anderson. 1986. Technological discontinuities and organizational environments. *Administrative Science Quarterly* (31): 439–65.

Weis, Sandra Gerson. 1965. Conditions for innovation in large organizations. In *Handbook of Organizations,* ed. James March. Chicago, Ill.: Rand McNally & Company.

Williamson, Oliver E. 1975. *Markets and hierarchies.* New York: The Free Press.

Wrigley, Leonard. 1970. Divisional autonomy and diversification. Ph.D. diss., Harvard University.

19

Artificial Intelligence and Expert Systems: Potential and Problems for Large-Scale Bureaucracies

Ronald M. Lee

BUREAUCRACY AS ARTIFICIAL INTELLIGENCE

Bureaucracy. In popular usage, the connotations are usually negative: large, rigid organizations, baroque, ritualized procedures, inability to adapt to changing needs and conditions in the environment.

A common complaint about bureaucracies is that they are inefficient. Requests are routed through numerous offices, each of which may have a backlog, leading to an accumulation of delays. Nonroutine requests are sometimes misrouted, creating additional delays. Errors in the request cause backtracking and still further delays. Other complaints are about the ineffectiveness of the system. In order to keep the complexity manageable, bureaucratic rules may be simplistic, covering only standard cases. Exceptional requests are either rejected or diverted to a discretionary authority. When there are many exceptions, a change in regulations may be called for. Because of the complexity already present, however, this is often difficult to do. Change is either resisted or made minimally.

On a broader scale, the very existence of a bureaucracy is sometimes criticized. Bureaucracies are often erected to perform a particular governmental or social function, and are thus protected from competitive challenges. They may grow to such size that the sheer momentum of their economic weight relative to the society carries them forward. An important aspect of this problem is a failure to effectively manage complexity. Bureaucracies are "sticky upwards." That is, they seem to grow more easily than they shrink.[1] Elgin and Bushnell (1977: 337) observe that "we have rushed to create bureaucracies of such extreme levels of scale, complexity, and interdependence that they now begin to exceed our capacity to comprehend and manage them." They argue that this has reached such proportions in many social systems that complexity, in its own right, has become the critical issue.

The term "bureaucracy," as both a popular and scientific term, has come to have a variety of often overlapping definitions. The definition used here is Weber's (1956/1978). To Weber, the process of bureaucratization is a shift from organizational management based on the interests and personalities of specific individuals, to one based on explicit *rules* and *procedures*. These rules and procedures are identified with *roles* in the organization rather than individual people. Bureaucratic organizations thus take on an impersonal, mechanical character. To Weber, this is a positive development leading to greater effectiveness and efficiency: "Bureaucracy develops the more perfectly, the more it is 'dehumanized,' the more completely it succeeds in eliminating from official business love, hatred, and all purely personal, irrational, and emotional elements which escape calculation" (Weber 1956/1978:975).

Bureaucracies are sometimes characterized as having a mechanistic, form of administration based on fixed rules and procedures as opposed to organic organizations, which rely more on individual discretion (Burne and Stalker 1961). Jay Galbraith (1973, 1977) offers a useful extension to this view. A currently popular theory of organizations is the information processing view, due principally to Simon (Simon 1955; March and Simon 1958). The key concern is how the organization copes with the *complexity* of its environment, given the bounded rationality (cognitive limitations) of its managers. Galbraith extends the information-processing view of organizations to a contingency theory approach. He regards the complexity of the organizations task as only one dimension of its information-processing difficulties. Another dimension is added to the organizational design problem, which Galbraith calls *uncertainty*. This refers to the degree of unpredictability of the tasks performed in the organization: "Uncertainty is defined as the difference between the amount of information required to perform the task and the amount of information already possessed by the organization" (1973:5). The importance of this relates to the organization's ability to plan or pre-program its activities: "The greater the task uncertainty, the greater the amount of information that must be processed among decision makers during task execution in order to achieve a given level of performance" (1973:4).

Galbraith classifies the nature of the organization's overall cognitive task (as well as any of its subtasks) on a two-dimensional framework of complexity and uncertainty. This may be viewed as a matrix (Figure 19.1) characterizing the different types of cognitive tasks that organizations face. In situations of high complexity but low uncertainty, the organization is able to plan and routinize its activities. These are the conditions under which bureaucracy is most effective. In situations of low complexity and high uncertainty, by contrast, the organization is constantly being surprised by changes in the environment. Here, the most effective form of administration seems to be one that relies heavily on the discretion of its employees. Burne and Stalker (1961) use the terms "mechanical" and "organic" to describe these contrasting forms of administration.

Figure 19.1. Task Complexity versus Environmental Surprise

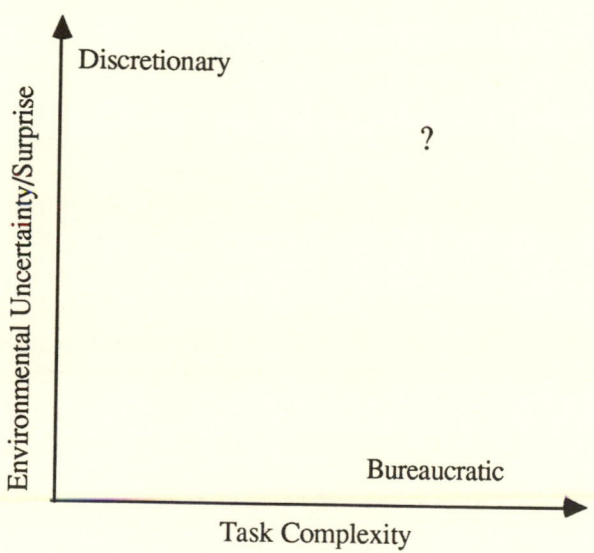

The problem, of course, is deciding what form of administration is appropriate when the environmental demands are both highly complex and highly uncertain. As observed, rationalization is the typical response to complexity. An apparent difficulty with rationalization, however, is that when a once stable environment becomes more uncertain, the organization seems to have difficulties derationalizing, that is, removing rules and procedures and relying more on individual discretion in order to become more adaptive. One factor is likely to be that it has reached a level of internal complexity that cannot be maintained in a less rationalized type of organization. The desired response would be to move quickly to another highly rationalized configuration. However, the complex of bureaucratic procedures represents a large-scale intellectual effort of many people over time. Bureaucracies are not built in a day. The time required to construct a new configuration may be too long compared to the rate of environmental change.

This suggests that rationalization is a thing to be managed, just as the organization manages other assets and technology. The information-processing metaphor invites a concept of "bureaucratic software." Bureaucratic software is the collection of rules, procedures, and job descriptions in the organization. The issue is whether this can be managed, perhaps drawing on the experiences from managing computer software. Indeed, the metaphor converges at the level of automation in the organization, computerization being an extreme form of rationalization. The advantages of a concept of bureaucratic software would be to apply such concepts as program libraries and various programmer aids to the design and maintenance of organizational rules and procedures. The eventual goal would be improved bureaucratic software engineering.

This raises the issue of language. Bureaucratic software at present is largely in a natural language form. However, it typically occurs in a restricted style and content, somewhat like the legalese of commercial contracts or legislation. There is little poetry in job descriptions and procedure manuals. The conjecture is that a substantial part of this could be codified in a more formal language, capable of mechanical inference. It is here that mechanical aids could be developed to aid in the adaptation of bureaucratic structures.

This chapter is about the technology of bureaucracies and its relationship to the management of complexity. Over the past several decades, bureaucracies have been eager consumers of new information technology. Indeed, they probably support the computer industry. Certainly, this technology has done much to improve bureaucratic efficiency. On the other hand, it has not helped at all in the management of bureaucratic complexity. Indeed, it has aggravated the problem by obscuring bureaucratic rules and procedures in the form of computer codes. (For instance, many have experienced the frustrations of trying to rectify a computer-generated billing error.)

This is both a representation problem and a modeling problem. It is a representation problem in that computerized rules and procedures need to be made more accessible and directly controllable by management. It is a modeling problem in that improved methods of systems analysis are needed to more effectively analyze and design complex bureaucratic systems. This is not a matter of refining present techniques. There is a need for more fundamental revision and extensions in the approach to such problems (Stamper 1979; Lee 1984a, 1984b, 1985, 1988). Bureaucratic systems are not merely information-processing systems. They are systems of organizational and social control. They convey more than data; they convey orders, commands, obligations, contracts, permissions, licenses, vouchers, receipts, prohibitions, waivers, and verifications. Our focus, therefore, is not on computer support for the information processing of bureaucracies, but rather on providing more effective technology for their *normative* operations.

BUREAUCRACY AS DEONTIC SYSTEMS

A currently popular view of organizational management (March and Simon 1958) regards managers as information processors. Taking the metaphor literally, a bureaucracy is an organization where the programs these managers and other personnel are to follow are in the form of explicit rules and procedures.

But the programming of people differs from the programming of computers. As observed repeatedly in the literature on organizational psychology and sociology (Maslow 1943; McGregor 1960; Cyert and March 1963; March and Olsen 1979), people are not naturally idle. They have their own individual interests, goals, and aspirations, which they seek to satisfy through their participation in the organization.

When these correspond to the interests and goals of the organization itself, we tend to regard their independent behavior as initiative, otherwise it is considered more as the dysfunctional pursuit of personal interest. The programming of personnel in a bureaucracy, therefore, differs from computer programming: It not only orders the execution of desired behavior, but *constrains* the performance of undesired behavior.

Considering the collection of rules, procedures, and plans of a bureaucracy as its software, its basic logical structure may be contrasted with computer software. Essentially, computer programs consist of commands to the machine. Under certain (data) conditions, the machine is to do this or else do that. If no conditions are met, the machine halts. The underlying logic is imperative: Without appropriate instructions, the default behavior of the machine is inaction. By contrast, bureaucratic software does not simply mandate desired behavior. It also constrains extraneous behavior not appropriate to the organization's goals. Bureaucratic procedures thus contain not only imperatives (duties, obligation) but also prohibitions and contingent permissions. A typical example might be that discretionary purchases by departments have a maximum limit of $1,000. Purchases above that amount must go through the purchasing department, have three quotations, and the like.

The underlying logic of bureaucratic software, therefore, is not simply a logic of imperatives. It has a more complex basis in a broader theory of action and normative behavior. Efforts to formalize these concepts have developed under the heading of deontic logics (the name is derived from a Greek term meaning should or ought; see Hilpinen 1981). These are a variant of modal logic that contain operators applying potential behaviors or actions.

Deontic logic has its origin in the classical philosophy of ethics. The modern development of deontic logic was initiated in the early 1950s by G. H. von Wright who coined the term, based on the Greek deontwz meaning "as it should be" or "duly." Deontic logic is a logic of normative concepts. Its major application, outside ethics, has been to the philosophy of law. It is here that the connections to contract law, and eventually to bureaucratic regulation, might be made. The first axiomatization for deontic logic was proposed by von Wright (1968). As a basic concept, he introduced the operator:

$$O\phi$$

read that ϕ is obligatory. Based on this, a notion of permission can be defined as its logical dual:

$$P\phi \leftrightarrow \operatorname{def} \sim O \sim \phi$$

That is, to be permitted to ϕ is not to be obliged not to do it. A related concept of prohibition was defined as:

$$F\phi \leftrightarrow \operatorname{def} O \sim \phi$$

That is, ϕ is forbidden if it is obligatory not to do ϕ. For completeness, we also add a notation for waiver (of an obligation):

$$W\phi \leftrightarrow \operatorname{def} \sim O \phi$$

That is, ϕ is waived if it is not obligatory to do ϕ.

The practical relevance of deontic logic in administrative contexts is to provide automatic inference in, say, contract arbitration or the interpretation of bureaucratic regulation. Such applications are useful in complex cases where the chain of connections would otherwise be difficult to follow. Thus the axioms and inference rules of deontic logic take on pragmatic importance that the system draws the correct and intended conclusions.

As applied to bureaucracies, these deontic concepts provide a useful explication of the degree to which an organization is rationalized. This is diagrammed in Figure 19.2.

Figure 19.2. Rationalization as Deontic Constraints

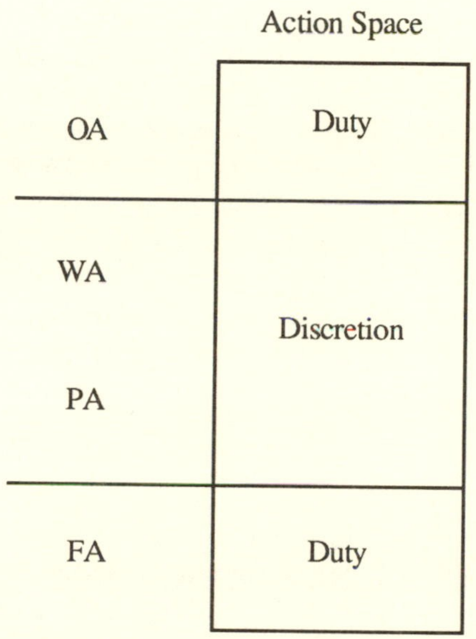

Action Space

OA	Duty
WA	Discretion
PA	
FA	Duty

If the range of possible actions is considered graphically as an action space, the important constraints on behavior are those actions that are obligatory and those that are forbidden. These prescribe the regulated behavior of personnel in the organization. The residual is discretionary behavior, that is, actions that are neither obligatory nor forbidden.

We may imagine the software of a bureaucracy—its rules and regulations—as a set of deontic rules governing the actions of its personnel. The question then arises: Where do these deontic rules come from? How do they change? While many of our actions are physical, others are (primarily) linguistic. A certain class of linguistic actions brings about a change in deontic status, what we call deontic performatives.

The linguistic concept of a performative was first introduced by Austin (1962) and elaborated by Searle (1969) and others. The performative aspects of contracts and financial instruments were discussed by Lee (1980, 1981). The relevance of performatives to office processes was first noted by Flores and Ludlow (1981). A performative is an utterance that not only conveys information but also, by its being spoken, accomplishes some socially significant act. For instance, the sentence, "I now pronounce you man and wife," when spoken by a priest during a marriage ceremony not only describes the relationship between the couple, but actually *creates* it. This example brings out several key features of perfomatives. One is that the state created by such an utterance is generally some type of social artifact. Obviously, the mere speaking of a few words has very little physical effect. Rather, it places one or more people in different states of social perception. Often, this involves a certain set of obligations, such as of fidelity or economic responsibility.

The roles involved in a linguistic utterance are usually cast as speaker and listener. However, in the case of performatives, the listener role must be divided between addressees and by-standers. Clearly, not everybody attending the marriage ceremony becomes socially obligated by the priest's pronouncement.

Also, it is not always the addressees of performatives who acquire the social obligation by the utterance. For instance, a major class of performatives is the class of *promises*, in which case it is the speaker who acquires the obligation. In other cases the addressee may in fact be an object: "I christen thee the *Queen Elizabeth*." These latter are, however, fairly rare types of performatives.

Linguists generally refer to performatives as a type of utterance, that is, a spoken communication. What is sometimes overlooked is that written communications, too, may be performatives. In these cases, however, the execution of the performative takes on a somewhat different character. In a spoken performative, the person making the performative is obviously identified as the speaker. In written performatives, the issue of authorship arises. Also, with spoken performatives the addressee hears the performative at the time it is spoken. Written communications, however, endure throughout time and so the addressee may receive the communication considerably later than when it was initially made. The question then arises: When during this interval does the performative come into force?

These issues of authorship and timing are commonly resolved by a very simple device, namely, the author's handwritten signature, accompanied by the date on which it was signed. The ritual of signing one's name to a document is so pervasive that its fundamental role is often not recognized. Indeed, as a rough heuristic, one can usually distinguish purely informative documents from those with a performative component by whether or not it has a personal signature. For instance, printed announcements or bulletins seldom have signatures; contracts to pay money (checks, etc.) always do. The effect of the signature is roughly the declaration: "I hereby acknowledge that my beliefs and intentions are accurately described by this associated text."

Signed documents, as performative instruments, also acquire a unique feature not possessed by their purely informative counterparts: The performative effect of the original signature is not carried over to its mechanical duplicates. For instance, in legal documents, such as contracts or wills, when several copies are made, each must be separately signed by the author(s) to have legal validity.

In the context of organizational procedures, the informative/ performative distinction can be refined further. One aspect of these procedures is certainly to transmit and store information. Another, however, is to control and standardize the behavior of the personnel involved. Procedures are thus means of standardizing the exercises of *authority* of certain individuals in the organization over others. Red tape, however, one particular form of authority, seems prominent. This is where a certain type of behavior is in general forbidden, except under special circumstances. The exercise of authority in these cases amounts to some person's evaluation of the circumstances and the granting of permission where appropriate. In many instances of red tape the action in question is divided into a number of subactions, each requiring separate permission. The delay or inaction inherent in the definition of red tape thus results not for reasons of information collection or processing, but rather due to the wait times in the personal queues of these various permission-granting individuals.

Various types of permission structures exist within organizations. A common example is the request of some department to purchase a large item. Often such a request must be approved by a number of individuals to verify that the item is technically sound, compatible with similar items in the organization or competitively priced. In each step along the way, the permission performance is inevitably signaled by the signature of the authorizing individual. Another common type of organization performative is order giving. Interestingly, this seems to be a more efficient process than permission granting. The difference seems to be that orders are generally given by a single individual to a number of others, whereas permission often needs to be granted by a number of people together for a single person.

The effect of these performatives is to create a change in deontic status. This is diagrammed in Figure 19.3.

Figure 19.3. Performatives Changing Deontic Status

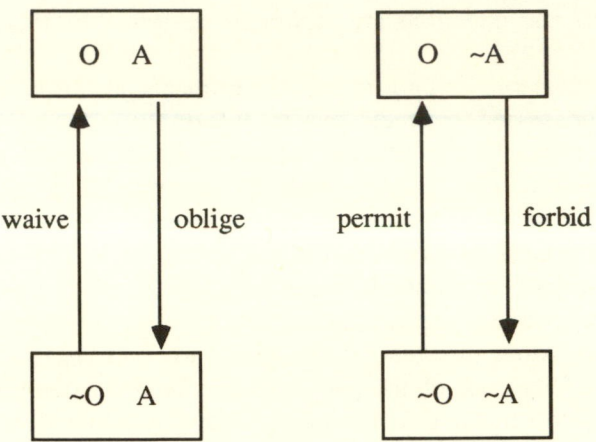

DEONTIC EXPERT SYSTEMS

Expert systems have become widely popular as a means of making complex deductions from rules expressed in an easily understandable IF/THEN format. A deontic expert system is one that makes inferences about deontic conditions. To illustrate, we introduce the following rule format:

IF<condition>
[AND <condition>] . . .
THEN <condition>.

Each <condition> represents a static property or relationship in the organization:

FACULTY(X)
SUPERVISOR(X,Y)

A <condition> may also be a deontic condition, indicated by one of the following forms:

OBLIG(X:C)
PERMIT(X:C)
FORBID(X:C)
WAIVEIX:C)

A single argument to a deontic condition is our notation for an action, X:C, where X indicates an individual (agent) and C is any condition, including other deontic conditions.

As an example, consider the set of deontic rules governing the use of a scarce resource, such as the office photocopy machine in a university department. During the times when this machine is "temporarily *not* out of order" there is considerable contention for its use. Here we consider how the written rules applying to this situation might be converted to automated form.

Written rule: "Any faculty member may use the photocopy machine."

rule:	IF FACULTY(X)
	THEN PERMIT (X:USE-COPIER)
fact:	FACULTY (Lee)
assess:	Lee: USE:COPIER
response:	PERMIT(Lee:USE COPIER)

Multiple conditions may of course appear in the rules. For example, another rule is the following. Written rule: "Staff may use the copier if they have special copy privileges."

rule:	IF STAFF(X)
	AND COPY-PRIVILEGE(X)
	THEN PERMIT (X:USE-COPIER)
fact:	STAFF (Fletcher)
	COPY-PRIVILEGE(Fletcher)
assess:	Fletcher: USE:COPIER
response:	PERMIT(Fletcher:USE COPIER)

Another kind of inference in a deontic expert system is default reasoning: When the supporting conditions of a rule cannot be proven, the converse deontic state is assumed. An example is the following. Written rule: "Students may not use the copier."

fact:	STUDENT (Dewitz)
assess:	Dewitz: USE:COPIER
response:	FORBID(Dewitz:USE COPIER)

A change in the conditions pertaining to an individual is brought about by an update to the system. If the system is assumed performative, then these update actions are deontic performatives, which actions may themselves be controlled by deontic rules. The role of the system is thus to enforce authority controls.

Written rule: "The chairperson may grant copier privileges to staff."

rule:	IF CHAIR(X)
	AND STAFF(Y)
	THEN
	PERMIT (X:COPY-PRIVILEGE(Y))
fact:	CHAIR (Dyer)
	STAFF (Brown)

update: Dyer: COPY-PRIVILEGE (Brown)
            UPDATE ACCEPTED
assess: Brown: USE:COPIER
response: PERMIT(Fletcher:USE COPIER)
update: Lee: COPY-PRIVILEGE (Quintus)
response: UPDATE REJECTED
explain: CHAIR(Lee) is not true

These update constraints may be applied recursively to model the delegation of authority. Written rule: "Chairpersons may delegate copier usage discretion to the associate chair."

rule: IF CHAIR(X)
         AND ASSOCIATE-CHAIR(Y)
         THEN PERMIT (X:
             PERMIT (Y:
                 PERMIT (Z:USE COPIERZ)))

However, since such recursive rules are difficult to understand, delegation is usually represented using intermediate deontic states:

rules: IF CHAIR(X)
          AND ASSOCIATE-CHAIR (Y)
          THEN PERMIT (X:COPY-DISCRETION(Y)).

          IF COPY-DISCRETION(Y)
          AND STAFF(Z)
          THEN
          PERMIT(Y: COPYPRIVILEGE(Z)).

          IF COPY-PRIVILEGE (Z)
          THEN PERMIT (Z:USE-COPIER).

MANAGING BUREAUCRATIC PROCEDURES

The conditions, hence the deontic status, pertaining to an individual may be modified by an update. Constraints on updates are enforced through other deontic rules. However, these are only static constraints. Often, constraints have a temporal sequence to them, that one action must be done first, *then* another, and so on. This leads to the notion of a *procedure*.

A representation commonly used in computer science to represent temporal sequence is a *state-transition network*. These are usually graphic, for instance, as in Figure 19.4.

In this example, at state 0 there is a choice between taking actions A or B. If state 1 is reached, there is a choice of taking actions C or D. A familiar example of state transition networks in management science is a decision tree. In this case, the node types are differentiated between choice nodes, indicating choices of the decision maker, and outcome nodes, indicating choices made by external events.

Figure 19.4. State Transition Network

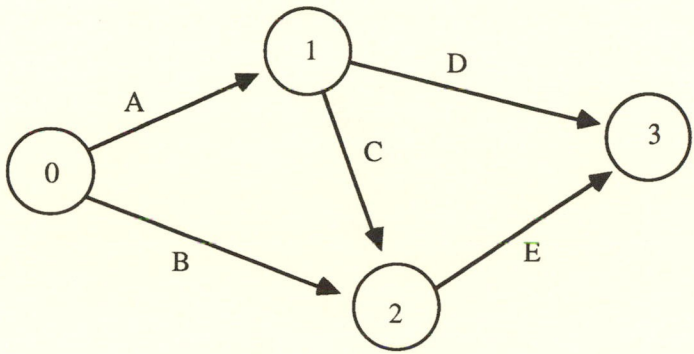

While state transition diagrams are adequate for modeling many procedures, an aspect they do not capture is *concurrent:* that various actions may occur while others are taking place. A different representation that models concurrency is a marked graph, as in Figure 19.5.

Figure 19.5. Marked Graph

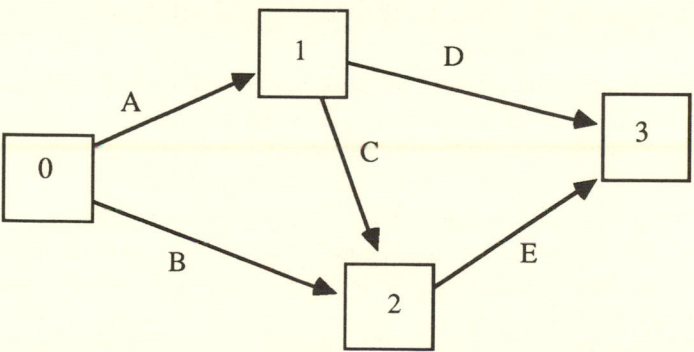

In this example, at node 0, actions A and B commence concurrently. When action A is completed, actions C and D may commence. When both actions B and C have been completed, action E may commence. A familiar example of marked graphs in management science is a PERT diagram. A marked graph, however, does not represent choice between alternatives.

A representation that captures both choice and concurrency is a Petri net (Peterson 1981). A Petri net is a graph representation having two types of nodes. So-called *place* nodes indicate states or substates of the system, and are drawn as circles. These correspond to the nodes in a state transition diagram and represent choices. A Petri net also has *transition* nodes, drawn as a vertical bar. These correspond to the nodes in a marked graph and indicate concurrences. A Petri net is a directed graph having these two node types in alternation as in Figure 19.6.

Figure 19.6. Petri Net

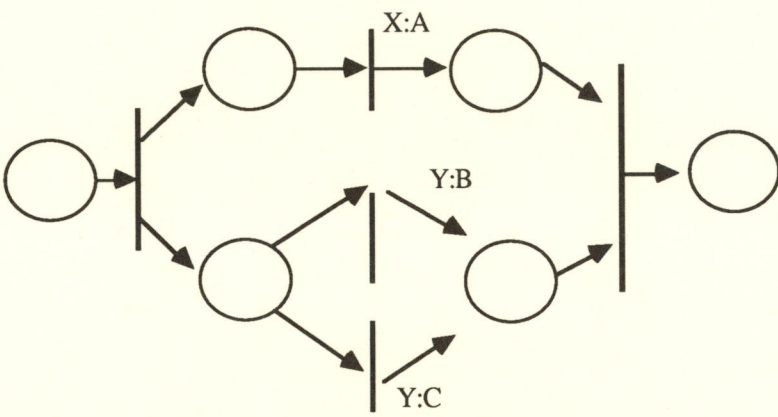

Note that actions are associated with transitions. In this example, party X does A concurrently with party Y's doing either B or C. Note also that transitions may be unmarked, indicating a null action.

Each place represents a substate of the overall system. The flow of activity in the system is indicated by drawing dots, called tokens, in the places. The overall placement of tokens is called a marking, and represents to total system state. For example, the initial marking of the above graph shown in Figure 19.7.

Figure 19.7. Initial Marking of Petri Net

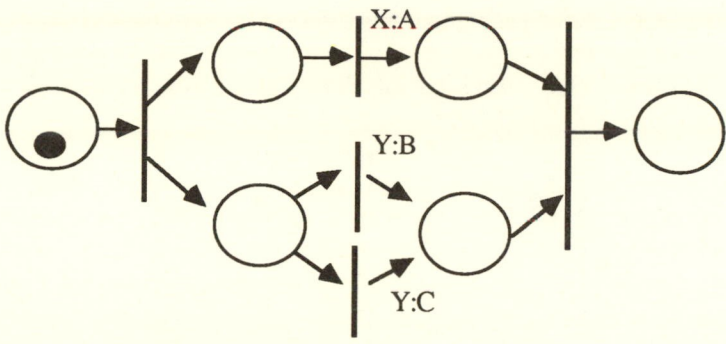

The transition is said to be enabled when all of its input places have tokens. In the case of null transitions, this is sufficient for it to fire, removing tokens from its input places, and placing new tokens in all of its output places, as in Figure 19.8.

Figure 19.8. Next Marking of Petri Net

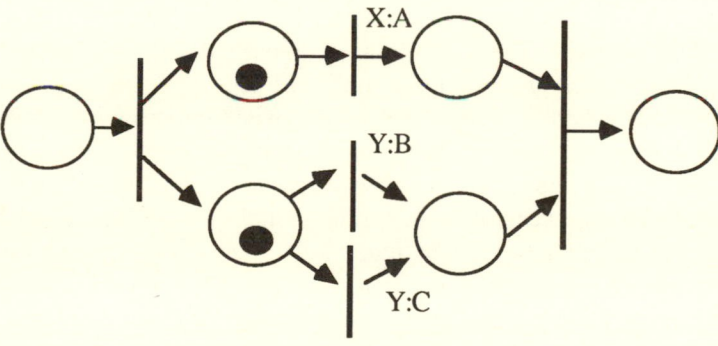

If the case of transitions with associated actions, the action must also take place for the transition to fire. For example, suppose that X does the action A, as in Figure 19.9.

The tokens of a Petri net are typically regarded as state indicators only. In bureaucratic applications, they often have the additional interpretation as the flow of documents. For example, the issuance of a multipart form may be regarded as a transition with multiple output places, a token representing each of the copies. Figure 19.10 is an example Petri net with a more realistic interpretation, indicating a university's procedure for faculty travel.

Figure 19.9. Marking of Petri Net after X Does A

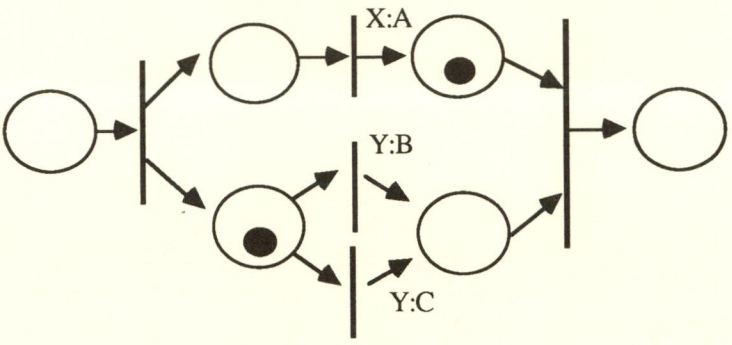

Of special interest is how a computerized system can aid in the development and modification of procedures. Here we make an analogy with computer programming. In developing a sizable computer program, a programmer often encodes several thousand instructions, all of which must work in harmony. How is this accomplished? Over the past two decades, much of the attention in programming language development has been to develop aids to this process. One important aspect of this is grammatical correctness. This applies at two levels. One, when the programmer enters an instruction that is syntactically incorrect, the system identifies the error immediately. This happens quite often—perhaps every five or ten entries— and eliminates a great number of errors at their source. The other kind of grammatical correctness is at the macrolevel—verifying the structure of an entire program or subroutine. For example, the system can identify nonterminating iterations and other clear mistakes. In other cases, the system identifies a pattern that is merely suspect, and gives the programmer a warning message. With these aids (and others) the program development process is aided considerably. Nonetheless errors may still be present: The system cannot guarantee total correctness. But it does facilitate development and modification by pointing out the error patterns it knows about.

For procedure development, we propose a similar kind of strategy. Corresponding to the single statement level of programs, the system controls the kinds of actions that can be entered, by developing a separate library from which actions are selected.

Figure 19.10. Petri Net for Travel Request

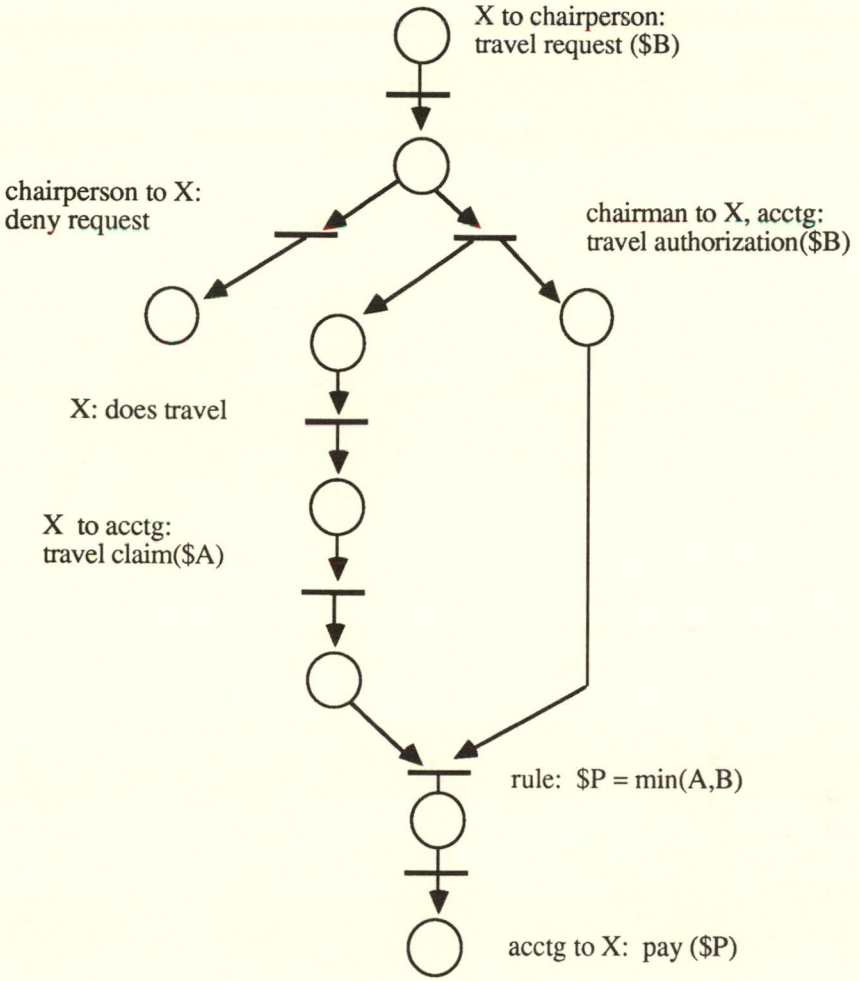

X to chairperson:
travel request ($B)

chairperson to X:
deny request

chairman to X, acctg:
travel authorization($B)

X: does travel

X to acctg:
travel claim($A)

rule: $P = min(A,B)$

acctg to X: pay ($P)

Of greater interest, however, is verification at the macrolevel—examining the composition of the Petri net procedure for errors. Of course, the system is able to identify graphical correctness, such as the alternation of place and transition nodes. But what we have in mind is more of a substantive verification—checking whether the sequence of actions being modeled can lead to undesirable conditions for the organization. These are of two types:

- undercontrol—conditions such as opportunities for embezzle-ment or collusion

- overcontrol—conditions where steps are taken that have no functional or control purpose, like superfluous copies of documents.

Our basic mechanism to accomplish this substantive verification is what we call an *audit pattern*. An audit pattern is drawn using the same Petri net notation as for procedures. However, the actions in the audit pattern may contain variables. Further, the graph of the audit pattern may be only part of that in the procedure, and need not even be a connected graph. Further, the audit pattern graph may contain additional transitions, contained in a segment of the graph surrounded by a dashed line. This is the *exception region* of the graph, indicating what can go wrong in the procedure (e.g., the inventory clerk steals the goods).

To illustrate the use of audit patterns, consider the following procedure. The situation is that a job foreman contracts with a laborer, called a roustabout, to unload materials for a certain hourly wage. After the work is done, the foreman brings a report of the hours worked to the company cashier, receives the wags, and pays the roustabout (Figure 19.11).

Figure 19.11. Procedure Example: Hire Roustabout

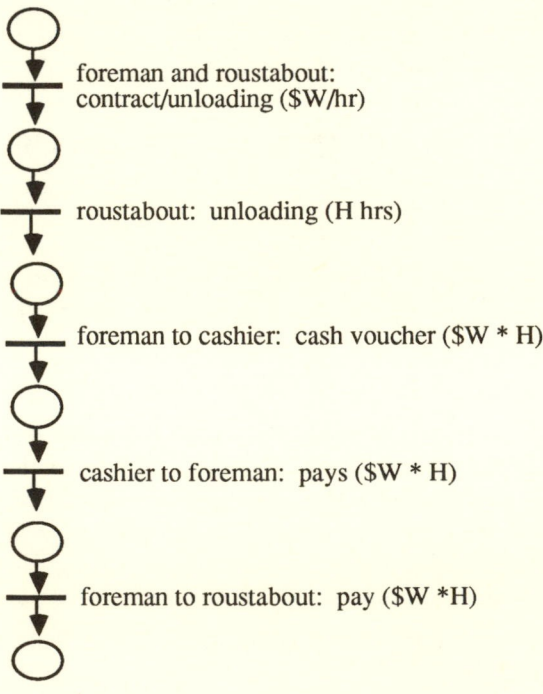

foreman and roustabout:
contract/unloading ($W/hr)

roustabout: unloading (H hrs)

foreman to cashier: cash voucher ($W * H)

cashier to foreman: pays ($W * H)

foreman to roustabout: pay ($W *H)

The weakness of this procedure is that the foreman may inflate the number of hours worked and keep the difference himself. This is portrayed in the following audit pattern shown in Figure 19.12.

Figure 19.12. Audit Pattern Example: Contract Work

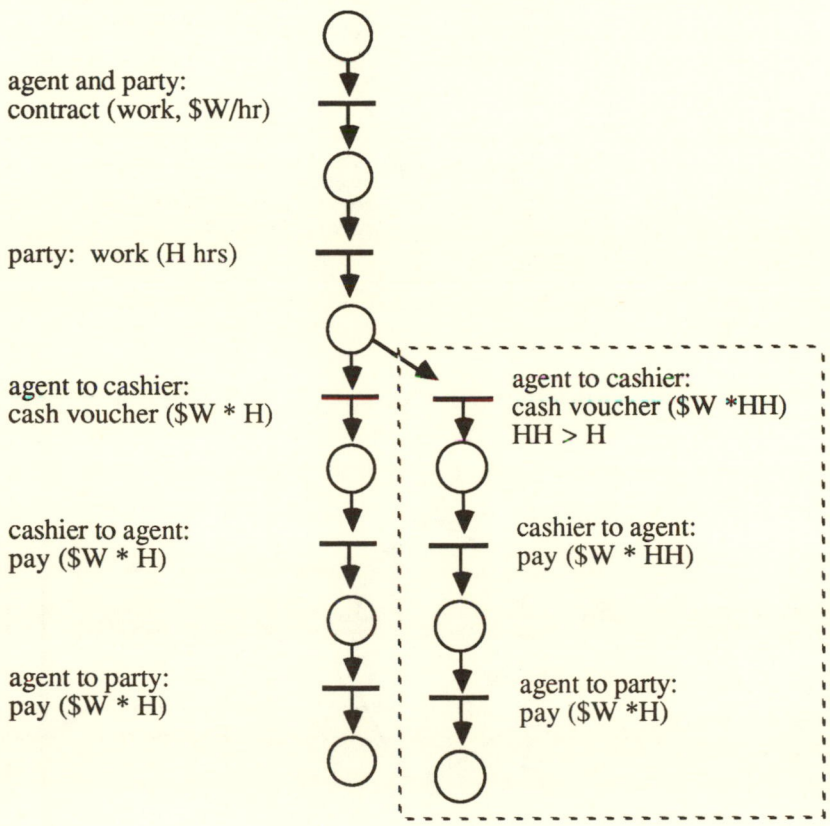

agent and party:
contract (work, $W/hr)

party: work (H hrs)

agent to cashier:
cash voucher ($W * H)

cashier to agent:
pay ($W * H)

agent to party:
pay ($W * H)

agent to cashier:
cash voucher ($W *HH)
HH > H

cashier to agent:
pay ($W * HH)

agent to party:
pay ($W *H)

Another example is the case of controlling cash for ticket sales. In this procedure, a clerk sells the tickets, reporting the sale to the ticket agent and giving the cash to the cashier. The ticket agent reports the sales to the sales manager, the cashier reports the cash receipts to the sales manage, and the sales manager reconciles the two (Figure 19.13).

This procedure is reasonably well controlled as it stands. However, one day the cashier becomes sick and the ticket agent is asked to fill in. Under this condition the audit pattern in Figure 19.14 is matched.

Figure 19.13. Procedure Example: Ticket Sales

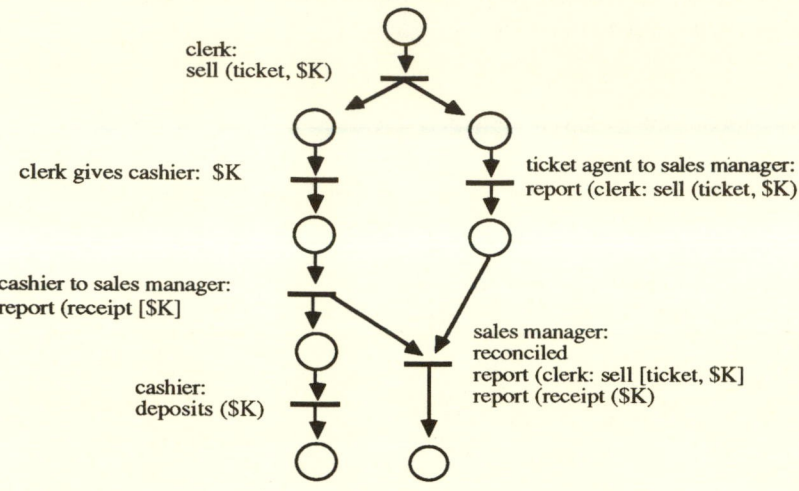

Figure 19.14. Audit Pattern Example: Agent Conceals Sales

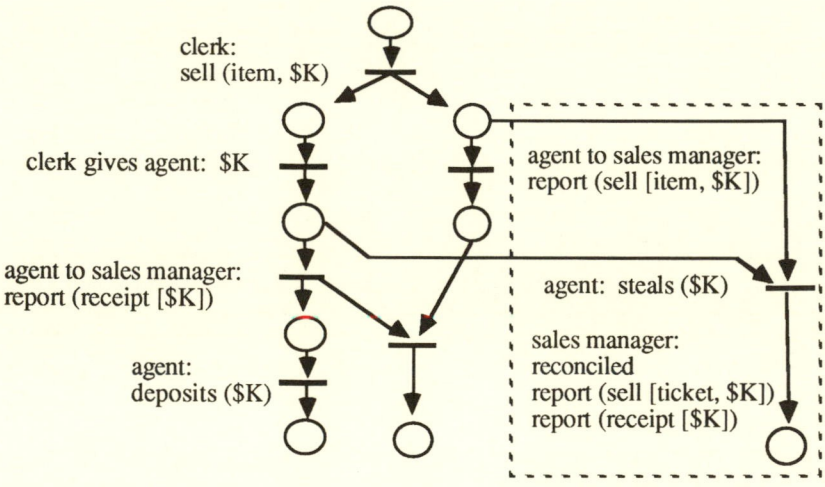

PROTOTYPE IMPLEMENTATION

A prototype computer program exhibiting the features discussed above is currently under development. In this section we illustrate how this system might be used to manage bureaucratic software. As a prototype, the main purpose of this program is to test the ideas and suggest further innovations. It may also be used as a CASE tool, for computer-aided software engineering of bureaucratic systems.

Developing a Deontic Rule Base

When the user executes the system, the following menu bar appears:

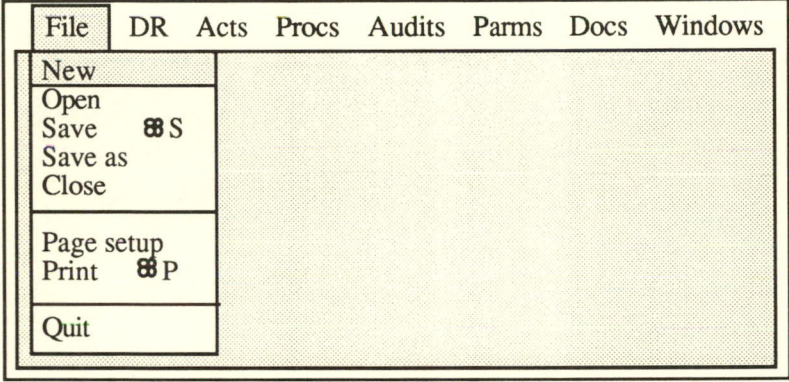

To create a new file of deontic rules, the user selects *New* from the *File* menu, as shown. The user is then prompted to give a name to the rule base:

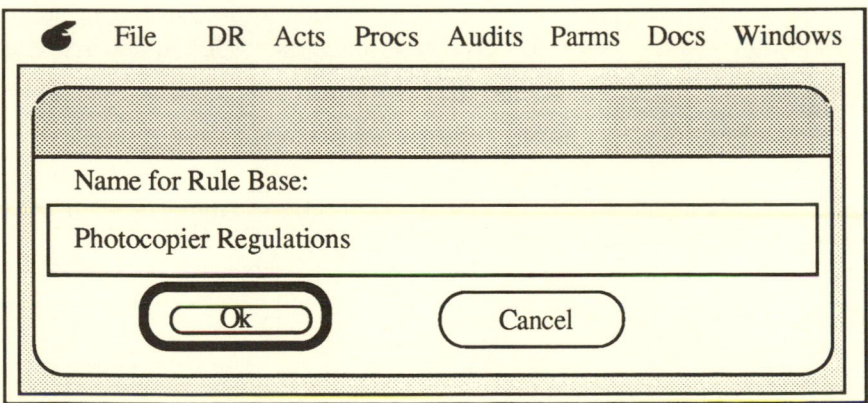

The user enters the deontic rules into a textual window such as the following:

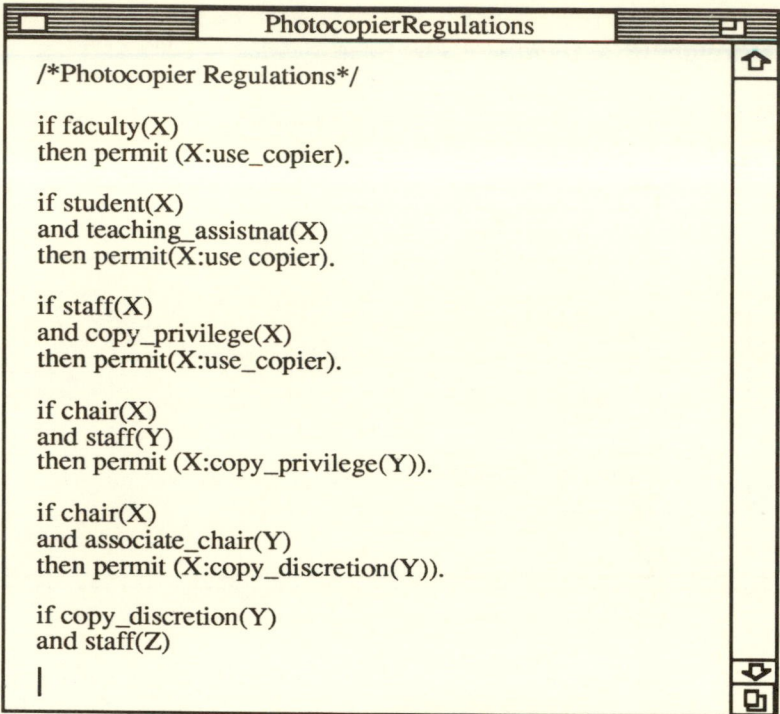

```
PhotocopierRegulations

/*Photocopier Regulations*/

if faculty(X)
then permit (X:use_copier).

if student(X)
and teaching_assistnat(X)
then permit(X:use copier).

if staff(X)
and copy_privilege(X)
then permit(X:use_copier).

if chair(X)
and staff(Y)
then permit (X:copy_privilege(Y)).

if chair(X)
and associate_chair(Y)
then permit (X:copy_discretion(Y)).

if copy_discretion(Y)
and staff(Z)
```

As can be seen, the syntax is much like that in the earlier discussion, except that constants are in lowercase, while variables are in uppercase. At any time in the session, the user may return to view this rule by selecting from the *Windows* menu:

File	DR	Acts	Procs	Audits	Parms	Docs	Windows	
							Clear Graphic Window	
							Clear Output Window	
							PhotocopierRegulations	
							Σ Output Window	

Using Deontic Rules

To use the rule base, the user chooses the *DR* menu (for Deontic Reasoning). After compiling it (*Compile*), the user may interact with the rule base using either *Assess* or *Update*, in the same sense as in the earlier examples. For instance, to assess the deontic status of a given action:

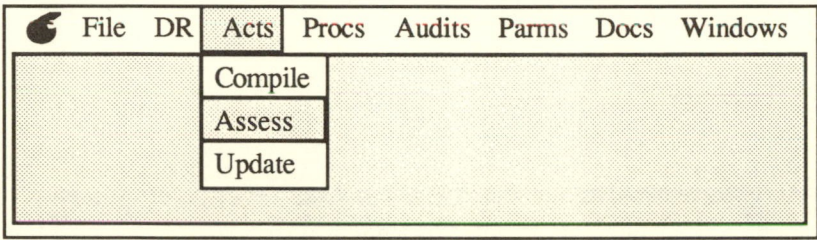

The system prompts the user for any unknown facts:

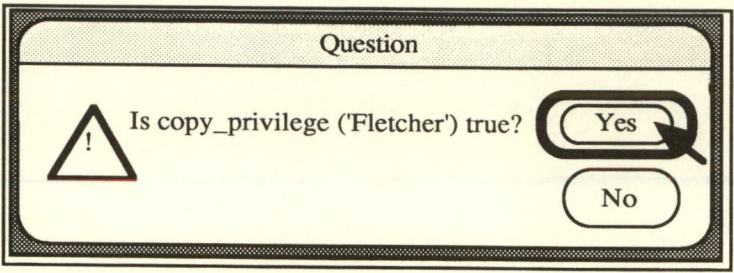

The results of this query are as follows:

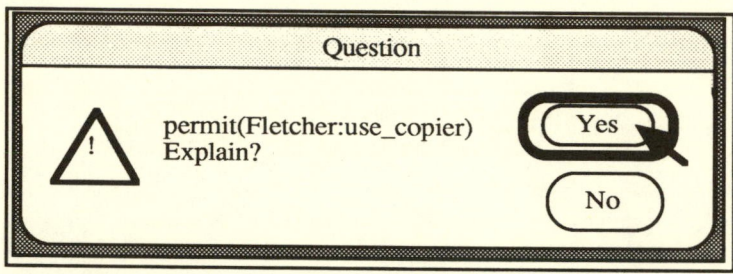

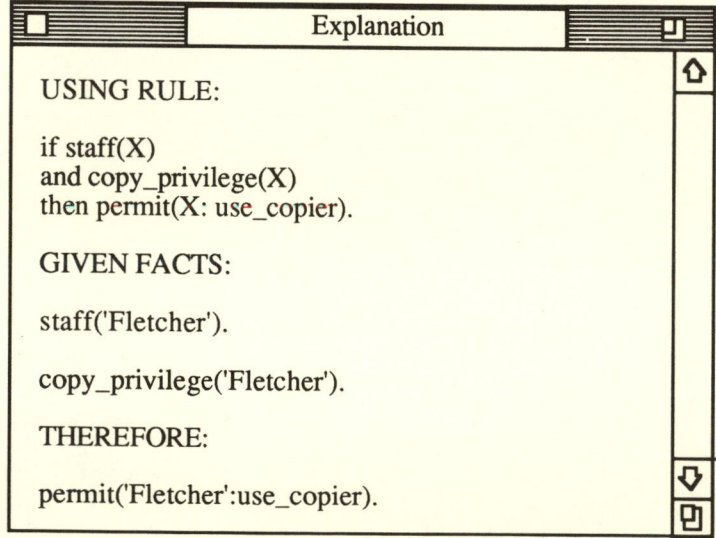

Developing Procedures

In developing procedures, the menus *Acts*, *Procs*, and *Audits* are used. The *Acts* menu specifies the basic vocabulary of actions:

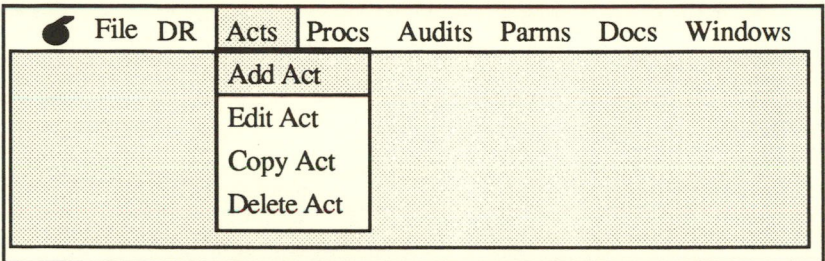

A key feature is the use of direct manipulation graphics for drawing the Petri net graph:

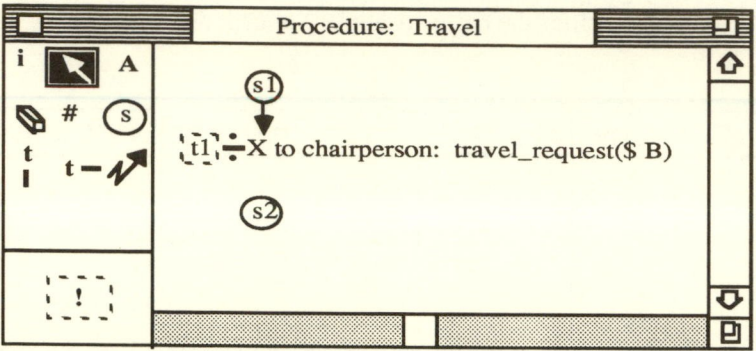

The upper right hand segment of this screen is the tools palette. The user clicks the mouse on one of these icons, and a different drawing functionality is produced. In this snapshot, the user is repositioning the first transition node. The completed Petri net for this procedure is as follows:

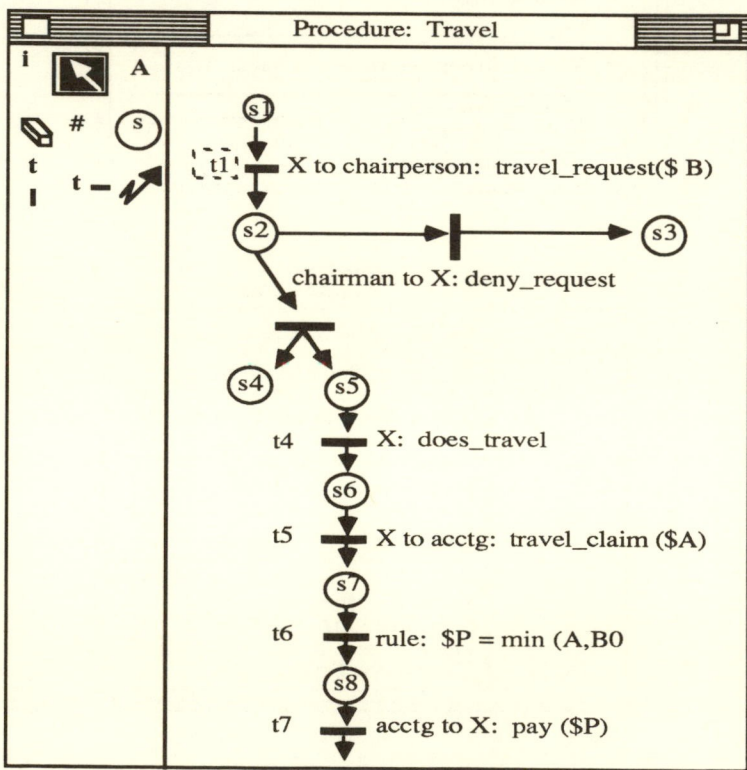

Developing Audit Patterns

The *Audits* menu is for developing audit patterns:

⚞	File	DR	Acts	Procs	Audits	Parms	Docs	Windows

Create Audit Pattern
Edit Audit Pattern
Compile, Show Assertions
Compile, Close Audit Window
Abort Audit Window

- -

Copy Audit Pattern
Delete Audit Pattern

- -

Save Audit Library
Save Audit Library As
Open Audit Library
Close Audit Library

Again, direct manipulation graphics is used in a fashion similar to that for procedures. A completed audit pattern is the following:

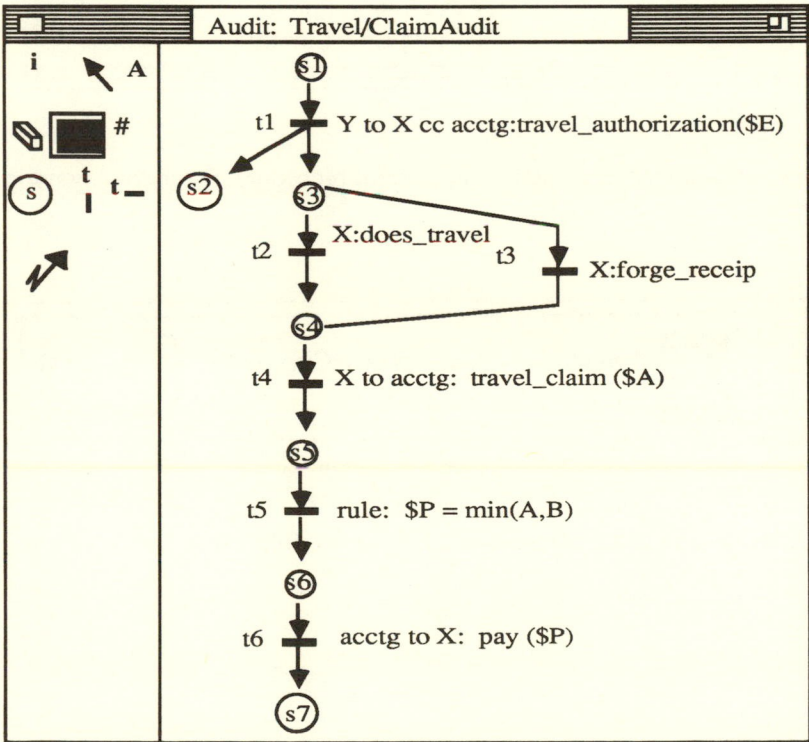

Using Audit Patterns

Audit patterns are used when the user the selects the *Audit Proc* window from the *Procs* menu:

🍎 File Fonts DR Parms	**Procs**	Acts Audits Docs Windows

Create Proc
Edit Proc
Compile, Show Assertions
Compile, Close Proc Window
Abort Proc Window

Audit Proc Window
Exec Proc Window

Copy Proc
Delete Proc

Save Proc Library
Save Proc Library As
Open Proc Library
Close Proc Library

If the audit pattern matches the current procedure, the following notice is displayed:

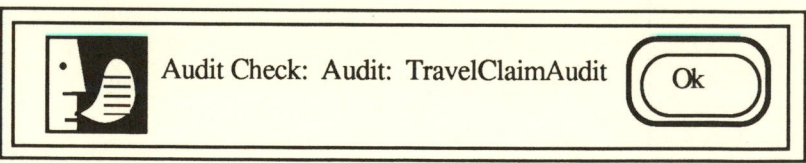

Audit Check: Audit: TravelClaimAudit   (Ok)

There is one *ptrans* for each transition in the graph being compiled. For the above example, the *ptrans* assertions are the following:

Σ Output Window

Procedure:

ptrans(t5, [s6], [s7], _43 to acctg:travel_claim($50)).

 ptrans(t4, [s5], [s6], _65:does_travel).

ptrans(t3, [s2], [s4, s5], chairperson to_91 cc acctg:travel_authorization($

ptrans(t1,[s2], [s3], chairperson to_118:deny_request).

ptrans(t1, [s1], [s2],_137 to chairperson:travel_request($_144)).

ptrans(t7, [s8], [s9], acctg to_164:pay($_170)).

 ptrans (t6, [s7], [s8], rule: $_193=min(_196,_197)).

Audit Pattern:

ptrans(_694, [_508], [_520,_514], _579 to _583 cc acctg:travel_authorization

 ptrans(_720, [_520], [_526], _605:does_travel).

ptrans(_740, [_526], [_532], _625 to acctg:travel_claim($_632)).

 ptrans(_760, [_532], [_538], rule: $_655=minP658, _659)).

ptrans(_780, [_538], [_544], acct to _679:pay($_685)).

Here, the terms with leading underscores are internally generated variables. An audit pattern is matched when the *ptrans* assertions of the audit pattern (outside the exception regions) are a subset of the *ptrans* assertions for the procedure matching unbound variables to constants.

Developing Electronic Forms

Electronic forms are much like the paper forms common in bureaucracies, except that the user interacts with a computer terminal instead of writing on the form. Such electronic forms are becoming common in various office system applications. A novel feature of our system is the use of direct manipulation graphics to develop the forms. Before (or during) the development of an electronic form, the user must specify the kinds of data fields it should contain. These data fields are called *parameters*, and are managed from the *Parms* menu:

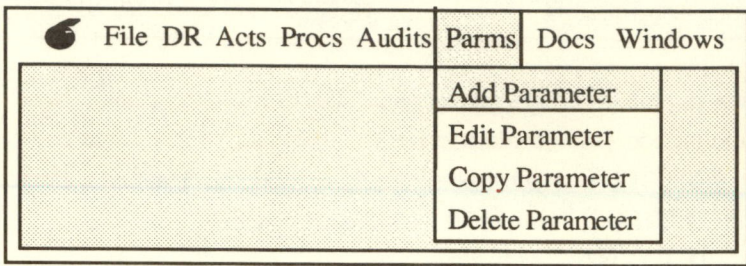

As shown, the specification of a parameter is itself an electronic form. To lay out the electronic form itself, one goes to the *Docs* menu:

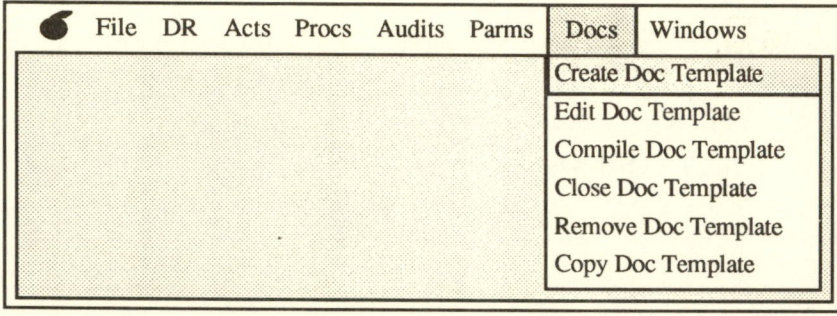

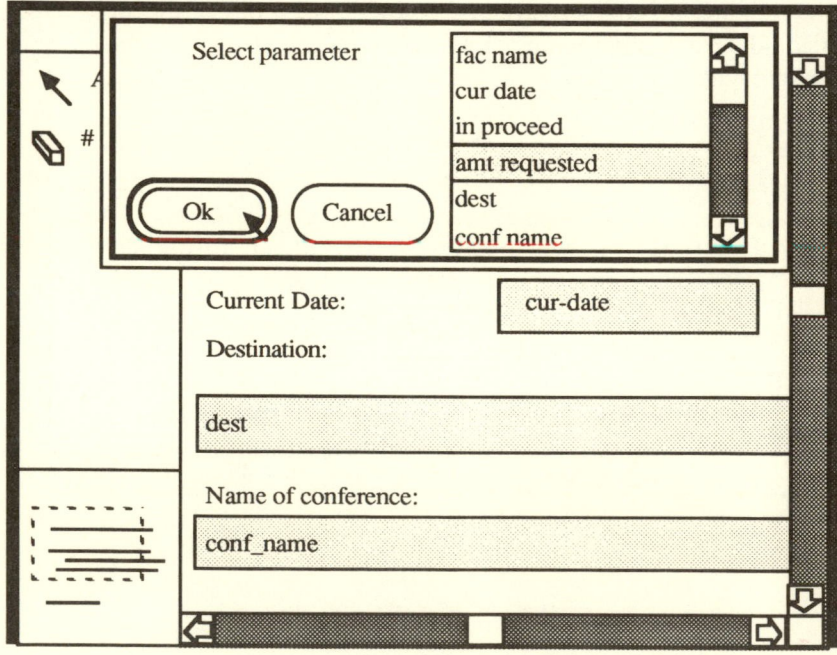

After choosing the # tool, one selects from a menu of available parameters. (Successive forms may therefore share parameters.) The system then places the label and the data field (as a shaded gray area) in the graphic portion of the window. The user may modify the layout by selecting any of these labels or data fields and moving them around. An example completed layout is shown next. Following that is the appearance of this form when it is executed for the user. After all the forms for a procedure have been prepared, the procedure can be executed in simulation fashion *Exec Proc Window* from the *Procs* menu.

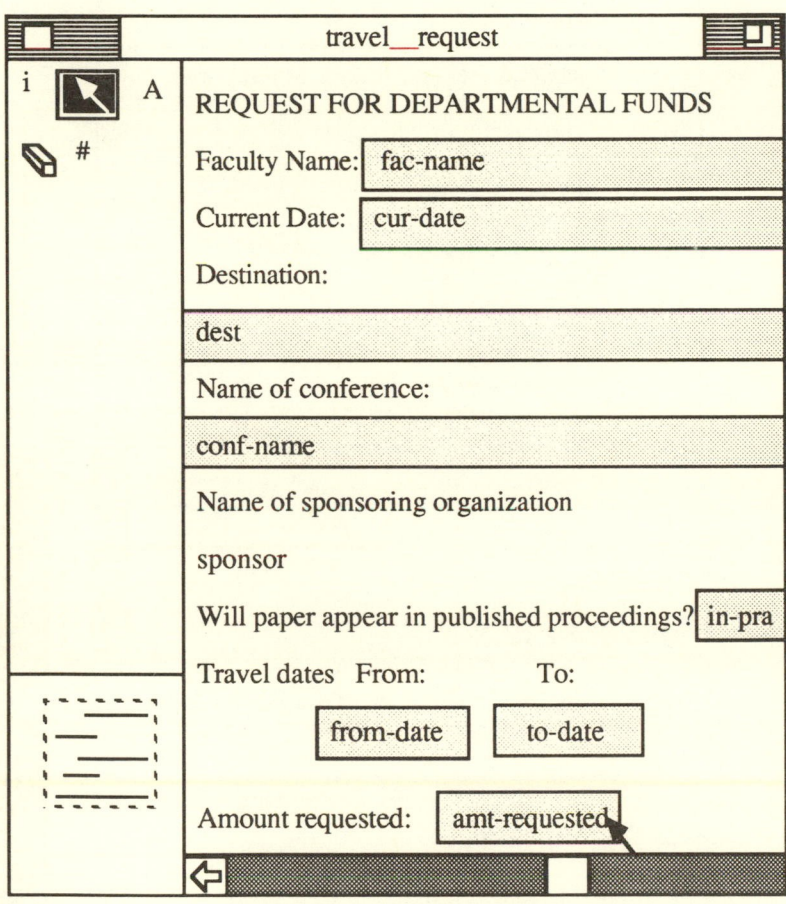

travel__request

REQUEST FOR DEPARTMENTAL FUNDS

Faculty Name: fac-name

Current Date: cur-date

Destination:

dest

Name of conference:

conf-name

Name of sponsoring organization

sponsor

Will paper appear in published proceedings? in-pra

Travel dates   From: To:

from-date   to-date

Amount requested: amt-requested

```
┌─────────────────────────────────────────────────────┐
│ ▣▤▤▤▤        travel__request        ▤▤▤▤ ▣           │
├─────────────────────────────────────────────────────┤
│ REQUEST FOR DEPARTMENTAL FUNDS                       │
│ Faculty Name: :Lee, Ronald M.                        │
│ Current Date:  8/3/90                                │
│ Destination:                                         │
│ Los Angeles, CA                                      │
│ Name of conference:                                  │
│ Generating Creativity and Innovation in Large        │
│ Name of sponsoring organization                      │
│ RGK Foundation                                       │
│ Will paper appear in published proceedings?  yes     │
│ Travel dates  From:          To:                     │
│              8/8/90        8/10/90                    │
│ Amount requested:  100                               │
│  ( Ok )                      ( Cancel )              │
└─────────────────────────────────────────────────────┘
```

FURTHER DEVELOPMENT

As mentioned earlier, this system is still under development. Some of the features yet to be included follow.

Graphical Simplification

Various shorthand graphical notations are possible to make the graphical composition of procedures and audit patterns faster and easier. One example is the case of directly parallel (as opposed to asynchronous) actions. Instead of:

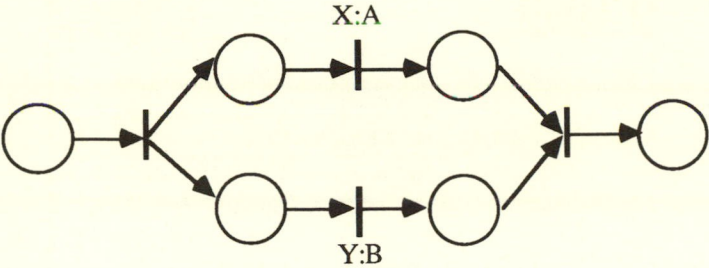

one might use the notation:

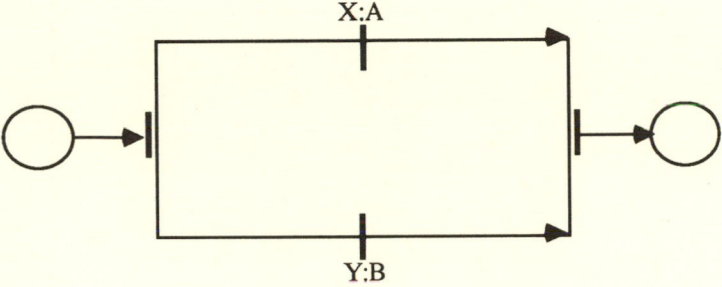

Modularization

Another issue is coping with larger Petri net graphs that do not fit easily into a single graphical window. A device to help manage graphical complexity is the use of modules, drawn as a box, which refer to a separately defined Petri net in subroutine fashion. For example,

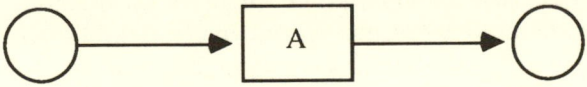

where procedure A is another Petri net:

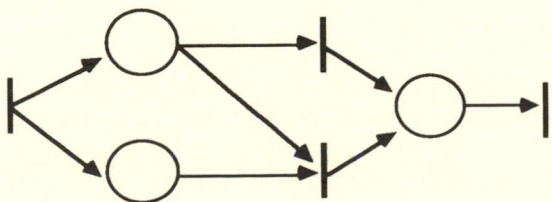

Abstraction

Another issue is generalizing the pattern-matching capabilities of the audit patterns. At present, the audit patterns are essentially a template on the actual actions, using variables to be matched. We plan to replace this with abstraction hierarchies on these actions, for example, that a money order or a travelers check are special cases of a check that are particularly reliable (hence a useful category in certain procedures). These, along with personal checks, are special cases of paying by check. This is diagrammed using another kind of graph common in artificial intelligence, known as an isa hierarchy:

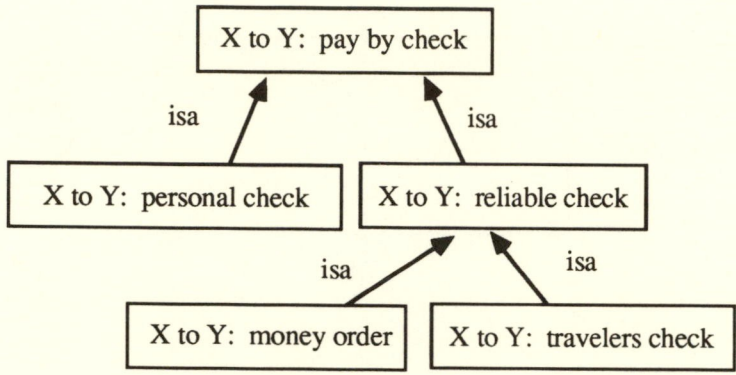

DEFEASIBLE DEONTIC REASONING

Earlier, the example of delegation of authority was illustrated regarding update constraints. Implicit in this is the notion of a deontic hierarchy, typified by the classical organization chart. When more than one deontic hierarchy pertains to the same action, the possibility arises of deontic dilemmas, where "you're damned if you do and damned if you don't." We would like to facilitate reasoning about deontic dilemmas, suggesting possible courses of action to the user.

MULTILINGUAL APPLICATIONS

The use of electronic forms in procedures has a side-benefit created by the fact that the information is structured by the form. Much of the difficulty of translation to a different language is removed. Following are several small electronic forms illustrating the same form in English, Russian, and Chinese. Further development includes applications to internal electronic contracting.

NOTE

1. To get a sense for the scale of this problem, consider the European Common Market bureaucracy, which is estimated to produce some 15,000 pages of official reports, regulations, and memos per day! Further, these are produced in four languages, so that the actual paper output is 60,000 pages per day.

REFERENCES

Abrahamson, B. 1977. *Bureaucracy or participation: The logic of organization.* London: Sage.

Austin, J. L. 1962. *How to DO things with words.* Cambridge, Mass.: Harvard University Press.

Burne, T., and G. M. Stalker. 1961. *The management of innovation.* London: Tavistock.

Cyert, R. M., and J. G. March. 1963. *A behavioral theory of the firm.* Englewood Cliffs, N.J.: Prentice-Hall.

Elgin, D. S., and R. A. Bushnell. 1977. The limits to complexity: Are bureaucracies becoming unmanageable?" *The Futurist* (December).

Flores, F., and J. J. Ludlow. 1981. Doing and speaking in the office. In *Decision support systems: Issues and challenges.*, eds. G. Fick and R. H. Sprague, Jr. Oxford: Pergamon.

Galbraith, J. 1973. *Designing complex organizations.* Reading, Mass.: Addison-Wesley.

_____. *Organization design.* Reading, Mass.: Addison-Wesley.

Hilpinen, R., ed. 1977. *Deontic logic: Introductory and systematic readings.* Dordrecht: D. Reidel.

_____, ed. 1981. *New studies in deontic logic.* Dordrecht: D. Reidel.

Lee, R. M. 1980. CANDID: A logical calculus for describing financial contracts, Ph. D. diss. The Wharton School, University of Pennsylvania.

_____. 1981. *CANDID description of commercial and financial concepts: A formal semantics approach to knowledge representation.* Laxenburg, Austria: International Institute for Applied Systems Analysis.

_____. 1984a. Bureaucracies, bureaucrats and information technology," *European Journal of Operational Research* 18: 293–303.

_____. 1984b. Automating red tape: The performative vs. informative roles of bureaucratic documents. *Offices—Technology and People* 2: 187–94.

_____. 1985. Bureaucracy as artificial intelligence. In *Knowledge Representation for Decision Support,* ed. Humphreys, P. Durham, England: North Holland.

_____. 1988. Bureaucracies as deontic systems. *ACM Transactions on Office Information Systems,* vol. 6 (2): 87–108.

McGregor, D. 1960. *The human side of enterprise.* New York: McGraw-Hill.

March, J. G., and J. P. Olsen. 1979. *Ambiguity and choice in organizations.* 2d ed.. Bergen: Universitetsforlaget.

March, J. G., and H. A. Simon. 1958. *Organizations.* New York: Wiley.

Maslow, A. H. 1943. A theory of human motivation. *Psychological Review* 50 (4): 370–96.

Peterson, J. L. 1981. *Petri net theory and the modeling of systems.* New York: Prentice-Hall.

Searle, J. 1969. *Speech acts: An essay in the philosophy of language.* London: Cambridge University Press.

Simon, H. A. 1955. A behavioral model of rational choice. *Quarterly Journal of Economics* 69.

Stamper, R. 1979. LEGOL as a tool for the study of bureaucracy,. *Proceedings of the IPIP TCS WG 8.2 Conference on the Interaction of Information Systems and the Organization.*

_____. 1985. A logic of social norms for the emantics of business information. In *Proceedings of IPIP WG 2.6 Conference of Database Semantics,* ed. T. B. Steel and R. Meersman. North Holland.

Von Wright, G. H. 1968. An essay in deontic logic and the general theory of action. *Acta Philosophica Fennica.* Amsterdam: North Holland.

Weber, M. 1956/1978. *Economy and society.* Berkeley, Calif.: University of California Press. Translated from *Wirtschaft und Gelsellschaft.* Guegingen: J. C. B. Mohr, 1956.

20

A Survey of Needs for Human-Friendly Fuzzy Systems

Akira Ishikawa

Fuzzy control is one of the most advanced areas in the application of fuzzy logic and systems. Already more than 120 applications of fuzzy control have been introduced in Japan. These are not limited to the more well-known examples of fuzzy control in subways, elevators, container cranes, and water treatment plants. Applications have also been developed for such diverse uses as golf diagnosis, computer-aided instruction, color print evaluation, and securities investment. Important applications of fuzzy control are now found throughout the service sector as well as in manufacturing industries. The quality, efficiency, and effectiveness of operational management have noticeably increased as a result of the emergence of fuzzy control.

In December 1989, we conducted a survey of the development and application of fuzzy logic and systems for process control, pattern recognition, and communication. Data were gathered on the number of researchers by area, the perceived importance of each theme, and the different views of professionals and laypeople. Based on the results of our survey, this chapter presents our analysis and recommendations regarding the future development of fuzzy technology, particularly the need for friendly fuzzy systems.

SURVEY OVERVIEW

Objectives

The broad objective of the survey was to identify needs among users of fuzzy systems. We did this in the three areas of human-friendly fuzzy systems: fuzzy control, fuzzy pattern recognition, and fuzzy communication. Ultimately, our aim was to facilitate development of the basic technology and to conduct effective hardware-oriented R&D. It is mandatory to visualize the needs for such systems and how they might evolve to ensure that R&D proceeds in the right direction. By identifying the direct and indirect diffusion of technology, we will be better prepared and able to conduct orderly R&D. For example, this kind of analysis may indicate the necessity of additional research in new theories and techniques outside the scope of fuzzy theory, such as robotics and numerical control.

Scope and Description

- The scope of this survey covered the areas of fuzzy control; fuzzy pattern recognition, including both mobile and immobile objects, and fuzzy communication.

- The time horizon of the survey was 1990 to 2000.

- The survey sample included members of the Japan Fuzzy Society, randomly selected members of the Information Processing Society, and a smaller group of foreign researchers. This sample group included researchers and professionals dealing directly with fuzzy logic and systems, as well as those in related areas.

- The sample size was 1,200 in total: 900 from the Japan Fuzzy Society, 100 members of the Information Processing Society, and 200 foreign researchers.

- The method used for the survey was to send out questionnaires in English and Japanese. The new Delphi method of sending the questionnaires twice was attempted at the outset, but abandoned due to the lack of time.

- The survey was conducted December 8–20, 1989.

Content

Forecasting-type surveys like this, whether designed to identify needs or new ideas, require that one organize the question topics in some kind of framework. There are two approaches: One is to let the survey respondents decide, and the other is to identify and select topics in advance, through deliberations of a working group, for example. We chose the latter approach. As a basic framework, we divided users of human-friendly fuzzy systems into public, business, and home domains. These domains were further classified into functional, industrial, and operational areas. For each area, we attempted to identify the needs of the users. Another consideration, in view of the fact our survey was to be conducted at year-end, was to limit the length of the survey in order to maximize the response rate and accuracy of the data. The questionnaire consisted of thirty-eight questions on fuzzy pattern recognition, thirty-two questions on fuzzy control, and thirty questions on fuzzy communication, as well as questions about the importance and expected applications of each research theme.

Response Rate and Respondent Profile

Despite the time limitations, the response rate was higher than expected. This reflects a relatively strong interest in fuzzy systems.

Among Japanese specialists, the response rate was 198 out of 1000, or 19.8 percent. For foreign specialists, it was 34 out of 200, or 17.0 percent. The survey audience was more diverse than anticipated, since the respondents belong to a wide variety of academic societies and associations. The distribution of respondents' ages was as follows:

Ages	Distribution (percent)	
20–29	25.8	
30–39	34.3	
40–49	25.8	
50–59	9.6	
60–69	4.0	
No answer	0.5	
Total	100.0	(N=198)
Average Age	37.6	

ANALYSIS OF SURVEY RESULTS

Number of Experts by Area of Research

Developmental research in fuzzy systems was divided into six categories, labeled A through F, each of which included at least two independent research themes. The number of experts varied considerably by theme. Obviously, the variance is affected by the scope of each theme as well as by curiosity and necessity on the part of researchers. Because of the scarcity of the samples available, we computed an average number of experts per category to arrive at a rough comparison, as shown in Table 20.1.

Table 20.1. Number of Experts by Categories

	Code	Average Number of Researchers*
General subjects in fuzzy control R&D	F	46.3
Human-friendly fuzzy control systems	E	38.0
Static pattern recognition of colored and 3-D objects	A	21.3
Dynamic pattern recognition of colored and 3-D objects	B	19.5
Visual recognition of 3-D objects (developmental studies)	C	14.7
Dynamic recognition of human expressions (developmental studies)	D	8.0

*Based on the average number of researchers in all subthemes.

Many more experts were engaged in developmental research in categories E (human-friendly fuzzy systems) and F (general fuzzy control) than in A through D (pattern processing and recognition). Further, in a comparison of E and F categories, within a specific area such as control systems, more experts were doing F-type R&D in application of fuzzy theory to general engineering system control than E-type research in human-friendly aspects other than engineering.

Importance and Prospects of Developmental Research by Theme

In analyzing the importance and prospects of each research theme, we have excluded those categories (C, D) in which fewer than twenty experts were involved so as to ensure the reliability of our data. We rank developmental research themes in order of perceived importance in Table 20.2.

In order to clarify the characteristics of our survey findings, we have constructed a graph (Figure 20.1) which plots "importance" along the y-axis and "prospects in 2–3 years (for significant work)" along the x-axis. The median of each group score is also plotted, forming a cross and quadrants.

This graph reveals three groups. (Naturally enough, there are essentially no experts working on themes that are considered both unimportant and lacking in prospects.) Here is a summary of the results for each developmental research theme:

Prospective and important themes:
- Fuzzy robust control
- Time saving in process control
- Static pattern recognition for objects

Prospective but less important themes:
- Fuzzy programmable control
- Static pattern recognition of letters and symbols
- Dynamic pattern recognition of letters and symbols

Less prospective but important themes:
- Preventive control via qualitative inference
- Control to deal with contradictory human communication
- Dynamic pattern recognition of objects
- Distributive control in CIM

If we look at Figure 20.1 more closely, some interesting contrasts appear. For instance, comparing T1 and T3 with T2 and T4, even when the object of research (pattern recognition) is the same, dynamic pattern recognition is seen as a more difficult theme than static pattern recognition. Furthermore, if we compare T1 and T2 with T3 and T4, recognition of tangible objects is considered more important than recognition of letters and symbols as cognitive objects. Looking into T5 through T10, we notice that qualitative inference and analysis of human communication are considered more difficult than engineering system control. One might call the applications of fuzzy theory to engineering system control "softwaring" *techniques or technologies*, whereas T5 and T6 are related to softwaring *common sense*.

Table 20.2 Perceived Importance and Prospects of Research Themes

(Percent of Respondents)	(Code)	Perceived Importance				Years to Obtain Results			
		High	Med.	Low	NR	2–3	5	10	NR
Static Pattern Recognition	A								
Object		66.7	26.7	3.3	3.3	60.0	23.3	10.0	6.7
Symbol		34.8	56.5	4.3	4.3	73.9	21.7	0	4.3
Dynamic Pattern Recognition	B								
Object		65.5	27.6	3.4	3.4	31.0	41.4	20.7	6.9
Symbol		35.0	55.0	5.0	5.0	60.0	25.0	10.0	5.0
Human-Friendly Control Systems	E								
Preventative control		70.0	27.5	2.5	0	32.5	45.0	10.0	12.5
Control to deal with		61.1	38.9	0	0	22.2	52.8	2.8	22.2
contradictory communication									
General Subjects in Fuzzy Control	F								
Fuzzy robust control		73.1	21.2	5.8	0	59.6	28.8	5.8	1.9
Time saving in process control		63.3	32.7	4.1	0	71.5	20.4	4.1	0
CIM distributive control		56.8	37.8	5.4	0	32.5	45.0	10.0	12.5
Fuzzy programmable control		44.7	46.8	6.4	2.1	55.3	29.8	4.3	6.4

NR = No Response.

We conclude that developmental studies with a wider vision on a long-term basis are needed. On the other hand, most experts regard themes involving applications of fuzzy logic to engineering systems as being ready for market within two to three years. This seems to indicate that fuzzy studies in this area are reaching maturity. In the near future, we anticipate commercialized fuzzy control systems will emerge in rapid succession, while the thrust of fuzzy research will shift from fuzzy engineering control to the applications of transcendental human thinking and fuzzy communication.

Figure 20.1. Classification of Themes by Perceived Importance and Prospects for Results

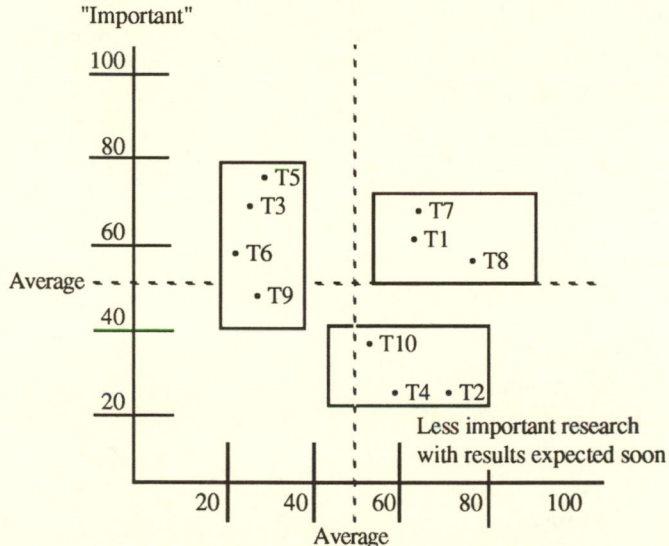

"Expected results in 2–3 years"

T1 = Static pattern recognition of objects
T2 = Static pattern recognition of letters and symbols
T3 = Dynamic pattern recognition of objects
T4 = Dynamic pattern recognition of letters and symbols
T5 = Preventive control through qualitative inferences
T6 = Adaptive control to deal with contradictory communication
T7 = Fuzzy robust control
T8 = Time saving in process control
T9 = CIM distributive control
T10 = Fuzzy programmable control

Differences of Opinion between Laypeople and Experts

We have tried to compare responses of laypeople with those of experts as to each theme's relative "importance" and "prospects within two to three years," as shown in Table 20.3.

Table 20.3. Difference in Perceptions of Experts and Laypeople Regarding Importance and Prospects of Research Themes

(Percent of Respondents)	"Important"		Expected Results "Expect 2–3 Years"	
	Experts	Laypeople	Experts	Laypeople
A. Static Pattern Recognition (SPR)				
Object	66.7	28.8	60.0	34.8
Symbol	34.8	27.3	73.9	52.5
B. Dynamic Pattern Recognition (DPR)				
Object	65.5	32.8	31.0	16.1
Symbol	35.0	21.7	60.0	23.2
E. Human-Friendly Control Systems (CS)				
Preventative control	70.0	33.3	32.5	19.2
Control to deal with contradictory communication	61.1	34.3	22.2	8.6
F. General Subjects in Fuzzy Control (FC)				
Fuzzy robust control	73.1	35.9	59.6	38.4
Time saving in process control	63.3	33.3	71.5	43.9
CIM distributive control	56.8	28.3	32.5	34.4
Fuzzy programmable control	44.7	31.3	55.3	37.4
Average	57.1	30.7	49.9	30.0

It is clear that more experts than laymen attach great importance to the themes in question and, moreover, that a greater number of experts believe results can be realized within two to three years. Although it may be natural for experts to ascribe great importance to their own research, the fact that they anticipate real results sooner than laypeople is very interesting. To interpret such a finding in a positive light, one might conclude that the laypeople is simply unaware of the real and substantial progress being made by experts in fuzzy studies. On the other hand, one cannot rule out the possibility that the experts are prone to evaluate their own prospects rather optimistically, getting swept up in the excitement of rapid developments in recent years.

ANALYSIS OF FUZZY THEORY APPLIED STUDIES

The Number of Researchers by Application Theme

In our study, application studies of fuzzy theory have been classified into fifteen groups, A through O, and two or more application themes are shown for each group. The average number of experts by group is shown in Table 20.4 to illustrate the relative distribution.

Table 20.4. Average Number of Experts by Theme

	Code	Average Number of Experts
Basic information processing	G	43.3
Basic linguistic processing	I	26.4
Realization of fuzzy control in public, private sectors	E	25.7
Pattern recognition (excluding images)	H	25.0
Human interface	N	21.5
Home automation using fuzzy control	F	20.7
Linguistic processing systems	J	19.0
Automated pattern recognition of colored objects	A	17.0
Automated dynamic pattern recognition of colored objects	B	15.6
Consulting	M	14.0
Communication of feelings	K	12.5
Functional support of movement and tasks	L	9.5
Home, educational, and leisure automation via static pattern recognition of colored objects	C	8.4
Home, educational, and leisure automation via dynamic pattern recognition of colored objects	D	8.2
Private databases	O	7.0

The greatest number of experts deals with theme G, Basic Information Processing, which aims at developing hardware environments to deal with ambiguous information. Other themes being studied by a large number of experts include I, Basic Research on Linguistic Processing, and E and F, Realization of Applied Systems of Fuzzy Control. In contrast, C and D, Home Automation Systems Using Pattern Recognition, and O, Private Databases are noticeable for the scarcity of experts researching them. These areas are closely related to object recognition, communication, and daily life. With the exception of G, Basic Information Processing, the distribution of experts in applications themes closely matches that in developmental research themes.

Importance, Prospects, and Technology Forecast of Application Themes

Table 20.5 summarizes the responses for each fuzzy applications theme in order of perceived importance. Again, those themes with fewer than twenty experts have been excluded from our analysis to help ensure statistical reliability.

Table 20.6 presents the range of responses (highest and lowest) for each category in the categories of "very important," "realizable within two to three years," and "not realizable without new technology." This helps illustrate the relations among perceived importance, realization period, and technological forecast. The range of values indicates the relative weight and scope of each theme.

What happens if we use the data on fuzzy applications categories in Table 20.6 to derive a graph as in Figure 20.2. First, in all themes except for pattern recognition, the perceived importance of each theme and its near-term (two to three-year) prospects for realization are inversely related. In other words, the more important the applications theme is, the lower the expectation of early realization. Conversely, the lesser the importance of a given theme is, the higher the expectation of realization within two to three years.

This graph also indicates clearly that application themes dealing with communication, G through N, are more important and difficult, being far from realization. This corresponds with the earlier finding for developmental studies that, although important, research in "qualitative inference" and "responding to human communication" would take be long-term and progress would be relatively slow.

Table 20.5. Summary of Survey Results

(Percent of respondents)	Importance				Years to obtain results				Level of technology required for results			
	High	Med.	Low	DK	2–3	5	10	DK	Old	Mid	New	DK
A. Static pattern recognition												
Visual systems of production robots in FA	84.0	16.0	0	0	64.0	20.0	12.0	4.0	80.0	16.0	4.0	0
Visual systems of automatic inspection in FA	80.8	19.2	0	0	61.5	26.9	7.7	3.8	23.1	57.7	15.4	3.8
Visual systems of robotic transport in FA	42.9	47.6	9.5	0	76.2	14.3	4.8	4.8	42.9	33.3	19.0	4.8
B. Dynamic pattern recognition												
Visual systems of production robots in FA	81.8	9.1	9.1	0	54.5	22.7	9.1	13.6	9.1	45.5	36.4	4.5
Visual systems of automatic inspection in FA	78.3	13.0	8.7	0	52.1	26.1	8.7	13.0	4.3	65.2	21.7	4.3
E. Automation via fuzzy control in public, private sectors												
Signal control systems for rail transport	66.7	25.9	3.7	3.7	63.0	33.3	3.7	0	29.6	48.1	22.0	0
Fire-fighting robots	62.5	29.2	8.3	0	20.8	50.0	16.7	12.5	8.3	66.7	20.8	4.2
Collision avoidance systems for ships	61.5	38.5	0	0	46.1	38.5	7.7	7.7	19.2	38.5	30.8	7.7
Aircraft control systems	60.0	30.0	10.0	0	35.0	30.0	35.0	0	10.0	60.0	30.0	0
Collision avoidance systems for automobiles	58.6	34.5	3.4	0	13.7	51.7	24.1	10.3	17.2	37.9	34.5	6.9
Flexible handling robots	56.0	40.0	4.0	0	60.0	36.0	0	4.0	24.0	48.0	28.0	0
Cooperative operations robots	54.8	41.9	3.2	0	22.6	54.8	16.1	6.5	9.7	45.2	41.9	0

Table 20.5 (continued)

(Percent of respondents)	Importance				Years to obtain results				Level of technology required for results			
	High	Med.	Low	DK	2–3	5	10	DK	Old	Mid	New	DK
Flexible speed control systems	54.2	37.5	8.3	0	62.5	33.3	0	4.2	16.7	45.8	33.3	0
Air conditioning systems	53.6	42.9	3.6	0	50.0	42.9	0	7.1	17.9	64.3	14.3	3.6
Posture control systems for drafting machines	53.3	46.2	3.8	53.3	0	30.0	10.0	6.7	20.0	50.0	26.7	0.3
Temperature control— furnaces	51.3	48.7	0	0	64.1	23.1	7.7	5.1	20.5	48.7	25.6	2.6
Machine control in plastics manufacturing	50.0	46.2	3.8	0	64.4	26.9	3.8	3.8	19.2	61.5	11.5	3.8
Highway gate control systems	50.0	52.3	7.7	0	61.6	38.5	0	0	30.8	46.2	23.1	0
Ship control systems	48.0	48.0	4.0	0	44.0	40.0	12.0	4.0	24.0	44.0	24.0	8.0
Optimum blending control	47.8	39.1	8.7	4.3	52.1	43.5	0	4.3	17.4	47.8	34.8	0
Running time forecast display	46.2	50.0	3.8	0	65.4	34.6	0	0	26.9	50.0	23.1	0
Acid wash schedule control	45.0	45.0	10.0	0	65.0	35.0	0	0	20.0	60.0	20.0	0
Unmanned test drive system	44.4	40.7	14.8	0	29.6	33.3	25.9	11.1	22.2	29.6	37.0	11.1
Unmanned vehicle with optimum route generator	43.5	52.2	4.3	0	43.5	53.5	8.7	4.3	26.1	60.9	8.7	0
Shortest-route selection by robots	35.7	53.6	10.7	0	46.5	42.9	3.6	7.1	32.1	50.0	14.3	3.6
F. Home automation systems closely related to daily life												
Conversion of handwriting to printing	52.2	39.1	8.7	0	26.0	56.5	13.0	4.5	17.4	34.8	43.5	4.3

Table 20.5 (continued)

(Percent of respondents)	Importance				Years to obtain results				Level of technology required for results			
	High	Med.	Low	DK	2–3	5	10	DK	Old	Mid	New	DK
Hot-water heater control	34.6	53.8	11.5	0	65.4	26.9	3.8	3.8	30.8	57.7	7.7	3.8
Intelligent car suspension	31.0	65.5	3.4	0	31.0	58.6	6.9	3.4	24.1	37.9	37.9	0
Self-tuning car engine	29.6	51.9	18.5	0	48.1	37.0	14.8	0	14.8	44.4	40.7	0
Multiple-zone A/C control	17.4	60.9	13.0	4.3	52.2	34.8	4.3	8.7	16.1	43.5	26.1	4.3
VCRs with auto recording pause for commercials	15.0	35.0	50.0	0	65.0	25.0	5.0	5.0	40.0	40.0	20.0	0
Automatic volume reduction system for TVs and audio	9.1	45.5	45.5	0	72.7	22.7	0	4.6	54.5	31.8	9.1	4.5
G. Basic information processing												
Inference computer based on common sense, language	86.0	14.0	0	0	9.3	37.2	34.9	16.3	0	14.0	79.1	2.3
PCs for fuzzy data processing	73.3	24.4	2.2	0	15.6	46.7	28.9	8.9	2.2	17.8	66.7	6.0
Mainframes for fuzzy data processing	71.4	26.2	2.4	0	19.0	42.9	28.6	9.5	2.4	11.9	71.4	7.1
H. Pattern recognition processing (excluding image processing)												
High-sensitivity touch sensors	74.1	18.5	3.7	0	18.5	51.9	18.5	11.1	0	22.2	66.7	3.7
High-sensitivity smell sensors	61.5	30.8	3.8	0	11.5	34.6	46.2	7.7	0	15.4	73.1	3.8
High-sensitivity taste sensors	59.1	31.8	4.5	0	9.1	40.9	45.5	4.5	0	9.1	91.8	0

Table 20.5 (continued)

(Percent of respondents)	Importance				Years to obtain results				Level of technology required for results			
	High	Med.	Low	DK	2–3	5	10	DK	Old	Mid	New	DK
I. Basic research in language processing												
Relevant structure of concepts expressed by common language	89.3	10.7	0	0	0	46.4	32.1	21.4	0	14.3	64.3	21.4
Relation between sensory stimuli and expression	85.2	11.1	3.7	0	3.7	37.0	37.0	22.2	0	22.2	59.3	18.5
Establishment of algorithms for interpreting sentences	80.8	19.2	0	0	3.8	34.6	38.5	23.1	0	23.1	53.8	15.4
Associative operations of words in common language	80.0	16.0	4.0	0	4.0	28.0	40.0	24.0	0	12.0	64.0	12.0
Algorithms for producing sentences from images	69.2	30.8	0	0	11.5	26.9	34.6	26.9	0	15.4	61.5	15.4
J. Linguistic processing												
Automatic summary production	70.0	25.0	5.0	0	20.0	25.0	35.0	20.0	10.0	35.0	45.0	5.0
M. Consulting												
Databases for questioning	75.0	20.8	0	4.2	12.5	45.8	12.5	29.2	0	29.2	50.0	20.8
N. Human interface												
OA input/output devices	54.5	45.5	0	0	18.2	40.9	27.3	9.1	9.1	22.7	54.5	4.5
Man-machine conversation	52.4	47.6	0	0	4.8	42.9	38.1	14.3	0	28.6	57.1	4.8

DK = Don't know or no response.

Table 20.6. Range of Responses by Category
(Maximum and Minimum of Experts and Laypeople)

(Percent of respondents)	"Very Important"		2–3 Years to Obtain Results"		"New Technology is Required"	
	Maximum	Minimum	Maximum	Minimum	Maximum	Minimum
A. Static pattern recognition (Automated systems in public, private sectors)	84.0	42.9	76.2	61.5	19.0	9.0
B. Dynamic pattern recognition (Automated systems in public, private sectors)	81.8	78.3	54.5	52.1	36.4	21.7
E. Automation via fuzzy control in public, private sectors	66.7	35.7	65.4	13.7	41.9	8.7
F. Home automation systems closely related to daily life	52.2	9.1	65.2	26.0	43.5	7.7
G. Basic information processing	86.0	71.4	19.0	9.3	79.1	66.7
H. Pattern recognition processing (excluding image processing)	74.1	59.1	18.5	9.1	81.8	66.7
I. Basic research in language processing	89.3	69.2	11.5	3.7	64.3	53.8
J. Linguistic processing	70.0 [=]	70.0	20.0 [0]	20.0	45.0 [0]	45.0
M. Consulting	75.0 [0]	75.0	12.5 [0]	12.5	50.0 [=]	50.0
N. Human interface	54.5	52.4	18.2	4.8	57.1	54.5

Figure 20.2. Correlations between Perceived Importance and Prospects by Category (percent of respondents)

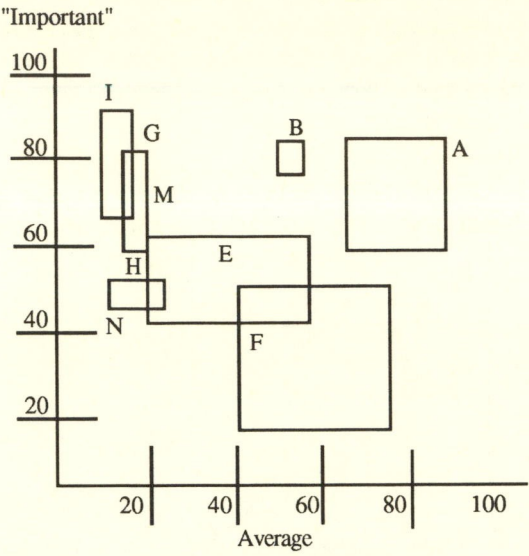

"Expected results in 2–3 years"

A = Static pattern recognition—automated systems in public, private sectors
B = Dynamic pattern recognition (as above)
E = Automation via fuzzy control
F = Home automation systems closely related to daily life
G = Basic information processing
H = Pattern recognition processing
I = Linguistic processing
M = Consulting
N = Human interface

Figure 20.3 plots realizability of fuzzy applications against the need for new technology. It is obvious again (and intuitively sensible) that realizability and need for new technology are trade-offs having an inverse relationship, with no exceptions. Further, themes dealing with communication, G through N, are in particular need of new technology. On the other hand, in the areas of pattern recognition, A and B, the need for new technology is not so high, since applications have come closer.

In addition, so as to show more clearly which applications require new technology most, the data on realization "possible with traditional technology" and "impossible without new technology" have been compared.

Table 20.7 ranks themes in order of importance from top to bottom, and in increasing order of dependence on new technology across from left to right. It is very clear that new technologies are indispensable for themes dealing with fuzzy communication, implying that we need to concentrate efforts in this area. New technologies and techniques in fuzzy communication applications are essential to the continued advance of fuzzy studies in general.

Figure 20.3. Correlations between Prospects for Results and Need for New Technology by Category (percent of respondents)

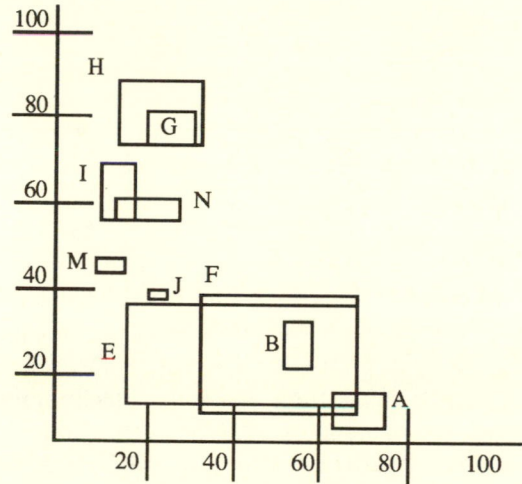

"Requires New Technology"

"Expected results in 2–3 years"

A = Static pattern recognition—automated systems in public, private sectors
B = Dynamic pattern recognition (as above)
E = Automation via fuzzy control
F = Home automation systems closely related to daily life
G = Basic information processing
H = Pattern recognition processing
I = Linguistic processing
M = Consulting
N = Human interface

Difference of Views between Experts and Laypeople

As with developmental research, experts in fuzzy applications have tended to ascribe greater importance to their work than laypeople and to be more optimistic about the time needed for realization. But a slightly different trend can be seen regarding three fields of fuzzy communication. Whereas experts and laypeople agreed on G (Basic Information Processing) and H (Pattern Recognition except for Images), experts view later realization of I (Linguistic Processing), except for the construction algorithm of sentences from images, as shown in Table 20.8. This may mean that expectations have risen much faster than actual-state-of-the-art applications, which may end up disappointing the public.

CONCLUSIONS

Based on the findings of this survey, fuzzy control is one of the most advanced areas in the application of fuzzy concepts and can be considered a well-established technology. Already a considerable number of real systems have been produced.

First, fuzzy control should be introduced for large-scale public use, rather than being the exclusive domain of talented engineers. For example, applications to automobile, vessel, and aircraft control to improve safety, effectiveness, and comfort are called for. Another need closely related to this, already being recognized but not adequately addressed, is to integrate fuzzy control with pattern recognition and sensor technology. Fuzzy control is likely to advance through integration with other technologies. Both basic and applied R&D in fuzzy pattern recognition have lagged behind other areas due to the necessity of larger memory and longer processing time for images than for letters and symbols, and for dynamic rather than static recognition.

Second, the application of fuzzy pattern recognition to family and individual life has lagged behind its use in factory and office automation. As domestic demand and consumer needs rise in importance, we anticipate increased diffusion throughout society.

Table 20.7. Comparison of Themes by Perceived Importance and Level of Technology Required

Level of Technology Required (Perceived importance)	Low (Possible with existing technology) ($\Delta T \geq 40$)	Medium (Partly possible with existing technology) ($40 > \Delta T \geq 20$)	High (Partially impossible without new technology) ($-40 < \Delta T \geq 20$)	Highest (Impossible without new technology) ($\Delta T \leq -40$)
High ($\beta \geq 70$)	• Static pattern recognition by production production robots in FA		• Dynamic pattern recognition by production robots in FA	• Mainframes for fuzzy data processing • PCs for fuzzy data processing • Inference computers for fuzzy d.p. • High-sensitivity touch sensors • Relation between sensory input and expression • Relevant structure of concepts expressed by common language • Associative operations of common language words • Algorithms for interpreting sentences • Databases for questioning
Medium ($70 > \beta \geq 50$)		• Static pattern recognition by transport robots in FA • Aircraft control systems • Cooperative operations robots	• Conversion of hand-writing to printing in OA equipment	• High-sensitivity taste sensors • High sensitivity smell sensors • Algorithms for producing sentences from images • Human interface OA input/output devices (voice & gesture recognition) • Man-machine conversation devices
Low ($\beta < 50$)	• Automatic volume reduction for TVs and audiovisual equipment	• VCRs with automatic recording pause for commercials • Hot water heater control • Multiple-zone air-conditioning control	• Self-tuning car engine	

(T = Percent responding "possible with existing technology"—"requires new technology."

Table 20.8. Difference in Perceptions of Experts and Laypeople Regarding Prospects of Communication Themes

Percent of respondents	"Expected Results in 2–3 Years"	
	Experts	Laypeople
G. Basic information processing		
Inference computer based on		
common sense, language	9.3	7.1
PCs for fuzzy data processing	15.6	11.6
Mainframes for fuzzy data		
processing	19.0	11.0
H. Pattern recognition processing		
(excluding image processing)		
High-sensitivity touch sensors	18.5	14.6
High-sensitivity smell sensors	11.5	9.1
High-sensitivity taste sensors	9.1	8.6
I. Basic research in language processing		
Relevant structure of concepts		
expressed by common language	0.0	6.1
Relation between sensory stimuli		
and expression	3.7	5.6
Establishment of algorithms for		
interpreting sentences	3.8	5.5
Associative operations of words in		
common language	4.0	7.1
Algorithms for producing sentences		
from images	11.5	5.0

Third, expectations have been high, perhaps unrealistically so, although more studies are needed to identify relevant areas. It is desirable to make a more in-depth analysis with a larger sample. In the area of fuzzy communication, vigorous research and development are expected in view of the rapid development of powerful computers of all classes and the increasing use for fuzzy logic in basic information-processing technologies. The emergence of such hardware, at a low level of sophistication, is expected shortly. More sophisticated hardware that can deal with common sense and natural language, a subtler area, will be longer in arriving, however.

Fuzzy communication techniques can also be applied effectively for human interface with computers, for the purpose of expression analysis that reflects nonverbal assumptions of humans. In addition, application of fuzzy logic should be considered for sensory products that depend on touch, taste, and olfactory elements. Applications to service and consulting industries might include the development of fuzzy data retrieval systems, initial medical consultation systems, and multipurpose care robots for the disadvantaged and the aged. Such robots need to be able to recognize patterns of "cues" as to the user's state of mind so that the comforting and preventive action may be taken in a timely fashion.

In developing human-friendly fuzzy systems, there is a need for confirmation of basic technologies that can satisfy needs directly and indirectly, exploration of their interdependence, and the discovery of developmental approaches that can maximize outcomes within a given time. Above all, international, cooperative, and synergistic research will be indispensable.

21

Discovery Engineering and Negotiating Organizational Change

Julian Gresser

In storybooks the inventor is portrayed as a solitary genius, sequestered in his (rarely her) laboratory, divorced from the hurly-burly of daily life. Recently, thanks to the U.S. Patent Office's Project XL and other innovative educational programs, invention is quickly becoming recognized as a skill that can actually be taught and readily acquired even by the average person. Indeed, many of our most important mundane products—the safety pin and bathtub, for example—attest to the uncelebrated inventive talents of the average person. This chapter investigates the proposition that invention is an acquirable skill, pointing out that not only invention, but also the allied processes of discovery and creativity are amenable to systematic intervention, and that these processes are particularly enhanced when pursued in groups. As will be seen, the new technology of discovery engineering may also have some interesting applications in the negotiation of organizational change.

FUNDAMENTAL PRINCIPLES

Discovery engineering is a system of techniques and procedures organized for the purpose of achieving discoveries and inventions and enhancing creativity. The word "discovery" (from the Latin *discooperire*, to uncover) connotes an unveiling or revelation of a thing that exists, if not in physical substance, at least in latent form within the mind. The roots of the word "invention" can be found in the Latin *invenire*, which originally meant "to find." If the discovery exists already in the above sense, our inability to understand is a kind of blindness. The focus of discovery engineering must thus be upon removing the shades that obscure sight.

One way of thinking about the process of discovery or invention is to visualize a gap or distance between the discoverer (D) and the thing discovered (D1). In the beginning, the gap appears great. In time, however, the gap closes and at the moment of discovery it vanishes entirely. At this point, D and D1 are one and the same. It is as though the discoverer reconnects to a hidden part of self, and there, meaning is created, when none apparently existed before. This ascribed meaning is what we refer to as "discovery."

Fallacies Behind Words

The first step in discovery engineering is to formulate an initial statement of the central problem or "discovery puzzle." Once clarified, the statement is pruned of its semantic "noise"— clumsy language that beclouds the eye of the discoverer. Next the "power structure" embodied in key words and sentences on which meaning hangs is analyzed and the major fallacies embedded in the linguistic structure isolated. Finally, the statement is transformed so that it more closely approximates and resonates with the discovery question.

In the history of science and many other fields there are numerous instances in which linguistic fallacy has proved a major stumbling block to discovery. For years ornithologists were convinced that whiteness was a property of swans, and when black swans were initially observed in Australia, they were assigned to the genus Chenopsis not Cygnus. Similarly, polio was misdiagnosed for years as a form of influenza. In both cases the principal obstacle was not the inadequacy of scientific knowledge per se, but rather semantic fallacy embedded in the linguistic structure of the problem's definition.

INVENTION, DISCOVERY, AND BRAINWAVE BIOFEEDBACK

If discovery or invention is within our grasp, but we simply fail to see it, one might naturally ask, "Where then is it?" Our answer is that it lies within the recesses of the mind, beyond normal consciousness. Then one will ask,

"What is consciousness and what is mind?" In discovery engineering, especially when supported by theta brainwave biofeedback, we learn to voyage through different levels of consciousness, there to find the discovery and to transport it back to ordinary consciousness, where it can be expressed and independently verified.

In brainwave biofeedback, an electrode is placed on the scalp over the left occiput, the visual area at the back of the head. When the eyes are open and thoughts or emotions are active, the left occiput usually produces beta brain rhythm at 13 to 20 hertz frequency. When the eyes are closed and intentional thinking is suspended, beta begins to vanish and an alpha rhythm appears, at 8 to 13 hertz. This indicates an "idling" stage of mind, sometimes containing daydreams. For most people, as training progresses and the body, emotions, and thoughts become silent, theta rhythm begins to appear, at 4 to 8 hertz. We call this "theta" or "creative" reverie. It is a state of consciousness where one experiences a detached feeling, a sense of just watching, of passive reflection, an attitude of simply allowing things to happen; most important, there is the sudden occurrence of strikingly vivid, life-like "hypnagogic" images.

It is often said that one can capture in a single image a one thousand words. Hypnagogic imagery (from the Greek *hynos*, to sleep, *agogeus*, to lead) condenses significantly more bits of word-information. Moreover, hypnagogic imagery occurs not only visually, but also in the form of smells, tastes, sounds, kinesthetic feelings, spatial perceptions, and emotions. Frequently hypnagogic imagery has a strong synesthetic quality in that it combines and crosses over traditional reference points for the five senses. Thus one "sees" sounds, "smells" colors, "feels" sights, and experiences multiple dimensions of time simultaneously. Hypnagogic imagery also has a holographic quality not present in ordinary two-dimensional images.

Historically, hypnagogic imagery produced in reverie has been the source of many important breakthroughs in science, technology, business, politics, and the arts. One of the most famous is August Kekule's account of his discovery of the ringed molecular structure of benzine.

> I turned my chair to the fire and dozed. Again the atoms were gambling before my eyes. This time the smaller groups kept modestly in the background. My mental eye, rendered more acute by repeated visions of this kind, could now distinguish larger structures, of manifold conformation; long rows, sometimes more closely fitted together; all twining and twisting in snake-like motions. But look! What was that? One of the snakes had seized hold of its own tail, and the form whirled lockingly before my eyes. As if by the flash of lightning I awoke . . . let us learn to dream, gentlemen. (See Willis Harman and Howard Rheingold, *Higher Creativity*, p. 41.)

As suggested by Kekule's report, the crux of discovery engineering lies in the understanding of the symbology. The average scientist, who does not possess Kekule's genius, might see the same snake swallowing its tail, but not find in this extraordinary image the clue to a breakthrough. The problem then is how to raise the level of consciousness of the ordinary person to find the answer "implicitly obvious" in the imagery.

Although the door to the creative unconscious mind is temporarily opened in reverie, it is still necessary for the discoverer to understand the meaning of information now available. For this purpose, a technique of interpretation is introduced by a facilitator somewhat along the following lines.

Suppose an average scientist in training suddenly encounters the above image of a snake swallowing its tail. The facilitator might ask, innocently and without a trace of judgment, *"What is a Snake?"* On hearing the reply and judging by the overall emotional feeling of the respondent, the facilitator might continue the dialogue with these questions: "What is a tail? What is the shape or structure of a snake swallowing its tail?" and so forth.

Once the imagery is carefully analyzed and reflected back to the discoverer, the facilitator might finally ask, "Suppose you integrate your responses. Do you find any connection to the discovery puzzle or do any insights come to mind either from the past, present, or possibly regarding some future event?" We have found that this critical probe frequently sparks an important insight.

Incubation and Dialogue with the Images

Once the discoverer learns how to contact the creative faculty through reverie and comes to understand the meaning of the images, the next step is to learn how to incubate or to present a discovery question and call forth a response. In this procedure, the discoverer enters reverie and poses the discovery question succinctly and clearly. After holding the question in mind for a short while, the issue is released and the discoverer waits for responsive images, which are then analyzed as discussed above.

In more advanced training, the discoverer can even learn to enter into a dialogue with the images. The discoverer will ask the image in reverie what information it wishes to convey and the image will respond, perhaps by transforming itself in some meaningful way. The technique of dialoguing is useful in that it allows the discoverer to remain "working" in reverie without returning to the distractions of ordinary consciousness.

INVENTING AND DISCOVERING IN GROUPS

Most people fear what they cannot control and are in terror of the unknown. For this reason, a voyage of discovery is best garrisoned in groups.

The voyage will demand patience, determination, courage, and resourcefulness. In groups, a sense of camaraderie develops, and with the startling realization that every horror of the unchartered mind is only mere perception, a feeling of collective relief. Then the process gives way to a sense of adventure, joy, and fun.

In group brainwave training, it is possible to measure the progress of each individual and the group as a whole by a special Fast-Hartley computer program and also to obtain data on the individual percentage times of beta, alpha, and theta brainwaves of the participants during the training session. As the training proceeds, each participant can keep track of important insights by pressing a pickle switch, reported by an arrow in the computer record. When reviewing the data, the trainee can correlate the point of insight with the brainwave pattern. Often this process helps jog the trainee's memory to recall other important inner experiences.

The psychological significance of an objective computer-generated record may be as important in discovery engineering as the data's more conventional uses. At least in the West, we seem so dependent on the objective world for proof of our reality that many of us are unwilling to believe or to thrust in our subjective insights or perceptions, however important or meaningful they may seem. Computer-generated data provides an important objective and verifiable reference point.

One of the most fascinating aspects of group biofeedback is the fact that after two or three sessions, a number of participants in a discovery team will invariably report the occurrence of similar images. This is highly significant because it provides an important signal that the discovery group is on the right track. When the heroic traits of individual character such as fearlessness and patience are imbued with the light of joy, and yoked further to the intentionality, will, and concentration of the group, we have found the effects on the "field" in which D1 resides to be profound.

NEGOTIATING ORGANIZATIONAL CHANGE

If discovery engineering can be used to build empathy within groups, can the technology also be used to effect organizational change?

Some years ago, an institutional client presented us with this question: How can the original mission of the founder be kept alive and expressed most effectively? To our surprise, the images of the group's members that responded to this incubated question contained many baleful firms: tea brewing, ship wrecks, swamps, a wolf's head protruding from a swamp, and toward the end of the program, a whirlwind. After processing this information with the team, which included the president and executive vice-president, it soon became evident, at least to us, that the images together foretold the advent of an imminent crisis. At the same time, some of the images expressed a tone or spirit of a revitalized organization and also concrete actions needed to place the entire enterprise on a fresh, and dynamic track. We included all of these insights in our report, which we submitted several weeks later to the president.

The warning was not heeded. As predicted, several months later a crisis ensued. The entire senior management, along with other members of the team, were dismissed.

These events occurred over three years ago. As I have reflected on this project, I have always remembered the president's failure to take effective action. Recently, however, I have come to realize my own company's shared responsibility.

Our work with this institution involved three classes of discovery. First was the assistance we rendered to the president and his key advisors in helping them discover that a problem in fact existed. Here we partially succeeded. Second was the president's discovery of how to fix the problem. Here again our group was helpful. Third was the actual process of taking those actions required to bring the discovery into practical reality. On this point my company was remiss, because we failed to help the president and his advisors negotiate a course of corrective action.

After several years of experience, one principle is now clear: The images that flow up from the mind in reverie are fragile. If their teaching is not grasped and acted upon, like bubbles, they will dissipate and dissolve into airy nothing. This principle seems as true for organizations as it is for individuals.

The question then is in what ways discovery engineering can help top executives take effective action. Although this application has never been systematically explored, our preliminary findings based on work with executives suggest that the technology may be useful, particularly when combined with other biofeedback modalities. For an action to be "effective" it must be taken pursuant to a clear mission and purpose, goals and objectives, and a plan. The plan itself must include a budgetary allocation not only of funds, but also of individual and organizational time. A strictly logical analysis will lead only to a partial enhancement. After a decision maker has identified clearly what the desired mission and purpose is, that same question might be presented to the unconscious mind in reverie as follows: "What is my *real* mission and purpose?" "What do I *really* want?" We have found that a decision can be greatly enriched by drawing on the insights embedded in the imagery.

Once a clear mission and purpose, goals and objectives, and a plan are in place, the next steps are the actions themselves. In my work as a professional negotiator, I have learned that "victory" in any transaction often comes to the party who maintains creative control over emotions. One learns to watch, almost with an attitude of wonder, as one's fears, joy or excitement arise beforehand. When one acquires this detached attitude of mind, one's mastery of the skill of listening increases dramatically. When one learns really to listen, we can penetrate the mind of our adversaries and find their deepest wishes and greatest pain. To the professional negotiator, the adversary's emotions are tools by which he or she can be tilted off-balance, and in the flux of emotional instability helped to discover that the pain can be allayed only by the adoption of *our* mission and purpose.

What contribution, if any, can discovery engineering make to helping top executives acquire this habit of detachment, which is essential to effective decision making? Detachment may be defined as the ability to see things simply as they are. In theta brainwave biofeedback training, a detached mind is prerequisite, for otherwise the images do not arise, or if they do, they will not speak to us. In short, the greater the level of detachment, the more meaningful and extensive the feedback. Detachment is also essential to the effective management of change. In negotiation, our adversaries' strength may also prove a decisive weakness, in the same way that great adversity unfolds significant opportunity. The discovery of this paradox is limited only by our poor ability to remove ourselves and see.

CONCLUSIONS

Discovery engineering involves a kind of superlogic that prunes linguistic structures of their semantic consolation and marries logic to a procedure in which natural imagery and other subtle information is first detected and then used to solve all kinds of problems and issues. Discovery engineering will appeal most to those who enjoy the process of discovery as an end in itself. For these explorers, the unconquered terrain of the human mind is as vast, treacherous, and challenging as the unexplored jungles of South America and Africa were to the conquistadors and missionaries of the sixteenth to nineteenth centuries, or as the oceans, outer space, and the microbial world are to scientists in this century. On a practical level, this new technology offers great promise for the design of basic and applied research, the manufacture of new products, and the revitalization of organizations. To realize its potential, however, discovery engineering must be linked to a program of training and coaching in effective decision making. For if the key decision makers are ineffective, the organization will not provide a hospitable environment; and even if, despite great odds, a significant discovery is made, it may languish, unrecognized and unrewarded. Discovery engineering can contribute, perhaps modestly at first, to helping executives develop those traits of character and behavior by whose grace even the most radical discovery will flourish.

22

Leadership for Creativity in Organizations: A Prototypical Case of Leading Multidisciplinary Teams of Professionals

Nirmal K. Sethia

One of the most critical determinants of organizational vitality and success in today's business environment is innovation. Innovation refers to the development of new products or processes. The essential impetus for innovation derives from creativity, which is the ability of individuals or groups to generate on a sustained basis significantly original ideas or solutions to problems. Creative work, especially formal and ongoing work in organizational settings, serves as a prototypical case of multi-disciplinary teamwork involving professionals. This is so because first, creativity requires a very high level of professional expertise based on specialized knowledge (Simon 1988). Second, creative work, because of its inherent complexity, is frequently a team endeavor (Briggs 1988; Mitchell 1989; Zuckerman 1977). Finally, such work often proceeds across the boundaries of more than one field of knowledge (Simon 1988; Kanter 1988; Levine 1989). Therefore, an understanding of the unique leadership challenges in facilitating creativity and maximizing its payoffs for the organization can provide a useful model for the effective leadership of multidisciplinary professional teamwork.

A BASIC CHALLENGE: THE ABUNDANCE OF "SUBSTITUTES FOR LEADERSHIP"

Exercise of creative leadership can be unusually problematic because of an abundance of "substitutes for leadership" surrounding creative endeavors. In one of the first delineations of the concept of substitutes for leadership, Kerr (1977) and Kerr and Jermier (1978) pointed out that in many instances organizational, individual, or task-situational variables substitute for leadership, and thereby reduce its importance and relevance. Creativity is a sphere in which leadership substitutes abound. At the individual level, creative people characteristically possess a great amount of expert knowledge, exercise autonomy, display a high self-image, and are primarily driven by intrinsic motivation (Amabile 1988; Barron and Harrington 1981; Martindale 1989; Sethia 1989a, 1989b). They also exhibit a marked desire as well as capacity for what Manz (1980, 1986) in a general context refers to as "self-management" or "self-leadership." For feedback and recognition, creative people consider fellow professionals to be more important than the organizational superiors. Moreover, their work absorbs and inspires them, and in any event, given its unpredictable and evolving nature (Gruber 1989; Simon 1988), it is not easily susceptible to supervisory guidance and control. Finally, in supporting creativity the organization has to allow considerable freedom and flexibility and adopt a long-term evaluative framework. Taken together, these characteristics and conditions indeed represent substantial substitutes for leadership.

Yet, leadership does play a crucial role in enabling and enhancing creativity in organizations. At the highest level in the organization, the vision and strategic goals of leadership determine if the organization will actively nurture creativity, or tolerate it with indifference, or "search out and destroy" it. Only when the top leadership is enthusiastic about radically new developments and values creativity will it provide the needed challenges and opportunities for people to be creative. The roles of Edwin Land at Polaroid and Steven Jobs at Apple in demanding and inspiring creativity have already become legendary (Sethia 1987). While the top leadership defines the overall cultural context for creativity, other levels of leadership that are closer to the day-to-day operations are likely to have a more immediate impact on creativity.

LEADERSHIP ROLES FOR CREATIVITY

Leadership that is effective for creativity satisfies the expectations of creative individuals, fulfills the demands of creative work, and integrates the creative effort with the goals and values of the organization.

Expectations of Creative Individuals

Creativity was defined earlier in this chapter as an ability. But to be understood in its full ramifications, creativity has to be viewed as a complex and higher-order ability that is a synergistic culmination of a host of more basic abilities and orientations (Perkins 1981: 245). The individual expectations that have to be satisfied by the leadership are rooted in these "core" abilities and orientations, which fall into two broad categories: cognitive and personality-motivational (Mumford and Gustafson 1988; Sethia 1989a, 1989b). The main cognitive expectations to be met are: being allowed to make full use of superior intelligence; having the opportunities to apply superior intelligence; having the opportunities to apply specialized knowledge as well as acquire new knowledge, receiving acceptance for idiosyncratic styles of thinking ("integrative" and "set breaking"); seeing value being attached as much to "problem finding" as to problem solving; and respect being shown not only to analytical and rational arguments but also to intuitive and aesthetic judgments. The main personality- and motivation-related expectations to be met are: appreciation for perseverance and self-motivated hard work; scope for curiosity and inquisitiveness; bearing with lack of certainty; guarding operational freedom and independence of judgment; support for risk taking; and furthering of intrinsic motivation.

Demands of Creative Work

Many of the demands of creative work arise from two well-understood facts about it: it is a very complex activity (Gruber 1989), and it represents the cutting edge of the field(s) it is anchored in. But there are two other equally important—and interrelated—facts about creative work. First, its success hinges on change or accidental occurrences (Gruber 1989; Simon 1988). Second, because of the element of chance involved, a particular project or piece of work is usually a part of, what Gruber (1989) calls a "network of enterprises"—a group of related projects or activities. Given these basic facts, creative work makes special demands on organizational resources (material and human resources, and time), and requires a highly organic, adaptable, and permeable structure (Sethia 1989a).

Organizational Imperatives

Even when creativity is greatly valued in an organization, it cannot be supported just for its own sake, and it cannot be supported endlessly. Therefore, selectivity enters in where the key decision makers place their bets, and how far they go with these bets. And when a good breakthrough is achieved—which may happen suddenly and unexpectedly—it is important for the organization to move opportunistically to exploit the new possibilities and identify future projects that can build on this breakthrough. It is for such reasons as these that Pake (1986) regards "technical taste" as an important factor in research management, and Simon (1988) emphasizes the value of a strategic orientation in management of creativity.

THE EXERCISE OF LEADERSHIP FOR CREATIVITY

On the one hand, creativity is accompanied by formidable substitutes for leadership; on the other hand, creativity involves stakes and demands that cry for "high power" leadership. The resolution of this apparent contradiction calls for a great deal of *creativity in leadership!* In this context two themes are particularly worthy of serious attention; one focusing on the distinctive abilities and orientations of those who can provide effective leadership for creativity, and the other focusing on how and by whom such leadership might be provided in organizational settings.

Characteristics of Effective Leaders

In discussing "creativity in leadership" Simon (1988) notes that a vicarious sense of accomplishment derived from the creative outcomes one has helped bring about constitutes one of the hallmarks of creative managers. Simon also points to three other important traits in creative managers: a sensitivity to opportunity (and the ability to exploit it), a strategic orientation (exhibited in an understanding of relevant future trends and setting of long-term goals), and a willingness to be adventurous and risk failure. Mumford and Feldman (1988) also have explored the distinctive attributes of creative leaders. In a complementary vein, where the focus shifts from "creative leadership" (that is, leadership imbued with creativity) to "leadership for creativity," McCall (1980) conjectures about a set of personal characteristics that may be expected to influence the success of those playing leadership roles in augmenting creativity in organizations. Aiming to be provocative rather than prescriptive, he hypothesizes that to succeed as a leader of creative people or projects one may have to be crafty, grouchy, dangerous, feisty, contrary, evangelistic, prejudiced, and spineless (McCall 1980).

Form and Locus of Leadership

It appears highly plausible that leadership for creativity has to be a team effort, involving different people in different roles. With respect to management of innovation, Angle and Van de Ven (1989) argue that "Innovations are not managed by one person (as often implied). It involves a team of managers (to manage innovations)." Further, they describe a model that balances four specific managerial roles in promotion of innovation: *sponsor, mentor, critic,* and *institutional leader*. They also note that these roles are likely to be performed by different individuals. What Angle and Van de Ven are suggesting about innovation would appear to be equally applicable to creativity. This suggests that in thinking about leadership for creativity, we may have to shift the focus of our search away from leadership as a quality or talent that is assumed to reside in a single individual in a given situation, and redirect it toward a vision of leadership as a vital stream of influences emanating from a constellation of people—some inside the organization occupying different hierarchical positions, others possibly outside—who individually fulfill some of the expectations of creative individuals, meet some of the demands of creative work, and satisfy some of the organizational imperatives that inevitably circumscribe creative endeavors.

REFERENCES

Amabile, T. M. 1988. A model of creativity and innovation in organizations. In *Research in organizational behavior,* ed. B. M. Staw and L. L. Cummings, Vol. 10. Greenwich, Conn.: JAI.

Angle, H. L., and A. H. Van de Ven. 1989. Suggestions for managing the innovation journey. In *Research on the management of innovation,* ed. A. H. Van de Ven, H. L. Angle, and M. Pools. New York: Harper and Row.

Barron, F. M., and D. M. Harrington. 1981. Creativity, intelligence and personality. In *Annual review of psychology,* ed. M. R. Rosenzweig and L. W. Porter, Vol. 32. Palo Alto, Calif.: Annual Review Press.

Briggs, J. 1988. *Fire in the crucible: The alchemy of creative genius*. New York: St. Martin's Press.

Gruber, H. E. 1989. The evolving system approach to creative work. *Creativity Research Journal*. 1: 27–51.

Kanter, R. M. 1988. When a thousand flower bloom: Structural, collective and social conditions for innovation in organization." In *Research in Organizational Behavior,* ed. B. M. Staw and L. L. Cummings. Vol. 10. Greenwich, Conn.: JAI.

Kerr, S. 1977. Substitutes for leadership: Some implications for organizational design. *Organization and Administrative Sciences* 8 (1): 135–46.

Kerr, S., and J. M. Jermier. 1978. Substitutes for leadership: Meaning and measurement. *Organizational Behavior and Human Performance* 22: 375–403.

Levine, J. B. 1989. Keeping new ideas kicking around: HP's free-thinking scientists help hone its market edge. *BusinessWeek,* Special Issue, 128.

McCall, M. W., Jr., 1980. Conjecturing about creative leaders. *Journal of Creative Behavior* 11: 225–34.

Manz, C. C. 1980. Self-management as a substitute for leadership: A social learning theory perspective. *Academy of Management Review* 5: 361–67.

_____. 1986. Self-leadership: Towards an expanded theory of self-influence processes in organization. *Academy of Management Review* 11: 585–600.

Martindale, C. 1989. Personality, situation, and creativity. In *Handbook of Creativity Research,* ed. J. A. Glober, R. R. Ronning and C. R. Reynolds. New York: Plenum.

Mitchell, R. 1989. Nurturing those ideas. *BusinessWeek,* Special Issue, pp. 106–18.

Mumford, M. D., and J. M. Feldman. 1988. *Creative leadership: Its nature and nurture*. School of Psychology, Georgia Institute of Technology.

Mumford, M. D., and S. Gustafson. 1988. Creative syndrome: Integration, application and innovation. *Psychological Bulletin* 103: 27–43.

Pake, G. E. 1986. From research to innovation at Xerox: A manager's principles and some examples. In *Research on Technological Innovation, Management, and Policy,* ed. R. S. Rosenblook. Vol. 3. Greenwich, Conn.: JAI.

Perkins, D. N. 1981. *The mind's best work*. Cambridge, Mass.: Harvard University Press.

Sethia, N. K. 1987. *Innovation: A corporate culture perspective*. Department of Management and Organization, School of Business Administration, University of Southern California, Los Angeles.

_____. 1989a. The shaping of creativity in organizations." In *Academy of Management Best Paper Proceedings: 1989,* ed. F. Hoy.

_____. 1989b. *The creative individual: Core abilities and orientations.* Department of Management and Organization, School of Business Administration, University of Southern California, Los Angeles.

Simon, H. A. 1988. Understanding creativity and creative management. In *Handbook for creative and innovative managers,* ed. R. L. Kuhn. New York: McGraw-Hill.

Zuckerman, H. 1977. *The scientific elite: Nobel laureates in the U.S.* New York: Free Press.

A Personal Summary
Robert Lawrence Kuhn

The chapters in this volume, and the presentations at the conference on which they were based, produced such a rich set of ideas and themes that it would be fatuous to attempt to encompass them all within a tight framework. Indeed, it is the diversity of topics and divergence of methodologies that endow creative and innovative management with both its theoretical power and practical applicability. Hence what follows are my own views, my own image of the emerging picture at this one instant of time, of creative and innovative management in both economics and politics at this inflection point in history.

I see *five* primary themes forging the leading edge of creative and innovative management:

PERSONAL FREEDOM AND INDIVIDUAL CREATIVITY

The primacy of the person is a fundamental driver. Unleashing people power is the key to organizational creativity, whether for a company or for a country. Enlightened leadership should do whatever it can to enhance people as individuals. Dynamic, adaptive bureaucracies stress participants not system, people not organization. Such realignment requires boldness for the individual, and risk for the institution.

COUNTRIES ARE LIKE COMPANIES, WHICH ARE LIKE UNIVERSITIES, WHICH ARE LIKE INSTITUTIONS

The similarity of large bureaucratic organizations in transition becomes startlingly clear. Descriptions of the corporation called General Motors, or the institution called Georgia Tech, or the government agency called NASA, or the country called China could each be mixed together and applied to each of the others. Managers seeking to induce creativity and innovation encounter the same issues, no matter the venue. The most remarkable characteristic of creative and innovative management is its organizational fungibility, its common applicability across all groupings of human beings irrespective of geography, sector, or class.

NO MODELS EXIST FOR CERTAIN PROBLEMS

Creativity is about being new and being different,[1] and hence it is sometimes impossible to generalize from historical precedents or case examples. Nothing in world history is truly comparable to what the Former Soviet Union must do in transforming a planned economy into a market economy. Similarly, there are no prototypes for the rapid technological obsolescence and huge numbers of knowledge-based workers characteristic of many modern industries. In this uncertain, ambiguous, constantly changing environment, third-party views are often essential. Independent experts can help derive signal from noise, seeing order amidst clutter and making meaning from chaos.

CREATIVE AND INNOVATIVE MANAGEMENT CONTINUES TO GROW AS AN ACADEMIC DISCIPLINE

The application of rigorous analytical techniques, and new ways of thinking through the complex problems of organizational creativity and innovation, demand multidisciplinary awareness. Longitudinal as well as horizontal studies must be made to assess the impact of time as a critical variable. Too often it is easy to have what appears to be "successful" creativity and innovation in the short term yield unsuccessful ultimate results in the long term. Creativity and innovation must always be means not ends.

NEW TECHNIQUES AND TECHNOLOGIES MUST BE EXPLAINED AND TESTED

Process is equal with content. Creative and innovative management is advanced by the development of new techniques and technologies. Information as a strategic weapon, artificial intelligence and expert systems, human resource planning and compensation, marketing analytics, brain waves, fuzzy logic—all these and more are part of the enlarging sphere of creative and innovative management.

A FINAL NOTE

I am often asked how we can help the *newly* emerging but still fragile democracies throughout the world. What should we support and how should we implement such support? In my opinion, *money should be spent on encouraging individual minds not sustaining organizational claims.* Let us put our first money into purchasing fax machines, copiers, personal computers, modems, and telephone systems—all the telecommunications tools that individuals can use independent of the state or any of its control-obsessed institutions. What will develop is the triumph of the individual, however rough the transition period that must be endured.

To conclude, I stress the first two themes of this volume. They are the two superarching themes of our age: (1) the dominance of personal freedom and individual creativity and (2) countries are like companies, which are like universities, which are like institutions . . . .

NOTE

1. Yuji Ijiri, "Creativity and Accountability in Management," in *New Directions in Creative and Innovative Management,* ed. Yuji Ijiri and Robert Lawrence Kuhn (Cambridge, Mass.: Ballinger, 1988).

Index

About the RGK Foundation

The RGK Foundation, established in 1966, provides support in the areas of medical and educational research, as well as academic excellence in institutions of higher learning. Support also goes for programs to raise literacy levels in our society and to attract minority and women students into math, science, and technology fields. The foundation has sponsored studies in several areas of national and international concern, including health, corporate governance, energy, and economic analysis. Major emphasis has been placed on research in connective tissue diseases, particularly scleroderma, and in areas that include spinal cord injury, autoimmunity, cancer, and blindness prevention. The foundation has also supported workshops and conferences examining the role of business in American society at many outstanding educational institutions, such as the IC^2 Institute at the University of Texas at Austin and the Keystone Center for Continuing Education in Colorado. Conferences sponsored at the Austin-based foundation are designed not only to enhance information exchange, but also to maintain an interlinkage among business, academic, community, and government. The RGK Foundation Building, which opened in October 1981, has a research library and provides research space for scholars in residence.

About the IC² Institute

The IC² Institute is a major international research center for the study of innovation, creativity, and capital (hence IC²). The institute studies and analyzes the enterprise system through the work of over eighty research fellows in an integrated and multidisciplinary program of research, conferences, and publications. Established in 1977, IC² links theory with practice by bringing together business, government, and academic leaders through an active international program of conferences, workshops, and colloquiums.

The key areas of research and study concentration of IC² include the management of technology; creative and innovative management; measuring the state of society; dynamic business development and entrepreneurship; econometrics, economic analysis, and management sciences; and the evaluation of attitudes, opinions, and concerns about key issues.

The institute generates a strong interaction between scholarly developments and real-world issues by conducting national and international conferences, developing initiatives for private and public sector consideration, assisting in the establishment of professional organizations and other research institutes and centers, and maintaining collaborative efforts with universities, communities, states, and government agencies.

IC^2 research is published through special reports, monographs, policy papers, technical working papers, research articles, and four major series of books.

About the Editor and Contributors

Robert Lawrence Kuhn is President of the Geneva Companies, the leading merger and acquisition firm for privately held companies. Dr. Kuhn is an international investment banker and corporate strategist, public speaker and business professor, and author and editor. He is editor in chief of the seven-volume *The Library of Investment Banking* and the *Handbook for Creative and Innovative Managers*; he is a recognized expert in strategies for mid-sized firms. As an investment banker, Dr. Kuhn specializes in mergers and acquisitions, financial strategy and structure, and new business formation. He is active in Japan and China, facilitating cross-border M&A and joint ventures. Trained in brain research, he speaks and lectures frequently and is quoted and published widely.

J. D. Aguera-Areas is Senior Scientist, Forensic Medical Advisory Service, Rockville, Maryland.

Bertram S. Brown is Executive Vice-President, Forensic Medical Advisory Service, Rockville, Maryland. Dr. Brown has been Executive Director of the National Institute of Mental Health and President of Hahnemann University.

Gennedy Filshin is Head, Regional Economics Department, USSR Academy of Sciences, USSR.

Eric G. Glamholtz is Professor, The John E. Anderson Graduate School of Management, University of California at Los Angeles. He is also President of Management Systems Consulting Corporation.

Julian Gresser is President, Discovery Engineering International, Sausalito, California. An attorney specializing in Japan, he has been Visiting Professor at the Harvard Law School and MIT.

Akira Ishikawa is Professor and Chairman, International Exchange Committee, Aoyama Gakuin University, Tokyo, Japan.

Richard N. Katz is Special Assistant to the Associate Vice President, Information Systems and Administrative Services, University of California.

Dyong Kong is President, National Research Center for Science and Technology Development, Beijing, People's Republic of China.

George Kozmetsky is Director, IC^2 Institute, The University of Texas at Austin.

Ronald M. Lee is Associate Professor, Management Science and Information Systems Department, The University of Texas at Austin.

Susan F. Lefkowitz is Administrator for Clinical Services, Executive Director of Faculty Practice, Georgetown University Medical Center.

Arie Y. Lewin is Professor, Fuqua School of Business, Duke University.

Humboldt C. Mandell, Jr., is Manager, Lunar/Mars Exploration Program Development Office, NASA/Johnson Space Center, Houston, Texas.

Gerhard O. Mensch is Director, International Institute of Industrial Innovation, Federal Republic of Germany. He is also Senior Vice President, German Finance Academy, Munich.

Helen M. Moye is Director, Central Office Personnel, Central Office Staffs, General Motors Corporation, Detroit, Michigan.

Yvonne Randie is Senior Consultant, Management Systems Consulting Corporation.

Arnold Reisman is Professor, Department of Operations Research, Case Western Reserve University.

Walt W. Rostow is Professor Emeritus of Political Economy, Department of Economics, The University of Texas at Austin.

Timothy W. Ruefli is the Frank C. Erwin, Jr. Centennial Research Fellow, IC^2 Institute, the Herbert C. Kelleher/M Corp Regents Professor in

Business, and Chairperson of the Management Department, Graduate School of Management, The University of Texas at Austin.

Dennis Schorr is Visiting Assistant Professor, The John E. Anderson Graduate School of Management, University of California at Los Angeles.

Paul A. Schumann, Jr. is President, Glocal Vantage, Austin, Texas.

Nirmal K. Sethia is Professor, Center for Effective Organizations, University of Southern California.

Hidesada Toriyama is Senior Vice-President of Public Relations, NTT Data Communications Systems Corporation, Tokyo, Japan.

Janos Vecsenyi is Professor of Policy and Strategy, International Management Center, Budapest, Hungary.

Richard P. West is Associate Vice President, Information Systems and Administrative Services, University of California.

Jerry Wind is the Lauder Professor of Marketing and Director, SEI Center for Advanced Studies in Management, The Wharton School, University of Pennsylvania.